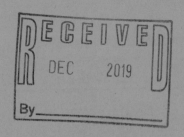

SHOW PEOPLE

SHOW PEOPLE

SHOW PEOPLE

A HISTORY
OF THE
FILM STAR

MICHAEL NEWTON

REAKTION BOOKS

For Lena

Published by
REAKTION BOOKS LTD
Unit 32, Waterside
44–48 Wharf Road
London N1 7UX, UK

www.reaktionbooks.co.uk

First published 2019
Copyright © Michael Newton 2019

Printed and bound in Great Britain
by TJ International, Padstow, Cornwall

A catalogue record for this book is available from the British Library

ISBN 978 1 78914 156 6

CONTENTS

Preface *9*

PART ONE: **THE SILENT STAR**

1 Mary Pickford: The Biograph Girl *17*

2 Pola Negri: Inventing the Star *29*

3 Charlie Chaplin: The Tramp *43*

PART TWO: **THE GOLDEN AGE**

4 'Asta' and 'Cheeta': The Animal Star *55*

5 Peter Lorre: Character Actor *67*

6 Fred Astaire, Ginger Rogers, Gene Kelly:
   A Star Danced *73*

7 Katharine Hepburn and Cary Grant:
   The Public Image *84*

8 Vivien Leigh: Ruinous Selves *93*

9 Veronica Lake: Half-obscured Faces *109*

10 Carole Lombard: The Screwball Heroine *115*

11 Greer Garson and Joan Fontaine:
    The Forgotten Star *120*

12 Orson Welles: The Film Star as Fragment
    and Failure *137*

13 Ingrid Bergman: Intermezzo *150*

PART THREE: **NATIONAL CINEMAS
– STARS FOR THE NATION**

14 Lamberto Maggiorani and Maria Pia Casilio:
   Absent Film Stars in Vittorio De Sica's Films *167*

15 Moira Shearer: The Marionette *174*

16 Gloria Swanson: Having a Face *183*

17 Ava Gardner: I Am Not an Actress *189*

18 Montgomery Clift: He's Not There *200*

19 Setsuko Hara: The Still Point *212*

20 Toshiro Mifune: Studying Lions *221*

21 Nargis and Raj Kapoor: My Heart Is Hindustani *226*

22 Giulietta Masina and Marcello Mastroianni:
   Nothing Is Sadder than Laughter *240*

23 John Wayne: How to Grow Old *250*

24 Audrey Hepburn: Frankenstein's Creature *261*

25 Marilyn Monroe: The Suffering Star *271*

26 Juanita Moore and Susan Kohner: *Imitation of Life* 280

PART FOUR: **NEW WAVE STARS**

27 Janet Leigh and Tippi Hedren: Torturing the Audience *287*

28 Audrey Hepburn and Cary Grant: The Strange Death
   of the Hollywood Golden Age *294*

29 Anna Karina: The Muse *299*

30 Celia Johnson and Julie Christie: The Adulterous Star *305*

31 Sidney Poitier: The Defiant One *313*

32 Dustin Hoffman: Little Big Man *322*

33 Woody Allen: The Director as Star *332*

34 Robert De Niro: For Real *340*

PART FIVE: **POSTHUMAN STARS**

35 Harrison Ford: *Blade Runner* and the Replication of
   the Person *353*

36 Maggie Cheung: Centre Stage *360*

37 Naomi Watts: *Mulholland Drive* *372*

38 Scarlett Johansson: A New Kind of Emptiness *381*

39 Shu Qi: A Placeless Heaven *388*

40 Andy Serkis: Lear's Shadow *395*
   Afterword *405*

   References *421*
   Acknowledgements *433*
   Index *435*

'No more festival of stars!' cried one of the more vociferous orators. 'What we need is a festival of dialogue!' . . . I was invited to speak. Organize a symposium by all means, I said, but don't forget what happened at this year's gala opening. The inaugural film had been a revival of *Gone with the Wind*, and when Clark Gable made his first appearance on the stairs of Tara the festival audience went wild with applause. Had his ghost appeared on the Croisette, pandemonium would have ensued. Show business couldn't dispense with stars.

ROMAN POLANSKI on the Cannes Film Festival, 1968,
in Roman Polanski, *Roman* (London, 1984), pp. 256–7

CLEOPATRA: Think you there was or might be such a man
           As this I dreamt of?
DOLABELLA: Gentle madam, no.
CLEOPATRA: You lie up to the hearing of the gods.
           But if there be nor ever were one such,
           It's past the size of dreaming. Nature wants stuff
           To vie strange forms with fancy, yet t'imagine
           An Antony were nature's piece 'gainst fancy,
           Condemning shadows quite.

WILLIAM SHAKESPEARE, *Antony and Cleopatra* (v.2)

There's no people like show people.

IRVING BERLIN

PREFACE

I n the Bollywood film *Fan* (2016), Shah Rukh Khan's film-star character, Aryan Khanna, declares, 'Without my fans, I am nothing.' A star playing a star, Khan riffs on his own enormous fame. Yet Khan also plays Gaurav Chandna, the 'super-fan', a young man given over to the karaoke appropriation of his idol, a man whose presence he performs on stage and whose image covers his bedroom walls. Aryan Khanna is Gaurav's god. In taking both roles, Shah Rukh Khan helps us to perceive the symbiotic relationship between star and fan. The film is about how one life may impose on another, either as an image that seduces, or, more frighteningly, as a stranger's bullying physical demand. Power seeps into both sides of this relationship, the power of fame and wealth that is the star's possession, the power to make and unmake the star that is the fan's prerogative. Moreover, playing both roles lets us feel how Khan, that distant film star, was himself once 'ordinary', just another Delhi boy like his stalker. Doubling proliferates through the film, even as, in one scene, the star plays the fan playing the fictional star posing with the waxwork of the original star at Madame Tussaud's.

The film fabricates a double take that draws on the essential divide in Khan's on-screen persona, one that has long combined both the gauche with the urbanely suave. In *Chennai Express* (2013), opposite Deepika Padukone, Khan plays a forty-year-old perpetual adolescent who contrives to turn his underdog's clumsiness into heroic self-assurance. Like Cary Grant, his poise and grace are ready to collapse into a sudden gracelessness. Khan began his career as a villain, became a romantic lead in *Dilwale Dulhania Le Jayenge* (1995), and now can move between comedy, action adventure and more challenging roles. He has embraced the actor's turn for self-transformation, becoming a man with Asperger's syndrome in the message film *My Name Is Khan* (2010) and a self-destructive drunk in *Devdas* (2002).

Fan's message is that we should live our own lives, not live through others, not even the others at home in the shiny fictions of cinema. Yet this humble truth is one that depends on the glamorous impact of the star himself. *Fan* emerged from a culture where the star system persists in unchallenged strength. In the world of Bollywood, the star is at once more removed from the world of his fans and readier to let himself appear to them. Just as his star-character does, Shah Rukh Khan similarly comes each Sunday to a raised stage built on the walls of his mansion and waves out, physically present, a man like them, to the mass of adoring fans below. They are his worshippers and his owners, the source of the capital that built the house, just as he becomes for them the potent source of shared dreams and aspirations. The fans gain a sense of connection; the star gains wealth and prestige, a life sustained by anonymous adoration. In *Fan* there's no conventional romantic interest beyond that forged between the two men that Shah Rukh Khan plays; by analogy, he's playing someone in love with himself.

Shah Rukh Khan's film – indeed the very fact of his fame upon which the film draws – shows how even now the age of the film star is still with us, even at a moment when the stars are readily critiqued or exposed, stripped out of a film they have already completed, as happened to Kevin Spacey in *All the Money in the World* (2017), or turned on for bad choices or despised opinions. This moralistic response to the star, this swift transformation from adoration to condemnation, has always been an element in our response to cinema. Since the beginnings of film-star culture, the star has been apt to turn into a source of scandal, someone to be built up and then pulled down. Love quickly hardens into hate. *Fan* likewise tells us of the star's power, but also of their vulnerability. The uniqueness they sell readily metamorphoses into hubris. Ultimately what do we want from the star, what role do they play for us among our public dreams, our private fantasies?

Fame proves transient; stars are soon forgotten. It is no longer a given that the cinema of the past will survive into a future beguiled by other, more compulsive forms of virtual world, or in a society that finds the values of old films to be wanting, or regrets the shabby lives, or the privileged gender or ethnicity of those who made them. Yet despite their apparent fading, still they endure, a continuing pervasive presence in the cultures that first celebrated them. As in Johann Peter Hebel's story 'An Unexpected Reunion' ('Unverhofftes Wiedersehen') of 1811, where an old woman encounters her long-dead love, embalmed still in all the beauty of his youth by the salt mines in Falun, cinema disinters the youth, the beauty of the past. Every film preserves a person as once did those salt mines. The star remains vivid there, even as we age: in my youth, I loved the 1970s David Bowie and Audrey Hepburn of the 1950s and '60s; they were once much older than I, then the same age, and now rather younger. The stars are caught in the dynamic stasis of those performances even as I, their viewer, find myself transformed by time.

This book hopes to be an extended critical meditation on the film star, carried out by means of forty separate essays covering fifty different stars. Each essay acts as an individual case history, examining the work and presence of many different actors from across the world. The book explores the film star as a type, a concept and a phenomenon. It does not attempt to provide an overview of film stardom as such, and still less an exhaustive account of all the myriad stars. It builds up a picture of film stardom from individuals and through responses to individual films. It aims not just at elucidating through practical examples the workings of the star industry, but at illuminating what moves us in a film, in an actor's performance. Its ultimate subject is cinephilia, that antiquated ardour. The book may consider the actor as auteur, the author of the film, but more than this it is concerned with our relationship with the film star as the source of our fondness for films. I would bring into the discussion of cinema what it means to fall in love with a film, with a film star, and to be sympathetic to the meanings that such devotion creates. This book explores the strange ecstasy of watching. The book's subject and its motivation takes in the relationship between 'the star' and 'the fan', the writer of this book being only a self-conscious, if wide-eyed version of the latter. People on-screen move us. And the person that engages us is both the part played, the character in the story, and the man or woman playing them. In cinema these two personae entangle themselves. The star's primacy over the role they possess has been long noted in cinema studies. The art historian Erwin Panofsky persuasively argues that in cinema the character is the actor, and the actor is synonymous with the character.[1] The role lives and dies with that actor, that star; many people may play Hamlet, but, as *Citizen Kane* shows us, only Orson Welles was ever Charles Foster Kane. It is Welles who moves us, as presently embodied in the fiction of the dynamically beleaguered self he plays. It is in part this interest, this residual feeling regarding the actor themselves, that is the basis of what is set out in these interconnected essays. I hope to articulate, as well as I can, as honestly, the impact particular people make on screen, their capacity to stir us, to make us think, to open up a possibility and to clarify a corner of the world.

As there is no possibility of being complete, this book deals with only a selection of the most influential and important film stars of the last hundred years. It unavoidably leaves out many names; however, I believe that the women and men included here are exemplary when it comes to considering what stardom and the idea of the person has meant on-screen. Though, perhaps inevitably, the book is largely American in focus, I have attempted to pay some attention to the ways in which stardom has existed worldwide: in Europe, in Taiwan and Hong Kong, in Japan and in India. In addition, this book especially focuses on those films that have taken the star and the meanings of acting as their subject, those times where stars appear in films that consciously advance an argument about what stardom is. It stands as a purposefully eclectic and even fragmented book, advancing its hypotheses on the sly and in relation to specific moments or films, a volume for dipping into, a world of cinema discovered.

In the culture of the last hundred years film stars have played many roles. They are the person as a product; they express a fantasy of wealth, glamour and importance; they are, as in Brad Pitt's memorable reported formula about himself, 'the void that fills the void'. This book examines the premise that film is not primarily the artistic expression of a writer or a director, but rather a vehicle for its stars. While necessarily aware, of course, of the cultural context of film and the workings of the star industry, this book is more concerned with the films themselves considered as works of art, and with the lives and the presence of those in them. I consider what films themselves have told us about 'stars' and about the person. In cinema, we enter into another's point of view, 'substituting, as it were, the eye of the beholder for the consciousness of the character'.[2] This marks a transition to an understanding of the person through 'the surface of things', 'a place where to see was to know'.[3] Later in this book, we will find Sidney Poitier saying that he wanted to make films where people left the cinema feeling that life and human beings are worthwhile. That is the immodest aim of this book too, and it also involves the hope that the reader may feel that cinema is worthwhile, with some of its value, at least, springing from the person of the star.

THE SILENT STAR

Mary Pickford before the looking glass, 1920, photographed by Alfred Cheney Johnston.

1

MARY PICKFORD:
THE BIOGRAPH GIRL

Once there were no film stars, there were only people on film. Mary Pickford was one of the very first of the stars, of this new kind of person. For all their resemblance to the theatrical celebrity and the operatic diva, there was something unprecedented and strange about these new arrivals. They were remote and intimate, though rarely seen in person, as much like literary characters as stage stars, rendered glamorous by distance, invited into our lives by their confidential ordinariness.

From the first, the strangeness of how film transforms people disconcerted the viewers of moving pictures. On first watching a film in 1896 the Russian writer Maxim Gorky was perplexed by

> the grey silhouettes of the people, as though condemned to eternal silence and cruelly punished by being deprived of all the colors of life. . . Their smiles are lifeless. . . Their laughter is soundless . . . It is terrifying to see, but it is the movement of shadows, only of shadows.[1]

Gorky's vision is an uncanny one, the moving-picture world becoming a kind of Hades as the person on film thins to a spectre.

A slightly later account offers another way of imagining what film does to people, not turning us to ghosts but catching something of a warm, fugitive human essence. In September 1904 Rudyard Kipling published 'Mrs Bathurst', a strange elliptical tale of a woman with an indefinable quality, an ineffable but inimitable 'It' that marks her out as irreplaceably herself. One of this short story's narrators goes to watch a moving film at a circus in South Africa, where 'the pictures were the real thing – alive an' movin.' Watching film of London Bridge in the morning, he suddenly glimpses Mrs Bathurst: 'There was no mistakin' the walk in a hundred thousand' and 'She walked on and on till she melted out of the picture – like – like a shadow jumpin' over a candle.' The film transmits the unique 'blindish look' she has, preserving in light that something that was hers, while not being her, merely a trace, both a mere picture and a mock-up of the real thing.[2]

There is some distance between what film theorists have thought that film was doing and what the film-going public believed about their experience. The critics have seen technique or ideology, while audiences have engaged with people. They have glimpsed, as those who adored Mrs Bathurst had glimpsed, something unique in the person on-screen, a quality alluded to there, even as it evades our comprehension.

Mrs Bathurst is not an actor, she's a passer-by, her trivial moment of being there an accident caught by the camera. As such she is typical of the early presence of persons on-screen. They were puppets, mannequins, and not expected to reveal through their external image a complex inner life. Those early bioscope models were anonymous, subordinate to the piece of film itself; indeed, the earliest films were 'performed by people who were anything but actors', sometimes literally just folk picked up in a café.[3] Erwin Panofsky remarks that the cast of a prestige 1905 production of *Faust* are 'characteristically "unknown"'.[4]

In the USA the film companies that made up The Edison Trust (the Motion Picture Patents Company) were in the business of selling the medium of film itself, and not the actors that appeared on it. Though the facts are disputed, some film historians have suggested that the players' anonymity was a strategy on the part of the production companies, one designed to reduce the players' power and influence and so suppress wages (though it seems that in fact only one company, Biograph, actively kept their actors' names hidden).

In Britain in 1911 one writer suggests that acting in film as a 'bioscope model' is a summer employment for unemployed theatrical actors and actresses, including understudies for the more famous, a lucrative sideline for the off-season. The same article suggests that this situation may change as audiences become more interested in those on the screen: 'Already leading French players pose to the camera in plays more ambitious than the run of animated picture plays of the past, and the probability is that sooner or later personality will count, even in this field of theatrical presentation.'[5] The use of 'model' and 'pose' in this article is typical of a cultural moment that saw what was done in film as closer to the static posing of photography than to the engaging representations of the stage.

Yet suddenly in the years between 1907 and 1911, with gathering regularity, there are signs everywhere of a new substantial interest in the life of the individual person on-screen. Personality began to count. The names given to the film process itself reveal much: if the Kinetoscope implied attention merely to what moves, 'bioscope' and 'biograph' bring the focus to an engagement with life, with the living person in movement to be gazed at, felt with. From 1909 the names of the players began to appear; from around this time the press began to talk of the 'picture personalities'. By 1914 *The Times* remarked on the practice of the film companies having exclusive contracts for famous actors, 'as it is felt that his appearance in a second film, even though the story is totally different, would militate considerably against the success of the first. It is apparently the actor, therefore, more than the story that the picture palace audience goes to see.'[6] In 1911 the Shakespearean actor Sir Herbert Beerbohm Tree was paid £1,000 to appear in a film version of *Henry VIII*, the money clearly being doled out to secure the actor's name and presence in the film.

The advent of the star represented a shift towards a sense that individual performers could sell a film, and that the public would pay to spend time in the company of certain actors. In this way, the first true film star was really Max Linder, the French comic actor and 'le roi du cinématographe', a dandiacal rentier with a truly worldwide fame. From 1909 his name was selling his films, a couple of years before Florence Lawrence and Mary Pickford, the two individuals customarily taken to be the first 'stars', were established in the public mind.[7] Crucially, Linder's fame consisted of the fact that he was seen as being indistinguishable from his screen persona: 'Max' was both a recreation of himself and an artful performance. It may not be accidental that stardom should first come to a comic, gifted as such a figure could be with the ability to play versions of the same character again and again in an ongoing series. (In a similar way, in 1914, the film comedian John (Jack) Bunny was reckoned by the *Saturday Review* to be more famous than any stage or music-hall actor.)[8] Soon Mary Pickford would reproduce an aspect of this path to notoriety by becoming an icon of herself, someone given to certain kinds of role, most notably her 'Little Mary' films for American film-maker D. W. Griffith, although the variation intrinsic in dramatic roles meant that this steadfast adherence to type was always broken up by difference from film to film. (In the early 1910s, however, there were adventure serials that, like the comedy films, featured an ongoing character/actor, such as Pearl White's *The Perils of Pauline* films.)

In 1910 Kale and Vitagraph began advertising their actors through lobby cards and posters.[9] From that year on the stars were promoted using placards and postcards (in imitation of a practice already established in relation to theatre stars), slides of the actors were screened between reels, press interviews began to appear, as did the newly arrived fan magazines. The first such magazines were the *Motion Picture Story Magazine*, launched in February 1911, and the *Moving Picture Weekly*, established in January 1913, though periodicals such as *Variety* and *The Billboard* had already been covering the film industry since the middle of the previous decade. *Motion Picture Story Magazine* was at first primarily interested in retelling film stories in prose, and merely took notice of the actors, alongside photographs providing snippets telling us, for example, that Miss Clara Williams, 'one of the most popular of the picture players', is 'an expert horse-woman, and a lover of outdoor life', or that Miss Alice Jones never acted before her appearance in films, or that Miss Florence E. Turner 'has won a permanent place in the affections of the picture public'.[10] Such magazines took an interest in the film actors and soon they were firmly enmeshed in the promotion of their personalities to the public, as well as offering readers, on occasion, the possibility to join the ranks of the 'stars' through talent competitions and 'Fame and Fortune' contests (Clara Bow and Mary Astor found fame in such a way).[11]

Some critics have badly wanted the emerging desire for the star to originate with the studios and the exhibitors, and not to have come from below, from the audience themselves. Richard deCordova, for instance, has argued that 'the "picture personality" was the result of a particular production and circulation of knowledge and that studio publicity departments, films and fan magazines produced and promulgated this knowledge'.[12] In this account, the star is really a capitalist dodge. Others have seen the origin of the film star as something determined by the audience's own yearnings.[13] Those who see the film star's emergence as dependent upon institutional practices or marketing techniques may well be right, and there is much evidence on their side. However, they would still leave unanswered the question as to why the idea of the star caught on with those to whom it was marketed. The audience were not suckers; they liked what they liked. Most plausibly, the film star was born from a composite of pressures: from the makers, from the exhibitors, from the magazines, and from the audience themselves.

For it would be hard to determine whether promotion by the film companies of their players stimulated or responded to interest by filmgoers. Either way, certainly the independent producers and the film companies extracted profit from the economic potential of the personality cult. An article in *Nickelodeon* in February 1910 suggests that the audience demanded 'a better acquaintance with those they see upon the screen', while the exhibitors 'are becoming more and more interested in the personnel of those with whom they have become so familiar in the image'.[14] 'Personnel' here is a curious choice of word, clearly touching on 'personality', while clinging to a sense of a broader company. Both for the exhibitors and the audience, the key shift appears to have been a growing curiosity, an interest in the actors as persons.

Richard deCordova shows us that there was no interest in acting in the films before 1907, as the emphasis still fell on the technology itself; it was the recording machine itself that was the artist. Then, about 1907, there arose a growing insistence on the work of human beings in the process, whether the director, the cinematographer or the writer. The most obvious trace of the human in the process was that of the people on-screen.[15]

At the same moment, around 1907–8, fiction and narrative forms overtook production of documentary forms. The turn towards narrative meant a turn towards acting, and also a turn towards a person understood not only as embodied in an instant, a passing glance like that which falls on Mrs Bathurst, but in the complexity of an unravelling story. As film became ambitious, it depended more on the talents of the players. Companies such as The Edison Company turned to actors from the stock theatre companies, moving away from freelance and occasional models. 'Personality' had arrived with the fiction film, with the expansion of the person enabled by narrative.

The narrative film meant more sophisticated acting. The Société Film d'Art, founded in 1908 in Paris, has been seen as the first attempt to make a self-consciously artistic cinema. In the USA their style of acting was touted in the very late 1900s as the mode to follow. Mary Pickford, however, would resist the broad manner of acting imported from the Pathé Company, aiming at something she saw as more natural, more understated. Pickford deemed her own acting style to be a relatively muted one; in contrast to the vogueish French school of 'pantomime' on-screen, she decided, as she put it, that 'I would never overact.'[16] This decision set Pickford somewhat apart. In contrast to later understandings of the difference between theatre and film, in the 1910s there are indications that theatre actors saw film playing as broad acting, as mime and pronounced gesture, and theatre as the place for subtlety and nuance.[17] This may be an instance of theatrical snobbery, however, for early film acting, of which Pickford's is a strong example, can better be described as both exaggerated and subtle.[18] Acting on film meant making the narrative clear, not bothering with complexity, and drawing upon the necessity to make things understood. While Griffith admired the French, his adoption of close-up also enforced a more naturalistic style of playing; less had to be signalled, as more could just be seen.

The interest in the actor on-screen soon became a fascination with all concerning the real person who was, and was not, shown there. The new notion of the performer depends upon the thought that this person we have seen and suffered or laughed with persists and exists outside the film. Film and its narrative provides evidence of a person elsewhere, in whom one might be interested, whom one might meet. In his short story Kipling's clubbish men recognize someone they know from life on-screen; around 1912 Mary Pickford was learning to cope with being recognized off it. Suddenly, even in private life, she was identifiably 'The Biograph Girl'. When this first happened, her instinct was to go to D. W. Griffith and demand a raise.[19]

So it was that around 1910 human personality changed. The public was ripe to fall for a star. There was Linder, there was Florence Lawrence, but quickly, more powerfully present than anyone up to this point, there was Mary Pickford. Even if we take on the fact that Pickford was pushed as a star where other actors were not, still a mystery remains about her stardom, about all stardom. Why did fame come to this person and not another? Why, in Cecil B. DeMille's phrase about her, did Mary Pickford 'fire the imagination of millions'?[20]

Mary Pickford, like all the early stars, like all stars ever since, was both the sum of her performances and someone incommensurate, additional, elsewhere.[21] For the film historian deCordova, the star emerges from the conscious knowledge that there's a distinction between the public and the private life – the star existing as a sign of that split. Moreover, what makes them mysterious is precisely what is glimpsed on-screen, the fact that the audience may feel that the unseen somehow is seen there.

Young Gladys Smith was a little girl in Toronto with a dead dad, left looking after a younger brother and sister, having been from an early age, in lieu of her grieving mother, the head of the house – indeed, as she once put it herself, 'the father'. (Her mother shared with young Mary the notion that her dead husband's features were preserved in her daughter.) Having walked out of the family home nearly three years earlier, her father died in 1898 of a cerebral haemorrhage following a blow to the head. Gladys was five years old; responsibility had come early. Years later her brother Jack told her, while she was in costume as Little Lord Fauntleroy, 'Mary, you've never really lived. And you don't know how to play.'[22] While very young, a lodger staying in the family's best room introduced her to the possibility of acting on stage. He was a theatrical producer for the Cummings Stock Company of Toronto and he wanted the two Smith girls to play schoolchildren in a production of *The Silver King*. To win over her hesitant mother, clinging to respectability as she was, the lodger took his landlady backstage to meet the company, convincing her that actors were just ordinary people. The mother was persuaded, Gladys made her debut, and her stage career was launched. Soon she was touring as 'Baby Gladys', before stepping, under the aegis of the producer David Belasco, into a Broadway role in *The Warrens of Virginia*. She was thirteen years old and it was only then that Belasco re-christened young Gladys Smith as 'Mary Pickford'. She blagged her way into working with the highly successful director D. W. Griffith; on their first encounter, he deemed her too little and too fat; she thought him a tad vulgar. Yet together, while she was still in her mid-teens, they would build in partnership a solid career for her, making an icon in motion.

Griffith drew out from Pickford an image of American youthful resilience, feisty and dreamy in equal amounts. Initially she was advertised without her full name and was only known as 'The Girl with the Golden Hair' or 'Goldielocks' and other pseudonyms. In 1913, in the 'Filmings' column of the paper *London Life*, she was still 'Little Mary' and 'the dainty Biograph girl'; crucially, the article that names her as such also retails gossip about her private life, revealing her age and the fact that she is married.[23] Audiences began to recognize her and to look out for her films. In December 1911 Mary Pickford was the first film actor to have their photograph on the cover of a magazine.[24]

One evening in 1914, driving up Broadway, she noticed the long lines at the Strand for her film *Rags*; the following week she drove by again when another actor's film was playing, and saw that no one was queuing. She bought a ticket and went inside and found the cinema half-full. The commercial implications of her fame could not have been clearer; her immediate response was to go to her producer, Adolph Zukor, and demand that from then on her films should be marketed separately as Mary Pickford films, 'not packaged with other Famous Players' films'.[25]

It is revealing that the first close-up that Griffith framed was of Mary Pickford in the film *Friends* (1912). When they saw what he had done, the heads of Biograph studio were outraged, as such shots meant that they were no longer getting their money's worth: they had paid good money to show the whole of Mary Pickford, not merely her face. But for the viewing public such shots were precisely giving the whole person, secluding the audience with the actor on-screen in a way that had hardly occurred before. Where earlier film-makers, like James Williamson with *The Big Swallow* (1901), had used the close-up as a kind of trick shot, and one where the person viewed was anonymous and disconnected from any complex narrative, Griffith closed in on Pickford in a moment of feeling, letting the shot seize that mood, communicating it between the actor and the watcher.

In time Pickford may have come to resent the insipid, indefatigable cheerfulness of such roles as *Pollyanna*, but still she was at her best in those 'glad girl' parts.[26] On-screen, of course, she was not, as one disillusioned visiting child noted during shooting, 'a real little girl', but rather enacted an adult's longing for childhood innocence, gambolling and pouting, gaily skipping across the screen, an irrepressible unbowed Little Nell for the twentieth-century public. Although largely remembered for her juvenile roles, her range was far greater than the legend suggests and in any case her childlikeness was not synonymous with blandness; in Griffith's *The Female of the Species* (1912), for example, she contrives to be, as she often was, at once waifish and tough. It is not surprising that her sturdy, resourceful persona in *Suds* (1920) inspired Astrid Lindgren to dream up Pippi Longstocking. Pickford played a practical miss most of the time, but one given to dreaming too. In *Poor Little Rich Girl* (1917), dosed with a sleeping potion, she flees her miserable life by hallucinating a fantasy world, a Garden of Lonely Children, the counterparts to her own isolation; in *The Little Princess* (1917), as Sara Crewe, she's again a lost girl, an orphan, but still a feisty dreamer, an artist weaving tales for the other children. On-screen she sought to challenge herself, doubling up roles in a virtuoso spirit, splitting herself in two, as lonely invalid and hardy street-kid in *Stella Maris* (1918), as both mother and son in *Little Lord Fauntleroy* (1921).

Again according to Erwin Panofsky, early cinema did not look to theatre for its inspiration, but rather turned to paintings, postcards, tableaux and waxworks, giving movement to these static forms, and combining them with plots derived from penny dreadfuls, popular songs and pornography.[27] Pickford's films in part exemplify Panofsky's assertion, given as they are to melodrama and mawkishness, even to the kitsch pornographic consumption of a faux-child, the erotics of sexless sentiment. Yet on the other hand, in Pickford's performances at least, there is no trace of the waxwork or the tableau, for to give movement to such forms is to see them metamorphose; instead we catch on-screen the glimmer of a warm mutability, the play of feeling on the features, the communication transmitted through the well-chosen changefulness in a human face. In *The Little Princess*, at one moment, an Indian servant invites a potential benefactor to come to the window, where on Christmas night they will be able to look on as Pickford and young ZaSu Pitts play out a scene of discovery and fantasy; 'only great happiness can come through the happiness of others', the Indian tells his companion. In that thought we find much of the appeal of Pickford, that she could embody vulnerability for the America of her time, but also a plucky patience, the ability to play for others a hard-won happiness.

Pickford may most often have been playing innocents and children, sufferers and survivors, but her approach to the trade she was in was canny and sophisticated. She was a self-fashioner, perhaps collusive with the public's wish that on-screen she should stay a child, but was anything but childish in her approach to the business of film. She shaped her own career, choosing scripts, writing and collaborating on them too, 'directing the directors'.[28] As the critic Molly Haskell declares, the 'childish ebullience . . . masks a calculating spirit'.[29] She stage-managed her own progress for the industry, capitalizing on her popularity to get the best possible deal. In 1910 she moved to Carl Laemmle's company IMP and began to appear under her own (assumed) name; and in 1912 she transferred to Adolph Zukor's Famous Players Company, while her weekly salary went up and up, from $40 per week in 1909 to $10,000 per week in 1916 (and with a $300,000 bonus).

Fame truly came in 1914 with *Hearts Adrift* and *Tess of the Storm Country*. It was these roles in particular that led Pickford to be called 'America's sweetheart' – the name coined on a poster outside a movie theatre by its owner, David Grauman; outside the States she was sold as 'The World's Sweetheart'. Her wartime propaganda film *100% American* (1918) is a signal indication of this young Canadian's assimilation into America's sense of itself. The power of the star was amply demonstrated by Pickford's campaign to raise money for the war effort by having people invest in Liberty Bonds; she toured with her fellow stars Douglas Fairbanks and Charlie Chaplin, collecting a fortune. Pickford wanted to be in control of things: she knew that she knew as much about film-making as any director. With Fairbanks, Chaplin and Griffith, she formed United Artists, a company that put the talent in charge. She married Fairbanks in 1920, the pair of stars thereby becoming the most famous couple in the world; they divorced in 1936. Once being recognized in public was a source of astonishment, but by the time of her marriage to Fairbanks it had become a necessity. Mobbed by fans, however threatening and frightening it seemed, was better than returning to the anonymity of the private person. She won an Oscar for her role in her first talking picture, *Coquette* (1929). Despite this success in the era of talking pictures, her career was about to take a slide and after some failures, especially a poorly received version of *The Taming of the Shrew* (1929), she knew it was time to quit.

In *The Little Princess*, the director Marshall Neilan expressly sought to capture the genuine advent of laughter in Pickford's features, the dawning of hilarity there.[30] The fascination fell on the changes in her face, the desire to observe and preserve them, the turning of fugitive expression into the permanence of film. Pickford was a 'sweetheart', with all that word indicates of chaste romance, of the gentlest desire. For Molly Haskell, Pickford embodied 'the virgin', a type of innocence. In this way her films from the late 1900s to the early 1920s bear witness to a lingering Victorian sensibility in cinema, that most new-fangled of forms. Modernity, it seems, contains nostalgia. In Haskell's view, Pickford's films offer a dark, lurid child's vision of the world – stark, hallucinatory, hungering after sweetness.[31] In Pickford's films we see indeed a bridge between a new world, where the human being – just an image – dilates in the flicker of strips of film, but still connects back to the old pieties of the nineteenth-century novel, the stage melodrama, the forlornly old-fashioned still alive in the cinematic person, this new-found Biograph girl.

2

POLA NEGRI:
INVENTING THE STAR

I n Gene Kelly and Stanley Donen's *Singin' in the Rain* (1952) the curtain rises on the entrance to Grauman's Chinese Theatre on the night of the film premiere of *The Royal Rascal* ('The Biggest Picture of 1927'). The crowd outside jostle and gawk at Monumental Pictures' galaxy of stars. First to arrive, to cheers and wolf-whistles, is Zelda Zanders, 'darling of the flapper set', an all-American feisty red-head, all teeth and tiara. But then a limousine pulls up and out sweeps 'that exotic star', Olga Mara, accompanied by her latest husband, the Baron de la Bonnet de la Toulon. Olga shimmers up the red carpet with a sternly decadent stare, her dress a simulacrum of starlight on a spider's web. Later at the after-film party, the boss of Monumental unveils an amusing curiosity to the assembled guests – a talking film. None of the film people are that enthralled. 'It's a toy,' says one. 'It's vulgar,' intones the haughty Olga Mara, as one might expect of a European who would discern in cinema the possibilities of High Art.

As the rhyme might suggest, Olga Mara could be standing in for Theda Bara. She would fit, in so far as Bara was truly Hollywood's original femme fatale, or, as they put it back then, Vamp. But Bara was never the real deal, merely a counterfeited version of European – and Egyptian – mystery and sophistication, and in fact was simply Theodosia Goodman, a first-generation American from Ohio. Anyway by 1927 she was yesterday's woman, the public having grown bored with her heavy-lidded intensities.

It's much more likely that Kelly and Donen were invoking the image of Pola Negri, who, if not Hollywood's first femme fatale, was certainly its greatest and one of the key figures of silent film cinema. In her career and her development we can see, perhaps more clearly than elsewhere, the invention of a new kind of person and of a new image of what a person might be, all contained in the concept of the 'film star'. Stars may burn brightly, but they quickly fade. In the greater world Negri's most lasting achievement may be that she was the person to invent and popularize the practice of painting toenails red. (That first morning when Adolphe Menjou saw her, he believed her feet were bleeding.) In the world of films, she remains an exemplary character, a test case for the understanding of how fame and cinema work.

In synopsis, Negri's life sounds almost inconceivably extraordinary; she seems a quintessential figure of fame, a living symbol of the silent age, caught between F. Scott Fitzgerald's penetrating glamour and the ironies of Joseph Roth. Her history was absurdly eventful; she asserted, 'My life truly has been a drama of great scenes.' Her biography was touched by Tsarist oppression, the German invasion of Warsaw in 1915, and the November Revolution in Berlin (shots and explosions from outside the cinema formed the background to the premiere of her film *Carmen* in 1918); she grew up in poverty, made a fortune and then lost most of it in the Wall Street Crash; she had a career in Poland, then Berlin, then Hollywood, then (after a brief sojourn in Britain and France) back in Germany; she married twice and divorced twice too; she was both Charlie Chaplin's lover and Rudolph Valentino's; two of the men she loved died suddenly and tragically young; her lovers were gamblers, crooners, actors, aviators; her two husbands were aristocrats; she was by turns one of America's most adored stars and a vilified hate figure; Ronald Reagan invited her to his inauguration; she was Hitler's favourite actress.

There's something legendarily profligate about her persona, a life apparently given over to embodying the 'star': she called her autobiography *Memoirs of a Star* (1970) and meant it. In an interview in 1970 Marjorie Clapp claimed, 'Pola Negri is a star and she intends to play that role as long as she lives.'[1] Now we have precedents concerning what that role would mean; less fortunate than us, the early 'film stars' had to define themselves from film to film, article to article, improvising the performance as they went along. It is clear from Negri's own words that her models were the divas of opera, ballet's great dancers, the turn-of-the-century theatrical star – Sarah Bernhardt, Eleonora Duse (both of whom she met). These offered apt prototypes for Negri's career; apart from the inescapable presence of the screen, silent films are far closer to ballet and grand theatre than they are to *Breaking Bad*. These figures epitomized a different order of talent, something qualitatively distinct from ordinary mortals; perhaps the pagan idea of the passing human being elevated to the gods, becoming one bright, particular star, coloured this concept of fame. Such exemplars were necessary, though both Bernhardt and Duse offered the young Negri the same bleak advice: one could choose perfection of the life or perfection of the work, but both were impossible; above all, she must expect to be unhappy in love. The very word 'star' summons up images of remoteness, of loneliness. The space between the stalls and the screen opens like the heavens circling the earth. In the valedictory 'Foreword' to her autobiography, Negri projects a strangely dislocated version of herself, peering out from some vantage point inside her public image, poised to become once again a private person. She regards her life, her profile: 'Where am I in all this?' she muses, and to the end an answer eludes her.

Those *Memoirs* are a masterpiece of misdirection, a book that is decidedly 'tuppence coloured' when it might have been 'penny plain'. As Mariusz Kotowski, her biographer, puts it, 'When she told . . . humorous stories with her dark and cracked voice, the truth was not always confirmable.'[2] Quite. She tells us that the house she had built in Hollywood was a simple affair constructed in an unassuming 'colonial style'; in fact, it was modelled on the White House. She modestly recalls someone addressing her as 'the most intelligent and responsive person I've ever met'. From her own account, she impressed Einstein, charmed Hermann Göring and captivated George Bernard Shaw. Often she seems to be providing a textbook example of confession as an act of self-exoneration. Negri had been accused by many people of doing many unpalatable things. She had to prove that she had truly loved Rudolph Valentino and not betrayed his memory, that she had not simply abandoned her native Poland, that she had never been Hitler's mistress (she was not) or otherwise been a tool of the Third Reich. In these indictments she faced an industry dedicated to the revelation of an actor's secrets or, failing that, to their invention.

She was born on 3 January 1897 in Lipno, Poland, as Barbara Apolonia Chałupec, the third (and only surviving) child of an upper middle-class Polish woman who had, to the family's horror, married beneath her by wedding a significantly younger part-Romany Slovakian tinsmith. For all her life, the daughter would remain strongly attached to her pious and tough mother, staying loyal both to her mum's Catholicism and her stoicism; in her films, as in her *Memoirs*, Negri was not given to self-pity. That toughness was soon required, for the father drifted into taking part in seditious activity directed against the Russian Imperialist occupiers; when Pola was only eight years old, he was arrested and, in time, exiled to Siberia. When he was eventually released, more than ten years later, he made no effort to contact his wife and daughter, having found a new wife. Her father's arrest plunged the young girl and her mother into extreme financial insecurity. They moved to Warsaw, where, after a rocky start, Eleonara Chałupec earned her rather scanty living as a cook to a wealthy Jewish woman. Yet even in poverty her mother retained her would-be aristocratic sense of style; when they finally moved out of a Warsaw slum, though they carried all they had by hand, their suitcases were faded Vuitton.

In 1911 the young Pola was spotted dancing on the street by a couple with connections to the world of ballet. On their recommendation the girl joined Warsaw's ballet school, where she distinguished herself; a possible career as a principal dancer beckoned, but was dashed when Pola fell ill with tuberculosis. A rich friend of the family paid for her to stay in a mountain sanatorium. There in its library she came upon the works of the Italian poet Ada Negri and, much impressed, adopted the writer's name. She also decided that if she were not well enough to dance, she would act. After training at the Warsaw Imperial Academy of Dramatic Arts, she made a great stage success playing the young Hedwig in Ibsen's *The Wild Duck*. Rather than going to the grand Warsaw theatre that wanted her, Negri opted to work in a small experimental theatre company. As a consequence of this risky choice Negri found herself recommended to Max Reinhardt, Berlin's great theatre producer and director, for a leading role in his forthcoming orientalist pantomime, *Sumurun*. One of the other actors in the piece was a rising star of German comic film, Ernst Lubitsch, then best known for his comic creation 'Meyer', an Alexanderplatz cousin to Charlie Chaplin's 'The Tramp'. Negri had already made a number of one- and two-reel films in Warsaw; through his connections to Paul Davidson's UFA studios, Lubitsch invited her to perform in a couple of full-length films: *Die Augen der Mummie Mâ* (The Eyes of the Mummy Ma) and as Carmen in a version of Prosper Mérimée's tale (both 1918).

A visit to her mother in Poland led to Negri's disastrous and rather inexplicable marriage to a handsome and dull Polish Count. According to her *Memoirs*, for all her on-screen flirting, she was at this point, at 22 years old, an inexperienced and sentimental young lady. In her hurry to marry, she failed to notice the Count's rather tepid interest in her or how oddly close her fiancé was to his sister. The marriage appears to have expired on its first night, but Negri was stuck with it; after TB, this was the next great threat to her promising career. Lubitsch saved her. On a visit to Poland he persuaded her to come back to Germany and make proper films with him. Her husband was more pleased than not at the prospect of his young bride going off to become a film star, and so Negri packed her bags and returned to Berlin. So was secured one of the greatest cinematic partnerships, as vital as Josef von Sternberg and Marlene Dietrich, Hitchcock and Ingrid Bergman, Scorsese and Robert De Niro.

Sternberg worshipped Dietrich, and Hitchcock adored Bergman; but Lubitsch was characteristically sceptical about the personal (as opposed to cinematic) qualities of his leading lady. In part that was due to the fact that, now a star, Negri increasingly granted herself the star's privileges. In her view tantrums and bad behaviour backstage was an avowal of personality made in order that she could then more effectively lose herself inside the character she was playing on camera. 'Accomplished artists,' she avers, 'cannot be equated to people simply because they happen to be people.'

The film she came back to make with Lubitsch was *Madame DuBarry* (1919); it was the film that made them both stars in America, and in doing so opened up German cinema – boycotted since the end of the war – to the world. With Potsdam's Sanssouci standing in for Versailles, *Madame DuBarry* offers history as reverie, as style; it's significantly closer to Sofia Coppola's contentedly anachronistic *Marie Antoinette* (2006) than to the researched instances of Paul Greengrass's drama-doc *Bloody Sunday* (2002). It entices us with images, seduces us with spectacle. Lubitsch's film graces us with a vision of history as purely personal. In effect, the causes of the French Revolution boil down to a lover's quarrel. Many years ago Lubitsch's lack of a truly political and historical sense somewhat troubled the film critic Siegfried Kracauer. He saw this film, and other similar 'historical' works made in Germany in these years, as a way of belittling the processes of history as 'an arena reserved for blind and ferocious instincts, a product of devilish machinations forever frustrating our hopes for freedom and happiness.'[3] Though fully aware of Lubitsch's humane sensibility and generous outlook, for Kracauer such an implicit philosophy as this was a highly dangerous one, liable to induce the kind of nihilistic fatalism that years later would bear fruit in the unopposed coming to power of the Nazis.

Part of the unspoken frenzy that Kracauer detects in Lubitsch is, as Caroline Lejeune once noted, a new insistence on the agency of the crowd, seen as a force in relation to which emerges the lonely single figure.[4] Lubitsch loves the crowds almost as much as he loves Negri and Emil Jannings (playing Louis xv); all three are cinematically thrilling, offering a type of pleasure to the eye. But more than that, Lubitsch's film offers a kind of fable about the film star and her audience, and in doing so provided Negri not only with her greatest triumph but with a film that would define her predicament.

Negri (or her ghostwriter, Alfred Allan Lewis) wrote, 'The kings had all died, leaving the realm to mummers.' Around this time, she bought some of the Hohenzollern diamonds, a film star literally taking on the trappings of monarchs. She plays du Barry with all the hauteur a small 22-year-old Pole can muster. She is beautiful but manifestly not bothered whether we find her beautiful or not. She fascinates the viewer; it is a pleasure simply to watch the passing emotions of her face, to see someone so eloquently equipped for the pantomime of flirtation. By our standards she's over the top, but her acting is not without its subtleties. She can look both dim and cunning, dreamy and on-the-make. Ernst Lubitsch's biographer Scott Eyman remarks: 'If it's possible for an actress to believably play a character who sleeps her way to the top and still remains innocent, Negri manages to pull it off.'[5] Yet for all the compassion the audience feels for her, in this film, it's du Barry versus the masses; she's both their representative and their enemy, possessing the wealth and elegance they yearn for and despise. She was at her best in performance mixing the class-contradictions of her own life, a young woman who had grown up in the slums, but with an eye always on her mother's foregone elegancies and the gilt and illusion of the stage. Often in her Berlin films, she is an interloper, a parvenue; though she may be ascending the ranks, she remains one of the people.

And in the end they kill her. The fascination that is also resentment finds its ultimate expression; in short, it's the perfect enunciation of the plight of the great film stars. In this reading of the film, Louis xv is the director, the envious court Negri's fellow actors, the mob the vengeful audience. Although at this stage of her career her persona entailed the refusal of suffering, it turns out that Negri will have to suffer anyway. The film ends fittingly enough with her beheading, the head flung to the crowd so that the last thing we see is that emotive face, decapitated and immobile. The camera lingers on the stilled face that had earlier fascinated it; the moment is the camera's and the audience's revenge.

There followed a number of highly successful films, but all the best are those Lubitsch made with her. In the first half of Negri's memoirs, for all her love of performance, she portrays herself as unworldly, consumptive, even shy; yet in her German films she's resilient, brazen and robust, a streetwise kid. With her pallor and her black hair, there's a touch of the young Siouxsie Sioux about her. Negri possessed the art of looking self-possessed; every grin, every deprecatory smirk offers us someone immeasurably pleased with themselves. She kicks off *Sumurun* (1920) with a come-hither look that, nearly a century later, makes me regret that I can't get up and go thither. That look of hers reminds us that in 1920s cinema it was eroticism that was the great subject, the novelty of the medium, and (despite Sergei Eisenstein and *Potemkin*) not close-ups of maggots in meat. She manifests, at least at first, a sexuality unshaded by sorrow or self-doubt, a person finding herself in pure play. There is a blithe anarchy in it all that it is hard not to admire. If she is a femme fatale, then she is one who

Pola Negri's come-hither glance in *Sumurun* (1920).

is visibly relishing her own ploys and processes; it is hard, and indeed pointless, not to enjoy them with her.

In those Lubitsch films she is not necessarily the romantic lead; in *Sumurun* she is not the title character, who is a more dignified kind of harem girl altogether. For all its pathos, Lubitsch's film version of Reinhardt's *Sumurun* plays like a comedy. It is an Edmund Dulac-style hallucination of the mysterious 'East', a fairy-tale Orient and therefore a vision of tyranny and absolute control – both the dominion held by the autocratic Sheikh, but also that operated in the interstices of power by beautiful women. Despite the despotic Sheikh, men are a sorry bunch here: eunuchs, besotted old men or feckless dreamers passively enthralled by their desire. It is Sumurun, the virtuous courtesan, who pulls her mawkish lover closer for a kiss and who engineers (with female help) her own victory; and 'The Dancer', played by Negri, proves a go-getting, upwardly mobile character. Yet here Negri comes to a sticky end, properly punished for her duplicity, while Sumurun's own deceptions are well rewarded.

It is a silly film, but a highly likeable one; its vision of the Near East reminds us that across the Alps Puccini was just beginning to write *Turandot* and so fabricate a similarly far-fetched version of China. It conjures up another kind of modernist art, one that comes out of the *Thousand and One Nights*, Hoffmann and Dickens, derived from burlesque and dedicated to pantomime, not dissonant or introspective, but spectacular, fabulous and only fragmented in so far as all films must be so.

The term 'femme fatale' suggests languor; a 'spider-woman' is presumably a patient creature, biding her time in her web awaiting victims. Pola Negri is nothing like that. Particularly in *Die Bergkatze* (The Wildcat, 1921), Lubitsch indulges Negri's energy and unleashes her capacity for fun. Although she was billed as 'The Queen of Tragedy', it makes clear how much her genius was for comedy. There are jokes about how the men like to be whipped by her, but she's a noticeably vivacious dominatrix, cheeky, a figure of mischief. Similarly, while playing Madame du Barry, Negri twice has a man blindfolded, she dresses in men's clothes and has the king act the part of a lady's maid. In *Die Bergkatze*, when she wants to gain the hero's attention, she chucks a snowball at him. Once again, as in *Sumurun*, she is a runner, darting around the possibly parodic expressionist-style sets, racing pell-mell up and down the staircases. Matching her energy, Lubitsch experiments wildly with the frame of the image itself, which becomes at various moments a pair of lips, an oval, an ascending stair and so on, and on. 'Das Mädel hat Schmiss' ('the girl's got pep'), we're told. Later the ideal Lubitsch woman – such as Miriam Hopkins in *Trouble in Paradise* (1932) or, especially, Carole Lombard in *To Be or Not to Be* (1942) – appeared as half-distracted con artists, mingling the beautiful and the daft. Here we see most clearly how Negri was a prototype for such characters.

Like most of Lubitsch's films, *Die Bergkatze* is a delight; it makes space for the kind of wistful melancholy that the tough-minded despise, though it's not hard to locate the tough-mindedness in it, with its alert acceptance of human frailty. It can even take pleasure in the self-absorbed silliness of human egotism. Yet *Die Bergkatze* flopped in Germany, its jokes about chocolate-box soldiers and its gentle endorsement of stylish cowardice unwanted by a defeated nation with a *Freikorps*. Even its vision of the mountains (and Lubitsch apparently loved mountains), the sacred Germanic space, transforms that sublime romantic symbol of purity into the backdrop to an absurdist, poetic farce. There is a touch of subversive social comment too: the robbers are prepared to sacrifice themselves for love; it is the bourgeois couple who are ultimately selfish and grab what they can.

Negri would rarely enjoy such on-screen freedom again. She left for Hollywood, the first European star to be bought up as a rare commodity, but once she got there it was clear the American film business did not know what to do with her. Although allowed a latitude not granted to American women, there would, however, be no place for her carefree sexiness. Here she really honed her ongoing public performance as a star, creating a reputation for desirable reclusiveness years before Garbo did so, spontaneously stage-managing her life. Her every move was followed by the press; her relationship with Charlie Chaplin played out in the papers and fan magazines; they were lovers in the headlines long before they had in fact got into bed with each other. With Bernhardt and Duse in mind, she grasped the necessity of managing the processes of stardom in order to sustain her career. Sadly, her role as a public figure was better managed than her film choices. She succeeded in getting a small number of good films made, typically with European directors: reunited with Lubitsch in *Forbidden Paradise* (1924); directed by Garbo's lover and mentor Mauritz Stiller in the lachrymose melodrama *Hotel Imperial* (1927); and, post-Hollywood, in German director Paul Czinner's *Street of Abandoned Children* (or *The Way of Lost Souls*, 1929), her only British film. Lubitsch without Negri would remain Lubitsch; Negri without Lubitsch was never quite so good again. A journalist wrote: 'To Pola, going back to Lubitsch's direction was like taking off a tight pair of shoes . . . He didn't want her to be beautiful or sympathetic.' Hollywood required both, on- and off-screen. Given the demands, it was only a matter of time before the love affair with the American audience ended. Stardom, it turned out, was not just a marketing exercise, nor was it a matter of stunning performances; it was a relation to the public, allowing oneself to exist as an image in the eyes of the crowd. The relation soured when the public turned critical.

The break came with Negri's well-publicized romance with Valentino. Their love affair was the publicity department's dream come true, an exotic counterpart to solid Douglas Fairbanks and Mary Pickford. It was Negri's public apotheosis and the cause of her downfall. On 23 August 1926 Valentino died from peritonitis following an appendectomy. If the public demanded heightened life and artifice on the screen, at a burial they required strict naturalism. At his funeral Negri wept, staggered and swooned (twice); she also paid for a huge bouquet of flowers spelling out her own name. The rumour was that the bouquet was sufficiently massive to make sure it would come out clearly in the press photographs. The film fans simply did not credit Negri's mourning; she was not in love, she was on the make. Then any residual goodwill granted her as 'Valentino's widow' vanished when she married another aristocrat, this time a Russian prince in exile, nine months after Valentino's death. The account in the *Memoirs* of this marriage to Prince Serge Mdivani makes odd reading. She seems to have sleepwalked into the wedding, bullied into marrying by her lover, his family and finally her mother. Why it happened is doubtful, but that it strained her relationship with American filmgoers is clear. She made more films, most of them commendable, but she was on the way out. The advent of sound was another blow, the Wall Street Crash and the demise of 1920s glamour and artifice yet another. By this time she was drinking copiously and perhaps indulging in cocaine too. Although she had successfully played 'ordinary women' (as in *Hotel Imperial*), women fans, in particular, wanted a more down-to-earth kind of heroine than it was supposed Negri could believably supply.

Sound was supposed to have finished her in the USA, yet her accent was no thicker than Dietrich's or Garbo's. Her voice, the husky essence of cigarettes and champagne, sounds perfectly fine in her 1930s German films. But Hollywood was unconvinced: Negri was yesterday's star. She went where the work was, first to London, then to Paris, and then on to Germany. She found a home in the Nazi-sponsored film industry, where she was both suspected (particularly of having too friendly connections with Jews) and a much-appreciated source of foreign income. Hitler loved her film *Mazurka* (1935); for a while he watched it two or three times a week, weeping regularly over its sentimental picture of a wronged mother.

With the advent of war Negri absconded via Lisbon on a refugee boat back to the States. She had arrived nearly twenty years before, a star greeted by crowds of press and well-wishers. Now she was no one, though a no one still burdened by the fact of being a 'star'. She made one appearance in a harmless comedy (*Hi Diddle Diddle*, 1943), but after that failed to find more work, turning down too many parts as wrong for her and not finding any that might be right. After a lifetime spent in Warsaw, Berlin, Hollywood, London, Paris, the Château de Rueil-Séraincourt and Cap Ferrat, she became an American citizen and spent her last three decades in San Antonio, Texas. Her last relationship was with Margaret West, the woman who first introduced country and western music to American network radio. There was one more film, *The Moon-spinners* (1964) with Walt Disney, but it was the independently wealthy West who ensured that Negri's last years were financially comfortable; she lived on money left to her by West for some 25 years. Negri declared that she and West were never lovers; most people now assume they were. Either way, it is reassuring to know that her last relationship was such a loving and generous one.

Negri was an early choice to play Norma Desmond, the decaying silent-film star in Billy Wilder's *Sunset Boulevard* (1950). There are various theories as to why she turned it down: perhaps she resented not being the first choice of all; perhaps she thought her potential co-star (at that stage Montgomery Clift) was wrong for the part; possibly she felt ridiculed by the script, which was very likely in part based on her. The role instead went to her once great rival Gloria Swanson (though the rivalry had very largely been a set of grudges concocted by Paramount's publicity department). Personally, I am glad she didn't choose to play the role, in part because Swanson is so good in it, and in part because it is clear that for all her toughness Negri might not have stood up against Wilder's cynicism. She genuinely loved the films the world appeared to have forgotten, and she was right to love them.

In her *Memoirs* there is a photo of Negri as a late middle-aged woman gazing at a younger flawless waxwork of herself as she had once appeared in the title role of *The Spanish Dancer* (1923). It might have been painful to see such a double – the contrast of success and its aftermath, of youth and age – except that Negri looks remarkably unworried, amused by this strange parodic doppelgänger of herself, this figure of fame. To some extent she bought into her own myth, seeing herself as part aristocrat, part 'gipsy'; yet something in her, as she had written, was watching the image from elsewhere. With others of her generation, she represented a new kind of woman, intemperate, passionate and shameless. She dreamt of playing Cleopatra, a role she never landed, but in any case was caught up by the press in a version of herself that answered to the chauvinist critics' view of that queen as a person without a centre, fickle, insincere, impulsive, up to no good. Negri had the artist's desire, the actor's longing, to be, as she herself put it, 'the world and everything in it'. For a few years she seemed to be achieving that ambition, creating so many people, so various, so irreconcilable. Even now, though she has been dead for more than thirty years, those selves remain, facets of a person who is the sum of her many performances, especially her prototypical performance as a star.

3

CHARLIE CHAPLIN: THE TRAMP

C harlie Chaplin spent much of his career refining and exploring one myth, one persona – that of 'The Tramp'. Between 1914 and 1936 he explored this character in film after film, honing the meanings implicit in this vagabond figure. Comedians often embody one ongoing character or character type across their films, whether they are Buster Keaton or Laurel and Hardy, W. C. Fields or Woody Allen. There is something sticky in the nature of such gag-based comedy, some way in which it depends upon an immutable, archetypal version of the self, a personality that refuses to alter, the self standing as an imperturbable fact in the world. Here eccentricity coalesces.

From his first appearance in *Mabel's Strange Predicament* (1914) to *Modern Times* (1936), The Tramp inhabits a hostile world, where antagonism is constant and the environment hostile. Chaplin declared that the 'theme of life is conflict and pain', and all his clowning drew upon that fact.[1] Yet he survives, gracefully maladroit, dodging the consequences of his lack of coordination with a dancer's agility. He's a ne'er-do-well who's a natural aristocrat; he is shabby-genteel, his life dedicated to the maintenance of dignity and the expression of gentlemanliness. In mythic terms, a tramp embraces poverty as non-conformity, in an unsettled and wayward shot at freedom. In *The Kid* (1921) the authority of the law is against him, bearing down on him as it would too on Jackie Coogan, another version of Chaplin himself, as a hapless orphaned child. There is something of the child about The Tramp, always there in the ill-fitting clothes, and this eternal boyishness marks him out as a romantic, but sexless adult. When it comes to fighting, he is weak, and being weak he has to be especially clever. Above material desires, his concerns are personal relations and the social graces; he is a singular fellow and an everyman. In the films he is an isolated figure, and out of that isolation he frames his appeal to the individuals in the crowd that make up the cinema audience. In a mass art form, he calls out for the very individual response that is love.

Chaplin's films depend on the distance, and the erasure of distance, between the film star and the unloved child. Chaplin's background comes into play in his films, drawing on the suffering experienced in his impoverished childhood, his time in the workhouse, the absence of his father, his mother's mental illness. Given that foundational sense of abandonment, as Robert Warshow once suggested, the question his films ultimately ask is, if you really knew me, could you still love me?[2] *City Lights* (1931), one of his two or three greatest films, dramatizes that question, this immodest plea. *City Lights* can stand in for dozens of Chaplin's films as The Tramp, indeed for much of his oeuvre. Though each film offers a variation on the theme of that character, this is because there is something unchanging about him. The Tramp is not a person in time, but a myth, an epitome of the modern self, trapped in history but unsullied by its passing.

After *City Lights* the historical world would impinge more and more on the comedic timelessness. In *Modern Times* (1936) an independent and broadly socialist response to the impact of the Great Depression permeates the film, even as it gilds that misery with the tinsel of fantasy. (That film at first had the working title *The Masses*.) And then in his first film without The Tramp, *The Great Dictator* (1940), history and contemporary politics are fully present with the lies of fascism exposed. *City Lights*, then, sounds the first notes of a slow swansong for The Tramp, a mature reflection on one of the century's archetypal figures.

In his short book on *City Lights*, Charles J. Maland recounts an anecdote about the filming of Chaplin's masterpiece.[3] The journalist

Erwin Kish had come to spend time with Chaplin. They were filming the pivotal scene in which The Tramp first meets The Blind Girl (played by the young socialite Virginia Cherrill). Kish relates that they shot this one scene three hundred times. Chaplin began using Kish experimentally as a sample audience member; he wished to discover if simply through mime and camera movement Kish could grasp the essential information that the scene must convey. The entire success of the film depended on the audience following the plot at this point. They must take in that the young flower-seller on the street corner is blind, that The Tramp falls in love with her, and that by sheer accident, due to her blindness, she should mistakenly imagine that he is wealthy. The meaning of the film that follows depends on her misapprehension, and The Tramp's instantaneous, improvised decision not to disabuse her about her mistake. Probably without letting his choice fully come to consciousness, he chooses to let her dream about him. This deceit could look seedy, though The Tramp's gentleness and his tactful shyness prevents our reading it that way. Still this choice is both culpable and cinematic, its meanings evoking truths about the nature of the films, of love, and of our relation to the film star.

In his commitment to mime, Chaplin becomes the film star who most self-consciously invites us to read him. This reading is an act of human solidarity; through it we discover our connection to others. It is a democratic appeal, one that depends upon what is universal in us, what is shared, an instinctive attunement to the meanings of gesture and glance and posture. It speaks to the individual in the mass, presenting as it does a man at the bottom of social structures who also, by dint of his gentleness and his eccentricity, stands somewhere beyond them. So it was that Chaplin clung to the artificial limitations of the silent film long after the rest of the world had switched to speech. Silence meant classlessness, meant an adherence to a global language of expression, one that breaks the boundaries of a merely national cinema. *City Lights* begins with a parody of the recently arrived talking cinema, pompous officials and a lady of leisure speechifying inanely at the unveiling of a pompous statue (all we hear is the buzzing of kazoos), the banality of their discourse answered by the dumb figure of The Tramp, snoozing unconcernedly in the statue's arms. Chaplin was the most famous man in the world because the entire world knew and understood him. He was available for their dreams. As he himself declared: 'I cannot conceive of my films as other than silent. My shadow appears on the screen as in a dream, and dreams do not speak.'[4]

Chaplin had the singular advantage for an artist of working in a truly popular medium, making mass art, while still moving and appealing to the most intellectual of audiences. Like Shakespeare, his work had to gather the approval of both the groundlings and of monarchs. His work at once delighted 'ordinary' filmgoers and D. H. Lawrence. In the anti-authoritarian instincts of Chaplin's films lies the assumption that film itself is not an authority. Chaplin's cinema retains its roots in circus, the sideshow and the music hall. He had begun as a stage artist (a fact evidenced everywhere in the distanced and unified spaces in which his scenes play out) and so retained the theatre performer's relation of intimacy to the audience in the gods. Time and again in *City Lights*, The Tramp looks out into the camera, striking up a little collusion, an understanding, between him and ourselves.

City Lights stands as a film that depends upon our ability to read visual clues and to understand inwardness by external signs. Yet at its centre is a young blind woman on whom all such nuances are lost. The world of mime that is Chaplin's element is a closed book to her. She acts as the limit to Chaplin's ability to move another, someone who cannot judge him by appearances but only by the generous deeds he performs. Her blindness makes her peculiarly the object of his gaze. The film is ready to point to the impulse to stare that informs it; the film's second scene shows The Tramp before a shop window admiring a nude statue of a woman with an attitude somewhere innocently between a connoisseur's and a lecher's eye. Windows are key stage properties in this film, dependent as it is on the painful contrast of being brought inside or shut out. Somehow The Tramp's enchantment rarely if ever appears seedy or voyeuristic; the tentative quality of his feeling for her, with a love almost purged of pragmatic desire, redeems his looking. There is perhaps a Dickensian pathos in the affection lavished on this blind woman; compassion prompts The Tramp, and not lust.

Her blindness is essential to our understanding of her; her character is designated as 'The Blind Girl', even though she closes the film with her sight intact. She's blind because being so she is all the freer to dream up her version of the benefactor who helps her. In her imaginings, which Chaplin filmed and then cut from the finished film, he stands as all that is conventionally handsome and noble, a fashion-plate version of masculine desirability.

Structurally *City Lights* has been dismissed as a sequence of amusing episodes, a gag-film committed only to creating situations that will make us laugh. It is called *City Lights* and it is a city film above all in its interest in randomness and accident; a man of the streets, The Tramp forms the two relationships central to the film by chance. In fact, of course, Chaplin consciously sets out the plot in a narrative exposition that juxtaposes two worlds and two relationships: that between The Tramp and The Blind Girl, and that between The Tramp and The Eccentric Millionaire. Chaplin moves between two material and moral universes, both predicated on help and the intimacy that help fosters. Both provide realms in which The Tramp helps another, looking after The Blind Girl as best he can, a hapless knight errant, and saving The Millionaire repeatedly from his abrupt and desperate suicidal impulses. Money defines both worlds, as the film dramatizes all those various ways by which we come by it: winning it, being given it, stealing it, working for it, or finding it. Otherwise these two realms exist through other stark contrasts: the girl belongs to the world of day, the millionaire to the night; the girl is single but romantic, the millionaire divorcing and hedonistic; the girl sells flowers, symbols of purposeless beauty, while the rich man chucks the flowers she sells aside; she has a home and a sweet grandmother, a relationship based on kinship and affection, he has a house like a nightclub and a hostile butler, a relationship based on the cash nexus; she affirms life and embraces optimism, where he teeters constantly on the edge of a suicidal despair. Above all, The Eccentric Million-aire's house is set back from the public street, a place with a locked door, privatized and separate, whereas her home finds itself in the shared privacy of a communal courtyard, its window constantly open to the world.

The central joke of the film, and the key to its resonance, is that both The Blind Girl and The Millionaire are unable consistently to recall or know The Tramp, and by extension the actor who embodies him. When he's drunk, The Millionaire adores The Tramp, hugging him close in a fierce, inebriated affection; but each time he sobers up, he can no longer recall the little man to whom he declared his undy-ing friendship. He stares blankly at an unremembered face and orders his eager butler to get rid of him.

There's an autobiographical impulse at work in *City Lights*. Con-sequently it almost played out in London, the town where Chaplin spent his impoverished childhood, before its locale shifted to some West Coast town, Anywhere, USA. It is autobiographical perhaps above all in setting out as myth the huge journey that Chaplin himself undertook from workhouse street kid to the biggest film star in the world. Having grown up in abject poverty, Chaplin was now a terrif-ically wealthy man. In the film it is The Tramp who mediates between The Blind Girl's world and The Millionaire's (these two characters never otherwise meet or see each other), and in reality Chaplin him-self was the common denominator between those distinct social territories. In trying to bring together the world of his childhood and youth with that of his maturity, Chaplin attempts in a fable to answer the doubt of the rich and the famous: will I be loved as the rich man, as the dream figure on the screen, or as myself, a lad from out of the London abyss?

Here we have the most famous man in the world who somehow, in different ways, is a person who, within the parable of this film, cannot be recognized or remembered. Later in this book we shall encounter other celebrated film stars who share the same fate of being forgettable. In its relation to the film star, cinema naturally dreads any kind of prosopagnosia, that cognitive condition in which we

Charlie Chaplin in the closing shots of *City Lights* (1931).

cannot recognize or recall faces. In 1931 Chaplin's face was probably the most recognized in the world, summoned up by a black tooth-brush moustache, a pair of marked eyebrows, a wavy cloud of hair; yet here he falls back into the condition of anonymity, somehow unable to be known or understood to be himself.

The closing scene of *City Lights* goes very deep into an explora-tion of the meaning of the film star's predicament, at least as Chaplin personified it for his public. With money given by The Millionaire and brought to The Blind Girl by The Tramp, she has had an oper-ation, regained her sight and bought a chic flower shop, where she works with her grandmother. With sight comes mirrors; we now see the former 'Blind Girl' checking her face in a looking-glass in the flower shop. She continues to expect the arrival of the mysterious benefactor who saved her, seeing him perhaps in the well-dressed and insipidly elegant men about town who come to her shop. Meanwhile The Tramp has gone to prison for theft of the money he brought to her. Newly released, he wanders the streets, unable to find her, for-lorn and lost. Suddenly, by chance, he finds himself in front of the store where she works. With the glass between them, a permeable bar-rier, for the first time they look at each other. He knows her at once, of course, but she, never having laid eyes on him, cannot guess that this comical, shambolic figure is the man who has loved her. As he stands before the shop window gazing at her, the film echoes that earlier moment where he had appraised the statue of the nude. Now the woman in the window has come to life, become a truly moving image in a moving film, able to engage with him, to answer his gaze, to mime to him the meanings that the glass barrier prevents him from hearing. With the window between them, she must do for him what he has done for us: she must mime her meaning and communicate without words.

She comes out to the street to give him a flower. He takes it, and she offers him a coin. Not caring for the money, he reaches out for her hand, and as she takes his hand into her own she finally 'sees' him. Returned to her blindness, by touch she realizes that this is the man who gave her everything. 'You?' she asks. He nods. He asks her if she can see. 'Yes,' she replies, 'I can see now.' Silently they look at each other, and the film ends.

But how does it end? What do her last words mean? She says, at once, three different things: she tells him that she is able to see; she affirms that she now sees him; and she lets us know that finally she comprehends it all. In seeing him, an edifice of illusion that she has built up about him shatters. Reverse shots that isolate each in their separate image emphasize their apartness. Chaplin asserted that comedy is a long shot and tragedy is a close-up (what he called 'insets'). Here as rarely, if ever, before, we see both of them close up. Brought in, we draw near to their heartbreak, the distance that permits laughter snatched from us. The Tramp stares at her, enraptured; that excellent critic James Agee declared what Chaplin does here to be the finest acting up to then in cinema.[5] But, putting himself in the third person, inside The Tramp, Chaplin himself later affirmed that he wasn't acting at all; he was merely looking at The Girl, watching the reactions in her face: 'He was watching and wondering what she was thinking and wondering without any effort.'[6] As The Tramp wonders, so do we. The cutting tells us that it's a tragic ending, and so does the minor key sadness in the music. Yet some have seen love or maybe only its younger sister, tenderness, in her expression; others feel the disappointment, even the devastation in her face. Her hand moves to her chest; elsewhere in the film this has been a gesture that signifies romantic love, but here it is somewhere between an embrace and a blocking out. Is there pity there? Gratitude? Loss? She has looked for love, she has imagined it and pictured the man himself. And now, instead, there is this small, desperate, comical creature. And what about his look? He is apparently elated, but does this mean that he cannot see the possibility of disappointment that is there? In the instant when she wakes from her dream, one of the dreams perhaps that Chaplin had declared his films had put on-screen, does The Tramp steadfastly, desperately, cling to his reveries concerning life? The moment presents another instance of his refusal to be defeated, but one that is no longer comedic and optimistic, but instead marks him out as deluded. Maybe he purely evades life.

And so a film that hinges on our ability to read the inner life in outer impressions closes with a gesture that seems radically unreadable. It ends without a resolution; that heartbroken refusal to resolve the ground between love and rejections commences our investigation of the movie star's meanings.

THE GOLDEN AGE

4

'ASTA' AND 'CHEETA': THE ANIMAL STAR

In 2009 a Hollywood memoir was nominated for the Booker Prize for fiction. The book was *Me Cheeta: The Autobiography*, a celebrity chronicle to shelve alongside Mickey Rooney's *Life Is Too Short* and Katharine Hepburn's modestly titled *Me*.[1] More importantly, the book's putative author is indeed 'Cheeta' (or, rather, 'Cheetah'), the chimpanzee star of just short of a dozen Tarzan films and the sidekick of American beefcake Johnny Weissmuller. Cheeta opens the story of his life by saying it will be a celebratory list, an expanded acknowledgements page. As it happens, of course, the book works out rather differently.

The author was in fact James Lever; so far it is his only book. Parody is a loving attack. *Me Cheeta* is a shaggy dog story, one that self-consciously sabotages its chosen genre. It hates Hollywood, it hates its stars and yet, like Cheeta and his keepers, at the end of the day it settles down to the silver-nitrate glow of some classic American movie. Only an avid film buff would have been able to collect so many scraps of trivia and disappointment to tear from the film world they loved; only the most pious fan could have devoured so many saccharine showbiz chronicles.

If the book despises the dream factory, it honours the dreaming itself. Not the least of its many virtues is that the book sends you back to the best of the 1930s Tarzan films. They are indeed magical and Cheeta (and his ghost writer) are persuasive in illuminating their charm. Nonetheless, watching them again, you find yourself surprised by things that *Me Cheeta* skims over or distorts. Were these really the films we used to watch on Saturday morning television? The pre-Hays Code pictures seem much more erotic and vicious than I remember. The jungle is part-idyll, part-nightmare. Naturally envious perhaps, Cheeta downplays his rival Maureen O'Sullivan's art deco sexiness (to the end of her life O'Sullivan would refer to Cheeta as 'that bastard'). Fascinated by flesh and bodies, those very first Tarzan films ogle both her and Weissmuller, presented as perfect specimens. The Africans too are there for us to stare at, ethnographic types categorized for the viewer. In the earliest *Tarzan* films O'Sullivan wears a costume so skimpy it holds the viewer in a perpetual state of mild agitated expectation. As one visiting roué to the jungle remarks, you keep believing you'll see something more, but never do. Although in fact you do. The scene in *Tarzan and his Mate* (1934) where O'Sullivan's body-double (Josephine McKim) swims nude with Tarzan offers a moment of pure beauty. The couple both seem so light, so effortless, so unforced. The later censored films offer a buttoned-up jungle: Jane's hemlines drop and she grows ever more brisk.

Violence occurs with regularity. Local helpers are dispatched in negligent abundance: consumed by cannibals, trampled by elephants, shot by disgruntled colonists. Even the whites aren't safe. Tarzan's jungle home is no place for pastoral softies. Each skinny-dipping spree ends in a struggle with a king-sized crocodile; rhinos disrupt picnics; love trysts are interfered with by lions. How was this carnage ever considered perfect entertainment for impressionable children?

One of James Lever's jokes derives from suspending disbelief and imagining that this mute chimpanzee, the last of the silent film comedians, has attained a voice – or rather, always had a voice, but kept shtum anyway. The incongruity entails a continual second glance; what everyone in the book assumes to be a dumb beast, we know is an acerbic observer of the human beings he encounters. Seen but not heard in life, in print he takes his authorial revenge.

The only problem with *Me Cheeta* turns out to be that it is too well-written. What in other, differently talented, hands would be a teasing joke on celebrity venality, or an exercise in pastiche, persists in wandering off into profundity. Though there are some very funny jokes here, the keynotes are melancholy and rage. Disgust tarnishes the glamour. Cheeta's stock of wisdom chiefly derives from two sources: books on animal behaviour and a myriad of sleazy anecdotes told by the stars of the Hollywood Golden Age. That these two wells of inspiration should be so strikingly similar is the abiding premise of the book: 'Life ain't perfect, as the one and only Wallace Beery supposedly told Gloria Swanson after raping her on her wedding night.'[2] It is with asides such as that one that we are told more than we ever wanted to know. Did Marlene Dietrich really wet herself whenever she laughed? Who cares? What does it have to do with the splendour of *Shanghai Express*?

The book employs a tested literary device. Cheeta is Voltaire's Huron, the Native American protagonist of his novel *L'Ingénu*, the wild outsider gazing on at the strangeness of modern life with unimplicated eyes. Cheeta, however, is a compromised outsider, an animal irreducibly different from us, but also a Hollywood player privy to secrets, a witness to scandal.

Me Cheeta is *Hollywood Babylon* with bananas. Is the misanthropy purely an impersonation, the kind of thing that an exploited and world-famous chimpanzee might feel, or evidence of the ghost writer's temperament? Either way, this is a puritanical book, dominated by righteous outrage. The quips work, the reader laughs, but they leave a sour taste; it is amusing, but bitter. In particular a puzzling repugnance to sex recurs, only one of the ways in which the book reminds you of Jonathan Swift.

Cheeta chooses to reimagine the Tarzan films as buddy movies, memorials to an inter-species friendship. Between genders himself (he's a boy but plays a girl), this chimp is an American dreamer, hankering after the timeless world of the jungle. Greedy whites may impinge on the sanctuary, but still it remains, unchanging and glorious. The repetitive use of stock footage in the early Tarzan films should not seem a money-saving flaw, rather it is the secret to the whole affair. It is always the same battle, always the same play. The guys just like to hang out. The chief threat to this bliss turns out to be Jane. Why do girls have to come and spoil the fun? Women bring the domestic, the ordered, the civilized; and all Cheeta wants is comedy, idle intimacy, to play forever with Johnny.

In dwelling on the sexual debaucheries of half-remembered leading men and starlets, the book summons up some savage enough indignation. However, strangely, it mostly avoids the one subject that might more likely nowadays arouse the ire of a viewer of the *Tarzan* films: race. A troubling primitivism saturates these films. They render African animals as spectacle, while simultaneously transforming the human inhabitants of the place into beasts. In *Tarzan the Ape Man* (1932) Jane's father declares of the local tribespeople, 'they have no emotions . . . they're hardly human'. Cheeta is in his own way an African migrant and the book makes some play with this idea. Moreover, at one point he compares himself to Hattie McDaniel, the Oscar-winning co-star of *Gone with the Wind*. But ultimately the racial politics of the films, and of the Edgar Rice Burroughs books they are based on, recede into a few jokes about the Gaboni, the African tribe that live on the outskirts of Tarzan's protected escarpment. As a child I had always naively believed that the films really were shot in Africa. It amazes me that Hollywood had access to quite so many lions and elephants. Yet now I know that the whole series was made in California, it is the extras that worry me. All those Gaboni and Jaconi tribesmen – were they really all locals from Watts and West Compton?

Rather than human oppression, the book is alert to the enslavement and destruction of animals. According to Cheeta, and he ought to know, the contradiction of human feelings towards death appear most vividly in our paradoxical relationship to our fellow creatures. This relationship, Cheeta asserts, is based on a combination of extermination and conservation, of tyranny and fondness. We eradicate a species in the wild and meanwhile preserve a few specimens in a zoo, a sealed-off sanctuary from the realities of death.

Cheeta, supposedly the longest-lived chimpanzee on record, pursues a one-ape campaign against mortality. Death only occurs, he argues, if you stop paying attention for a moment; it's a giving-in.

Safeguarded in his model home, with Don the guardian to pet him, Cheeta lives out the long American retirement. It's a twilight zone of Turner Classic Movies and hospital visits. Meanwhile on film and in the book, he lives on, preserved. While there is only one end to a biography, a memoir finishes of course with its author alive and having the last word. The others have gone, but Cheeta is still there.

The chimp talks intriguingly about the process of cinema. Actors are paid to make-believe. Animals naturally cannot do that; they are before, or beyond, pretence. The Tarzan myth celebrates unself-consciousness; growing up free in the jungle, a feral child outside civilization's discontents, Tarzan combines the superiority of the human with the natural vigour and grace of the beast. In those films of the early 1930s, Johnny Weissmuller was an adept at conveying this unity. In watching him you feel the casual beauty of someone incapable of posing. It was his fame as an Olympic gold-medal-winning swimmer that brought Weissmuller to Hollywood and cinema screens. He was no actor; he was a physical presence. As Lever writes, 'He wasn't *bland*. Rather, he had attained a hard-won shallowness where

A publicity shot of Cheeta with Maureen O'Sullivan and Johnny Weissmuller behind the scenes of the film *Tarzan the Ape Man* (1932).

other humans never got beyond "depth".' Other Tarzans were never so good, least of all his successor, the louche ex-Princetonian and alleged child-abuser Lex Barker. Weissmuller was inimitable. He was relaxed enough even to use his own unfeigned woodenness as an expression of the role. He said of himself, 'The public forgave my acting, because they knew I was an athlete . . . They knew I wasn't make-believe.' Film favours such poise; the camera ultimately shows the person just being. Even with hardened performers there remains this unassimilated presence, and the camera reveals not only what is staged, but what cannot be hidden. Unwittingly looking forward to the recent *Planet of the Apes* films that will end this book, Cheeta disdains the CGI-animated brutes that may humanely replace real animals in film: film should present the actual thereness of the animal, of the star, transposing a life onto the screen. The book plays with such ideas freely. Imitation and spontaneity are two of the axes around which its moral vision turns.

Animals on film can be seen to express this unembarrassed ease. This is powerfully the case in the *Tarzan* films, where an ape-actor interacts with an ape-man. *Me Cheeta* laments the lost animal stars: Trigger, Rin Tin Tin, Asta, Pal, Champion the Wonder Horse and all those anonymous beasts, like the horses reportedly killed in the making of Tony Richardson's *The Charge of the Light Brigade* (1968). If Weissmuller adopted Tarzan's inarticulacy in real life in order to finesse away moments of awkwardness, then Cheeta more radically collapses the split between actor and role. Though he may be some other ape named Jiggs, really he is undividedly Cheeta. He plays himself, and the ghost writer plays him.

The star is, the book's epigraph tells us, not quite a human being. Not less than human, not more – merely something different. Or rather, with one exception, the stars in Cheeta's eyes are decidedly less than human, more than a little bestial. They dress up as chimps, have sex like bonobos; their smiles are automatic responses, 'fear-grimaces', remarked on by a Desmond 'Cheeta' Morris, like the elaborate courtship displays, the behaviour of the alpha males. They are no other than an animal.

There are in fact only two human beings in Lever's book: Johnny Weissmuller and Cheeta. The others are monsters of egotism, lecherous grotesques caught in the vivid glare of an anecdote or cut down to size by some sharp gibe. The friends, the wives, the co-stars aren't real to anyone. Everyone is shabby, reprehensible. They are the kind of people that gossip retails, the sullied selves dealt with in barroom tales, and Cheeta recoils, sickened by all of them. But one.

For *Me Cheeta* is a kind of *Lolita* (the tongue taking a trip down the palate to tap on the teeth), a record of a child star, a paean to the USA, an outsider's appropriation of the American language and, above all, an unrequited love. The book is an ode to Johnny Weissmuller, a letter from an unknown chimpanzee. Johnny moves in another element, like a bather into cleanness leaping. He learned his characteristic head-held-high breaststroke as a boy swimming outside in Chicago, keeping his chin up to avoid the shit floating in the river. Film encyclopaedias may label him a 'swinger', talking of the failed marriages, the Vegas years, but none of that matters; he rises above it all, wondered at by his hairy co-star, his buddy, the best friend he ever had. In this sense the book is, after all, what it begins by telling us it will be: an acknowledgement. In an act of pure generosity, Cheeta shifts the centre of his life to another: an American, an Olympic swimmer, a Hollywood star, a wild man so beautiful that he redeems our otherwise grubby species.

*

> I think Crab my dog to be the sourest-natured dog that lives
> . . . He is a stone, a very pebblestone, and has not more pity
> in him than a dog . . . I am the dog. No, the dog is himself,
> and I am the dog. O, the dog is me, and I am myself . . .
> Now the dog all this while sheds not a tear nor speaks a word;
> but see how I lay the dust with my tears. (*The Two Gentlemen
> of Verona*, II.3)

The animal star may seem to undermine the central thought running through this book that the film star once represented an ideal version of the human being. In fact, it simply renders that thought more complex. For what the animal star does is to throw the category of the person into question, perhaps extending it beyond the human as such. In films, we give our sympathy to all kinds of non-human characters, taking in animals, aliens, robots, ghosts or spirits. There are limits to such connections; perhaps the zombie resides on the far side of identification. But on-screen the ape or the dog certainly live in the ambiguous borderland between similarity and strangeness, humanized creatures that remain other and animal.

In Lever's novel, one of the animal stars that Cheeta worries over is Asta the dog, the star of *The Thin Man* series of films, Leo McCarey's *The Awful Truth* (1937) and Howard Hawks's *Bringing Up Baby* (1938), a Wire Fox Terrier scurrying about an urbane world. Though a dog, Asta became a genuine star in his own right, a selling point for the films in which he appeared. In his films, the dog acts as a roughening element in the sophistication, humanizing the cosmopolitan world with a touch of something warm and unruly.

Both the *Tarzan* films and *The Thin Man* (1934) emerged from the realm of pulp fiction. *Tarzan* was pure Imperialist pulp-horror, a genre given over to the exotic, to sensation as such, bound up in scenes of titillation and violence. *The Thin Man* films draw on the writing of Dashiell Hammett and hard-boiled fiction, though on-screen it transmutes those origins into something highly sophisticated and knowing, a triumph of artifice and wit, closer to P. G. Wodehouse and Anita Loos than to *True Detective*.

The first *Tarzan* films and *The Thin Man* are key texts of Hollywood cinema before the imposition of the puritanical Production Code (otherwise known as the Hays Code). Where *Tarzan and his Mate* (1934) exemplifies the licence of the period, *The Thin Man* stands poised between sexual knowingness and post-Code indirection. The film busies itself with defining marriage, taking place in a world confused by infidelity and divorce; among the many separating and compromised couples, William Powell and Myrna Loy represent marriage's best hope, a union sustained by wit and the freedom preserved in an ironized trust – and a plentiful supply of cocktails. In

The Thin Man and *The Awful Truth* (1937), Asta acts as kind of glue for a sparring romantic couple, an animal taking the place of a child. (In *The Thin Man*, Powell and Loy pose for a photograph with Asta as a family group.) Critics have suggested that the tightening of the Code created 'screwball comedy', displacing a humour based on physicality into one based on language, and then again on a displacement in language, crude facts metamorphosed into wit by the need for innuendo and indirection.

The dog star's relation to this play of desire proves fascinating. In *The Thin Man*'s closing moments it turns out that on a train journey to California, Powell has talked too long, keeping a honeymooning couple (including a fashionable Maureen O'Sullivan) from their marriage bed. Powell and Loy themselves head for their bunks. All through the film the couple have slept in chaste twin beds, Asta sleeping beside his mistress. Loy suggests that the same thing is going to happen tonight, but Powell has other ideas. He throws Asta onto the top bunk, where the camera follows him, and, unseen by us, presumably gets into bed with Loy. It's not twin beds tonight; and the dog, in the compartment with them, and still seeing what we cannot see, decides to share our modest, knowing exclusion: bashfully, discreetly, he covers his eyes with one paw. And so the film ends with an urbane gag performed by, perhaps manifest in, a dog.

It is a great ending to the film, indeed one of the greatest endings of all Hollywood comedies, and one that draws our gaze to the peculiar position of the animal star. In Shakespeare's *The Two Gentlemen of Verona* we find an entirely different use of an animal actor. Here the dog, Crab, in each performance famously upstages his human owner, the servant Launce, purely by being apart from human feeling, deadpan, inexpressive and unmoved. Launce loves the dog and feels sorrow for his master's sufferings; yet Crab the dog apparently feels nothing, but merely sits and looks, a living point of contrast with human yearning. Both Cheeta and Asta operate in an entirely opposite way. Both give us an image of human emotion glimpsed either in parody or in real resemblance. In *Tarzan and his Mate* Cheeta mourns his dead mother; elsewhere in other films he is jealous, exuberant, sad, enacting

Asta, between Myrna Loy and William Powell, in a publicity shot for *The Thin Man* films.

a bestial version of human finer feelings. Similarly, that final moment of *The Thin Man* presents an animal apparently showing human shyness and shame. The Asta films, like the *Tarzan* films, seek in their different ways to bridge the gap between human and animal, bringing on to the artifice of the screen humanized beasts, shy, cowardly, even witty. Both Asta and Cheeta are animals, instinctual creatures. This immersion in instinct acts ironically in relation to the coming toughening up of the Hays Code, the set of rules that would, among other things, deny the instinctual, the bodily, and aim to suppress mention both of what is immoral in us and also of what is animal.

W. C. Fields's famous quip that an actor (or comic) should never work with children or animals derives its pith from the fear that it is precisely these who will steal the scene from you. They do so by being 'cute', a charm that comes above all with being unselfconscious. Entirely natural, Asta and Cheeta are shown to be performers too, manifesting a mock-up of human feeling and artifice, an artless imitation of our artfulness, a natural display of natural feeling. They may perform this, but they cannot be said to act it.

For while animals can perform, can they 'act'? This seems to me a crucial distinction, particularly in Asta's films where very often human beings are shown as trying to appear other than they are, either to evade accusation in a detective plot, or because they have an unreal sense of who others truly are or who they themselves are, as befits the comedy of suspicion in *The Awful Truth* or the comic collapse of identity in *Bringing Up Baby* (1938).

Animals can neither be sincere nor insincere, honest nor deceitful. They cannot pretend at all. They just are. This is what is caught in the fabrication of the screen, this direct immersion in being as such. Everyone else, the human actors, the human stars, are caught up in self-consciousness and pretence.

So it is that we may call Asta or Cheeta an animal actor, but in a real sense they do not act at all. Their on-screen presence is the effect of training, the widening of behaviour to include tricks that can be called up by rote. Asta both represents such training and in the film itself refutes the automation that it implies: William Powell, one of her owners, attempts to show how well-disciplined his dog is. 'Sit', he says, 'sit'. Asta remains unmoved, still standing. Powell considers: 'Stand', he orders, and at once Asta sits. This both draws on and denies the fact of training's rigours; Asta looks free, even rebellious, and yet fully constrained.

This is why the animal star is of such interest in itself and in relation to our exploration of the 'human' qualities embodied in the star. Asta (also known as Skippy) and the multiple embodiments of the character Cheeta exist in relation to a proliferation of names and animal performers: there is not one Asta, not one Cheeta, but many, including, in the case of the ape, human actors concealed inside monkey suits. Though the original Asta was in his own way unique, there were in time still other Astas. A concept of self cannot quite pertain to these animal stars, who are easily interchangeable. Hitchcock spent years looking for a Grace Kelly type, falling back on Vera Miles, or Kim Novak, as he must, and Woody Allen has doubled himself in

Kenneth Branagh, Will Ferrell, Owen Wilson and many others; yet all the time we know the person these stand-ins are doubling for, the person they are, and the person they are not.

The star is a symbol of human uniqueness. Asta and Cheeta are both unique, and generic; perhaps any well-trained fox terrier or chimp can be them. Acting emerges from the discrepancy of a name, that having the name we were born with we then choose to play under the name of a fiction. The player plays someone else, choosing as themselves to pretend to be an other. It is vital that when talking or writing about cinema, one instinctively elides character and actor, the star and the part they play. These merge, while remaining distinct. We know that they are playing parts, even as we confuse person and character.

With Asta, the character is the animal, the animal is the character, and it itself knows no distinction between the two. Even sex does not matter. Pertinently, Asta's name (and gender) is an uncertain matter; he's a male dog with a woman's name. First named Skippy, he then took on the name of the Danish silent-film tragedy queen Asta Nielsen, known in Germany as 'Die Asta'. (Asta Nielsen was herself able to go beyond gender, famously playing the lead role in a cross-dressing Hamlet (1921).)

In radically different ways human stars transcend the boundary between person and role. In talking of Rio Bravo or Some Like It Hot, we say that John Wayne does this, or Marilyn Monroe says that; afterwards the characters' names may slip our minds, but the stars who play them rarely do. In any case, Wayne and Monroe are already known by names that are themselves fictions, behind which Marion Morrison or Norma Jeane Mortenson perhaps linger. These are people living in relation to a name, whether granted by birth, by family belonging, or one self-chosen. But animals are only given names, and only in that sense have them. They may answer to them, but few would argue that their identity is embroiled in their name. Asta too was once a famous name, even though it was a borrowed one, and an indeterminate one, drifting between 'part' and animal, and one animal and another. So he lives on-screen, a star, an animal and an intervention in the fiction wherein he plays.

5

PETER LORRE:
CHARACTER ACTOR

The history of Peter Lorre shows us that, in coming close to the nature of the icon, the film star can also easily fall into the state of becoming a caricature. The clear-cut uniqueness of individuality always threatens to metamorphose into mere eccentricity. For such figures, being distinctive is both what is most marketable about them and what entraps them.

Peter Lorre's career hit its peak almost instantly with his role in Fritz Lang's masterpiece *M* (1931). Talking about *Peeping Tom* (1960), the movie that effectively wrecked his career, Michael Powell remarked, 'it is a very compassionate film'; it just happened to direct its compassion at a serial killer.[1] *M* depends upon the same paradox; its *coup de théâtre* tests the limits of our pity, inviting us to share, if we can, compassion with a crazed murderer. Played by a youthful Lorre, this would be the first, the greatest and most representative major role in a career that in its own unique fashion goes to the heart of what makes the movies so intriguing and so potent.

M concerns the pursuit of a child-killer loose in Berlin. What is unusual about this film is that, frustrated by the police's lack of success, gangsters and career criminals unite to track down the predator themselves. In part, moral revulsion motivates these underworld gumshoes, though it is also clear that killing little girls is bad for illicit business. There are too many raids and too many police on the streets. The madman must be stopped, so everyday larceny can continue.

M still amazes. It influenced dozens of later films, yet it remains strikingly unlike anything else. It is hard to think of many other mainstream films that are so radically decentred, so reluctant to grant us a hero. Yet it is an unexpectedly methodical, measured picture; dreaminess only attaches, just off-centre, to the spaces where the killer himself moves. The film's subject-matter could not be grimmer, yet Lang enlivens grey emptiness with an Otto Dix-like burlesque energy. Around the random murders, the film homes in on Berlin's melancholy, a landscape of puddles and prostitutes, a silent city, that hush broken by bells or shrieks, the tap-tap of a tool being sharpened, or haunted by the killer's eerie whistling of Grieg's 'In the Hall of the Mountain King'. Yet against this frosty atmosphere, the film revels in its satire, its playful equation of cops and robbers. The criminals so much enjoy hunting down Peter Lorre that we tend to forget why precisely they are doing so. These hunt scenes are oddly relaxed, even frivolous in a slightly chilly way; the criminals are simply getting down to work. The only vital passion belongs to Lorre: while the criminals are rational figures, he releases despair and fury, a rage that finds its echo in the crowd that faces and judges him.

It is a film about murder that pays close attention to the business of living. For those who know Berlin, there is something beguilingly moving about the glimpses of the city's life: the Mickey Mouse figurines in the *confiserie*, the list of prices in a café, the faces of invalids and beggars. It is a 'city film' at the end of the grand era of city films, though the city it depicts is a dark, troubled, paranoid one. Above all there are the glances into a child's metropolis of toyshops and school gates, of hurdy-gurdy men and balloon-sellers. Lang looks on at a childhood world, seen from above and at a distance, not with the children but observing them. *M*'s child victims are strangely on the edge of things, unknown by the film, hardly ever seen close up. The film's final spoken moral, 'we must take more care of the children', is one that remains relevant and with which nearly all will agree. Yet as an ending it feels somehow off-key, a heartfelt plea that is also a platitude, and that does little to resolve the weird energies of the film itself.

The first time we really see Lorre, he is before a mirror, darkly enjoying acting weird, pulling faces, indeed literally pulling his face, turning himself into an other that he regards. It might be said that he would act out that craziness, professionally, for the next thirty-odd years. Lorre had not quite come from nowhere: *M* was his fourth film. But those other roles had been slight affairs and in *M* he was the closest thing to being the movie's star. Here his relative obscurity enabled him to personify anonymity: practically unknown on-screen, he could also be frighteningly invisible on the streets. One message of Lang's film is that anyone might be guilty; until he is at last marked out, the child-killer is an everyman. It is one of *M*'s unintended ironies that in the end the killer should have one of the most distinctive and caricaturable faces in movie history, as identifiable encapsulating the macabre as a drawing in a Bugs Bunny cartoon as he was in peering around Sydney Greenstreet's substantial shoulder. Far from appearing anonymous, Lorre presented one more way in which cinema discovered uniqueness. There was only ever one of him.

Lorre looked like a sleazy baby, his face registering every passing petulance, ready to drop from a sudden hopeful grin down to a sulk. When acting, he seems haunted, shiftless; he moves between an uncanny calm and fits of restless mania. This instability might be traced back to the desperate rhythms of his life as a morphine addict. His style depends on rapid transitions, his talent for letting an emotion leap towards its opposite. Dramatically this proves vivid, but it also leaves us with a sense of the characters he plays as purely reactive, puppets of expression.

He was born as László Löwenstein in Rosenberg, Hungary, in 1904. He fled the prospect of a life as a bank clerk for the stage, training in Vienna and making his debut in Zurich, before being discovered by Bertolt Brecht. Lang's film made him a star, but stardom was no defence against the Nazis and in 1933 he fled to Paris. All but broke, he was rescued by a meeting with Alfred Hitchcock. All the English that Lorre knew that evening was 'yes' and 'no', but he impressed Hitchcock largely by using the first of these two words as often as possible, and by falling about with laughter every time he guessed that yet another of the English director's anecdotes had reached its punchline.

So it was that three years after *M*, in his first English-language film, Lorre was endangering children again, kidnapping a teenage Nova Pilbeam in the first version of Alfred Hitchcock's *The Man Who Knew Too Much* (1934). Remarkably he learnt to speak English while he was playing the role. He is outstanding, a precursor of Graham Greene's Pinkie, a wicked boy with a blonde (or grey) streak in his hair. He offers the threat produced by the apparently unthreatening; small, plump, frail, he nonetheless conjures up a strangely devious menace. Quite rightly Lorre stole the show, transforming what had begun as a bit-part into the movie's dynamic centre; when the film was advertised, it was Lorre's face that dominated the poster. Curled and moustachioed, he is almost as great in another Hitchcock film, *Secret Agent* (1936), based on Somerset Maugham's Ashenden stories of 1928, and a film of marvellous moments. From Hitchcock he would pass to Hollywood, where he would become one of the era's defining stars.

Peter Lorre making faces as the murderer Hans Beckert in Fritz Lang's *M* (1931).

Two versions of Lorre face each other in uneasy connection: there's Peter Lorre (rhymes with 'Gomorrah'), respected Brechtian actor, versus Peter Lorre (rhymes with 'sorry'), Hollywood's epitome of everything foreign, alien and charmingly toad-like. Lorre could stand in for any kind of suspicious foreigner – from *Secret Agent*'s 'The Hairless Mexican', through (improbably) going Dutch in *The Mask of Dimitrios* (1944), acting Russian (as Raskolnikov) in Josef von Sternberg's *Crime and Punishment* (1935), to being *The Maltese Falcon*'s (1941) Joel Cairo, a man with many passports, all equally implausible. In *Secret Agent* John Gielgud hunts for a concealed German spy, though that movie's real secret German-speaker is Lorre himself. The East End shoot-out at the end of *The Man Who Knew Too Much* inevitably recalls the Sidney Street siege and memories of murderous continental anarchists; here Lorre was an émigré actor touching on the nation's darkest fantasies of an immigrant intrusion. In the late 1930s he achieved great success churning out a series of mediocre, if charming, crime films as the inscrutable Japanese detective Mr Moto. He is prone to murmuring sagely, 'Ah, so!' and offering up improbable lines such as (describing a drawing) 'What harmony and colour. Truly this is a voiceless poem.' At the time this kind of thing went down well. After all, Lorre was inescapably alien, a man to whom the usual rules and social conventions may not apply. In *Secret Agent* moral scruples perturb the decent English, while, killer and clown, Hispanic Peter Lorre finds the murder business ludicrously comic. A dozen national stereotypes from boys' weeklies had coalesced in one man.

Mr Moto was an archetypally chaste detective, a Japanese Father Brown. Though he could be lascivious in *Secret Agent* and *Strange Cargo* (1940), or erotically obsessed in Karl Freund's *Mad Love* (1935), on-screen sexlessness suited Lorre, who was rarely (if ever) allowed a successful romantic relationship. On set with Hitchcock he was nicknamed 'The Walking Overcoat', because the long coat he wore all but trailed on the floor so that it seemed to be wearing him (though it may not have been so much the coat that was long, but rather that Lorre was short). There are traces of a miniature Mezut Özil about him; he might be Steve Buscemi's granddad. Yet all such resemblances are faint; the essential quality of the man is unrepeatable.

Some have felt that the Mr Moto films wrecked Lorre, turning him from a highly inventive character actor into a Hollywood hack, even though some of his most memorable roles (including *Casablanca*, 1942) post-date them. He played best with a great foil, his ridiculous relish for excess up against John Gielgud's elegant Home Counties restraint, his penchant for improvisation unnerving the stage actor's disciplined regard for the script. In *The Man Who Knew Too Much*, matched by Leslie Banks, Lorre cannot help but steal each scene; he is a physically present actor, often, you feel, surrounded as he is by the pallid English, the only one in the room with a body. Paired by Warner Brothers in a recurring double-act with the imposingly corpulent Sydney Greenstreet (they have been memorably described as 'the Laurel and Hardy of crime'), Lorre found a home in film noir, a genre recep-tive to grotesque vigour and the eccentric variety of life.[2] Though both are excellent in *The Maltese Falcon*, their first outing together, the prize goes to Greenstreet, who quite literally fills the screen. Elsewhere honours are more even, though it is precisely the contrast between the two men – the secret connection present in the contradiction of types – that was the key to their mutual achievement.

At his best Lorre occupied that uneasy territory between the silly and the sinister. He was a great star, a quintessence of the enchanting variety offered up by mid-century films. If an air of disappointment hangs around him, encapsulated in the box-office failure of the one film he directed, *Der Verlorene* (The Lost One, 1951), then that too is somehow intrinsic to the vision of the world summed up by his image. It is unfortunate, but appropriate, given his world-weary, hangdog demeanour, that one of his last films was titled *The Sad Sack* (1957). He succeeded at embodying human un-success. None of his charac-ters get what they want, unless it is to kill and be caught like Lang's urban murderer. He died in 1964. Given his chaotic and driven life, it is miraculous that he survived so long. It is our luck that he left behind so many versions of himself, doubled, distinct and yet all instantly recognizable as Peter Lorre.

6

FRED ASTAIRE, GINGER ROGERS, GENE KELLY: A STAR DANCED

'A star danced, and under that I was born.'
Beatrice in William Shakespeare, *Much Ado about Nothing* (II.I)

O ne of the key ways in which cinema has reflected on the movie star has been by taking fame itself as its subject. Nowhere is this truer than in the great Hollywood musicals, from the wonderful sequence of films made in the 1930s by Fred Astaire and Ginger Rogers to the great works of the 1950s, dominated by Astaire still and by Gene Kelly. In these pictures the great fear is that of anonymity, of living the unnoticed life; what will save you from that obscurity is becoming a singing and dancing star on film or stage, and love, a love that expresses itself in dancing. The dance film, like so many of the films discussed in this book, shows the ordinary to be extraordinary through the image of the star. Cinema discovers them. The dreaming actor, the hard-working hoofer striding into Broadway looking for success, these are the talismans of the musicals, from the beginnings to *La La Land* (2016). *Easter Parade* (1948) repeated the premise with Astaire taking a lowly chorus girl, Judy Garland, as his new dance partner to show that he can dance with anyone, and make anyone a star. This process of discovery, this launch into fame, happens in worlds (Broadway, Hollywood) where the exploitation of performers is the expected thing. The musical's triumph is to transmute this exploitation into joy.

Ginger Rogers could just be an ordinary gal, not too remote from the folks in the audience. Fred Astaire stands too as an average guy who, without losing his ordinariness, becomes elegant, endowed with immense grace. Film finds this long-chinned, thinning-haired man and makes him mesmerically attractive, just as his dancing plays on the transformation of ordinary movements into dance.

Sometimes, as in Vincente Minnelli's *The Band Wagon* (1953) or Gene Kelly and Stanley Donen's *Singin' in the Rain* (1952), the plot turns on a further process of transformation – that the star who is already a star can only remain so by once again metamorphosing. Gene Kelly must adapt to the new world of talking pictures; as Tony Hunter, ageing film star, the ageing Fred Astaire must reinvent himself and come back into contact with youth, as personified by Cyd Charisse.

But it is vital that this process of discovery of a star or of the star's reinvention come into touch with dance. Above all, dance in these films means enchantment. In Shakespeare's *As You Like It* melancholy Jacques asserts, 'I am for other than dancing measures.' It's bewildering to discover that every Shakespeare play, including *King Lear*, ended with a jig, moving seamlessly from gouged-out eyeballs to cutting a caper. That closing dance expressed concord, delight, a measured order in things. Yet Jacques seeks to exile himself from pleasure and community, he won't let dance help him step up towards the sweetness of life.

In American films dance wants to assert the place of the individual, to find a space for their freedom, their spontaneity and their capacity for improvised joy. It makes its stand against automation and pompous authority. Above all, it does so by being deliciously silly. By avoiding dancing, Shakespeare's Jacques refuses the embrace of his own foolishness. At some point, near the beginning, while watching even the best musical, a moment will arise when it will all seem sublimely daft. From the first ten seconds, Jacques Demy's *Les demoiselles de Rochefort* (1967) strikes you as preposterous – it is just all so vivid, there is just so much dancing, it is all so pink – but, by the moment Gene Kelly arrives, the absurdity has won you over.

Dance on film could really only emerge properly with sound, and the synchronization of the human body to music, a natural form enabled by a technological innovation. In Fritz Lang's *Metropolis* (1927), the robotic workers jerk in rhythm with the machines they service. It looks like dance, but one forced through the sensibility of totalitarianism. The men who shift are turned away, faceless, their movements a mechanized parody of the freedom found in spontaneous motion. The Busby Berkeley musicals of the early 1930s, despite their all-American sheen, present a similarly anonymizing view. Berkeley's amazing dance sequences swallow up individual dancers into a chorus; it could be the opening ceremony of the Beijing Olympics or a band of North Korean cheerleaders. These are moments not built to the human scale. Seen from above, people lose themselves here in the making of a design, absorbed into sudden stars or ephemeral flowers. Those sequences refuse to let you follow one particular dancer; the figures are just an organized crowd. In Berkeley's films that were otherwise tough, down-at-heel works, spectacle dissolves the story. This is dance at its most abstract, an almost mathematical form – Berkeley reputedly referred to these sequences as his 'homogeneous quadrangle equations' – closer to Cubism and Futurism than to the traditional Hollywood movie. This abstract quality carries through in a less extreme form to most dance films, expressed in their fascination with the way that bodies inhabit space. To take one example, Mark Sandrich, the director of several of the Fred Astaire and Ginger Rogers films, had studied engineering at Columbia and planned his dance sequences using blueprints, the human element cut out to a pattern.

Always the battle was between the self and that which would deny it. In *Modern Times* (1936), when Charlie Chaplin cavorts and pirouettes around the production line, he offers an anarchic, individualistic riposte to Henry Ford's *Metropolis* world in which he finds himself, deftly transforming factory work into ballet (on a visit to Hollywood in 1916, Vaslav Nijinsky told Chaplin that he was a dancer). Similarly, in *Shall We Dance* (1937) Fred Astaire furthers the dancer's revolt against mechanism, syncopating his body to the pistons, wheels and turning-rods of a steamship's engine room, a gleefully human imitation and transcendence of the machine. What was abject in *Metropolis* becomes pure enchantment.

If the mechanical was one enemy to human flourishing, another was the threat of being reduced to being one of the mass. All classic

Hollywood cinema involves the paradox that each movie is cut out to the type of genre, its uniqueness threatened by the fact that it is a production-line product. Likewise, as Lincoln Kirstein suggested, one problem in dance, therefore, was foregrounding the star, or the couple, against the anonymous chorus, 'the mass background'.[1] In *Top Hat* (1935) Astaire distinguishes himself from a chorus line of identically dressed elegant men, all in top hat, white tie and tails, that uniform of sophisticated pleasure. First, he does so by a virtuoso tap dance with a cane and then, more brutally, uses the same cane to gun down the faceless others like so many ducks in a shooting gallery. There can only be one star. Yet later Astaire would play a variation on this same theme, during the same song, and with pretty much a similar routine: doing 'Puttin' on the Ritz' again in *Blue Skies* (1946), Astaire, the star, passes through a mirrored room that doubles him to a space where he dances with a chorus of eight Fred Astaires, the star opposed to, and identical with, the mass behind him – even though that 'mass' consists of his own multiplied image.

Ginger Rogers was open to becoming doubled too, once given over to the apotheosis and the reproductions of cinema. In *Shall We Dance* the performer Linda Keene (née Linda Thompson), played by Rogers, finds her true self confused with the publicity around her, just as elsewhere in the film she, the living celluloid woman, becomes confused with a showroom dummy version of herself. At the film's climax Astaire dances with myriad versions of Ginger Rogers, the female chorus hidden behind masks of the star, anonymous women taking on the face of fame; the woman behind the last Rogers mask turns out to be Rogers herself. She's counselled 'not to make a spectacle of herself', but the film and the business behind stardom determines that a spectacle is precisely what she shall become.

In *Singin' in the Rain* the fate of Kathy Selden (Debbie Reynolds) reflects this same possibility of being lost in film. Kathy begins as a chorus girl and through her own merits, as well as the transformative effects of being loved by a male star, she slowly ascends to stardom. Yet the threat of losing her voice to that of her arch-rival Lina Lamont

(Jean Hagen) troubles this rise to renown. Even here the possibility that film will hollow you out emerges, ripping apart the union of image and voice that comprises the person on-screen.

Fred Astaire's and Gene Kelly's presence could not be more different; they are the two poles of the musical's American male. Astaire was natural, nuanced, elegant, endlessly skilled, but nonetheless vulnerable, capable of delicacy, and sly, a wistful vision of a down-to-earth showbiz aristocrat; notably, his original dancing partner was his sister, Adele. Contrariwise, Kelly was extrovert, expressive, muscular, sharp-witted, democratic; his original dancing partner was his brother, Fred, and ever after he was as comfortable dancing with another man as with the central woman. Astaire inhabited a tangible fantasy world; Kelly's dream places were just as unreal, but came tinged with a nod to reality – the sailor on leave, the backstage low-down on the dream factory.[2] Kelly brought ambition to the dance film, wanting it to grow and develop beyond the tinsel timelessness of an Astaire and Rogers film. If there was something sappy about Astaire, there was a potential graceful toughness in Kelly's on-screen presence. Although it may seem ridiculous to mention it, somehow the scar on his left cheek, a relic of childhood, endowed Kelly with something rough, individualized and real.

If the dance film celebrates the individual person, the star, it does so always in relation to the couple. The dancer seeks a partner, a co-star; opposites attract. Astaire only made sense in relation to another; as has been often said, the dance numbers in an Astaire–Rogers film are the love scenes. Katharine Hepburn remarked on Astaire and Rogers, 'He gives her class, she gives him sex.'[3] This sense that the person requires balance, relatedness, permeates the great Hollywood musicals. Rogers was at her best dancing with Astaire, and though he found other partners, including the non-dancing Joan Fontaine, as well as Judy Garland, Cyd Charisse and Audrey Hepburn, Astaire's iconic relationship is with Rogers. The two are bound together, united as Fred and Ginger; indeed, the plot of *Shall We Dance* focuses on the simple question as to whether this couple are married or not, imagining romantic permanence for their on-screen relation.

The sexual politics of the great musicals is a murky business. So often the plot turns on the flirtatious encounter, the street-level simulation of the process by which the star is picked out from the masses. Pick-ups proliferate in the musical, as it imagines flirtation and seduction in the public space of the street or the bar. The man forces himself on the woman and we partake in the oppression of being chosen. The dancer proves himself in this way to be a red-blooded male, and the woman's resistance is always headed for inevitable capitulation; the stake in the couple the movie will cherish prevents any other outcome. Strangers come together; a partnership forms; someone ordinary finds themselves transformed by love; the star finds – and makes – another star.

When not matching himself against the machine and winning, Astaire was often inviting the censure of the stuffy, a classless American guy in *Top Hat* (1935) up against the pompous upper-class Englishmen obeying The Thackeray Club's rule of silence. There is disapproval too at the end of the 'Singin' in the Rain' dance, in the policeman who moves Gene Kelly along. In such moments the dancer stands for a natural pleasure of which authority disapproves. Kelly affirmed that 'dancing is a compulsion from within more authentic than the forms imposed from without'.[4] He had begun his career as a dance teacher for children and something of the teacher always remained with him. In *Anchors Aweigh* (1945), when he instructs the cartoon Jerry Mouse in how to dance and in that way give up being a grouch, the film celebrates the childlikeness in dance, the capacity to achieve unselfconsciousness through playful imitation. Dance becomes a way of sharing, an act of display and virtuosity that at its finest and freest feels curiously without ego.

Dance belongs with the most natural, authentic expressions of the human being, something that rises above language and rules. Kelly believed that every kind of person possessed their own style of movement, all of which could be heightened and made expressively manifest in dance; for instance, a muscular truck driver should dance in a truck driver's way. For Kelly dance was always an expression of the individual, something arising from the uniqueness of the American

Fred Astaire and Ginger Rogers, elegantly together, in *Swing Time* (1936).

self. There was a democratic appeal in this thought, a sense that the totality of American experience could in theory find a place in dance.

In relation to dance, two tensions held the Hollywood musical together. The first involved the relation between the white film stars and the largely anonymous African American dancers that they in part imitated. This was a boundary that could rarely be brought to light, though the 'Slap That Bass' sequence and the shoeshine dance in *The Band Wagon* (1953) did their best to present it, however problematically. In the shoeshine scene, Astaire shares the dancing honours with an African American shoeshine guy (played by Leroy Daniels), but only Astaire sings. More disturbingly, the Bojangles of Harlem sequence in *Swing Time* (1936) shows the big star blacking up and appropriating (even as he celebrates) the work of 'anonymous' black dancers.

On the further side lay ballet. The American celebration of the natural entailed a suspicion of European classical styles, seen as suspiciously French or, worse, Russian. Such foreign highbrow imports were viewed as dubious, especially if compared to the national vigour of the cakewalk, vaudeville and tap. The streetwise dance world, vulgar and free, squares up against elitist pretensions. In *Shall We Dance* Pete Peters (Astaire) doubles as 'Petrov', the pretentious ballet star; in *The Band Wagon* Astaire's character fears that Cyd Charisse's ballerina will look down on the vulgar world of Broadway theatre. Yet dance in the American musical was always also in love with the ballet world that it sometimes affected to despise. In particular, the final ballet in *An American in Paris* (1951) and the 'Broadway' ballet in *Singin' in the Rain* show American popular art seeking to match European achievements. Elsewhere on stage, Agnes de Mille's choreography for *Oklahoma!* in 1943 and the home-grown ballet of Aaron Copland's *Rodeo* (1942) – and Eugene Loring's choreography for Copland's *Billy the Kid* (1938) – were all establishing a peculiarly American version of classical dance.

This vivid, demotic art offers a glimpse of a world without consequences, where all suffering comes to the comic resolution of joy. So it is perhaps that the dance film is at its very best when most removed from life. The dance critic Lincoln Kirstein suggested that the technology of film would open up the fullest possibilities for dance, by which he meant 'a treatment of human bodies comparable to the way Disney treats his puppets'.[5] The German writer Heinrich von Kleist's thought that the best dancer was a marionette, because only they possess utter unselfconsciousness in their movement, finds an echo here. There is something persuasive in that idea, not least because one of the greatest filmed dance sequences remains that of the hippopotami and the crocodiles in *Fantasia* (1940), just as in 'I Got No Strings' Walt Disney's Pinocchio is one of cinema's freest dancers, surpassing – as only an animated puppet could – all the limitations and constraints of the body. (Similarly, for *The Red Shoes* (1948), the cinematographer Jack Cardiff sped up Moira Shearer's pirouettes, making impossible physical feats happen.) Yet, of course, to nearly all the audience, Astaire, Rogers and Kelly were already operating at a level of skill that defied any attempt to match it; their hard-won excellence beyond imitation. In the early 1930s Hermes Pan, Astaire and Rogers's choreographer, resisted attempts to make the dancers' moves simpler and therefore imitable by ordinary dancers; the steps, like the man and woman who executed them, were there for the audience's astonishment.[6]

For all the insistence on naturalness, the dance film is as busy celebrating artifice; after all there is also nothing more unnatural than suddenly breaking into a dance. The moment when someone begins to sing or dance, and the invisible orchestra strikes up, the musical shatters within its artifice a flat conception of the real. The Astaire– Rogers films take place in a studio-enclosed world, an illusory realm of chic, upper-class leisure, with men of the people in top hats and tails. In the past, Hollywood film was far more welcoming to dance than it is now, with some few exceptions, because it already welcomed and made room for the theatrical, the unnatural and the artificial. Dance films work best in the cinema, with conditions as close as pos- sible to the size and vividness of theatre. In the 1930s, '40s and '50s, at a time when songs could be sung in drama films like *The Big Sleep* (1946) or *Rio Bravo* (1959), the premises of the musical were part of the vocabulary of film. Later, as naturalism and authenticity became key values, the dance film somewhat dropped away, although, in the spirit of Jacques Demy's 1960s musicals, Damien Chazelle's *La La Land* (2016) stands as one attempt to put together dance and the new taste for the real.

The dancing star forms an ideal subject for film, as both cinema and dance commit themselves to the image of the human being in motion. The dancer exaggerates one vital component of the film star, the presence in them of physical grace. In ballet exaggeration exceeds itself; close up, the make-up looks grotesque, the plots are melodra- matic, the gestures pronounced. It is both vibrantly physical and

Gene Kelly playing it cool in a publicity image from 1949, the year of *On the Town*.

oddly unreal. It allows us to imagine an unlimited freedom for the limited body. The meaning of dance arises from our embodiment, transfigured into style. We watch this body now, attaining its brief almost-perfection, one that must be lost. To film ballet and dance alerts us to the vanishing, even as it, through the greater permanence of film, denies it. Both depend upon the pathos of the image, the person held in this passing moment.

Dance is as close as the human gets to being like music; the body transforms into the instrument the music plays. It is pure expression and, like music, it rejects no one. It is at its best in the single take, where you see the performance as a performance, well away from *Flashdance*-style trickery. Film gives us a trace of dance's magnificent physicality, just as dance brings something essentially theatrical to cinema.

But it is more than performance that the dance film hails; it commends and applauds play. When Gene Kelly sings 'Singin' in the Rain' he is clearly on a Hollywood set. Yet in our imaginings it is a Los Angeles street, just like the real streets that Kelly and Stanley Donen had shot in while making *On the Town* (1949). The dance film was just then moving out on location, and the street was becoming the stage. As Kelly dances, and the rain falls, he shows that to dance on the street is to transform it, to claim back the urban space as one briefly dedicated to frivolity and mirth. Watching this scene with my eight-year-old daughter, she remarked, 'he's just like a kid'. Here the sophisticated star shows themselves also imbued with essential playfulness. This film, and all the great dance films, ultimately point towards this great transformation, an alchemy in the person, in the world, that with a touch of rhythm and a gesture of style transmutes the world to delight.

7

KATHARINE HEPBURN AND CARY GRANT: THE PUBLIC IMAGE

'Katharine Hepburn jokingly said, "Cary? He's just Cary. He's a personality functioning."'[1]

As we have seen with the musicals, it is crucial to the understanding of the classic Hollywood star that very often they existed not only as individuals, but as one side of a couple. Particularly in the realm of comedy, stars live in relatedness. With a few exceptions, such as in John Huston's *The African Queen* (1951), with her ostentatiously improbable relationship with Humphrey Bogart, Katharine Hepburn's most memorable films are those where she shared the star billing with either Cary Grant or Spencer Tracy. The Tracy films define themselves through the troubling of what cannot help but come across as an at-heart-untroubled intimacy. No matter how badly these two get on, we know that essentially they get on well. More intriguing to me, at least, are the four films that she made with Cary Grant: George Cukor's *Sylvia Scarlett* (1935); Howard Hawks's *Bringing Up Baby* (1938); and *Holiday* (1938) and *The Philadelphia Story* (1940), both again directed by Cukor. In this sequence of films we watch two of the most vital stars of the Hollywood Golden Age come into being as themselves, defining their own screen presence both in relation to each other and to the audience. With Grant in particular, this was a matter of finding a way to place and project himself on-screen. For Hepburn, it was an affair of toning down a character already strongly in place, of modifying herself in such a way as to sidestep society's conventional and delimiting judgement.

Cinema audiences warmed to certain couples for reasons that are imbued with the essential erotics of film. The films that Hepburn and Grant made together display and analyse the nature of 'romantic love', investigating and enacting affection and intimacy. We watch their love trials from a distance, immersing ourselves in the hypothesis of a fictional affair. With Spencer Tracy, as in other famous screen relationships, such as Bogart and Bacall, or Warren Beatty and Julie Christie, the doubling of a real-life liaison colours the connection on film. With Grant and Hepburn we know that we are in the realms of fiction, of acting. We watch these comic lovers and perhaps fall a little in love with them ourselves. If we cannot share the possibility of desire for them, then we stand outside the energies of the film; we must imagine ourselves in love.

In this regard Katharine Hepburn is an intriguing case, as someone whom for a stretch of her career the public was supposed not to love. She was too alien, too classy, too stuck-up, someone who was imagined to be beyond the touch of common connection. Grant was the democratic gentleman; Hepburn, at first, the Bryn Mawr republican aristocrat. As critics have long argued, her great coup – and it was one she stage-managed herself – was to win the audience's affection, to make herself 'lovable'. By her own choice, she entered into an erotic contract, an affectual relation, with the audience.

That found 'lovability' can seem a capitulation to prevailing, and unjust, notions of what makes someone attractively 'womanly'. Entering the erotics of cinema, of stardom, Hepburn may be thought to have sold herself short, to have compromised her character in an attempt cheaply (and lucratively) to win hearts. What was striking about Hepburn was how unlike everyone else she was. Talking to Peter Bogdanovich, George Cukor recalled Hepburn's first screen test:

> For example, Katharine Hepburn: when we first saw her test, there was something about her; no one like her had been seen before: she had a very sharp way of talking; she wore her hair in a very peculiar way, and she really wasn't the current idea of a movie star at all, in her manner or in anything.[2]

She had come to be seen as an eccentric figure, someone outside the customary rules of femininity. She had to negotiate her unlikeness to other people, her exceptionality, in a film world that both needed that difference and yet sought to contain it in films that depended upon the identification of the audience and the star. As I have suggested, it is noteworthy that Hepburn's most renowned films are with a limited set of leading men (Grant, Tracy, Bogart), whereas it is hard to think of a leading lady from the 1930s to the '60s with whom Grant did not play. They would include Jean Arthur, Joan Fontaine, Ginger Rogers, Marilyn Monroe, Grace Kelly, Eva Marie Saint, both Katharine and Audrey Hepburn, Deborah Kerr, Rosalind Russell, Irene Dunne, Ingrid Bergman and so on. His most committed on-screen relationships were with Mae West and Katharine Hepburn, two women united in their strength, though their enactment of it on-screen could not be more different. Perhaps the difference in the number of Grant and Hepburn's partnerships itself reflects thoughts about men and women in the period, as well as the economics of the film industry. Couples are good box office, particularly where they exist in relation to the machinery of public relations and the gossip columns.

These gender biases work in many ways in our understanding of the star, both as an individual and as part of 'the couple'. As societies are constructed along the lines of 'gender', these contrasts, these placings, are framed within common (and diverse) understandings of the customary roles of women and of men. These understandings are necessarily contingent, limited and bound to what any specific culture can allow to be expressed. Yet also possibilities emerge together that present the image of an escape from what Max Weber termed the steel-hard casing of culture ('das stahlhartes Gehäuse'); narrative and image, the perceived presence of these particular persons, open up fugitive impressions of desire and interest. It may be pertinent that the couple at the centre of these four films are bisexual, and are directed by a gay man (Cukor) and a man perhaps similarly bisexual (Hawks); a scepticism about the naturalness of gender conventions might well flow from these facts.

Despite what will be said in the afterword about the 'Dream House', that brothel of Hollywood dreams, by 'erotics' we need not imagine a crude desire for 'the star' as merely an instrument for our lust. Rather I mean that cinema is a place where we reach towards another, where we hold an impression of that person in mind, an interest tinged by the appeal of a perceived loveliness. Grant was always sexually desirable. He first came to prominence playing a man who 'could be had' by the worldly wise Mae West. Ever after he appealed to straight women, gay men and, in a dim, unspoken manner, gay women and straight men too. He was uncomplicatedly sexy, virile in a comfortable way. It was a perplexing element in Hepburn's on-screen presence that she could seem hardly sexual at all, attractive without evoking thoughts of sex. Out of this contrast between them, the four films they made together make a space for the finding of themselves and of each other.

Sylvia Scarlett is a perplexingly bad movie, intriguing but lifeless. Both Grant and Hepburn produce that same feeling of displacement and disbelief you have when you see an old photograph of a new friend; can they really once have seemed so? Hepburn spends most of the film disguised as a rather thin and unattractive lad: 'I'll be a boy, rough and hard!' she irritatingly declaims. There are attenuated shades of Shakespeare's Rosalind and Viola here (in her early forties Hepburn was to play Rosalind on stage in New York). Her mother dead and on the run with her ineffectual father, the two of them pal up with a cockney con man, Jimmy Monkley, played by Grant. His London accent is not bad (and faintly recalls the BBC *Strictly Come Dancing* judge Len Goodman), yet Grant, the Bristol working-class lad, looks out of place playing an Englishman; his affect, the aspirations he would embody, would best find themselves in the context of America.

The film does not flinch from the romantic tensions released by Hepburn's cross-dressing; she is pursued by a woman who thinks she's a boy, kissed by a woman who knows she's a woman, while Grant, who thinks her a boy, wants to go to bed with her (him) as 'he'd' make a good 'hot-water bottle'. Her main affair is with the wavy-haired, dapper gigolo painter, played by Brian Aherne, who shows a considerable interest in him (her). As in that other cross-dressing comedy *Some Like It Hot*, the question is who loves whom; desires form and fade, and the possible relationship between Grant and Hepburn doesn't happen, as they find other loves, or other makeshifts for love. Like *Some Like It Hot*, too, it is a film about acting, Hepburn 'performing' gender in ways that would make the feminist theorist Judith Butler proud, and the runaways living as con men (creating scenes to win cash) or as singing Pierrots. When Hepburn has a moustache painted on her smooth lip, both she and the girl who paints it have film stars in mind: does she want to be Charlie Chaplin or Ronald Colman? An actor is being figured as an actor here in ways that make the film a hall of mirrors, reflecting back, but not yet winning desire.

Grant was the best thing in *Sylvia Scarlett*. In their next film together, *Bringing Up Baby*, it would be Hepburn who would be released into action, turning her neuter presence into a moonstruck yearning. Here the sexlessness has been transferred into Grant, playing Professor David Huxley, a preoccupied and desiccated palaeontologist pledged to a marriage without entanglements 'of any kind' with the passionless Miss Swallow. It is the first of three films that Hepburn and Grant made together that explore the idea of the 'wrong engagement': someone has found themselves the wrong fiancé/fiancée and needs to be rescued from the bad marriage they are about to make. Each time, from now on, it must be clear to all that it is Hepburn and Grant who must be together, and the films work solely for the legitimation of their choice, the establishment of the two individual stars as a star couple, of two people united in a marriage. As Peter Swaab has pointed out in his excellent account of *Bringing Up Baby*, part of the poignancy involved in the uniting of these two characters is the peculiar isolation in which they live before they meet each other.[3] Grant spends time with dry bones and the stiff Miss Swallow; Susan is a society girl without much society, playing golf alone, with a distant brother, no sign of any parents, and no friends to confide in. Certainly in her late twenties (or, as Hepburn was, in her early thirties), we learn that she has never loved anyone before.

As 'Susan Vance', Hepburn pursues David Huxley (Grant), playing with him, indeed making him play, taking him from the world of the museum into the screwball realm of games. It would be hard to say who is the main protagonist here: they exist together, flying and chasing each other; she rips his coat, he tears her dress; she steals his clothes, he dresses himself in hers.[4] The more he ignores her, the closer she gets. Audiences may find Susan's single-minded pursuit annoying and consider her unsympathetic. Or maybe Hepburn finds that strange middle ground between being lovable and being maddening. They become like children together, lost in the silvered Connecticut woods. Grant's role is first to embody an endlessly baffled dignity, making him the butt of the joke. As its director Howard Hawks himself declared, a comic film aims solidly at the humiliation of the man.[5] Here it is Grant who cross-dresses, putting on Susan's negligee, and in the process loses all sense of who he is. In screwball, as in Shakespeare's romantic comedies, a spell of not knowing who you are proves part of the salutary process of becoming the person you ought to be.

Grant is truly himself here. The whole thing plays on the presence or absence of his identity, and with that the presence or absence of David Huxley's glasses. It is vital that (as would later happen to Audrey Hepburn), Grant's/Huxley's attractiveness is something that is not a given, but must be discovered on film – and here it must be Susan Vance who discovers it. He is a spellbindingly attractive man who does not know that he is handsome. Only we and Susan know it. Between *Sylvia Scarlett* and this movie there came Leo McCarey's wonderful *The Awful Truth* (1937), the movie where Grant found himself, finally able, as Pauline Kael put it, 'to project his feelings of absurdity through his characters and to make a style out of their feeling silly'.[6] He's an actor who finds acting ridiculous and this self-consciousness became a kind of gift, the holy ghost of irony that would turn him into the greatest film star of his generation.

It has often been argued that in the films he went on to make for Hitchcock, Cary Grant represented an ideal alter ego, the man he might have liked to be. The paradox is not that this was largely what he represented for a substantial percentage of the American and

Katharine Hepburn and Cary Grant flirting and fighting in *The Philadelphia Story* (1940).

European cinema public, but that it was also something that Cary Grant came to represent for Cary Grant himself. The star's persona became a shining possibility too for one Archibald Leach, the young, dispossessed man from Bristol with a mother in a psychiatric hospital who had once dreamt him up. Later in life, Grant remarked, 'I suddenly realized that I had spent the greater part of my life fluctuating between Archie Leach and Cary Grant, unsure of either, suspecting each.'[7] 'Everyone wants to be Cary Grant,' complained Cary Grant; 'even I want to be Cary Grant.' Such statements play on the slippage between Cary Grant (or Archie Leach), the person, and 'Cary Grant', the public image. In these late 1930s films, as Kael suggests, Grant began to place his scepticism about acting into his performances. He was always that strange creature, an actor who looked on at his acting, even while he embodied Hollywood's acting perfection. He was in the role and outside it, the part he was playing and himself – though that self too was perhaps a figment, an index of modernity's possibilities placed on-screen. He fitted Katharine Hepburn well, because both of them were so consciously engaged in the invention of themselves as stars, as living people on-screen.

Grant's persona fitted screwball and was made for romantic comedy as such. He combined urbanity with fun, elegance with acrobatics and could cling to a dignity that was happy to see itself collapse into folly. Their next film, *Holiday*, maps out Grant's aptitude for the comedic world, beyond money and possessions, the real world of life and discovery and natural passion. Hepburn's a citizen of in that realm too, and the film only concerns their mutual discovery of themselves as residents there, while Hepburn's character's sister (Grant's fiancée at the start of the film) belongs to the world of cash and conventions. Hepburn's sister is never going to win the struggle to be with Grant, for after all she's no star (played by the unremarkably attractive Doris Nolan), and no living, lively person either. On the other hand, Grant and Hepburn belong to an aristocracy of the curious, the passionate and the fully alive. Perhaps their place in that elite is itself suspect, the worst kind of snobbery – that is, a spiritual one. Perhaps it is only an act they put on, a part they play, and nothing to do with the people they really were. Yet in watching the film it is hard to shake off the sense that this is truly about them, actually about Grant and about Hepburn – as part and person intertwine and form an image of human potential.

Yet despite these great roles, while Grant's position was unassailable, Hepburn's career looked finished. She was, famously enough, put down as 'box office poison': simply put, when she was in a film, cinema managers believed they lost money. She took refuge for a short while on stage and there acted in Philip Barry's *The Philadelphia Story*, the play that would, when made into a film, seal her place in the pantheon of Hollywood stars (she would in time win four Best Actress Oscars, and be nominated for twelve).

Katharine Hepburn could not do otherwise than appear intelligent on film. Her persona became that of the woman who is wild and interesting enough to guarantee happiness to a man, but whose apartness, independence and modernity makes men unhappy. Therefore she must sacrifice some small part of that reserve – but by no means all. In remarking on this, I'm strongly indebted to Molly Haskell and Maria DiBattista, who have argued that Hepburn lives on-screen as the exceptional woman who must accept that she is also ordinary.[8] In this she reverses the fantasies in play in the 'women's pictures' of the period, which were busy locating the extraordinary in the everyday.

The Philadelphia Story permits a mass attack on Hepburn in the character of Tracy Lord, a society lady on the eve of her second marriage. One by one all the men in her life – her father, her ex, her fiancé – deem her to be essentially remote, cold, posh and virginal. The film takes in here the criticisms that audiences are supposed to have shared. Hepburn, however, transcends this attack by revealing herself in the second half of the film to be lovably extraordinary, mortal, warm, with feet of clay and as given to mistakes as anyone else. Hepburn had been herself and then gone 'gooey' in the middle. That was her own ploy, a conscious gambit to break up and rebuild her compromised persona. In this film poshness need not put us off; the man of the people is a heel. It's the aristocracy of true individualism that counts. In this way the film provides a textbook example of the manipulation of the public image – in a movie that itself considers the intrusion of the media into private life (Tracy Lord's society wedding is to be covered by a sleazy gossip magazine).

Saved from her own perfections, and her quest for perfection in others, Tracy drops her aspiring nouveau riche fiancé and instead marries again her first love, played by Cary Grant. She returns to the person she once was, but renewed, human, ready to be loved forever by him – and by us. The movie turns a goddess into a human being, an independent woman into a wife, and an actor into a star.

8

VIVIEN LEIGH: RUINOUS SELVES

Every great Hollywood star is both an actor and the embodiment of a myth. For all that they are also profoundly ordinary people, their legend depends upon a human uniqueness. But film has transformed them, turning their selves, their talents, into an individual archetypal narrative, one seen both in their films but also in the public knowledge of their private lives. The myth of Vivien Leigh, one of Britain's very few genuine women 'movie stars', is memorable and dark, her life a rise-and-fall story, centred around the consequences of what was then called her 'manic depression', around her vulnerability, her 'promiscuity', her ageing. Her films themselves similarly want to tell us stories about suffering and resilience, about surviving and about being punished for doing so.

Leigh was born in Darjeeling in 1913. A colonial childhood was followed by boarding school exile and the fatal bug of theatre. Her ambition was hardly deflected by an early marriage and motherhood at nineteen – in her diary, she noted, 'Had a baby – a girl'. She was learning acting on her feet, changing herself into something remarkable. But still her early films are all forgettably average; only a devotee could detect traces of a future Blanche DuBois in them. In the benign, if dull Elizabethan swashbuckler *Fire over England* (1937) she plays opposite Laurence Olivier for the first time. The two had just fallen in love, but the expectation that the film might contain some Humphrey Bogart and Lauren Bacall style fireworks soon fizzles out. Leigh has little to do but run about or pine, a petulant source of frustrated energy.

But only a year later there are signs of greatness discovering itself. Tim Whelan's *St Martin's Lane* (1938) (released in America as *Sidewalks of London*) enacts a parable of fame, fixed on the greasepaint ambitions of London's theatreland. Leigh plays Libby, short for Liberty ('like the Statue', she helpfully informs us); the name is of course a significant one, for a woman's pursuit – and missing – of freedom is one of the central elements of Leigh's work. In analysing Liberty's path from street busker to potential screen star, the film shows the men around her wanting to market a freshness felt in her, one that they immediately treat as suspect the moment it actually comes to be sold. Libby retails her personality, but is trapped in a double bind: authentic, but duplicitous; frail, but mercenary. The film wonders whether she would not have been better off never making it, choosing to loiter instead with her platonic mate and fellow busker Charles Laughton, rather than flirting with Rex Harrison and aristocratic backstage Johnnies. Leigh and Laughton here are beauty and the beast, Esmeralda and the hunchback. They are like playful children: Laughton seems an overgrown boy, brimming with sweaty self-belief, while, in her beret and shirt and tie, there's something schoolgirlish about Leigh.

Leigh's corblimey Cockney accent is considerably less convincing than Scarlett O'Hara's Georgian drawl; it is an enacted Englishness, pretty much akin to what the film itself would like to sell. With its no-nonsense nostalgia for the gutter, the film clings on to a kind of light-hearted pessimism; 'Everything's luck and good temper . . . and if you can take a joke,' booms Charles Laughton with bullish stoicism, before tacking on the glum coda, 'The whole of life's a joke.' This grimly chipper mood was the 1930s English version of the can-do optimistic gleam offered by Hollywood and *Gone with the Wind*.

Gone with the Wind depends equally on the presence of Clark Gable, Olivia de Havilland and all the others involved, yet there is some truth in the thought that it is centrally Leigh's film. To comprehend this film takes us to the heart of an understanding of Leigh and her persona. Like Liberty, Scarlett O'Hara is another plotter, another survivor. Here Leigh's great weakness is also her strength: she always looks like she's acting – pulling faces, looking sulky, producing those incorrigible dimples. There is much wrong with *Gone with the Wind*: its racial politics, its slippery view of American Civil War history, its mingled adoration for and suspicion of its central heroine. Yet for all that it remains one of the most vital, entertaining and beguilingly beautiful of all classic Hollywood films – and, more than anything else, it is the mercurial verve of Leigh's performance that brings it to life.

Before it was a classic film, *Gone with the Wind* was a classic PR stunt. The film's producer, David O. Selznick, announced that he would launch a nationwide search for the young woman who would play Scarlett O'Hara, its heroine. The move provoked a furore. Margaret Mitchell's 1936 novel was already a national best-seller – it seemed that everyone was reading it – and now the desire to star in the film version proved irresistible. As in a proto-*Pop Idol*, lines of would-be Scarletts queued up for fretful screen tests, each dreaming of Tara and stardom. Letters poured in to the Selznick studio recommending starlets for the role; one even suggested someone almost unknown in America, the British actress Vivien Leigh. The fact that nearly every player in Hollywood, as well as a substantial proportion of the book's readers, imagined themselves as Scarlett O'Hara defeated the possibility of an easy choice. It seemed that Scarlett was both an everywoman and a frustratingly elusive character to cast. Katharine Hepburn, Bette Davis, Lana Turner, Paulette Goddard, all were nearly right and yet failed somehow to capture the required quality. Through a mixture of cunning, determination and strategic 'good luck', Vivien Leigh nabbed the role in a way that might have appealed to Scarlett herself. The search for the film's star apparently ended in fairy-tale fashion. Leigh was 'spotted' in the watching crowd on the night that filming began, with discarded Hollywood stage sets blazing around her in simulation of the burning of Atlanta. Her being there was hardly fortuitous, but rather a mixture of her own wiles and the sense of theatre of the producer's agent brother, Myron Selznick. The flame-lit moment sums up something about the film; from the tattered legend of the event something fabulously disreputable shines through. But as a legend of discovery it is entirely apt for *Gone with the Wind*, likewise a mingling of over-the-top spectacle, spontaneous passion and conscious artfulness.

Gone with the Wind is a national memorial to American forgetting, a film that now resurrects two legendary pasts, the lost American South and the classic Hollywood movie. Both are institutions that have kept going while clinging to the idea that their glories have already departed. The South has founded its identity on a noble defeat, and though American film may always be banking on the next blockbuster, the medium itself increasingly looks like a mausoleum of past marvels. At the heart of both the myth of the South and of Hollywood lies the vanishing vision of a certain kind of femininity: wily, quick-witted, resilient, conniving and wonderful.

In making its allegory of the old South, the film entangles a long-standing misapprehension in a Technicolor pageant. It presents the fortunes of Scarlett O'Hara, one of three daughters of an Irish American (and Roman Catholic) slave-owning plantation family in Georgia. Scarlett loves the wan Ashley Wilkes (played by Leslie Howard), but Ashley, it quickly turns out, is betrothed to another, the antithesis of fervent, flirtatious Scarlett: the Quakerish, quivering and ever-sincere Melanie Hamilton (Olivia de Havilland). For the rest of the film, and although she marries three other men (the first out of pique, the second out of necessity), Scarlett nurses her ardour for Ashley, convinced that he feels the same way about her, but is only restrained by his sense of honour. Her third husband is a more serious contender for her love: Rhett Butler (Clark Gable) is Scarlett's male counterpart, just as devious, just as heated as herself. He's no gentleman, but then she's no lady. However, beguiled by Ashley, dismissive of sexual desire and apparently hostile to the idea of motherhood, Scarlett resists this man she has married. These passions play out through the apocalypse of the American Civil War, a conflict that calls upon all Scarlett's resources as she fights for her own – and her house's – survival.

For all its gaudy big-screen splendour, *Gone with the Wind* is a film that works best in its intimate scenes. Here the film foregoes its flames and sunsets and draws in on the intricacies of its central character as embodied by Leigh. The other leading parts inevitably revolve around Scarlett, real in themselves, yet there to cast a light on her nature. A thread of impulsive gestures, of pettish epigrams, she is the reckless heart of the film. Near the beginning, having playfully beckoned him into a room for a private conversation, Scarlett is rejected by Ashley, the man she loves. Leigh plays the scene as an unripe grand passion, striving with him; it is an oddly unbalanced moment, with the woman making the running but up against the infuriating rule of Ashley's spineless determination. He sits on the left of the screen, the zone for waverers in classic Hollywood cinema, irresolutely regarding her but full of apparent self-confidence, facing her as she stands on the right, tentative yet absolutely decided. She persuades, she confesses herself, she shows her strength in her willingness to surrender, and all he can do is agree that he loves her while feebly evading her. Her fervour confronts his measured acceptance of his own lack of it; in rage at his baffling refusal, she slaps him. When Ashley stalks from the room at last, Scarlett hurls a vase in fury against the far wall of the room. As it smashes, up from the sofa where he has been concealed all the time rises Rhett Butler, the man she will eventually marry. 'Has the war started?' he asks her. Like the audience, he has heard the whole scene, and he offers her and us a sardonic interpretation of its outbursts. He is comically concerned, faintly amused and flirtatious. Though she responds like any good screwball comedy heroine with fiery repartee, a signal for any 1930s audience that the two are made for each other, this time it is Scarlett who flees the room. In one scene the film has presented us with the path that Scarlett will follow.

Yet for all the compressed magic of this, the mystery is that this character and this small love-confusion should require that great background of the war and those epic colours, and that these convoluted amorous pursuits should depend upon and find their place within such a magnificent tapestry. It is not so much that the film explores the relation of the self to history, but rather that history itself should seem a vision that both undoes Scarlett's character and provides a projected glory for her losses. The film unspools the destruction of something (of Scarlett's – and Leigh's – youth, the South's grace) but does so in such a way that the unravelling appears a thing of beauty. Margaret Mitchell's book was less wide-eyed, its ending provokingly bathetic and hard: Rhett Butler simply abandons Scarlett. For its own ending, the film had to go beyond that famous moment where he strides off, telling her in a masterpiece of censorship-eluding scansion, 'Frankly, my dear, I don't *give* a damn', and instead chooses an optimism as robust, as wild as its own fervid sway. 'Tomorrow,' Scarlett persuades us, 'is another day.'

This story draws upon the allure of the South and is by now the most famous example of its sustaining myth. Yet if Scarlett, and Leigh, are to be taken as the embodiment of that sweet untruth, then the film subtly transforms the illusion. It gives us neither triumph, nor a gracious downfall, but rather a stoic manipulator. This is a feminized South, where to be most successfully feminine is to be the best player of a confidence game. The men are compromised cavaliers, their courage curiously ineffectual: Rhett may save Melanie and Scarlett from the ruins of Atlanta, but he then promptly leaves them to their fate in the middle of hostile territory. Yet the film nonetheless adheres to a vision that its own complexities would dismantle.

Gone with the Wind was a magnificent folly, a film made frenziedly, a fabrication of breakdowns and Benzedrine. It represents the triumph of artifice, the South of the 1860s concocted on a Hollywood lot. While the book was an ante-Modernist throwback, a 1930s riposte to Harriet Beecher Stowe, the film lovingly and necessarily embraces the possibilities of technology, made from a fabric of process shots, images and cuts. Watching it, you are quickly drawn into a semi-resistant, somnolent state, drugged by colours sweet as candy. The soft image of black children fanning drowsy Southern belles beguiles, like a Burne-Jones painting commissioned by George Lincoln Rockwell, the theatrical *Führer* of the American Nazi Party. The whole works like an opera, complete with its overture and entr'acte. In its first phases it is the sweep of the movie that is so alluring and so suspect; the astounding unreality of it all immerses you. Sitting through Stephen Daldry's *The Reader* (2008), it proved tough to resist the thought, 'Those poor Nazi guards, they really suffered.' Watching Fleming's movie, you are similarly corralled into feeling, 'Those poor plantation owners, they really had it hard.' If the ultimate meaning of *The Reader* is the frailty of art, that reading changes nothing – all that Chekhov, all that Tolstoy, and they still both remain moral idiots – the ultimate message of *Gone with the Wind* is art's potency, the shiny complicity of the moving picture.

It is a complicity that would, if it could, float free of direct involvement with the South's self-image or politics. Signalling aristocratic poise, three of the film's four stars were in one way or another British, and both Hattie McDaniel and Clark Gable were born outside the South. (Gable pluckily refused to attempt a Southern accent for the role.) The Pittsburgh-born producer of the film, David O. Selznick, constructed an outsider's rendition of the South's defiant requiem. The footage of the film's Atlanta premiere reveals just how out of place and ill at ease Selznick looks there, a Jew in Georgia; it was the first time he had ever set foot in the South. This was an American epic made by someone ostensibly outside its power. Selznick was uneasy about the story's aptness to be read as a white parable of the essential goodness of the slave-owning South. In the days of Kristallnacht and Dachau, he was acutely aware of the nature of racial prejudice. Other towns than Atlanta were burning now. The film tries its best to alleviate the tacit racism, banning use of the 'N word' and repressing direct mention of the Ku Klux Klan. Yet the real world would draw out the story's latent meanings, irreducibly embroiled as they were in Margaret Mitchell's novel, that American Bible. The black stars of the film would not be invited to the Atlanta premiere; in the Southern version of the film's printed programme, Hattie McDaniel's image was quietly excised. Most painful of all, at the dinner where she was awarded her Oscar for Best Supporting Actress, McDaniel sat at a table apart from the film's white stars.

The core of the fable lies with Scarlett's ambiguous collusion with the desires of men. It is a tribute to the power of Mitchell's conception and of Vivien Leigh's playing that Scarlett should remain such a multifaceted character. Here a British woman plays a classic

American conniver, the epitome of national contradictions. A heroine for the Depression years, she is not least American in being, in the end, a free marketeer, a flirtatious worshipper of Mammon. (Ever since the novel's publication critics have noted how vigorous Scarlett O'Hara and noble Melanie Hamilton echo Thackeray's presentation in *Vanity Fair* of Becky Sharp and Amelia Sedley.) *Gone with the Wind* sells us an old understanding of the South. In the film's terms, slavery is not a degraded element in a noble system, rather its existence promotes and protects that nobility. Southern courtesy requires the subjection of the blacks. Without it, the South – and Scarlett – become the image of their own Northern antithesis, as a feudal system gives way to the free labour of the Yankee world. Scarlett enthusiastically embraces this change, and as soon as is possible she becomes a happily exploitative entrepreneur. There are, perhaps, parallels here with the position of the film star, and therefore of Leigh herself, committed to embodying beauty and to the production of art, but that art itself being a commercial enterprise, a grace for sale.

Like the film star herself, however, Scarlett lives an economic life, her identity chiefly revolving not around cash, but around men, though in the circumstances the two are apt to be confused. It is undoubtedly an 'iconic' romance, though the retrospective icon flattens out the weird turns of the love plot. For most of the time Scarlett refuses her connection to Gable's Rhett Butler, choosing instead the comforts of unrequited desire elsewhere. The talismanic images of the picture, its bodice-ripping poster of Clark Gable taking Vivien Leigh in his powerful arms (replayed in the 1980s poster where Reagan embraced a swooning Maggie Thatcher), all suggest that this is where the overriding passion burns. However, for most of the film Scarlett herself appears to think otherwise, obsessed as she is with Leslie Howard's pithless Ashley Wilkes; she's a Cathy who prefers Linton to Heathcliff. Likewise, it is not so clear how much Rhett's passion is for her. At the end of both halves of the film, Rhett forsakes Scarlett, rejecting the promise of love: the first time, she misjudges his high-minded motives; the second time, he misinterprets her. On both occasions the abandoned Scarlett struggles on, making good, or looking set fair to do so.

Scarlett may marry three times, but in each case it is a throwaway gesture, a means of giving nothing of herself. The initial two husbands prove fortuitously expendable: the first carried off by measles, the mutton-chopped second dispatched off-screen by wicked carpet-baggers. Watching the film now, Scarlett's refusal of sexual pleasure is intriguingly mystifying. Her avoidance of such intimacy now looks not so much neurotic as insurrectionary. When Rhett threatens to crush Scarlett's skull, the film confronts us with his abiding horror at her recalcitrant otherness, entangled with the on-screen otherness of the star, at once intimate and remote. Why can't she just do as she ought? Rhett and the audience want her to play the game of love with him, and yet she will not do so according to the rules. On several occasions, when Rhett proposes kissing her, in one move she shuts her eyes, throws her head back, puckers up and waits. These are comic presages of the marital rape scene to come and Scarlett's post-coital morning stretches and smiles that follow; unwilling perhaps, the film seems inclined to imply, to own up to her own desire, Scarlett seems happy to let herself be overwhelmed. While this scene has deservedly formed the test case for critical debates about the film, equally extraor-dinary is the moment where Ashley finally kisses Scarlett. For a moment she becomes strange to us, letting go of the tension of long-ing, laughing, weeping, collapsing, desiring. 'You love me,' she repeats, in manic relief, 'You love me.'

In a famous reading of the film, Molly Haskell introduced Scarlett as a 'superfemale', like all the best Southern belles: a demonic coquette playing within society's structures, a self-exploiting rebel.[1] She also bears traces, through Mitchell's biography, of the tomboy, also some-thing of a personal myth for Haskell, who has written often of just such a phase in her own life and of the troubles of having to surrender its vantages.

Though rightly concentrating on Scarlett, in her book on the film Haskell is characteristically fair to the film's other main characters too.[2] She does justice to the complex goodness of Olivia de Havilland's Melanie, placing the serene power of a character who offers us an alternative vision of uncomplaining fortitude. Haskell is equally astute on the ways that the film exposes the feebleness of men. There are those early nonentities of doting husbands, those perfect hunks yammering boyishly for a war that will wipe them out, those endless lines of wounded and helpless Confederate soldiers. The film would rather show us hospitals than battlefields. For many, the epicentre of male fragility is the Peter Wimsey-esque Leslie Howard as Ashley Wilkes. Haskell has previously written of the now long-faded attraction of the 'Ashley-figure', and she may be one of the last to feel a faint trace of desire for this heroically vague Englishman. Most now will plump for Rhett. Yet, as Haskell persuasively argues, grinning Clark Gable is in fact the most surprising addition to this spineless bunch, the movie both assuming and casting doubt on his previously unstoppable sex appeal. The film consistently 'unmans' him and he becomes over its length a weeping, frustrated, insecure, pram-pushing figure, surrendering to fate and accepting that Scarlett is one woman that he will never get to love him.

Although it begins with slave-market-and-magnolia sweetness, the film by no means stays there. In fact, it quickly launches out into a Thomas Hardy-like sequence of calamities. Miscarriages, falls, premature deaths, mistaken marriages and misunderstandings proliferate; the rich colours grow luridly Gothic. As the scene darkens, Scarlett correspondingly transforms from vain flirt into an admirable, though admittedly equivocal heroine: she flees the hospital where the wounded soldiers suffer, but sticks by Melanie, abiding by her promises. She coolly kills a marauding Yankee, in a moment that still staggers us with its rapid violence; saintly Melanie participates happily in clearing up the deed. (This man, the only Northern soldier we see, is a villainous figure intent on rape and pillage; no viewer of the film ever grieved over his murder.) Meanwhile history is remade as spectacle; the wounded crowd the earth, Atlanta burns.

The film mourns the loss of a world, one manifest in the various attitudes and characters of Scarlett and Melanie, Ashley and Rhett. It presents a fabled country, a feudal order of gallantry, chivalry and slaves. But the grace shrivels. When the film opened in England in April 1940 it must have been hard not to project the loss of a mythic

European sweetness onto the screen, something just then being erased by the destruction of war. The film's three British stars could have fostered this identification. Olivia de Havilland has remarked that, in an echo of his role, Leslie Howard's unmistakable sadness in the film was the product of his anxieties about the coming war, a conflict that would see his own death in a military air crash. Joseph Goebbels banned the film, suspicious of its propaganda for lost causes. After the war, when it was seen in the countries of once-occupied Europe, the film there too looked like a masterwork of the aftermath. It stands with Roberto Rossellini's *Germania anno zero* (Germany, Year Zero) 1948) and Carol Reed's *The Third Man* (1949) as a film that explored the end of a civilization. Whether these prophetic forebodings were always present in the film, or are fortuitous resonances found in its spacious plot, it is part of the richness of *Gone with the Wind* that it could so soon be open to new interpretations.

Gone with the Wind remains Leigh's central role, the part that defined her career and secured her position in the history of American film. Moving on from its heights would prove difficult, yet Leigh continued to perform the complexities of being a woman on film, a person in a society with a divided view of what it meant to be a woman at all.

Having divorced their respective spouses, for a long time Leigh was absorbed into the smiling public image of 'The Oliviers', in love and famous for it, a sanctified, theatrical confection of a marriage. Naturally Olivier wanted to play opposite her: Leigh might have made a fantastic Cathy in William Wyler's *Wuthering Heights* (1939), but, if she and Olivier had gotten their way, would have been terribly miscast as the gauche second Mrs de Winter in Hitchcock's *Rebecca* (1940).

Instead she took the role of ballet dancer Myra Lester in Mervyn LeRoy's *Waterloo Bridge* (1940). This was a three-hankie First World War weepie that proceeds like a Hardyesque 'Satire of Circumstance', a sick joke about providence, luck and doom. It presents a somewhat muffed debate about the value of living life on any terms, with Robert Taylor's inexplicably Americanized Scot affirming an enraptured optimism against Leigh's gloomy English assumption that what can go wrong will go wrong. In plot terms, Leigh's pessimism would appear

Vivien Leigh insouciantly regal as Cleopatra in *Caesar and Cleopatra* (1945).

to win out. Through one terrible mistake (the misinformation that Taylor has been killed at the front) and one masochistically obtuse scene of cross-purposes between Myra and her fiancé's mother, our heroine's life plunges into poverty and prostitution. When Taylor unexpectedly returns, Leigh hopes that she can pick up where she left off. Only of course she cannot; she is a fallen woman and, as such, there is only one thing to be done with her. Myra's sin is one that cannot speak its name; no one ever explicitly mentions how Myra has been paying the rent. 'You don't have to tell me,' moans Robert Taylor, when realization finally comes.

It is all desperately sad and yet somehow the film wants Taylor's bright sense of life's possibilities to survive even losing Myra. At the start of another world war he is left behind to walk the bridge again, to shed a nostalgic tear and summon up a resolute half-smile of remembrance. For ultimately the film is happy to consign fallen Myra to suicide. It enjoys her defeat by letting us wallow in it; her extinction is sentimental, accompanied by the sweetness of a tear.

This was Vivien Leigh's favourite role and it is certainly one of her most significant ones. There are few of her films that so clearly express the contradictions of her essential myth. Here the strong investment in her essential innocence mingles most obviously with the horror that she is in fact 'corrupt'. It offers an innocent's progress. The film plays on the undeniable appeal of her freshness, but shows it becoming tired, jaded. Ballet is the perfect medium for young Myra and for Leigh; it is a physical art dependent on hard graft and strength that must give the appearance of ethereal delicacy. Like a film star, Myra moves from a performance of gracious prettiness, adored and remote from earthly concerns, to an assumption that she is available for any man and as such is worthless, unless redeemed by self-destruction. It is an actress's film that more than most exposes the contradictions in the public consumption of the great Hollywood women stars. Vivien Leigh's genius was to embody a startling vivacity, a quality of naturalness; yet it was also always apparent that this was a performance, an exposure of the self. Like all stars, she was a published person.

The ironies of her position were next best expressed in the British-produced adaption of Tolstoy's *Anna Karenina* (1948). By rights, this really ought to have been a fantastic film. It was shot by the gifted Henri Alekan, who had recently photographed Jean Cocteau's *La Belle et la Bête* (1946); Julien Duvivier, one of the period's great French film-makers, directed; Constant Lambert wrote the music; Jean Anouilh collaborated on the film script. And at the centre of it all is Leigh, truly at her very best, indeed better almost than she had ever been.

Yet the film fails to be great. It is not its heaviness that mars it – for central to its meaning is a woman cushioned and trapped by brocade, antimacassar and frills, the ceilinged sets deepening the sense of confinement. Ultimately, it is wrecked by the miscasting of the uncharismatic Kieron Moore as Vronsky. Though too old, Olivier would have been infinitely better. By this point Peter Finch, Leigh's new lover, could also have brought much more to the part, and Olivier might more suitably have been cast as the cuckolded Karenin, a role that fell instead to his great friend Ralph Richardson. Art was imitating life; the Leigh myth was blending the screen and the gossip columns.

It is particularly amazing that Leigh's performance here comes only a few years after she starred in Gabriel Pascal's cinema version of George Bernard Shaw's *Caesar and Cleopatra* (1945). Here she still relies on the trick of looking absurdly pleased with herself, in possession perhaps of some private delight in her own public beauty. Knowingness is Cleopatra's keynote, so too, as with Scarlett, are her rapid turns of feeling, with Leigh moving dizzily from the plaintive to the petulant, from the dominating to the despairing. The whole film pivots on its own delightful unreality, balanced with a Shavian ethic of pragmatic truth-telling. The film tells it like it is, while showing us a Technicolor land that never existed outside a studio.

To have passed from this to the thoughtfulness and seriousness of her Anna Karenina is remarkable, but that three years later she would up her game once more in playing Blanche DuBois in Elia Kazan's version of Tennessee Williams's *A Streetcar Named Desire*

(1951) is extraordinary. It is simply one of the greatest pieces of acting in any American film. Leigh had lived to unite in one career the acting styles of two distinct worlds – moving from playing against dinner-jacketed Rex Harrison suavely proffering a cigarette to Marlon Brando bellowing in a ripped T-shirt. She had passed from theatricality and urbanity to passion and 'the authentic'. (Olivier would have to wait years before following her by playing Archie Rice in John Osborne's *The Entertainer*.) There can hardly have been two such very different Southern Belles as her two Oscar-winning performances as Scarlett O'Hara and Blanche DuBois; where one survives, the other goes under. With Blanche, Leigh finds a space for insecurity, for the elusive sense of failure in her. She seemed to be putting her disintegration on-screen: Leigh is felt to suffer, as Blanche suffers. It was a high-risk activity, but also a sign of things to come. Her later films play out again and again the cruelty of ageing, the sense of failure, of missing out on the feast of life. As happened to Montgomery Clift, her films became preoccupied with the wreck of her once astonishing beauty. Yet the long tailing-off of her career should not conceal from us that she continued to be a great actor to the end of her life, and that for a while on film in a handful of performances she had brilliantly held together the contradictions both of her own personality and of the beloved, and envied, Hollywood star.

Veronica Lake looking sultry in an image for *Sullivan's Travels* (1941).

9

VERONICA LAKE:
HALF-OBSCURED FACES

I n Alfred Hitchcock's *Shadow of a Doubt* (1943) the heroine's book-
ish little sister settles down to say her bedtime prayers. In rapid
succession, she asks for heavenly favour for her dad, her mum,
her sister, her brother, and Veronica Lake. As this implies, Lake was
simply one of the biggest American stars of the war years; 45 years
later, in *Who Killed Roger Rabbit?*, her iconic looks are still central as
a memory of the 1940s, the long blonde hair, side-parted, the tresses
falling down on one side, half-obscuring her face. You can still pur-
chase a Veronica Lake wig. Young women truly wanted to be Veronica
Lake. That haircut was so often imitated that the war-time u.s.
government had to forbid it officially; too many women were getting
their hair caught in the machinery in the munitions factories. In noir
films such as *This Gun for Hire* and *The Glass Key* (both 1942), alongside another tough blond, Alan Ladd, she was essentially cool, a tiny
femme fatale, emotionally withdrawn, unreadable, holding the screen
but hidden. (The noir fatal woman was often small: in *Out of the Past*
(1947) Robert Mitchum quips with Jane Greer, 'you're not very tall,
are you?' 'I'm as tall as Napoleon,' she replies. 'And cuter, too,' says
Mitchum.)

Lake was a noir heroine par excellence because the brutal emotional freeze of noir was in her very bones. In *The Glass Key* she flirts
on remote, imperturbably aroused, chastely chill. In *The Blue Dahlia*
(1946), scripted by Raymond Chandler, Alan Ladd's character remarks

that she's a woman who every guy believes he has seen some place; 'the trick,' he adds, 'is to find you.' Yet despite this apparently destined connection, the romance here is as ever perfunctory. In all these films where Ladd and Lake are paired, other things draw our attention: male friendship and the loyalty between men, the masochistic endurance of punishment. Meanwhile, Lake is that 'unexpressive she', an uninvolved symbol of desire, sketched in to fill the place required by some long-imagined dream of femininity, without letting us feel that she is truly that greedy dream's fulfilment. Playing in the supernatural comedy *I Married a Witch* (1942) Lake has something uncannily otherworldly about her, even as – for once – she is driven by a passion, one thrust on her by her warlock father's spell. Yet even here, as in the films with Ladd, what was most present on-screen was how composed and yet not quite there she was, how unruffled and how desperately collected.

Yet of all Lake's films, it seems to me that the one that most interrogates her on-screen persona and has most to say about the role of the film star is Preston Sturges's wonderful, almost completely satisfying satire on the movie business, *Sullivan's Travels* (1941).

It is a strange feature of the best comedies that all are somehow engaged with comedy's impossibility, with the fact that the optimism and joy it offers as art may be unfindable in the real world. Tragedy is far less concerned with its own ontological status; it never apologizes for its assumption that the world is a dark place. Paradoxically perhaps, comedy can be less complacent regarding its vision of things. For the Greeks and Romans one defining characteristic of tragedy was that its plot was drawn from history, while comedy derived from the realm of fiction. Real life, they believed, fails to provide material for comedy.

So it is that in the best tradition of 1930s and '40s comic film, notably reaching even Bob Hope and Bing Crosby's *Road* films, *Sullivan's Travels* is a movie that wants to let on that it is just a movie. Three times in this film we are in a cinema audience watching people watching films. Sturges's story concerns John L. Sullivan (Joel McCrea), a highly successful comedy movie director, who decides that he wants to make a passionate and tragic film (*O Brother, Where Art Thou?*), a work that will realize the sociological and educational potential of cinema. As this may indicate, he is a comedy director without a sense of humour. His studio bosses think the idea stinks, and besides what does Sullivan, a well-heeled college graduate and very wealthy man, an American success, know of suffering? Sullivan agrees and decides, like the boy in the fairy tale who went in search of fear, that he will dress up as a tramp and go out into the world to find trouble. He is practically a knight setting out to find adventure, a version of the Prince in Mark Twain's *The Prince and the Pauper*, or like the sultan in Izak Dinesen's story 'A Consolatory Tale' (published a year after Sturges's film) who, disguised as a beggar, goes out from the palace to taste life as a common person in the city he rules. Rather than finding work in a factory, like Simone Weil, and taking up a position at the bottom of the social structure, Sullivan chooses to become a tramp, a figure of independent poverty on society's romantic margins. (George Orwell's *Down and Out in Paris and London* had appeared only nine years before.) Naturally enough, Sullivan's search proves an abortive one: he cannot get free of his wealth and privilege; he remains a tourist in the suffering world. What he does find is The Girl, played with low-voiced sultry sweetness by Veronica Lake.

She is broke and in trouble, and so, apparently, is he. In an edge-of-town diner she buys him coffee, a sinker, and some ham and eggs. This small, quixotic gesture of kindness is one of many that pattern the film. It is unique, though, in so far as its results are purely positive: after all, it enables the romance that sweetens the movie. As the studio boss at the movie's beginning points out, a film ought to have 'a little sex in it'. Yet it is a cutely sexless romance; there is not even much of an epicene kink in her dressing up as Sullivan's sidekick boy-tramp. Sullivan is just too preoccupied by suffering properly to notice her. When they first meet she only really gets through to him as a suitable object for his compassion: a poor defenceless kid, beaten by Holly-wood, and on her way back to Palookaville. The fact that she seems not at all defenceless and is in fact busy showing practical compassion for him hardly troubles his earnest altruism.

Lake is a wannabe movie star who will end up getting her break through Sullivan's supposed death (more of that later). There she is, one of America's movie sweethearts playing someone doomed to be forever nameless (she remains 'The Girl' throughout), a person unable to penetrate the holy places of Hollywood. Why is she even in the film? No one's sure. A policeman asks Sullivan how The Girl fits into this picture. 'There's always a girl in the picture,' he testily replies; 'haven't you ever been to the movies?' Her presence in the film affects nothing; in plot terms she could be removed from the narrative and nothing would be altered. And yet, her condition of namelessness, her aspiration for movie fame, her companionable love for Sullivan, and her not easily seen face are the heart of this film. As Andrew Sarris has noted, Sturges can expose the generic silliness of Hollywood movies and then, in the same movie, write some of the sweetest low-key love scenes on film.[1]

Sullivan's Travels breaks one supposed rule of comedy: it includes a violent death. On the edge of a train depot, a tramp coshes Sullivan and robs him of hundreds of dollars that he's been distributing to the down-and-outs at the depot. The thief even takes his shoes. As he crosses the rail tracks with the money, the tramp drops the $5 bills. As he panics and tries to gather them up, a train pulls in. He is caught 'like a rabbit in the headlights', as Sturges's script puts it, and struck down. The scene plays out like a moment in a thriller; we are watching it happen, but also do so, vitally, from inside the tramp's perspective, inhabiting his desperation as he tries to work out which way to run. Waking from the blow, Sullivan cannot remember who he is; like other film stars in this book, he loses himself and his name through amnesia. Confronted by a security guard, he fights back and knocks the man down with a rock. He is taken to court but, confused and nameless, he cannot defend himself adequately and is sentenced to six years' hard labour. Meanwhile the tramp's body has been found, unrecognizable after the accident: in the heel of his pilfered shoe, put there for safety, is Sullivan's director's card. Sullivan, it seems, is dead. Finally Sullivan has got what he believed he wanted; he has found trouble and become nameless. And the otherwise nameless tramp has become him. He has died for Sullivan and as Sullivan, and Sullivan has passed into his real world.

In the harsh confines of the prison camp Sullivan comes back to knowledge of himself. He shouldn't be in prison: a tramp may be sentenced to six years for assault, but a film director would never be. Justice may be rigged, but he has lost his privileges and his credentials. Now he is as much without a name as The Girl, a generic convict, a 'Richard Roe'. He has to prove he is who he is, a film-maker, and not a victim of the plot. He has become properly what he pretended to be: not an actor of poverty, but truly poor. The film forsakes all jokes; it takes on the conventions of film realism; comedy has passed its limits and become its opposite. Sturges has achieved Sullivan's aim and fabricated a film that abandons comedy for 'the un-comic realities beyond it'.[2] At his lowest ebb, in a church hall, through the active kindness of the black congregation, Sullivan watches a Disney cartoon with the other convicts and finds himself laughing with his fellows. The moment attempts to justify comedy as necessary escape; it also provides the impetus for Sullivan to effect his own escape. He declares himself to be his own murderer and the resulting publicity saves him – this nameless man has his photograph recognized in the paper (by The Girl, of course) – and his fame restores him to fame. Comedy has reasserted its basic principle: there is no trouble so great that you cannot get out of it.

Sullivan's resurrection also gets him out of his loveless marriage (one that only took place for the tax breaks), for his duplicitous wife has swiftly married again. He is free now to marry The Girl and effect Hollywood's necessary romantic closure; Jack finds his Jill and the audience leave satisfied. The film has abandoned comedy to reassert it at the finish. Yet Lake remains The Girl, nameless to the end.

In his wonderful book *'You Ain't Heard Nothing Yet'*, Andrew Sarris notes how Sturges throngs the world of his films with an extravagant multiplicity of characters.[3] In his films America is a congested, cluttered place; it is a comedy of the crowd, of fascinating faces. As you watch *Sullivan's Travels*, your eye constantly passes beyond Joel McCrea's preoccupied handsomeness, even beyond Lake's fine features, to the faces of the extras and bit-players, especially those playing the tramps and convicts, the congregation of the African American church. You glimpse here people from outside the world of cinema, faces with histories that stretch back before there even were moving pictures. Yet there they are in the movie, signs of a reality that the sheen of Hollywood cinema can hardly contain. André Bazin argued that in all this Sturges ironizes the American class system; more recently Maria DiBattista has seen him as only reinforcing that same system; both might agree that in either case this film shows a readiness to open out and look upon other faces from other lives.[4] One of cinema's earliest discoveries was that of the iconic human face, blown up to huge size, an image of personhood and allure, of an inwardness portrayed and withheld, an inaccessible beauty, only perhaps to be attained by looking. How else could we catch hold of another's face? The film ends with McCrea's and Lake's smiling faces, secure in stardom, caught up in the artifice of film. Around them appears a myriad of those faces that have haunted the margins of this movie. Those faces appear about them, the last signs of a process that the movie has entered into and then transcended, a comedic doubling of the star with the ordinary person, the director-prince with the nameless beggar, Veronica Lake with The Girl. Sullivan's privilege here is not quite Lake's: in becoming a wife, she will gain a name, but in what sense is it hers? Less tormented than Sullivan, she is nonetheless in a starker position. The film has told us how corrupt and meaningless is the process by which a young woman becomes a Hollywood star. Lake could be anyone; anyone might be Veronica Lake. She is special and anonymous. These are not her travels, though she is a fellow-traveller for two of Sullivan's four journeys; this is not her resurrection.

10

CAROLE LOMBARD: THE SCREWBALL HEROINE

Carole Lombard remains one of the greatest American comediennes, a movie star too daffily diffident to be 'starry', a glamorous character floating above glamour. Irony was her essence, a subversive force on which she drew: at her best she acted someone acting. In Howard Hawks's manic early masterpiece *Twentieth Century* (1934) she shows herself already an expert in the comedy of style. Hawks takes the well-established premise that theatre acting looked ghastly in the talking picture and makes it the basis of a comedy. Lombard plays an amazing film actor playing a theatre star. The joke about theatre people here is that they are always acting; it is a joke that would return, as we will see, in Lombard's last ever movie. Her character Lily Garland (née Mildred Plotka) is an invented person, her stage name imposed on her by Oscar Jaffe (played by John Barrymore), her autocratic, would-be Svengali of a director. Here theatre represents a place where men control women; Lombard shows her independence by quitting its constrictions for the supposedly woman-centred world of Hollywood. There she becomes a famous face, someone who adorns the covers of at least a dozen fan and gossip magazines. Later, in *To Be or Not to Be*, she would appear again as someone mediated by the stardom industry, her photograph found in newspapers and cigarette packets – they even named a soap after her. Secretly, however, she is a person at some distance from the goldfish-owning, farm-loving persona she enacts in interviews. In *Twentieth Century*, as a film star

Not collaborating, just acting: Carole Lombard in *To Be or Not To Be* (1942).

now, she is apparently free of the man who 'discovered' her. However, after running into him again on the Twentieth Century, the train from Chicago to Grand Central Station, she falls back into his clutches and ends the film, perhaps happily tricked, once again being directed and controlled on the New York stage. It is a film that sets out the power play in the directorial relationship. Playing the director, Barrymore's most terrible fear is that he too may have to be an actor, and yet he is condemned to spend his life in relation to them. Barrymore plays the role with a gloriously excessive momentousness; he believes he is in the greatest tragedy ever performed, even though the stakes are just the cash required to fund another play. Lombard hardly has his seriousness, but she is not mugging it up either. She is both inside and outside the role, a borderline position she would make her very own.

As an actor, Lombard flourished when she was playing at the limit of good taste or the edge of credibility. Who else, in William Wellman's *Nothing Sacred* (1937), could have done so much and been so goofily sympathetic as a small-town young woman pretending to be dying of a terminal disease in order to be feted by a New York newspaper? In that film she personifies comedy's resistance to death, above all how it resists taking it seriously. Yet this act of cheek comes across as dizzily elated and anything but sacrilegious. Many remain convinced that this movie really undermines that decorous social collusion and cohesion provided by the canons of taste. One mark of being civilized is the ability to know when to avoid the obvious joke. Taste, like comedy, depends on the cohesion of an audience, that which they share, and that which can be tested to see if they share. It is apt perhaps therefore that Lombard's last movie, finished just days before her death in a plane crash, should be one that critics at the time derided as 'tasteless', a category confusion in the guise of a movie.

Set in Nazi-occupied Poland, while Poland still was Nazi-occupied, Ernst Lubitsch's *To Be or Not to Be* (1942) dances on the boundaries of what comedy can safely take on and make use of. Comedy necessitates exclusions: there can be no evil, no death, no intense, unrelieved suffering. Yet it also embraces the small stuff that tragedy would transcend, including the body's weakness and vulnerability and messiness; failure; shabbiness; folly and our little egos. The war itself is a tragedy, but it is therefore also a kind of play too, one that demolishes the limits set by the censor. Can one make a comedy about the suffering in Poland at that time? The circumstances there might be thought to invalidate all art, and yet in many senses, as *Sophie's Choice* would later show, a tragedy may be more kitsch, more sentimental than any farce could be.[1] As Bertolt Brecht remarked, regarding the clownishness of Hitler,

'One may state that tragedy deals with the sufferings of mankind in a less serious way than comedy.'[2] Lubitsch, an exiled German Jew, engages with the war as comedy and, after all, what else can a great comic artist do, other than to fall silent.

In the face of genuine evil as enacted by the Nazis, what may comedy achieve? It can collude in the darkness, as the Internet troll does; it can express laughter's mockery of the enemy; or it can assert another set of values to which evil can have no access, values intrinsic to comedy itself: humour, humility, clarity of vision, affection and the potential for forgiveness of our petty vices. As William Blake put it, 'There is a Moment in each Day that Satan cannot find.'[3] Comedy may even be said to assert the place of art itself as another order, a kind of free and artfully spontaneous vision not allowed for in the Nazis' view.

Three or four times in *To Be or Not to Be* comedy collapses in the face of horror or cruelty. The miracle is that it returns. Laughter does not force itself upon us, but wins us over again. Lubitsch miraculously brings back a note of sweetness, hapless charm, generous forgiveness and folly. The film seals over again its bond with the audience, one that has been sobered and left alone by harshness. The movie celebrates the community of theatre and exists for the parallel community of the cinema audience; few films call out so strongly to be watched in the presence of others. In this celebration of the group, Lombard is the off-centre star at its centre, content in her humour and as the embodiment of comedy's wayward affirmations.

As *Twentieth Century* had so magnificently demonstrated, Lombard was at her natural best playing an actress. And Lubitsch's movie is likewise a classic comedy of the theatre, a work that shows reality permeated by its art. Lombard's husband in the tale, Joseph Tura (Jack Benny), is a terrible ham who believes, in his self-conceit, that he is a 'great, great actor'; as circumstances show, in his real-life performances with the Nazi enemy he may indeed be the great actor he credits himself to be. The film's complex plot enables variations on the theme of duality and repetition, present both in Lubitsch's touch with jokes that rely on their retelling, imbued each time with a new twist, and also in the doubling of actor and role. In the course of the film, as well as taking on Hamlet, Benny will perform both himself and a Nazi officer, and play in different scenes both sides of a doubled conversation, both as Professor Siletsky, sinister Nazi spy, and 'Concentration Camp' Ehrhardt, head of the Gestapo in Warsaw.

The film invites us to confuse art and life, merging the Gestapo HQ with a Warsaw playhouse, and Hitler as played by a spear-carrying actor versus the real tyrant himself. Lombard is entirely at home in this topsy-turvy, over-the-top world. Irony permeates her relation to the screen; she gives the impression always of being mentally elsewhere even as she is fully present. As she had in *Twentieth Century* and *Nothing Sacred*, she expresses here the perfection of screwball's vision of the world and of her own art. She is an artist who draws our eye to the fact that it is mere art, but still plays it from within. In an excellent short book on *To Be or Not to Be*, the playwright Peter Barnes speaks of the movie's commitment to a theatrical style in which the actors, operating in an unreal world, with a fake stage sky and a palpably studio-bound Warsaw, have to convince the Nazis who inhabit that same world with them that they are real.[4] Lombard's an actor playing an actress acting. She is a schemer and a dreamer, someone who flits above accusations of adultery as if they hardly concern her, who celebrates with us the beguiling vitality of flirtation. As in *Twentieth Century* and Hitchcock's *Mr and Mrs Smith* (1941), she is a woman who might evoke sexual jealousy and who yet exceeds the limiting control that such jealousy longs for. She cannot be pinned down, not even by the fictional worlds she plays in. No one who ever watched these films would want to judge her; all we can do is sit back and be joyously amazed.

11

GREER GARSON AND JOAN FONTAINE: THE FORGOTTEN STAR

'The world forgetting, by the world forgot.'
Alexander Pope, 'Eloisa to Abelard'

'Will Avellandea ever forget about me in this way? Here is where the mystery lies: before beginning to forget she has to remember, she has to begin to remember.'
Mario Benedetti, *The Truce*

Two films of the 1940s featuring major stars of the decade focus our attention on one unusual problem for the woman star and for the characters they play: the possibility that at any moment one might fall into the abyss of being forgotten. As we have seen, such anxieties already play out in Chaplin's *City Lights*. Joan Fontaine in Max Ophüls's *Letter from an Unknown Woman* (1948) and Greer Garson in Mervyn LeRoy's *Random Harvest* (1942) embody fascinating examples of this curious and emblematic fate.[1] (This was Garson's favourite among her own films, perfect in her view for its pathos, a film that could have been written for her.)[2] Both films draw upon literary texts – Ophüls's movie reimagines Stefan Zweig's own *Brief einer Unbekannten* (1922) and LeRoy's film dramatizes James Hilton's best-selling novel, also called *Random Harvest* (1941). Hilton's novel owes something, in its turn, to Rebecca West's story of an amnesiac infantry officer, *The Return of the Soldier* (1918). The web of resemblances does not end there, for the movie of *Random Harvest* stands as a sibling to Mervyn LeRoy's other great film, *Waterloo Bridge* (1940), discussed in Chapter Eight in relation to a third British Hollywood star, Vivien Leigh.

In different ways, both Ophüls's film and *Random Harvest* portray this curious trauma of being forgotten. In *Letter from an Unknown Woman* Stefan Brand (Louis Jourdan), a philandering, washed-up concert pianist, is preparing to run from a duel with a jealous husband when he receives a long letter, indeed a kind of suicide note, from Lisa (Joan Fontaine). She tells him she has loved him all her life and indeed, after one night spent together, has become the mother of his child, a son who has just died. Her long passion for him, however, has passed entirely unregarded: she loved him, but he never knew her, and each time they met could barely recall her, or otherwise could not even remember her at all.

In *Random Harvest* a shell-shocked officer (Ronald Colman) back from the Western Front is confined to an asylum, suffering from complete memory loss. He can neither recollect his own name nor recall anyone connected to him. On Armistice Night he escapes from the Melbridge County Asylum and wanders into the local town, Melbridge itself. Here, confused and lost, he meets Paula Ridgway (Greer Garson), a young actress. Rather than have him returned to the asylum, Paula takes the vulnerable man under her wing and offers him a place with her theatrical company. She names him 'Smithy'. Following an incident in which 'Smithy' lashes out at the company manager, the couple flee and set up home together in a coastal village. They marry. One day 'Smithy' goes to Liverpool for a job interview. Following a car accident, he recovers his memory and realizes that he is Charles Rainier, the rich heir to a thriving industrial business. In regaining his identity, however, all memory of everything that has happened to him since his amnesia began is in its turn forgotten. When he regains his memory, and 'Smithy' transforms into Charles Rainier, he becomes involved with a much younger woman, Kitty, played by the tragic and short-lived actress Susan Peters. (Kitty is only fifteen years old when she and Charles first meet.) Meanwhile, Paula tracks him down and, deciding not to lay claim to him until he remembers her, is working under the name of Miss Hanson as his faithful secretary. He has no idea that they were once married, nor that Paula has since given birth to their child, a little boy who has died. Realizing that he cannot marry Kitty, for the shadow of his unremembered past lies between them, Charles instead proposes marriage to Miss Hanson. It is a practical, passionless arrangement – so passionless, it is hard to tell if the contract between Miss Hanson and Charles Rainier represents a marriage or a business merger. After some months together, feeling their marriage is hopeless, Paula and Charles seem set to part, when a return visit by Charles to Melbridge prompts memories of the past he has lost. He hurries to the village where he first lived with Paula and there they reunite, becoming again the married couple they had once been.

Many films similarly explore the unsettling relation between amnesia and love, though not always with any profundity of insight. To take only one example, Peter Segal's *50 First Dates* (2004), starring Adam Sandler and Drew Barrymore, ineffectively combines a Don Juan figure who forgets the tourists he seduces with a local woman who, due to an improbable brain injury, at the start of each new day forgets him. Other films, notably Michel Gondry's *Eternal Sunshine of the Spotless Mind* (2004), with its willed forgetting, have gone somewhat deeper. Yet only *Random Harvest* and *Letter from an Unknown Woman* seem to me to have turned this theme into a searching examination of the nature of desire and of film, and simultaneously of what might be a woman's position in love and the film star's on the screen.

There is perhaps a curious link between the moment of these films and a wider concern with political forgetting. George Orwell's *1984* appeared in the same year as *Letter from an Unknown Woman*. It is hard to detect a political significance in Ophüls's film, yet Orwell's concern with how people may be made to vanish from history, with the resulting insignificance of the individual life, carries resonances that reverberate in this film. Joan Fontaine's unknown lady too is someone threatened with becoming a non-person, someone permanently occluded from view.

In these films Greer Garson and Joan Fontaine find themselves forgotten. It is the source of their on-screen suffering. Yet what is so bad about forgetting? To varying degrees, nearly everyone forgets people to whom they were once close; lovers drift apart. Regarding

A forgotten Greer Garson ignored by Ronald Colman in *Random Harvest* (1942).

infancy and early childhood experience, everyone on earth is an amne-siac. Relations are often transient: as W. H. Auden put it, 'hearts that we broke long ago/ Have long been breaking others'.[3] Moreover, everyone is, at one time or another, forgotten. In *The Human Condition* Hannah Arendt suggests that the dread of being forgotten was central to ancient Greek cultural and social life; only through 'shining deeds', or the making of lasting words or artworks or by the passing of laws, some few attain a place within memory. The rest of us find ourselves lost in the ongoing circle of life, living and dying, and are soon consigned to the void of forgetting.[4]

The extraordinary are remembered; the ordinary, immersed in their unremarkable lives, leave no trace of themselves. In this way Garson and Fontaine's characters (stand-ins for the actors themselves) express a common human fate. The forgotten one occupies a position within which they are brought profoundly face to face with the human condition. In their powerlessness they experience the fact that all and everything is forgotten. This idea is more likely to elude the forgetter, who might feel lifted up into a position of strength and cease to bear in mind their own propensity to vanish.

In *Letter from an Unknown Woman* and *Random Harvest*, being forgotten is a severe form of being unrequited: the love that the woman feels is not just spurned, but unnoticed. Unrequitedness was the default mode of the era, that age of the torch song, of 'These Foolish Things', 'I Get Along Without You Very Well' and 'They Can't Take That Away From Me', an aesthetic replenished by intimate regret, by pointless, painful remembrance. So it is that the strange paradox of unrequitedness operates in these films, the mingled selfishness and selflessness of love. Particularly in Fontaine's case, unrequitedness makes love look greedy. Even though it consciously seeks reciprocation, it cannot help but lay bare the egotism in desire. She manifests some of the same ambivalence we see in A. E. Housman's poems of forlorn desire, that wonderful melding of love and venom, the passive

'I've seen you before': Louis Jordan recalls Joan Fontaine in *Letter from an Unknown Woman* (1948).

124

aggression that festers within an unreturned love. Fontaine's Lisa stands as a figure of patient suffering, yet it can prove hard to shrug off the sense that her pain is masochistic and therefore grants her some harsh reward. Yet such devotion, as in Greer Garson's case, may also appear as the most selfless kind of love. Affection becomes an act of service, an abnegation, and a desire that no longer expects its fulfilment. The great paradox of love, that it at once gives and seeks to take, here rises to the surface.

Trying to explain why he had never wanted children of his own, a friend told me the following anecdote about his brother and his brother's children. His brother told him that, though it was hard being a parent, no moment in his life had been so great as when his child came up to him when he was sitting on a playground bench and handed a leaf to him, saying 'Daddy'. And my friend then faced me and said, 'and this revealed to me the utter egotism of love'. I can understand what this friend meant, and take his point. Yet I would also want to add that he perhaps missed something in reducing the love in this example to mere egotism. When we love someone, we want recognition from them, we make a claim, though I would hope we do so in order to recognize them in turn, and to accept their reciprocal claim on us. In love, we belong to each other.

Perhaps we live, we flourish, through and within the claims we make on others and that we accept that others have made on us. As Wittgenstein remarked, 'love is not a feeling'. It may be the bonds, responsibilities and mutual concern that frame the realized life. Yet success comes by choosing not to enforce or insist on those claims, and only lovingly to fulfil the duties. *Letter from an Unknown Woman* worries over the concert pianist Stefan Brand's refusal of such appeals: Stefan fails as a musician because he fails to commit to his art, much as he fails to commit to any one woman; otherwise, *Random Harvest* wants to show us what it means to become responsible for another person.

Yet to choose such a claim when the other is unable to meet it invites a particular pain. In these films a choice awaits us: to remember and to be miserable, though life will consequently gain in significance;

or to forget and be lightly cheerful, though life will seem meaningless. It is a version of the choice that the trolls offer Peer Gynt: when confronted with the possibility of gaining all he wants at the price of really seeing the world as a troll sees it, Peer refuses. Choosing humanness is to choose knowledge; to choose to remember is to choose to know who you were, where you have been, and what you have done, to let your eyes see what your hand did.

Questions of knowledge, however, are not simple matters in these films, which tend to dissolve identity and to throw even the reality of things into question. In Zweig and Ophüls, the forgotten one writes the letter. The power latent in being the one who describes falls to them. (This is especially striking in Zweig's novella, where the man is not a concert pianist, but a novelist. He may be the professional writer, yet the unknown woman's narrative displaces his.) Being the one to write the letter is indeed a potent position in regards to forgetting, for it might be said of human lives that only the text survives. Our written words – and cinematic image – linger when the self is gone. Words and cinema preserve us, while confronting us with forgetting. For texts too are forgotten. And movie stars that were once household names are now only recalled by a few.

Yet to be the one to tell the story may be both a victory and a curse. To the forgotten one, the past is full, is a tale, and the present is empty except for holding the trace of that continuing craving, is merely a place where the story of the past may be recounted. Moreover, while it may be Lisa's confession, its object and its effect is to reveal Stefan to himself, his venality and superficiality, in contrast to her fidelity and depths. Two of them were parents, both of them lost a child; but only one of them realized that fact.

Texts also distort the reality they appear to preserve. In *Letter from an Unknown Woman* Ophüls brings together the dead voice of a woman and the camera's recording eye. His use of a 'subjective camera' invites us to share the central character's anonymity and the way in which she is cruelly forgotten. This might invite a painful identification, were it not for the fact that the anonymity we share is one inhabited by a film star. In this manner, we experience the glamour of rejection, a marginalization ennobled by its being entwined with fame. Further, Ophüls's use of a first-person point of view brings in the possibility that what we are seeing is infused with one perspective on matters, and may not be the objective truth, but even a deception.

This possession of the story raises the question: who is stronger, the lover or the beloved, the unrequited or the adored? Both films invite us to live with a sense of loss, and to ask whose loss it is. Stefan's vulnerability is something he himself never comes to feel; only as a reader, a viewer of the film in which he stars, does he come to recognize just how hollow his show of strength was. *Random Harvest* is one of those many texts about the Great War that stressed not masculine heroism but a man's vulnerability. 'Smithy' (as played by Ronald Colman) is as easily led as a child, as unsure of social rules as a gauche boy, halting in speech. Like many figured as film stars, 'Smithy' is a person without connections or friends. He is a type of the abandoned kid. We first see him meeting people who might be but are not his parents: 'I would have liked to belong to them,' he intones.

If the man is vulnerable here, then Greer Garson was the ideal film star to soothe his troubles. As an author Hilton favoured a beguiling sentimentality when it came to women, many of whom offer an uncomplicated deliverance for the man. Hilton was strongly linked to Greer Garson's career, being central to her three most important films as the author of both *Goodbye Mr Chips* (1939) and *Random Harvest*, as well as the scriptwriter for William Wyler's *Mrs Miniver* (1942), based on Jan Struther's novel. So often in her films, Garson's velvety voice promises rescue. She was typecast as a lovely and sexual woman bewilderingly offering herself to succour ineffectual men. In *Goodbye Mr Chips* she was waiting to be discovered on a forlorn mountainside, giving hope to the story's romantic no-hoper. In *Mrs Miniver* she impersonates the tender sturdiness of the domestic, its proposed ability to outlast all storms, including those whipped up by the Nazis. In *Random Harvest* 'Paula Ridgway' is the one person to whom 'Smithy' can talk (he is silent and tongue-tied with all others). Here, she is an actress playing an actress, someone who (like 'Smithy' himself) adopts an identity not her own, 'Paula Ridgway' being merely a stage name. Maybe the film wants to tell us that only an actress would be so forward with a strange man; perhaps it wants to investigate lightly the connection between the character and the person who plays her.

Garson's tangible warmth and tender sexiness play very differently than Fontaine's cooler screen presence. The latter's acting habitually involves a kind of simpering, a disconsolate play of the eyebrows, a greedily modest faraway glance. The more restrained she is, the better she was. Fontaine often played a young woman oppressed by the lack of possibility in her life, someone constricted and thwarted (as in her films for Hitchcock, *Rebecca* and *Suspicion*), and therefore kin to many in the audience. She is a Cinderella who believes she doesn't want to go to the ball; her Prince is the handsome, sophisticated film star. Fontaine achieved glamour by looking as though glamour was something beyond her, a way of being to which she could not hope to aspire.

These films tell us that women are forgotten and that men forget. All would be well if the men would remember or if the women could blank over the past. That women are forgotten by men was also for a long time true of their position in the artistic canon, the achievements of women writers and artists lost where those of men were more likely to be preserved. Clearly there is an ideological pressure in this on-screen forgetting, a consequence of cultural expectations around gender. There is also the rumour of the invisibility of women's desire, its supposed inability to affect things in the world, but to become instead a form of waiting, a patient and perhaps unrewarded service.

One could feel compassion for Fontaine, a passionate affection for Garson. Unloved in the movie, both were available to be loved by those in the audience. Enmeshed in this lovableness is perhaps a baser desire, the objectifying lust that traps women on film in a subordinate position. Yet these films offer an interesting pre-emptive revision of Laura Mulvey's theory of the male gaze, her thesis that cinema involves the stultifying pleasure of the men looking, a look that both objectifies women and condemns them to seeming lacking.

Here we have women who are regarded and unregarded, looked at and impossible to see. What we watch is the process by which they are ignored. In *Random Harvest*, for Charles Rainier, Paula has become invisible. When she re-enters the film as his secretary Miss Hanson, Colman/Charles for a long while does not once look at her, for all that she looks at him. Other men appreciate her, but Charles cannot see her. Here, in both films, the woman is the watcher and the man is the mysterious, gazed at, elusive figure. In these ways these films both exemplify and, I believe, revise Mulvey's highly important idea.

Being overlooked was, in particular, Fontaine's fate and the substance of her public persona. At the start of her career she was chiefly known as the sister of the more famous and, at first, more successful Olivia de Havilland. On the set of *Rebecca* (1940) Hitchcock let her know that her leading man, Laurence Olivier, would rather have been working with his lover, Vivien Leigh. (In his next film, *Pride and Prejudice*, where again he hoped to star alongside Leigh, he was further annoyed to be playing opposite Greer Garson.)

By 1948, however, Fontaine was a slighted younger sister, who was also an Oscar winner in her own right. And Lisa is not so invisible as all that. She becomes a model at a dressmaker's and in so doing suddenly transforms herself into someone who men stare at, admire and comment on. Moreover, Stefan does not entirely forget her; in fact, he does notice and vaguely recall her. But he notices her in the same way that all men might and does not see her as a person with a history, a soul, but merely as a passing attractive and charming woman. On their one night of passion we approach her on the street corner through Stefan's point of view. His first words to her are, 'I've seen you before,' and it's hard to tell if they indicate a true memory or a pick-up line. Yet Stefan's regard for her is broken, intermittent; as Lisa tells him, 'you never noticed me.'

All these threads have their own obscure psychological meanings. It seems apt that, though he didn't live to read *Random Harvest*, Freud was a James Hilton fan. Both films are pregnant with psychoanalytical resonances. As Lisa, Fontaine's a woman on a one-night stand who can still appear innocent, maternal, childlike and pure; on

Christmas Eve, the night that will end with her having sex with Stefan, we first see her standing by a Madonna in the freshly falling snow. Her putative 'childlikeness' is crucial to this effect. In *Letter from an Unknown Woman*, Stefan stands in for the father, who is absent from the film itself but a dominant force in the character's memory. The affair is Oedipal not only for Stefan but for her, too. She is an Elektra, and even a Jocasta too, a woman who may be seen to love her son suffocatingly. Contrariwise, Garson cannot help but look like an adult: in fact, she lied about her age throughout her career, lopping a few years off so no one realized that she had made her screen debut at 35.

On the other hand, Joan Fontaine's characters were apt to live out this confusion between a father and a lover. In *Letter from an Unknown Woman* Fontaine plays herself both at the film's beginning as a child and later as a mother, occupying two positions in life, and both sides of the Oedipal divide: on their one date Stefan tells Lisa, 'I see you as a little girl . . .' For much of Hitchcock's *Rebecca* (1940), that Freudian fantasy of the daughter-figure replacing the absent and deathly 'mother', Olivier persists in treating his much younger bride, Joan Fontaine as the second Mrs de Winter, as a child. In her second film for Hitchcock, *Suspicion* (1941), Johnny (Cary Grant) impersonates as a joke the voice of Fontaine's character's father, enacting the older man's imagined disapproval. Certainly in Ophüls's film we understand Lisa (Fontaine) in relation to her father, seeing her on the carousel with Stefan not journeying but in a fiction, passing pictures of places they might have visited in reality and hearing of how she once did the same with her father, looking at travel brochures, but never in actuality travelling. When they decide to go around the carousel again, Stefan remarks to her, 'We'll revisit the scenes of our youth.' For her, it's an almost life, an existence spent as a perpetual dependant.

As we have seen, Stefan vaguely remembers Lisa, but cannot place her. Everything that Stefan and Lisa do is a reprise of something forgotten. He tells her, 'How else could we dance that way if we haven't danced together before? But then I'd remember you.' Love affairs naturally begin like this, with a sense of fatality, of destiny, of people linked together. One particular face moves us and not another. Lisa brings this sense of fatality into her understanding of their relationship. She often talks as though matters are out of her hands, beyond the reach of choices. She has been given her destiny and it so happens it must be a tragic one.

In Freudian terms this 'memory' of a person whom it seems will answer all our needs is easily explained. What we remember is not this new person, but the parent they pledge to re-embody for us. Such a return promises us that there might be a healing, but never an attainable presence, one that arrives in the present but is already imbued with the past. The person's coming assumes the guise of a homecoming. So it is that in Stefan's great love speech to Lisa in the carriage outside the opera house, he casts her, and fails to cast her, as the one who will answer every unspeakable wish: 'You can help me . . . the face that lives somewhere, just over the edge of memory.'

Given this strange recalling of the parent in the new person we desire, it is striking that in these two films both Fontaine and Garson play mothers who lose a son. The fact nourishes both films' Freudian bent. This is especially the case in Ophüls's film, which shows us Lisa's very close relations to her son. The boy's last farewell ('I'll see you in two weeks!') exactly echoes Stefan's words of parting at the Vienna station earlier in the movie. These lost boys might be thought to evoke the dead son, Mamilius, in Shakespeare's great drama of loss and recovery, *The Winter's Tale*. There a husband forgets the person his wife truly is. He jealously hurts her and, wounded by that hurt, his son dies, his daughter is banished and his wife apparently succumbs to her grief. In the end both the daughter and the wife are restored by means of a theatrical enchantment; yet young Mamilius is one person who cannot return, a death that cannot be overruled. There is a 'Mamilius' figure, in each case a dead son, in Rebecca West's novel *The Return of the Soldier*, in Ophüls's film and in *Random Harvest*. The dead children here represent the price paid by a fracture in the self, the future that cannot be recovered when the self loses its past.

In *Random Harvest* Greer Garson as Miss Hanson lets her errant husband know, 'You haven't even a memory . . . The best of you, your capacity for loving, your joy in living, is buried in a little space of time you've forgotten.' Of course, these words have their application to others and might be considered a common statement of our relation to our own youth. In West's *The Return of the Soldier*, forgetting permits a return to an outgrown state, to youth, a stage of being perhaps preferable to the compromises of a settled middle age. We can easily imagine someone saying of themselves, 'At that time in my life, I was at my best, and lived most fully. But that time is gone, and I have forgotten how to live like that.' Such a statement might provoke scepticism and we could find it self-dramatizing, unreal or despondent. Yet we could also credit it and understand its potential truth. In *Random Harvest* young Kitty reminds our amnesiac hero, 'You used to say you hated business.' 'Did I?', ponders Charles, recalling for us how we forget our own past attitudes, the things we once felt or held to be true. Charles is a man who has forgotten that he was once in love.

The man that Miss Hanson loves and cries for is the bewildered soldier 'Smithy', not the rich Charles Rainier, and therefore a man who may be said not to exist. As an actor, Colman's fugitive reserve is ideal to express the lack of passion he's supposed to live through. Miss Hanson also loves Charles perhaps, but only in the sense that he can be felt to be identical to 'Smithy'. Paula knows what she wants, telling us that, 'I want him as he was. I want his love.' In these ways *Random Harvest* speculates about what we do when we love someone. If Rainier doesn't love Greer Garson when she's Miss Hanson, we might ask, 'why not?' Has she changed or is he so changed? Was he deluded before? Or has he come to his senses? At the very end, when they recognize each other, they do so under their false names, not as Margaret and Charles, but as Paula and 'Smithy'. This may suggest that love is the subjective fake that Auden imagined that the middle-aged find it to be. They are their 'real' selves again, but it is difficult to discern if they are not just back inside a dream.

Yet it would indeed be hard to determine which is the real person, 'Smithy' or Charles Rainier – two people with nothing in common except that they are both played by the same actor. What unifies them is their mutual relation to that construct of gentlemanly romance, the Hollywood Englishman, Ronald Colman. In the end all three figures are united, Colman and 'Smithy' and Rainier, in the final recalling of the love he once had. Love and the actor become intertwined elements in the achieving of a unity.

Random Harvest makes it clear that it is in the resurrection business. Again and again it informs us that Smithy is a dead man, or a man as good as dead. In a pub a brandy is pressed on him with the words, 'Drop of the good stuff, that is – bring anyone back from the grave.' In the course of the film 'John Smith' is pronounced officially 'dead', and the marriage between him and Paula is dissolved. People here are 'ghost-ridden', 'prisoners of their past'. Charles wonders, 'Isn't there something morbid in burying one's heart with the dead?' In Liverpool, when an accident brings back his memory, he both dies and 'comes back from the dead'. By this means, by the outrageous unlikelihood of its plot, *Random Harvest* is a film that passes beyond the limits of the credible; it is a tale of a marvel, a fairy tale of the Great War, a story that could only happen in a once upon a time.

Few films now would so readily dispense with credibility. *Random Harvest* presents a key example of the period's wonderful unconcern with the real, the strong readiness to turn a movie into a dream, and, I would argue, a dream about film itself. Indeed, what is most interesting, and for the concerns of this book, most vital about the processes of forgetting and remembering on display in these films is what they say, not just about the particular examples of Fontaine and Garson, but about the film star, and especially the woman film star as such.

'Smithy' has forgotten who or what he is, a man without a name or an identity. The audience, however, are unlikely to forget that he is Ronald Colman, a perfect and perfectly desirable film star. These films play, once again, with the central paradox of the film star: that they are ordinary, as we all are, and hence forgettable; and that they are also exceptional, exemplary, presenting the possibility of a full human life, one worthy of the lasting attention of art and fame.

Fontaine and Garson are exceptional because they are stars, though on-screen they play the part of the ordinary. In doing so they transform both the category of the ordinary (telling us both that anyone can be like a star and that ordinary people are steeped in the fabulous) and the category of the exceptional (it is merely another form of the ordinary, and contains ordinariness in it like a cancer).

At the time it was apparent that Garson and Fontaine were not likely to be forgotten by a lover. Their stardom ensured their lasting-ness as a presence in a life. Some seventy years have passed, however, and now, in another level of meaning added to the film by time, both Fontaine and Garson are to most people, other than those aged over sixty or to younger fans of 1940s cinema, certainly forgotten. With the Internet there for us, we are in a strange position: everything is avail-able, but nothing has impact. Cinema's 'long tail' offers a myriad of digital traces, all present but without power. Everything is there to be seen, but so few ever see it. What once seemed a paradox – how could anyone forget being married to Greer Garson? – has altered. Now if we watch the film deprived of the resonances provided by the stardom industry, we see not Garson, but 'Paula', the actress subsumed at last into the character she played.

The film star was once unforgettable because the claim they made on us was one secured by their garnering of our love, their aptness to evoke desire, the perceived enchantment of their charisma. These ele-ments remain in place in an old film, perhaps, but must now exist without the machinery of publicity and marketing that once sustained them. If Garson now seems lovable, or Fontaine fascinating, it must be either an awareness of the history or the force of their performances, really the image of themselves, and their relation to the screen that secures them our engagement.

Cinema is an art of forgetting. How hard it can prove to remem-ber a film! The details foster endless disagreements: everyone sees things differently, everyone remembers it in their own way. With the literary text, we can point to chapter and verse. Now, with video, DVD, Blu-Ray and online versions, we may (still less easily) do this now with the cinematic text. But for many years this was not the case. The film was once a performance, an event unfolding in time, and like anything bound by time, it was always already moving into the past, into forgetting.

Early theorists of pop, like George Melly in *Revolt into Style* (1970) or Nik Cohn in *Awopbopaloobop Alopbamboom* (1969), pointed out the essential commitment to novelty in pop culture. Pop was dedicated to the 'now': last year's hits, last year's fashions were already over, un-hip, dead. The past only existed as a repository of styles ready to be appropriated again for this season now. This immersion in newness was part of pop's relation to youth, its belonging to the year zero inhabited by this year's crop of the young. Before it acquired the distorting background of a history, cinema too once belonged to this pop world. Films were released, made their impact and were gone. They were only ever seen again in small repertory theatres or in film clubs, or by means of a re-release. Before television started buying old films in bulk, the world lived cinema's newness and therefore its transience.

Indeed, the film star might be understood as the world's earliest version of the pop culture person, an individual commensurate to their own image, a sum of passing gestures, a committedly transient and malleable human being. In the early twenty-first century, perhaps wrapped up in our digital selves, the sense haunts us that we exist somewhere between being an image, a performance for others and a product (our intimacy something to be sold). Our bodies are not ourselves, but are ours, our possession, and therefore an alienable thing, another commodity, more or less desirable. Films and the stars themselves were precipitating causes in the establishment of this sense. Since the invention of cinema, this perception of ourselves has been further fostered by the triumph of a 'neoliberal' model of the market and by the properties intrinsic to the establishment of an online self. Celebrity is fame that cannot rise to the level of remembrance. Celebrities flow with the current, and we know already that in the future they will be forgotten. The interest that David Bowie and Madonna showed in the movie stars of the 1920s, '30s and '40s was not an accident but a striking indication of their own indebtedness to the cinematic human being, a person that was no more than the totting up of a series of gestures and condensed narratives. There was little room to grow old in this medium, committed as it was to the fashion of the moment. One part of the importance of Cary Grant, Katharine Hepburn, John Wayne and Meryl Streep (and some very few others) is that they found, against the grain of cinema's ephemerality, a way to develop inside the fleeting medium and grow old.

Remembering old film stars is not just nostalgia for another time's 'now', but an answer to a human claim. In these films Fontaine and Garson act the sorrow of being forgotten, and reach out in that sorrow to call out for our attention, for the gaze and the compassion due to human suffering, even here in its hypothetical, fictional mode. Cinema was long invested in that claim, its essential premise being that we need to look, and sometimes that we ought to do so. In a culture of distraction, and by means of a form that has supposedly deepened this fall into distraction, film has also, by a strange paradox, placed its weight on the other side of the scales and upheld the Proustian belief that life justifies itself in memory, and above all in the transmutation of memory into art, of the evanescent person into the permanent star. Film has stood against modernity's flattening out of the individual life, this loss of faith in the human as such. For all that it entangles human beings in the belief that we are no more than a profitable image, cinema, at its best, and even sometimes at its most mediocre, has engaged in the transfiguring of the person, a process that involves a recognition of the complexity and reality – and transience – of the whole human life.

12

ORSON WELLES:
THE FILM STAR AS
FRAGMENT AND FAILURE

I n Jonathan Swift's *Gulliver's Travels*, Gulliver finds himself in the
kingdom of Brobdingnag, where the people are some 60 feet tall.
Scale is everything; swollen to gigantic proportions the human
face becomes rough, pitted, the seemingly immaculate skin unmasked
as imperfect. In the twentieth century Brobdingnag transformed into
the picture house, a place for the pygmy public to stare up at the great
stars. However, far from seeming less perfect, the enlarged human
face seemed more wonderful, smoothed-out by celluloid, unattainable. Yet still strangeness clung to these super-sized persons, those
colossal faces.

Orson Welles grasped this strangeness and so returned us to the
Swiftian vision. In his films the human face that cinema loves and
dwells on unmasks its potential for ugliness; blown up to the size of
the cinema screen it looks not enchanted and godlike, but all too
human and flawed. Time and again the alienated gaze of his films
confronts us with the astonishment of the human face, there in his
use of close-ups that come in too close. Somehow the angle of vision
is out of kilter, and we see only the spit and stubble, the pockmarks
and pores. This disabused image of people extends into Welles's
understanding of character. Unlike some Hollywood directors, he
never lost sight of the blemishes in the human face and the human
soul. He is one of the few film-makers of the American 1940s and
'50s who is never kitsch. Reduced to Lilliputian proportions on TV

or a computer, his films really belong to the big screen, depending as they do on questions of scale, the proper size of the human being.

Welles's genius too was larger than life, a man with a talent always threatening to burst the bounds of the studio system it was supposed to flourish in. He was not only one of the most striking and inventive film-makers who have ever lived, but a highly curious example of the film star, operating within mainstream cinema while simultaneously dismantling all our conceptions of what a film star might be. Just as Welles's films began with words, with the things that his people say, so Welles's presence rests in large part on the growling, rumbling baritone of his voice. It is a curiously physical voice, one that summons up the body behind it. That feels apt, for in watching Welles's work over the decades, from *Citizen Kane* (1941) to *F for Fake* (1973), the metamorphoses of that body turns out to be where the attention lingers. On-screen, Welles embraced the collapse of his own handsomeness: the face's wrinkles and carved-out lines, the grizzled hair, the ever-expanding waist. In *Touch of Evil* (1958) Marlene Dietrich fails to recognize Welles in the police detective Hank Quinlan. Puzzled by the amazing degradation of that body, she lets him know, 'You're a mess, honey,' merely voicing what the audience was likely already thinking. Already in *Citizen Kane*, Welles had pictured the process of his own descent into age; he began his screen-acting career as an old young man, and he reached the summit of it, in *Chimes at Midnight* (1965), as a young old man, playing Falstaff, that corrupter of youth, that All-Hallows summer.

Many of the contradictions of Welles's position as a 'star', and of film stardom as such, are contained in the extraordinary expanses of *Citizen Kane*. The film announced Welles as a film star, and yet it flopped. It is naturally felt that stardom only exists in relation to popularity; an unknown film star is a contradiction in terms. With a cast largely drawn from Welles's Mercury Theatre troupe, this is a film without any stars, although both Welles and Joseph Cotten afterwards became such. Instead it has actors, people demonstrably performing. At this early moment in his career Welles was both renowned and undiscovered, a figure caught between fame and a relative obscurity. All art belongs in a commercial framework, an object of trade. Yet for cinema this can feel particularly true; Hollywood was an industry, retailing the finest dreams money can buy; success was measured in receipts and grosses.

The star is a marketable commodity. Many of the films explored in this book express an awareness of this fact, but few do so with such sceptical panache as *Citizen Kane*. The film sets out to reduce a life to art, to dissect the mystery of personality, to unpack the heart of Charles Foster Kane. In this process it also anatomizes and conceals a parallel examination of Welles himself, the star both present in and distinct from the part he plays.

The question asked in *Citizen Kane* is how do you screen a life? How do you tell a story of an existence? The clue to it all is, we are told, the word 'Rosebud'. It can seem that no one hears it said but us; it is a lonely last word shared between the audience and Kane. If this is the key to the mystery, only we see it turned. At the end of the film only the audience learns a 'solution' it supposedly offers (it is suggested it is no kind of solution anyway), seeing the fire burn its traces away from Kane's childhood sled. 'Rosebud' turns out to be a mere trade name. The emotional resonances that adhere to the word entwine themselves around a product, a manufactured good. Love clings to things, to objects, as symbols of something that they are not. So it is too that our love grips the commercialized work of art, the star themselves, the vendible product made by the power and prestige of Hollywood.

Through it all we regard Kane and trace Welles in him, a man whose context lies in film. The movie happily juxtaposes techniques, merging newsreel pastiche (and a kind of history of cinema concealed in it) and the nostalgic style of reminiscence. Deep focus shots replace the close-up of 1920s and '30s cinema. Deep focus corresponds to one element of modernist narrative, that is, stream of consciousness; here on-screen as in the novel, more than one thing, one element is present to us at once. We are not immersed in a face, we watch someone present with others, perhaps as important as himself. As the film critic André Bazin once suggested, the peculiar force of deep focus is that it brings ambiguity to a movie by letting the audience itself choose where to look, though it remains still only a choice among the options provided by the director.

Classic Hollywood film has been derided for its apparent object-ification of the women who appear in it. Yet of all films, *Citizen Kane* expresses a palpable lack of interest in the female body, in female beauty. The hired dancers may parade through the newspaper office, but our eye is led away from them, moving back to Charles Kane. Despite the fact that the film involves an adulterous affair, there is a strange absence of a direct sexual interest. Kane's interest in young Susan Alexander looks largely paternal, driven more by fondness and sympathy or the urge to control, than a simple physical lust.

Strange consequences follow from the casting of Dorothy Comingore as Susan, Kane's paramour. Comingore was a minor comedy actress, known for B-westerns and Three Stooges films; after *Citizen Kane* she found only three more supporting roles before being blacklisted by McCarthy in 1951. She was a competent actress, but she was no movie star. For Welles didn't want a co-star; he had pre-viously tested strippers for the role, seeking a kind of 'cheapness' for Susan. He bullied her, as a kind of speculation, a game, hoping to induce in her 'the look of crushed hatred' he wanted (in the elegant phrase coined by one of Welles's biographers, David Thomson).[1]

The erotic interest that would normally flow towards the female star is here directed towards Kane instead. Our focus falls on the man, on Welles's body and looks. Norman Mailer declared of Welles that 'when [he] was young, [he] was the most beautiful man anybody had ever seen'.[2] Stardom is eroticism, a response to and a containment of 'charisma'; in *Citizen Kane* that charisma purely emanates from Welles. In political life this was the age of charisma, most notably in the appeal of fascist demagogues and totalitarian dictators. *Citizen Kane* lives off this appeal to the emotional intoxication made by perfor-mance, and also throws it into question. Kane is a man who performs constantly to others, for example in the 'Declaration of Principles' scene, where even when alone with his two closest 'friends' he is styl-ishly and hammily enacting himself before them, striking a rather unconvincing pose, and then wincing inwardly at the fact that it nonetheless convinces.

It is Welles's presence that constitutes the film's meaning, and the analysis of it that marks its success. It assays the nature of his charm. David Thomson's line on the film is, to me, a persuasive one. He suggests that the movie offers a critique of Welles conducted by Herman J. Mankiewicz and John Houseman (his older Mercury Theatre collaborator), a critique which Welles then transformed into a self-conscious exploration of himself. He performs his own surgery, narcissistically cutting into the image of charm, vitality and power that he presents. And so Welles plays with his own ageing, and dramatizes his own position of independence at RKO. Kane versus 'the trusts' mirrors the artist up against the studio. His ultimate endeavour was to make a studio film that would subsume or destroy the Hollywood studio film, taking over the box of tricks that is cinema, much as Kane takes over *The Inquirer.* More than this, in doing so he makes a film that simultaneously enshrines and shreds the image of the star.

The film perhaps critiques the American pursuit of happiness, a progress measurable in terms of bank balance and column inches. Kane achieves wealth through luck (ill-luck) and not through his own efforts. It is a film interested in wealth as a cause of failure, unpersuaded by money's ability to realize the self. Indeed, cash proves a handicap in that process of self-development. Money distorts us, suggesting a propensity to failure in the true realm of exchange.

Hollywood finds an echo in Kane's dream home, Xanadu. Both contain an accumulation of European myths and tales and artefacts and people, a proliferation of objects and lives and illusions. Xanadu is a kind of film set, the site of a confusion of things and styles, a world of replicas.

The star's remoteness parallels that of the archetypal tycoon. Both live lives removed from the ordinary member of the audience. Fame surrounds both, and the film manifests the public's relation to the star, a self that exists in relation to us only in terms of its publicity, its image, its projection. Both the star and the tycoon are fantasized figures, caught up in the directed dream that is film. Kane is rich, but acts with the aggrieved quality, the wounded ego of a frustrated man; he can never realize the possibilities he desires. No one could. Partly that is because one message of the film is that money merely multiplies desire, without easing it. Caught in the possibilities of the dreamed world, Kane gradually erodes. Once he meets Susan he becomes dead, obsessive, humourless, a shadow of the young man he was; distorted by wealth and power, he shows himself unable to reach another person.

Thompson, the journalist who pursues the story on Kane, acts as our representative. Talking with Peter Bogdanovich, Welles said of him, 'He's not a person. He's a piece of machinery.'³ He's the man in front of us at the cinema; his facelessness (we never really see what he looks like) means that he can never be a character in his own right. The film does not concern the investigator, it is about the investigation – which is ours too – and the relation of that investigation to the person investigated. An understanding of the media is found in this, a pursuit of 'truth' that is also the manufacturing of consent, of an audience, a public – much as Kane's paper *The Inquirer* manufactures a war. The size of the headlines makes the news. Kane comes into being as a man of the newspapers and newsreels, and ends as a man dissected by them. In these processes, journalism is a shadow of Hollywood itself.

If the media makes these people, and then makes up the story of them, it does so in a peculiarly obtuse and indirect way. Kane, like all movie people, is a character pieced together from scraps, from scenes. He is brought to life by a thousand cuts. Modernism fractures narrative, and the modernist process permeates the very nature of a movie, a work of art constructed from separate strips of film, from discrete moments. Cinema is the modernist art form at its starkest. Yet few films place film's fragmented nature so boldly before us; *Citizen Kane* is closer to Joseph Conrad's disintegrated novels than to anything produced by classic Hollywood (Welles had initially planned that a version of *Heart of Darkness* would mark his film debut). Film creates a language for narrative, one itself predicated on the cut, on fragmentation, on broken performance. The completed film establishes permanencies from a self broken up into detached images, epiphanies, gestures and scenes. These are not even played in order, but are ordered later, the continuity established in the editing room. Kane, like Welles, is a broken figure unpersuasively made to seem whole.

These are selves constructed on a screen. Kane emerges from a set of competing narratives: the opening shots, the newsreel, the various tales by his friends, his banker, his butler and his lover – but never by Kane himself. Film makes identity objective, exterior; it views us from the outside. We are what others see in us, and what we perform before those others. Even a privacy exposes itself before us, the audience.

Welles in Kane is an actor directed by himself: storyteller, director, actor and character. The film divides roles, even as it divides selves. Kane is a double man, in a film where all is doubled: two sleds; two visits to Susan Alexander; two visits to Xanadu; two wives; two (or more) beginnings to the film; two friends; even two fathers, a real one and a bank.

When Kane first meets Susan, he makes shadow puppets for her. To us their meaning is obvious, yet Susan cannot guess their meaning. In a vignette, the moment enacts a parable of the film itself – and of all film. 'You're not a professional magician, are you?' she asks him. Kane was not, but in a way Welles was. The director was a Prospero; pretty soon Kane will be directing Susan's performance and life too. Regarding his investment in her, he declares, 'We're going to be a great opera star'. He can no longer distinguish 'you' from 'I', her stardom from his own. Susan's magnificent and continual riposte is, 'What about *me*?' Susan, like Dorothy Comingore, was no star, or was only an imitation of one when placed in relation to Kane, to Welles. Though the public ignored the film, Welles's stardom was set by it. He would spend the next decades exploring its implications.

Following the abortive release of *Citizen Kane* and the mutilation by the studio of his next movie, *The Magnificent Ambersons* (1942), in America Welles was forever hampered in his career as a director, while his life as an actor – and voice-over narrator – more or less flourished.

For a while he was both a studio problem and an authentic film star, to the delight of the gossip columns married to another star, the forces' sweetheart Rita Hayworth. Soon he fell away from being a leading man and launched into a lifetime of cameos and special appearances, the kind of actor who could salvage a film with a few good scenes. Yet in a clutch of films – *The Lady from Shanghai* (1947), *The Third Man* (1949), *Touch of Evil* (1958), and his Shakespeare films, especially *Chimes at Midnight* (1965) – he was much more than that, being there what he had once been in *Citizen Kane*, an exemplary version of the compromised person, the perfect embodiment of our imperfection.

Directed by Welles as well as starring him, *The Lady from Shanghai* is a film noir composed of sweat and sleaze. It begins with a threatened gang rape, takes us to a man who wants to be murdered, and leaves us in a crazy, shattered realm where killing seems just an expression of desire. The very inventiveness of the camera here makes the film seem sordid, trapping us inside a place of moral and visual distortion. Only a couple of years after Hiroshima and Nagasaki, the Bomb haunts this movie, lending an everyday story of marriage and murder an apocalyptic darkness. Watching the film, it becomes hard to shrug off the knowledge that people are incomprehensible, their motives obscure, their meaning occluded. At the end the film bewilderingly slips into using Mandarin, while Welles's character watches, drugged, a Chinese opera, an art form 'naturally' understood by the locals in the audience, but that is to him a baffling confusion. Everyone's ugly in this film, except the leads of course, and especially the sublime Rita Hayworth, though her beauty (at Welles's insistence – he made her cut off her long red hair) appears a concoction, a made-up peroxide blonde with sculpted eyebrows. Among the drooling and pop-eyed men, only her skin is smooth and clean, though the flesh looks as though it has been carved from sugar icing. In this realm of confusion, Welles plays Michael O'Hara, the Hemingway-esque, independent man, a romantic dupe in a world where to be alive is to be in pain. Welles's Irish accent is, to my British ears, an embarrassment of the Dick Van Dyke order, yet he here conveys as he could so well an injured sensibility, the pudgy naivety of a boy half-grown up into the life of the corrupt.

Though his films tender a darkened sense of others, in this fabricated world Welles was himself both ringmaster and victim. As an actor Welles was at his best playing some saloon-bar Candide. Though he often played 'villains', he always brought to such roles a boyish *joie de vivre* that grants even the blackest characters a youthful unworldliness. He could find innocence in evil, and there is no better example of this than his wonderful performance as Harry Lime in Carol Reed's *The Third Man* (1949).

Lost inside *The Third Man* I can still imagine myself, just as I used to as an adolescent, as Holly Martins (played by Joseph Cotten), the foolish, well-meaning idiot that he is. And perhaps my entire romantic life has been coloured by my teenage admiration for Alida Valli as the elusive Anna. Yet I never dreamt for a moment that I could be Harry Lime, for between him and this viewer lay the unleapable chasm of charm. Like Welles, by some ineffable magic Lime just makes everything seem such fun. Welles denied that cinema acting should be in essence understated, and indeed the keynote of all his performances is that of gusto. He was a man who couldn't turn himself down. Though he never looks stagey, and has none of that hitting-the-back-of-the-theatre impact that can make Laurence Olivier look overblown on film, he nonetheless fills the screen, simply by letting us share something of the energy and power that was part of who he was and part of how he performed himself to others.

After years away from Hollywood, *Touch of Evil* was Welles's comeback film; in commercial terms, it didn't work out, but as a movie it is an amazing piece of work. While *The Lady from Shanghai* ushers us into strangeness, *Touch of Evil* places us inside a world of oppression, where bullies thrive and intimidation is the rule. It is a noir that is genuinely black-hearted, the romantic colours of the genre blooming over only its two fading film stars, the worldly-wise Marlene Dietrich and Welles himself, playing the good bad cop Hank Quinlan, a man who puts convictions and his hunches over the inconveniences of the law. It is arguably Welles's finest performance. He works wonders here; to take only one example, whenever anyone offers him some booze, as a reformed alcoholic he replies curtly 'I don't drink,' until one time, when all is collapsing, he says it and only then catches sight of the whiskey glass he has just drained. Then comes the marvel of his performance, for somehow Welles registers the jolt of the fact with an entirely blank face, signalling his own fall by apparently making no sign at all.

All Welles's films feel delirious, replete with a weirdness that breaks up the standard Hollywood fare and shatters it into fragments, into a pattern of visionary shocks. In *Touch of Evil* this hallucinatory intensity is especially strong; its Beatnik thugs are out of a David Lynch nightmare and the screen seems as drugged as its victimized heroine, played by Janet Leigh, who, as in *Psycho*, displays her customary bad luck in choosing motels. Yet the drugs turn out to be not hallucinogens or narcotics, but sodium pentathol, the 'truth drug' – much as Welles's dark imaginings perhaps offer the unvarnished truth about things.

There's a touch of lament, an end-of-season feel about *Touch of Evil*, the last great film noir of Hollywood's Golden Age. The film contrasts the pianola ('it's so old, it's new') with rock 'n' roll, and the faded glamour of the old stars, of Dietrich and Welles, with the new guys, the virile emptiness of Charlton Heston, the heavies' hip brutality. Old Hollywood was busy beginning to die, though maybe only Welles yet knew it. From now on his career lay back in Europe, and he became through the 1960s and into the '70s a great European arthouse film director, still creating masterpieces.

Chief among them is his version of Shakespeare's *Henry IV* plays, *Falstaff: Chimes at Midnight* (1965). As a young man Welles had put on Shakespeare's Histories with the Mercury Theatre. Their self consciousness about the possibility of staging a real life had perhaps fed into *Citizen Kane*. Now 25 or so years later he returned to incorrigible Falstaff. *Chimes at Midnight* has so much that's good – John Gielgud as Bolingbroke and one of the greatest, most brutal battle scenes of cinema – but in one respect it seems seriously deficient: it lacks laughter, and laughter is Falstaff's essence. Despite his humour

Orson Welles and Rita Hayworth, doubled and duplicitous in *The Lady from Shanghai* (1947).

and his humanity, Welles's view of the world was too dark to bring out this element in the old fat knight. Yet he truly embodies other equally vital aspects of the character. In conversation with Peter Bogdanovich, Welles declared that everyone acts all the time, and that in each and every conversation we are busy performing ourselves.[4] Though this no doubt has its general application and its Shakespearean resonances, nonetheless it feels less of a universal statement and more of a self-diagnosis. For Welles and Falstaff have much in common: both of them live as actors on the stage of everyday life, as self-dramatizers, as players.

In the European theatrical tradition actors began by playing types, not individuals. Plays that glanced at specific persons did so scurrilously, satirizing named and local figures. Instead the theatrical company offered generic roles based on physique and 'type', from 'the soubrette' to 'the male lead'. These traditions can be seen in the *commedia dell'arte* and on into early twentieth-century repertory companies. Plays mirrored a social view of human beings as defined by classes, genres, by typicalities and common characteristics. Actors may be typecast. We can plausibly say of someone that they *should* have played Falstaff or Rosalind or Iago, even though they never did so. Casting can follow exigencies of the person, as in opera a career can be determined by the relative heaviness of the natural properties of a voice. Falstaff is an ideal role for this conundrum, for surely no other character in theatre history is so unique, so vastly well coined as a distinct and inimitable person. Falstaff stands for personhood, in his eccentricity and boundless will simply to express the fact of his being there. It is not accidental that among all Shakespeare's characters people have argued that his is a portrait that glances at an authentic original – Sir John Oldcastle – and also to the peculiar presence of the original actor who played him, that burly buffoon William Kempe.

And yet critics have also argued for the generic quality in this character, the fact that the role alludes to the emblematic figure of 'The Vice', a stock character from the morality play. One version of the actor is that they may be a stock figure in a stock company, as in the *commedia dell'arte*, where physicality and temperament categorized the individual under standard types. In Falstaff, therefore, Welles embodied a person who both expressed the very nub of that concept, and yet also manifested elements of an older, non-individualizing version of the self – determined by class, generalities, estate and kinships.

Watching the entertaining TV series he made, *Around the World with Orson Welles* (1955), you see just what a glorious flirt Welles was, how much he enjoyed acting the role of raconteur. Michael Parkinson's chat-show sofa is already beckoning. Yet when he talks to a group of Chelsea Pensioners he seems somehow out of place, a Falstaff sat with Shallow and Silence, but where the quiet dignity of the old men, the settled proprieties of their beliefs, exposes their interviewer as a man betrayed by his own eloquence. Yet what eloquence it was! Welles is one of the few civilized voices in cinema, a Europeanized American, a preserver of urbane values. There is a touch of Henry James about him, as well as of those mid-century American writers, Hemingway and Fitzgerald, those wide-eyed cynics and sophisticated dreamers. Talking to the Chelsea Pensioners, one mentions that they are officially 'living in independent retirement'. 'Great word, "independent",' remarks one of the old soldiers. 'Yes, it is,' agrees Welles. Everything about the worlds he summoned up in film and in his acting, the uniqueness and humanity of that sustained vision, shows that he meant it.

13

INGRID BERGMAN: INTERMEZZO

Young Ingrid Bergman grew up on camera, the compliantly posed and playful subject of her painter-father's appetite for film and photography. He even filmed her as a small child paying her respects at the grave of her mother, who died when Bergman was three years old. Her father died when she was thirteen her parents thinned to images, all that was left of them. Brought up with film as she was, from the very beginning of her career she possessed a startling capacity to not fear the camera. More than most, later she fell for directors – Victor Fleming, Roberto Rossellini – and for the photographer Robert Capa, drawn to men who recorded the world through film. The camera she played to was no neutral observer, but recalled the watchful eye of her adoring father. More intriguingly, she herself was a compulsive maker of films, producing hour after hour of footage of those briefly shared portions of her children's fleeting childhoods.

She was left, a lonely timid kid, given to escape her bashfulness through play's yearning pretence, acting already with her dolls, inhabiting personae so as to assume a face before the world. The desire to live a life of imagination vivified Bergman's acting, giving her its absorption, the vulnerable joy of play-acting. The primal place of make-believe offered a refuge from a world beyond her control, a sanctuary from shyness.

I trust it is not condescending to remark that Bergman, for all her manifest womanliness, remained on-screen in some part of herself a child. In that regard, I hope to bring out something of the aristocratic freedom expressed in her, something of the impulsiveness, the insistence on the rights of freedom. In fact, this 'childlikeness' in her also has its political consequences, as she is thrust into a world where on-screen others (both men and women) will dominate and infantilize her, in part because of that longing to live an unfettered life. In her films she is too often made to pay the price for pursuing her feelings.

Despite funny moments in *The Bells of St Mary's* (1945), early on her genius was for drama and until the mid-1950s she did not shine in comedies, where, after her Rossellini period, Jean Renoir's *Elena et les hommes* (1956) and Stanley Donen's *Indiscreet* (1958) marked a new direction for her. Previously, in *Journey to Italy*, her character is accused of not having a sense of humour, and while that was plainly wide of the mark concerning her as a person, that's undoubtedly true of many of her roles. In most of her great 1940s films, humour's irony about the self is something she does not appear to possess.

Ingrid Bergman reveals more vividly than almost any other actor how strongly our interest in the film star entwines with our concern for a person as such. That personhood, that unique quality, elusive – and merchandisable – finds itself preserved in film, the flickering shrine to the pathos of our having been here. In his essay on 'Stage Illusion', Charles Lamb noted that the best acting, and the most nearly perfect scenic illusion, occurs when 'the actor appears wholly unconscious of the presence of spectators'.[1] The great actor beguiles us into believing that they do not know they are looked at, so taken up by the play as seemingly to live inside its artifice. In the late 1930s and the 1940s, when Bergman made her indelible impact on Hollywood, there were very few stars who could do this. The Hollywood stars – and, in comedy, this was one of their great strengths – were all too conscious. They constantly performed themselves, enjoying our gazing at the mirage they made, leaving us with the feeling that even in bed they posed. Contrariwise, Bergman possessed a mystical insouciance; in Patrick Kavanagh's phrase, she was 'Caught out in virtue's naturalness'.[2] She gave audiences the pleasure she found in that absorption in the play. The very opposite of her great Swedish forerunner, static Garbo, with her face held up as a mask of itself, Bergman was beautiful in part by dint of not appearing to care whether she was beautiful or not. Watching her, the imagination comprehends that seeming unconsciousness to be an innocence: something that transcends whatever we know of her private life, or of her characters' slippery scruples. Moreover, her ingenuous apartness appears to the viewer as a sense of that character's story, of their life in time. The actor who poses, the image proffered, is unvarying; they adopt a stance for their own portrait. Bergman, however, shows signs of a history that cannot be reduced to a sign.

In this regard, a crucial moment occurs in the Nativity play scene in Leo McCarey's *The Bells of St Mary's*, a movie happily lodged between sentiment and transcendence. Here the camera records children acting out in their own way their own self-devised Nativity play, with the least possible intervention of the director. Lost inside a moment, the children play to the camera, but do so naturally, playing out the play with all the virtues of acting, of spontaneous make-believe. The scene veers towards the 'cute', but involves something beyond cuteness, an improvised, spontaneous, unscripted wholeness of performance. Here Bergman merely watches the children 'acting', her own response shown to be scripted, an artifice. With the children, however, it is clear that the words they speak would be different every time. The situation is imposed, an artifice too, but the acting they make up comes naturally, against all constraint – and when they sing 'Happy Birthday' to the baby Jesus, they do so of their own accord.

All this takes place in a film that seeks to evoke in the viewer, perhaps no less cynical in 1945 than now, the childlikeness of faith, of idealism. These qualities find their expression in Bergman's character, her benign, idealistic, childlike belief a breathing admonishment to the movie's sick millionaire, a man motivated only by selfishness and greed. Given this insistence on the natural, it is intriguing that Bergman here for once plays a Swede, even singing a song in Swedish, letting the audience hear her mother tongue, her native voice.

McCarey's film would have us realize the joy of simply 'being', as the child's essay on the five senses quoted by the film has it, letting us share in the delight of living. Bergman's acting is central to that delight.

At the age of 21, a young theatre student in Stockholm with an already burgeoning movie career, Bergman married, after a three-year courtship, Peter Lindstrom, a young dentist (he went on to train as a brain surgeon) some seven years older than herself. In the context of this early marriage the affairs she pursued through the late 1930s and the 1940s in Hollywood make complete sense, seeming not sordid, but a kind of seizing of life. She was as innocent as a guided missile. Her strong regard for Joan of Arc is apt, as there was something dangerous in such single-mindedness, that ardent pursuit of a destiny, of someone guided by a voice.

It is not hard to discern the myth she lived out in that classic run of films from *Intermezzo* (1939) to *Indiscreet* (1958), that version of a self that Robin Wood named the 'Bergman thematic'.[3] This is most palpably a matter of her being both refreshingly 'natural' and constrained, a victim of masculine control, even as she offers an image of the possibility of a life without control, one of extemporaneous and impromptu freedom. As Wood points out, the 'natural' is as much a construction as the 'glamorous', in a person capable of combining the 'nice' and the sexual, the 'natural' with being a 'lady'.[4] In Alfred Hitchcock's *Notorious* (1946) the distinction between 'being a lady' or not consciously becomes a point of discussion for the film.

Bergman would become in time the epitome of the film star as living scandal. Her affair with Roberto Rossellini marked her out as a fallen woman, even with a call in Congress that her films be banned from America. Her divorce was doubly darkened in the public's eyes by the fact that for several years she abandoned her young teenage daughter. Bergman was a mid-twentieth-century 'fallen woman', subject to the same taboos as her forgotten Victorian predecessors. Through transgression, the star turns into a scandal – a cause for offence – someone in their own worldly way 'holy', yet behaving in an unholy way, and thereby discrediting the sacred itself.

What is most curious is how the films she made up to the time of her departure for Italy and the end of her first marriage themselves seem dry runs for that crisis. The Rossellini scandal concerned the destruction of the built public image on-screen, yet also fulfilled the adulterous promise of many of her films. From the very start Bergman sometimes found herself placed in a moral grey zone, somewhere between exoneration and condemnation. She could play saints and fallen angels. Above all, like many of the great Hollywood women stars of the 1930s and '40s, 'Bergman' lives as a figure of independence and dependence, indeed of modernity. Yet she remains old-fashioned in her moral commitments, as in her commitment to romantic yearnings. She may be someone who will 'dare anything' (as she declares in *Intermezzo*), but in the end she does 'the right thing'.

Her first film for David Selznick was Gregory Ratoff's *Intermezzo*, a remake of her role in a Swedish film that had been released some three years before. The premise is that she is Leslie Howard's accompanist, and then his mistress – the adoring support to his starring role as concert violinist. In practice, however, as far as the movie is concerned, she's the virtuoso and he's the second fiddle. The two actors are almost playing in different films. Howard proffers the audience his perpetual air of defeated dignity, a vintage version of middle age bottled for consumption. Meanwhile she's all youth, all expression, holding nothing back, playing the last movement of a sonata as though it were the finale of a symphony. It all makes Bergman seem peculiarly alone, her presence a naivety that the others gaze at or draw upon, though there is nothing in them of equal weight that could reciprocate it. Only the young actress who plays the child servant Marianne (Maria Flynn) comes close to Bergman's spontaneity, placing the Swedish star as closer to the vigour and freedom of children than to the perpetually dignified demeanour of these sad grown-ups.

Following *Intermezzo*'s success, Bergman did a series of unspectacular and forgettable films in which she remained dully girlish. Therefore in *Dr Jekyll and Mr Hyde* (1941) Bergman intervened in the Hollywood sweetening of herself, making a playfully sour transformation into vulgar, flirtatious Ivy, giving herself over archly to the filthy laugh and a leering, lecherous vivacity. This choice of parts broke up the consistent and dull image that Selznick had been fostering and allowed her thereafter to play a much wider variety of roles. And then in any case came Michael Curtiz's *Casablanca* (1942), the classic idea of a classic Hollywood movie.

Casablanca, like Hollywood, is an international zone, a place open to all the talents. Nationality does matter here, in this parable of wartime commitment, with the Germans seen as stein-swilling patriots and the French countering with a nationalism of their own, the Marseillaise versus a beer-hall lied. It is important that Bergman's earnest husband, Victor Laszlo (played by Trieste-born Paul Henreid), is Czechoslovakian, but more important still that his mission is fought for and alongside the French, the Norwegians, the Russians, the Poles, and will be carried on in that international city New York.

So it is that *Casablanca*'s backstory belongs to another stylized realm: Paris, the capital city of forgetting. 'Who are you really?' Humphrey Bogart's Rick asks Bergman's Ilsa Lund, but she demurs from making a fit reply. It's written into their affair that there are no questions about the past. Though that occluded past remains present, even as it is not told, the rule is no questions, that nothing should be told. Back there 'Rick' is 'Richard', another romantic being. Though we are given three options, one of them 'romantic', Rick never reveals why he has lived so long in Europe or is now holed up in Casablanca. For Bogart is a Byronic hero for film noir days, a man rendered bitter and heartless by some obscure hurt.

In the absence of histories, the Hollywood actor becomes a more vivid persona, a trope, a style, in this movie of strongly styled character actors – Peter Lorre, Sydney Greenstreet, Claude Rains, Conrad Veidt – all playing to type because 'types' are what they are, though that belittling word hardly sums up the strength and flamboyance they live out on-screen. As Umberto Eco once asserted, *Casablanca* lives as its own icon, a series of quotable excerpts, a range of disconnected peaks.[5] Among this feast of archetypes, for our purposes what fascinates is how Bergman so naturally joins the party, that someone dedicated to demolishing the idea of 'type' from within, and who had so recently broken her type-casting in *Dr Jekyll and Mr Hyde*, should here seem so mythical, so standard, so passive, so caught up within the pack of cards that Hollywood offered when it came to showing living people.

Here, as so often, Bergman is another 'other woman', an adulteress that may still grasp the audience's sympathy. In the end she defers all her dark transgressive power to Rick, who decides for her, shows masculine strength where she has become feminine, weak. That weakness would be taken to its furthest possible point in George Cukor's *Gaslight* (1944). This later film reverses the trajectory that Bergman's Ilsa Lund follows in *Casablanca*: that is, she begins weak and discovers strength and purpose at the movie's conclusion.

Given her personal history, it is noteworthy how often Bergman played motherless women, instead tied to fathers or father figures (dead or alive), or romantically attached to older men: the teachers in *Intermezzo*, *Gaslight* and *Spellbound*, the dead father in *Notorious*. From the start of *Gaslight* the film has already brutally disposed of two mother figures: her biological mother, who is accused of having been insane, and her murdered aunt, the woman who brought her up.

When it comes to *Spellbound* (1945), while my admiration for Hitchcock remains intense, there is no doubt that he does not serve Bergman well here. She labours under the weight of the director's boring fetish for blondes, having to play 'cold' and then to endure a constant barrage of harassment censuring that implausible coldness. She seems more at home in the estranging nun costume she is made to adopt in McCarey's *The Bells of St Mary's*. The latter is also in its own cute way a film about the tenuousness of male control, with Bergman as Mary Benedict, the dutiful Sister Superior nun usurping masculine privilege. It is part of the questioning of gender roles that Bergman's character was a former tomboy. Certainly it is in doubt if Bing Crosby as Father O'Malley is 'in charge' of the school ('Well, I have some authority,' he demurs). Yet the world of the film makes such challenges merely charming, entirely soppy.

Like *Gaslight*, and as with the later films *Anastasia* (1956) and *Indiscreet*, Hitchcock's *Notorious* (1946) is a film about a confidence trick, about taking someone in through acting. As such it stands as a movie about being an actor and about being directed. Bergman's character is encouraged by the American secret services to pretend to fall in love and then be a faux-dutiful wife to a Nazi agent played by Claude Rains, so as all the better to spy on him. Cary Grant and Bergman notably consider the plot as their 'little theatrical plan'. Though Grant's character, Devlin, himself a government spy, is in love with Bergman's character, he sourly wonders how honest, even how 'sluttish', Bergman's character's play-acting is. *Gaslight* had put Bergman in the place of the audience, since we are manipulated with her. Simultaneously, the crucial thing in Hitchcock's spy film is that the victims of the plot somehow always knew that it was a plot, always suspected the deception that was being worked upon them. As Claude Rains's mother declares, 'I knew, but I couldn't see.'

Within the action, *Notorious* makes Bergman into an actor forced to improvise feeling, to 'fake it' (as Hitchcock would advise her to do on set). We not only gaze at Bergman, we share the film with her: the confidence trickster here works on behalf of the audience. Bergman is actor here, and sufferer, a beleaguered, poisoned figure. By performing her feelings she takes in another person, though in time she too will be taken in – and taken over. The film enshrines the ways in which we allow ourselves to be deceived by art. What is striking is that Bergman, who acts so much by not appearing to act, should in these films be reinvented as either actor or audience. Identification means both desire and compassion, both the sharing of a viewpoint and concern for a fate. It is a film about training a woman to perform, or about exploiting her innate ability to do so. In that sense it is a dry run for *Vertigo*. A near-contemporary essay by Maurice Schérer (that is, Éric Rohmer) remarks that Hitchcock was quite uninterested in the film as a thriller, and that the movie's aim is to exploit the resources of Ingrid Bergman's face.[6]

Her last 'Hollywood' film for a while, though in fact it was a British production, Alfred Hitchcock's *Under Capricorn* (1949) has Bergman living in nineteenth-century colonial Australia as the aristocratic alcoholic Irish wife of the man who was once her family's groom. Herself a natural aristocrat and an independent soul, Bergman plays out here a class relationship that brings with it dependence, isolation and separation. Joseph Cotten as the groom and Bergman are living a lie, caught up in what they need to present in order to be a couple at all, each responsible for the other's guilt. Once again her character proves hard to pin down in moral terms, perhaps or perhaps not having an affair with her old childhood friend, played by Michael Wilding, a chap as posh and as clubbable as herself. Bergman is fantastic in the film, consciously acting her socks off, and yet the whole thing feels drably underwhelming, a reprise of things she had already done as well as they could be done, in *Gaslight* for instance. Again Bergman was ready to make another break, to reproduce in a different key her flight from Sweden to Hollywood. A flirtatious fan letter sent to the newly acclaimed Italian director Roberto Rossellini led to her working with him, and more powerfully to the international scandal of her divorce and remarriage.

In *Stromboli* (1950), after all that Hollywood artifice, that constructed Hitchcockian world, Bergman is absolutely believable because things are so relatively stripped down. Watching her you gain the sense of a life lived in that person, the impression of depth, of apartness, of guilt and ambition. In the films she made for Rossellini she is somehow once again an 'actor' and not a 'star', and yet how inescapably a star she remains. Although after *Stromboli* Bergman sometimes felt at sea adapting herself to Rossellini's style, still she was striving against the superficiality of Hollywood films – and coming as a 'star' to the neo-realist 'purity' of Italian cinema of the time, finding a different kind of holiness than the schmaltz offered in *The Bells of St Mary's* or *Joan of Arc* (1948).

Made during the storm that swelled up about her affair with the Italian director, *Stromboli* presents the impossibility of a private life, both for its main character, Karin, the Lithuanian refugee married to an Italian solider so as to get out of the camp she is in, and the star who plays her. Roberto Rossellini's film concerns 'Karin', but it is as much about Bergman's own status as outsider, a wife consorting with 'whores', a woman failing to be modest.

Ingrid Bergman as Alicia Huberman, a spy despite herself, in Alfred Hitchcock's *Notorious* (1946).

A star is somebody for whom the public and private self, the character performed and the person performing, have become so entwined as to be inseparable. Bergman had had a string of affairs before, but they were 'private'; this 24-carat love affair with Rossellini played out in public – almost as a battle with Anna Magnani, Rossellini's previous adulterous lover and the great actor at the centre of Rossellini's first classic, *Rome, Open City* (1945) and his *L'Amore* (1948).

Karin – and Bergman – lives her life in the atmosphere of disapproval. *Stromboli*'s plot is almost Gothic – a young woman incarcerated, spied upon. Karin moves from one place of constraint and unfreedom to another, from the barbed wire of the refugee camp to the remote volcanic island. Even the camp is freer, cosmopolitan in its own shabby way, warm with the solidarity of its uprooted women. On the island everything is rooted, with traditions inherited, a way of life passed on like her husband's icon of the Virgin Mary (given to him by his mother) and his collection of family photographs.

In *Stromboli* Rossellini and Bergman explore the erotics of compassion. Like Karin, its heroine, this movie sexualizes sympathy. Pity becomes the hope of rescue, and Karin considers that hope only lives where desire is kindled. So it is that she flirts with the priest, seeing him as the man he is, and not understanding that God's pity works otherwise. Meanwhile, the community she lives in polices sexuality, publicly mocking the cuckold or the whore, standing in judgement against the aberrant. Karin believes in the evoking of sympathy, because she herself has so much of it. Karin's pity overwhelms her and comes to life in situations where the islanders see only neutral destruction. The ferret that attacks the rabbit and even the bloody plight of the tuna fish touch her, despite the fishes' strangeness, with their metallic gleam, thrashing in the water like machines. The film asks of us how much pity we feel for the exceptional person. Always when faced with such natural aristocrats, resentment may creep in. This troubled pity for the outstanding in fact frames much of the conundrum of our relation to the star.

In Rossellini's *Journey to Italy* (1954) Bergman appears, almost for the first time, as someone tired out by life, gripped by the harshly mediocre vice of middle age. Redemption hovers around her, but never fully reaches her, even as the film's final reconciliation appears forced, uncertain, as the couple try to reach each other again amidst a surging crowd.

In 1956 came her Hollywood comeback film, Anatole Litvak's curious *Anastasia*. After the stringencies of the Rossellini films, it is strangely welcome to find her in a film that commences with a view of a shadowed Paris in 1928 that is straight from an operetta. Far from the existential emptiness of *Journey to Italy*, we are back in a Hollywood chocolate-box picture of abjection and suffering.

Anastasia proves to be another film about the directorial relationship, the actor's malleability, and the permanent essence in them that defies the malleable. Yul Brynner plays the confidence trickster and the director figure, turning a woman without an identity into a simulacrum of the lost Russian princess Anastasia, perhaps the last survivor of the Romanov dynasty. Bergman's character is 'cast' in the role of a perfect play, and her mentors self-consciously understand the deception they practise to be pure theatre. She fills herself out with his desires, and yet – echoing the trace of reality in Bergman's acting, the fabled and fabulous illusion of the natural self – she might truly be the Anastasia she is called upon to fake. Bergman is ideal for this character caught between acting and the real, the part the perfect mirror to her myth as a performer, both a consummate artist of invented gestures and someone indefinably and irreducibly their real, natural self.

All this furthers a suspect fantasy of a controllable woman, with her identity dreamt up as being a fiction that a man makes. Bergman shows herself complicit in this fantasy even as her frightening honesty unmakes it. She both plays the game and shatters its limits.

Anastasia itself unstably shifts from genuine location shooting in Paris or Copenhagen to sets that stand as gratuitous confections of the real. What is most curious is that Bergman's character both colludes with the process and stands beyond it – both acting on demand and perhaps convinced that she is what she plays, and, more than that, perhaps truly is so. The movie ends with the marvellous Helen Hayes announcing that 'the play is over', leaving us with the uncertain impression of a strange, self-conscious film, a key text in the decadence of classic Hollywood, where films were growing apt to expose the secrets once concealed.

Stanley Donen's *Indiscreet* (1958) paired her up again with Cary Grant, and takes its place as part of a pattern in her work that both flirts with adultery, while aiming to soften its moral compromises. It is a film about a middle-aged affair between an unmarried theatre star and a roving economist (played by Grant). Cary Grant's character wants to protect Bergman's character's 'reputation' (much as Grant had publicly stood up for Bergman in the post-Rossellini years of her 'disgrace'), and so a kind of dance is done over whether they are having sex with each other or not. It is another confidence trick film, with Grant pretending that he is married, so as to avoid commitment, and therefore acting (or, rather, lying) to her, and she then certainly acts for him, staging a deception to make him jealous.

From now on, although she kept working right up to the end of her life, Bergman would not add much to deepen her reputation. In *The Inn of the Sixth Happiness* (1958) she's back playing a kind of saint, and therefore assumes a no-nonsense dignity, a hygienic grandeur, touching again on that aspect of herself already shown in *The Bells of St Mary's* and *Joan of Arc*. She was comically vivacious in writer I.A.L. Diamond's *Cactus Flower* (1969), won an Oscar for Best Supporting Actress for *Murder on the Orient Express* (1974), and took a role somewhat related to her own history in Ingmar Bergman's intense *Autumn Sonata* (1978), enacting on-screen the famous and neglectful mother that she perhaps was in her own relationship to the four children she left behind through divorce or ambition for acting success.

Bergman herself was an unrooted person happy with the romance of rootlessness. In her diaries Bergman described herself as a 'bird of passage', committed to the heartfelt pursuit of freedom.[7] Consistently in her films Bergman plays the 'foreigner': a German American, a Lithuanian, an Irishwoman, anything but someone from 'here'. Yet most of all she belongs to the utopian no-place that is found among the other worlds of Hollywood film, a land of make-believe as romantic and elaborate as any that she had invented as a young orphaned girl, fighting against shyness with fantasy, already choosing through the imagination a life of perilous liberty.

NATIONAL CINEMAS –
STARS FOR THE NATION

14
LAMBERTO MAGGIORANI AND MARIA PIA CASILIO: ABSENT FILM STARS IN VITTORIO DE SICA'S FILMS

In order to comprehend the phenomenon of the film star, it seems necessary to consider how those films work that deliberately do without them. This chapter is a 'control experiment', in which we shall consider the absence of the star. The actors in the films I will now discuss show up failings in the type of the 'movie star', inadequacies intrinsically related to what could be seen as the paltriness, the manufactured quality of the humanness that the stars present and endorse. Here the acting non-actor is not less than the star, but more. The anonymity preserved in these films – and exploded by them – posits an authenticity, a reality, a closeness to life itself. And yet these films nonetheless 'elevated' their actors to something approaching stardom; certainly both Lamberto Maggiorani and Maria Pia Casilio would afterwards find their lives moved into the realm of cinema. Casilio played successfully in films through the 1950s, typecast for the main part as a peevish, plaintive country girl. Maggiorani was only hired by De Sica on the understanding that after filming he must return to his work at the Breda munitions factory. Though he did so, he soon lost his job during a restructuring at the plant (likely in part because his employers believed him to be wealthy following his role in *Bicycle Thieves* (1948)). He found work as a bricklayer, while keeping his hopes alive of a movie career, one that failed to realize itself, beyond a few minor roles and a part in Pasolini's *Mamma Roma* (1962), his life derailed by the movie he had made.[1]

Lamberto Maggiorani as a desperate man in *Bicycle Thieves* (1948).

Much of the sadness of life aches in the Italian director Vittorio De Sica's films, and much of the beauty too. It is one of the small mysteries of cinema how De Sica (1901–1974), a lightweight actor (and very handsome man) accustomed to playing sentimental leads, should go on to become one of Europe's greatest tragic film-makers. It is as though Hugh Grant might suddenly metamorphose into Ken Loach. Yet links remain between the comedic ham and the neo-realist trage-dian. De Sica enthusiastically carried his actor's talent into his directing style, instructing his amateurs on the way to perform, enacting the parts to embody for them how things should be done. There's a story that on set in bed with Marcello Mastroianni he once played Sophia Loren's part, lying underneath the attractive star, and demonstrating to the two of them how he needed them to kiss.

Though De Sica went on to work with Mastroianni and Montgomery Clift, Loren and Jennifer Jones, there are no film stars in his first masterpieces, those extraordinary neo-realist works of the late 1940s and early '50s. Offering to finance *Bicycle Thieves*, David

Selznick wanted a bankable star to help him recoup his investment and suggested Cary Grant should play the unemployed hero; De Sica demurred, and countered with Henry Fonda, perhaps impressed by the downbeat grit that actor had displayed in John Ford's *The Grapes of Wrath* (1940).[2] Fortunately for all concerned, the deal with Selznick fell through, and De Sica was free to use the photogenic possibilities of authentic unknowns. Such a decision was hardly a new one in film – and documentaries such as those by Robert Flaherty, films like *Menschen am Sonntag*, or Humphrey Jennings's *Fires Were Started*, or the early films of Roberto Rossellini had similarly more or less dispensed with the familiarity and bankability of 'the star'. Some of the democratic impulse produced by the war was in this move away from stardom as well as the embracing of something local, something emphatically Italian, a turn towards the community as hero over the essential individualism embodied in the singular star.

Denying himself and his audience movie star glamour, De Sica was instead casting according to the authenticity of a face. Lamberto Maggiorani, the gaunt leading man of *Bicycle Thieves*, was a factory worker; Carlo Battisti who played the aged Umberto D. in the film of that name, truly was a retired university professor. Young Maria Pia Casilio did not really even want to be in a film; sitting in on the auditions for *Umberto D.* she was spotted by De Sica. To get out of it, she demanded what she imagined would be a prohibitive fee, only to find that the studio was prepared to pay it. Her reluctance somehow adds to the authenticity of her performance – a gesture towards avoidance, a *nolo episcopari* that is all but impossible to imagine in a Hollywood context. No film star could have lived on-screen as these people do. After all, as De Sica asserted, there are millions of characters, but only fifty or sixty movie stars; it seemed to him a strange illusion that so few people could faithfully embody the experience of so many. Yet for all the appeal to the genuine, that factory worker and the university professor are here not themselves, but players, as much bound up in an artifice as Cary Grant or Henry Fonda. For these are films that tell the truth about the contemporary world not as a documentation, but through the conjured illumination of poetry.

There is a four-minute sequence in *Umberto D.* (1952) that seems to me close to the heart of what is best about film-making, what is most poignant, gentle and attentive in it. Reluctantly enough, the housemaid Maria, played with superb indolence by Maria Pia Casilio, has woken early. She sits up in bed, rubs her tired eyes, puts on her housecoat and traipses down to the kitchen. There she stands by the cooker, strikes a match and lights the gas. Something draws her attention and she moves to the windows. As she does so the camera, from without, moves in towards her, until we look at her quite close-to, looking out. She watches a white cat on the forlorn, early morning rooftops, the ragged rear walls of tenement houses. Her face is serious, perhaps unreflecting, perhaps stoically sad, maybe holding the flicker of a resigned half-smile. She moves back from the windows, takes a jug from a dresser, fills it with water, positions it on the gas flame. As she waits for it to boil, she touches, experimentally, curiously, her newly pregnant belly, her breasts that her pregnancy are changing, and she looks up, lost in thoughts that we may guess at but can hardly know. There are the faintest trace of tears in her eyes. She takes some coffee beans and a grinder, and sits down to grind the coffee. She puts out a bare foot to close the kitchen door and keep the noise of the grinding inside. But then a noise from outside reaches her; she wipes her eyes, stands up and goes to the door, and sees the old man Umberto D. in the act of leaving the house. And with this the sequence ends. Within it, nothing happens. And yet this quiet moment, this still interlude of the ostensibly tedious, is at once the deepest, the lightest, the most far-reaching of scenes. It engraves an everyday beauty, it sketches the feeling of a whole life. For some, it might be highly boring, just someone going about their day, but for those willing to watch with it, it opens up another person's world, and grants us the gift of seeing this person now, both performing ordinariness and unveiling its maybe unsuspected wonders.

These early films – especially *Shoeshine* (1946), *Bicycle Thieves* and *Umberto D.* – are among the glories of European cinema. They are all tragedies of miscommunication. They celebrate the human condition while unveiling its tragic flaws. In *Shoeshine*, events turn first on a

Maria Pia Casilio as 'Maria', facing the morning in *Umberto D.* (1952).

deception and then on the separation of two boys, great friends placed in different cells when confined to prison. Apart from each other, each loses trust; words miscarry and cannot be heard so as to be understood. Here, as elsewhere, De Sica presents people who cannot reach each other through language, but stand hopeless and encased in their position in the world. They try to enlist or persuade others, find help, a loan or support in their loneliness, but no help comes. Acts of charity short-circuit; sympathy fails to achieve its aim. De Sica was an expert on the subject of being disregarded. His characters are invisible persons made visible to us. The lack of what would be to others very small sums of money drives them to desperation; the loss of a bicycle can destroy a whole life. Harried by oppression and poverty, his protagonists fall into acts of moral compromise; the heroes must become that which their conscience condemns – a snitch, a bully and thief, a beggar. His people are too flawed to be the pitiable saints some repute them to be. The sadness here is not inevitable; it is a consequence of a social structure, a political pathos.

At the same time that in America Arthur Miller was making *Death of a Salesman*, in Italy De Sica was exploring too the troubling radiance of failure. In watching *Umberto D.* or *Bicycle Thieves*, we are both taken inside the particular life and yet never lose sight of the fact that even now such tragedies are playing out for real somewhere. The central figures embody a general defeat and yet remain absolutely unique. This impression of the individual life finds itself in De Sica's eye for detail, etched into the surface of things like the scratches on the kitchen wall where, in *Umberto D.*, each morning Maria Pia Casilio as the pregnant housemaid strikes the matches to light the gas. They are all great urban films, leading us within what is, to middle-class audiences, the unseen city of the poor: the pawn shops, the cramped and ramshackle apartments, the fortune-teller's boudoir, the markets, soup kitchens and social clubs. The films permit us to penetrate both this teeming metropolitan world and also to enter the individual life, drawing us in by an attentiveness to sorrows to which we might otherwise fail to attend. The films lay a claim on us, with the unemphatic persuasion that we ought to bear witness to such tragedies.

In the midst of these harrowing and marvellous explorations of defeat, De Sica and his hugely talented collaborator, the screenwriter Cesare Zavattini, turned to make a fairy tale. The very funny fantasy film *Miracle in Milan* (1951) gives us Totò (Francesco Golisano) and Edvigie (the adorable Brunella Bovo), two improbably sweet holy fools. De Sica's films often looked into the depths that abide in simplicity. He liked human beings most when they are unguarded, naive and possessed by a simple faith in life. He wanted to manifest a kind of trust before things, one that often fails, but at least is there to fail. It is in the shoeshine boys' love for the horse they save up to buy, in Umberto D.'s fellow-feeling for a lonely pregnant girl and for his pet dog; it is the compassionate openness that allows us to love others. Yet he also shows the endearing selfishness in simplicity too, the child-like egoism, the guiltless need for small indulgences. Few film-makers help us to share so completely the pleasure of food: I get hungry every time I watch the son lingering over the mozzarella in carrozza in *Bicycle Thieves*. Everywhere in his films De Sica communicates a democratic delight in what delights everyone; his films presuppose that outdated concept, the normal heart, one that finds a natural sympathy with children, the old and life's discarded ones. *Miracle in Milan* may be a film obsessed with numbers – lottery numbers, multiplication tables, the price of a bid or a bribe, the figure that might express the imagination's largest possible fortune – but in the end it sides with that which cannot be counted, but can only, for all its fragility and its inability to find a place in the world, be counted on.

Some might recoil at the prospect of having their hearts warmed in this way. Yet *Miracle in Milan* never forgets how hard life is, and how in the end the only escape for the poor is to take to the skies and leave the confines of the earth altogether. In film this provides a fairy-tale uplift; in contemporary Athens or Caracas it would be just as hard to pull off. Zavattini and De Sica know that the film offers consolations that only a work of art could offer. We are shown people paying to watch a sunset, that stereotypical classic Hollywood ending, or handing over 100 lire to be told by a charlatan reader of faces that they are amazing people: 'who knows what you'll become!' This plays like a necessary moment of cinematic self-critique, the film telling us that it knows such flattery is what cheap films perennially offer us. Yet De Sica himself very rarely falls into this trap; rather his pictures affirm human dignity without insinuating (as Hollywood might) that this means we shall receive extraordinary rewards. Rather, in De Sica's films people go unrewarded; the story takes us beyond the moment of loss and leaves us only with the small resolution to keep going that sometimes comes in loss's wake. At the close of *Bicycle Thieves,* when driven beyond despair, the father and son take each other's hand as they move among the anonymous crowd. It is a symbol of human compassion and solidarity that proves almost unbearably moving. Yet as they walk on, they are lost to view. They truly vanish as no star ever vanishes. They have each other, but they are gone, returning back to the authenticating anonymity from which the film had, for its brief length, delivered them.

15

MOIRA SHEARER:
THE MARIONETTE

'O body swayed to music, O brightening glance,
How can we tell the dancer from the dance?'
W. B. Yeats, 'Among School Children' (1926)

hen film-makers Michael Powell and Emeric Pressburger
approached Moira Shearer to appear in their new film
The Red Shoes (1948), they were met with what might have
seemed a baffling indifference. For, perhaps unlike most young people
of the time, Moira Shearer had no desire to be a film star. Rather she
wanted another kind of life, another kind of fame, as a ballet dancer.
This young Scottish dancer rather looked down on the films. Unwilling to be a film star, and believing the premise of *The Red Shoes* – that
there was a profound conflict between art and life – to be an entirely
silly one, it took the persuasion of her mentor Ninette de Valois, the
founder of the Royal Ballet, to make her accept the role.

Given all this, like Maria Pia Casilio in Vittorio De Sica's *Umberto
D.*, Shearer was a non-actor compelled to act. Unimpressed by cinema,
Shearer found herself starring in one of the films central to cinema's
implications and entrancement. Yet her conquered reluctance to act
rhymes with *The Red Shoes'* deepest concerns. In being a film ostensibly about ballet, it slips covertly into becoming a film about film
itself. Above all, it merges the ballet star with the movie star, and sets
out to investigate the relationship between the maker and the character, the director (or writer) and the player. While beguiling us with
utter beauty, this is a film that invites the possibility that we might
reject film as such. The strength of its demand upon us to give ourselves up to the spell that cinema utters can provoke resistance to

that invocation. This movie tells us that film, art, the stardom complex, the order of society itself, require a woman to constrain. Melodrama depends upon the woman being caught up in what must appear to be an impossibility. Trapped between irreconcilable opposites, it shows us that there is nothing left for her but to choose her own death, falling into an oblivion that makes all odds even.

Ballet may come into Hollywood musicals, but the ballet film, such as *The Red Shoes*, follows rules all its own. Dancing should be care-free, but such films portray the dance world as the home of suffering, whether through toil and anxiety as in Robert Altman's *The Company*, or as pure Gothic in Dario Argento's *Suspiria*. Behind every adaptation of *Ballet Shoes* there looms a *Black Swan*. These are largely films about dedication to art, where dancing means compulsion, pain or a shimmering illusion.

The Red Shoes had a long gestation. In the early 1930s the British movie mogul Alexander Korda first conceived the idea, wanting a ballet film based on the biographies of Sergei Pavlovich Diaghilev, the impresario behind the dance company Les Ballets Russes, and of Vaslav Nijinsky, his star male dancer and his lover. When Nijinsky married, Diaghilev dismissed him from the company. The initial plan for the film might have kept the love between men central to the story, with Paul Muni as Nijinsky and Charles Laughton (himself a gay man) as Diaghilev. The plan was revived in the late 1930s as a vehicle for Merle Oberon, with whom Korda was in love, at which point the Hungarian émigré Emeric Pressburger wrote a script. Once again, the project languished. In the early 1940s Pressburger, now teamed up with Michael Powell as the film company The Archers, considered making the film themselves, but let it drop until the post-war period, when for £9,000 they bought the rights to Pressburger's script. The war was over and the film-makers (and, it would turn out, the audience) yearned for a subject that might play in the absence of war's pressures. The tale unravels in an apolitical world, a realm of glamour. As Powell would write, 'we had all been told for ten years to go out and die for freedom and democracy, for this and for that, and now that the war was over, *The Red Shoes* told us to go out and die for art.'[1]

Moira Shearer dancing as the ballerina Victoria Page, with Léonide Massine as the shoemaker in *The Red Shoes* (1948).

By the time it was finally made what fascinated Pressburger was the opportunity to put the making of a work of art on film. In doing so, this would become a film that put to question the nature of such art, the very condition of film itself, and the paradoxes that imbue the position of the woman star.

For this would be a film about the making of a star, the turning of a person, both with their willing complicity and against their interests, into an actor. Art and performance would absorb the living self. Pressburger considered that there was something religious in the film. Following *Black Narcissus* (1947), Powell and Pressburger's Gothic fantasy of a house of courtesans transformed into a nunnery, the cinematographer Jack Cardiff proved able to see the young ballet dancers as themselves nun-like: dedicated, ascetic, renunciatory.[2] Lermontov, the movie's dance impresario, informs us that ballet is his 'religion'. This spiritual strain corresponds to the film's mysterious atmosphere. It is a film deliriously given over to excess, present in the exaggerated make-up and gestures of its ballet stars; these are people prone to mime their selves in everyday life. Melodrama and extravagance here are naturalistically explained away as the way that people work in the world of the ballet. The hallucinatory realm of 'The Red Shoes' ballet itself (designed by the expatriate surrealist painter Hein Heckroth) is merely the most obviously extreme part of an artwork that seeks to transform the physical world and stable identity: everything and everyone here might become someone else, much as in the ballet, the man facing Vicky, the ballet star, might be her fellow dancer, or the shoemaker from the fairy tale they are dancing, or Lermontov, the impresario, or Julian Craster, the composer of the music to which she dances and her lover. Rooms here are so often mirrored, the looking glass doubling the world as a screen up there on the screen. The picture seems to conjure up an enchanted space, where theatre itself appears uncanny, a haunted doubling of the real, beyond the workaday world.

In the film, the young, aristocratic dancer Victoria Page (Moira Shearer) joins the ballet company run by Boris Lermontov (Anton Walbrook). Impressed by some quality of passionate self-abandonment that he glimpses in her during a matinee performance of *Swan Lake*, he casts her as the principal dancer in a new ballet, 'The Red Shoes', a fairy-tale piece based on Hans Christian Andersen's fable of a young woman who finds herself wearing the long-desired red shoes, which possess her and hold her fast, condemning her always to be dancing. In the end, as Lermontov explains, she dies. During the rehearsals for the ballet, to be performed at the Opéra de Monte Carlo, Vicky falls in love with its young composer, Julian Craster (Marius Goring). When the couple marry, Lermontov is furious, his plan to make Vicky into the greatest dancer of the age thwarted by her 'adolescent' love for a young man. For a while Vicky gives up her career, becoming subsumed by the apparently passive role of being her husband's muse, though still she retains her vivifying passion for dance. Travelling back to Monte Carlo, one year after her marriage, Lermontov persuades her again to perform in 'The Red Shoes'. This last performance will claim her life.

Shearer's disenchantment regarding movie-acting perhaps lay behind the strange emptiness of her performance in *The Red Shoes*. She is strikingly cool, held back from us. Vicky's relative silence throughout the film may be put down to the fact that she was no trained actor. (As Lermontov says to her, 'I will do the talking, you will do the dancing.') Instead, she exists most fully in the mute performance offered by dance, a form of acting locked into the body itself, its communicative presence. She is the dancer as star, the star as the dancer, and so it is that she manifests the paradox of the player, someone central to the work of art, its interpreter, and yet not its primary creator. The composer requires the musician, the scriptwriter and director needs the player. Ballet, like much of 1940s film, shows itself to be at the service of the woman star. On stage we see that the male dancer supports the woman, holds and furthers her dancing; he is not what counts. When Vicky dances in 'The Red Shoes' ballet with a succession of men, each is faceless, undistinguished; the spotlight is hers.

The claim that Powell and Pressburger (and Heckroth and Brian Easdale, the composer, and Jack Cardiff, and Léonide Massine and Robert Helpmann and Shearer herself) are staking here is that the gestures and images of ballet might open up a complex, associative kind of storytelling. Can ballet be said to have a meaning? A narrative art in the nineteenth and early twentieth centuries had long been in the process of becoming an abstract one; for all its apparent modernity, 'The Red Shoes' piece proves actually an old-fashioned kind of ballet, a neo-Romantic form of modernism, as committed to fairy tale as *La Sylphide* or *The Nutcracker*. The thought that movement in relation to music would itself construct a story – and be (in the film) a story within a story, a competing narrative that replicates the film as a whole in miniature – is a mere aspect of the film's greater storytelling, its parallel commitment to the shock of sudden glances, to the made-up face, the dramatic pose. The ballet sequence is both a strange interlude in the film and the strongest example of its visual methods. After all, film treasures motion and constantly refuses the stillness of the single photograph. The dancers themselves found it hard to adjust to the disrupted flow of filming that broke up the coherence of the unitary performance. A concept of the person unravels here, one in which dream and gesture, fantasy and the real intertwine, much as a shot of the auditorium metamorphosing into a raging sea connects to a 'realistic' backstage shot of the dancers in the theatre's wings (Powell had named the dance piece 'an original Freudian film-ballet').[3] Film's literalism ceases to pertain, anything can become anything else: the dancers charmed to flowers swaying in the wind, a cloud drifting in the sky, a white bird flying (as Julian predicts will happen when he discusses his music with Vicky). This dissolution most affects Vicky herself, who both hallucinates the performance she gives and is its troubled heart.

Most of Shearer's subsequent life on film reprises the dilemmas exposed in *The Red Shoes*. In *The Tales of Hoffmann* (1951) she dances the role of Olympia, the mechanical doll who enthrals a human lover, another version of the puppet-self that in *The Red Shoes* she had danced as Coppélia. In those moments, Shearer represents the beloved as art object, as a 'dead thing', one that 'never was alive' (to quote Hoffmann's tale) but that represents an image of life, like a person trammelled in the spool of a film. Her role in *The Story of Three Loves* (1953) similarly replays the conflict between love and ballet. Above all, Michael Powell's serial-killer film *Peeping Tom* (1960) acts as a dark furtherance of the mysteries present in her first film. With its film-maker killer, *Peeping Tom* renders explicit the implicit murderousness of cinema, and the casting of the German actor Karlheinz Böhm (billed as Carl Boehm) as Mark Lewis, a Teutonically accented English-man, echoes the presence in *The Red Shoes* of the Austrian Anton Walbrook. Above all, Moira Shearer's cameo role as Vivian revisits the stresses of her debut. Now she's an understudy, a double, for the lead in a film. When the studio closes for the day, she meets Mark, a camera operator on the same film, in order to make a show-reel that might secure her position before the movie camera. What she does not know is that Mark intends rather to film his murder of her, so as to record forever the fear that precedes it and the transition of a living woman to the animated lifelessness of film. Like the 'glamour model' who will be Mark's final victim ('Make us famous' are her last words), Vivian longs to be 'the star', even though, as Mark tells her, all stars are lonely and the greatest stars are the loneliest of all. Though she claims already to be lonely, for once Shearer nonetheless embodies a self-assured warmth here, a spirited presence, that is all the more poignant for the fact that at the end of the scene Mark coldly kills her. In doing so, Mark projects into her the same fear that he himself experienced as a child and that his scientist father clinically recorded. Shearer's a double for the man making the film, a stand-in for a terror that haunts him. Every murder Mark performs is a kind of suicide. All this reimagines cruelly what Lermontov inflicts upon Vicky Page. As in *The Red Shoes*, after her death Shearer/Vivian again becomes an absent presence on-screen, there still in the movie studio, though her corpse is invisible within a stage prop trunk.

In the passionate instant in *The Red Shoes* when, alone in his Paris hotel room, Lermontov strikes the mirror into which he gazes, he assaults himself as an image. Alone there, in that ornate suite, with-out Vicky he has become a blank. The blow comes out of rage, perhaps out of a narcissistic self-erasure. Diabolic, he hates love as such, reck-ons life to be 'so unimportant'. Like Mark Lewis in *Peeping Tom*, he wants to absorb all others into his work of art and so take possession of them. When he strokes and circles a statue of a dancer's bound foot, he caresses a fetishized object that manifests all he cannot possess. The separation of others from him ends as those others, especially Vicky, become puppets. It is a strange diagnosis regarding the condition of being a director, and on the part of Michael Powell both *The Red Shoes* and *Peeping Tom* carry the force of a self-scrutiny so strong that it rises to self-accusation. In cinema, in art, one person gives life to another. Yet, these films wish to tell us, such a gift involves a sinister claim, a desire to possess the soul of that character in a spirit of domination, to turn them into a creature for film. At times Lermontov seems a species of vampire, existing in shadow, pallid, protected from the light by dark sunglasses, shades that conceal his watching eyes.

The astonishing final minutes of *The Red Shoes* take us into a realm where the standard conventions of waking life break up and fracture into dream, or theatre. On the night when Vicky is to dance 'The Red Shoes' again in Monte Carlo, Julian Craster, her husband, comes to the theatre to reclaim her for their marriage. In the dressing room, Julian and Lermontov contend over her, one speaking up for romantic love, the other for the renunciation and madness of art. Both men are happy to bully her, much as Powell bullied Shearer on set, producing for real the tears she cries on camera. Trapped between the two, weeping, oppressed, Vicky appears to choose a life of dance and not of relatedness. Julian stiffly departs, planting mechanically a kiss on her forehead. As Vicky leaves the dressing room the red shoes she is wearing seem to take possession of her, though they sweep her not towards the stage but back to catch her departing husband. In time to the shunting engine of the train that pulls into the station to take Julian away, Vicky scutters down the steps outside the theatre, dances towards the overhanging terrace and then flings herself off, Anna Karenina-like, into the path of the arriving train.

Moments later, just as we expect Vicky to take her place on stage, instead Lermontov steps in to replace her. All the coolness and control, all the facade of his social self, has broken up. Mechanically, reduced to the hapless marionette to which he would have reduced Vicky, he forces out the announcement to the audience of her death. Yet the ballet goes on without her, *Hamlet* without the prince, the spotlight following on stage a lack where the living woman should be. The person – the star – that held the centre is gone; and all that remains is the men mourning, still observing her spotlit absence.

16

GLORIA SWANSON:
HAVING A FACE

S tars shine and are forsaken. Once famous everywhere, I think most people would struggle to put a name to an image of Pola Negri or Asta Nielsen, Ava Gardner or Montgomery Clift, even Faye Dunaway and Gene Hackman. In this regard, as remarked on earlier in this book, the film star was one of the first inhabitants of the temporary world framed by 'pop'. If film belongs to the transience of pop, it may not be a coherent proposition to grant it a history.

Billy Wilder understood this from the start. He felt that old films could never make sense to the young, except as remakes, because the later viewer could no longer place the stars. The context of their other performances shimmered and dissolved; the star would dwindle into the character they play. The films that Hollywood then made were never thought to be monumental, permanent works of art. They were designed to play for a week, and then to vanish. Before TV, long before video, DVDs and YouTube, there was often no way even to watch old films: in those days, a re-release was an event.

In this unhistoried world of the cinema, this place of fashion, film preserved the passing instant. In particular, Wilder's *Sunset Boulevard* (1950) relays a history that is still a living present, the blanked-out 'waxworks' who play morose games of bridge at Norma Desmond's mansion, all once international stars. It evokes Hollywood as a forgotten history in a place where the movie industry was less than forty years old. Legends have accrued on the shallow soil of its streets.

Schwab's drugstore, one of the movie's key locations, was where Harold Arlen had written 'Somewhere over the Rainbow', and where a drunk Scott Fitzgerald (like *Sunset's* narrator, another writer doomed by Hollywood) had collapsed only a decade before.

Sunset Boulevard lives on as a key fable of Hollywood stardom, one of those modern fairy tales that immortalize for us a notion of this glittering world. The film tells the tale of a struggling screenwriter, Joe Gillis (William Holden), who escapes his debts by becoming the lover of an ageing, wealthy and all-but-forgotten silent movie star, Norma Desmond (Gloria Swanson), living in decadent isolation in a mansion off Sunset Boulevard. The house's only other inhabitant is Max (Erich von Stroheim), the butler, but once Norma's director and husband. Feeling constricted by Norma's overbearing love, Joe becomes involved with his best friend's fiancée, Betty Schaefer (Nancy Olson), stealing away from the house and collaborating with her each night on a movie script. The two co-writers fall in love, but rather than expose Betty to the compromises of marriage to himself, Joe disillusions her, showing her the ways in which Norma keeps him. With Betty gone, he nonetheless decides to leave Norma and she, unable to accept that anyone might abandon a 'great star', shoots him dead.

Sunset Boulevard evokes several genres, being a noir, a melodrama, a Hollywood picture, a black comedy (briefly Mae West was considered for the Norma Desmond role) and a Gothic tale. As in any haunted house movie, there's an organ, with Max playing Bach's Toccata and Fugue in D minor as any Igor might. Gothic unveils a world where the past haunts the present, contemporary America shadowed by its own suppressed histories. Film itself, this film reminds us, is Gothic, a bearer of the past into the now.

With its opening shot *Sunset Boulevard*'s camera dips into the gutter and it will figuratively squat there throughout the movie. Hollywood is that gutter-world, a low place where cynics conspire to fabricate dreams. Here people opportunistically exploit each other, the self is bought and sold, as a toyboy lover, as a writer for hire, as a commodity on-screen. The faded screen goddess Norma is herself a dreamer, a consumer of her own image, allied with the cinema audiences who once worshipped her, having become the object of their, and her own, fantasy.

It was always going to be hard to find an ex-star willing to play Norma, happy to take the risk of exposing themselves to ridicule as a has-been. They tried for Pola Negri and Mary Pickford before Gloria Swanson claimed the role. Swanson shifted the balance of the movie, encouraging Wilder and his co-writer Charles Brackett to put Norma centre stage. Swanson brings a perfect physical presence to the film, imperious and petite, dominant and vulnerable. Her face communicates emotion as readily as does Charlie Chaplin's (and she mimics Chaplin to amuse Joe, donning trousers, painting on, as Katharine Hepburn's Sylvia Scarlett had, a masculinizing moustache), registering disdain, indignation and longing in mesmerizingly rapid shifts of expression.

Faced by Norma's plight, her extremity, we might laugh at her, fear her or pity her. The film invites us, at times, to see Norma as monstrous, with her hands weirdly contorted into claws, the dark glasses that scour out her eyes, the peculiar wire contraption of her cigarette holder. Reproducing textbook Oedipal strains, the hero Joe Gillis hesitates between two women, the older woman against the young, rapacity against naive romance, the vamp against the bobby-soxer, and the star versus the ingénue. Norma here is the suffocating mother, the woman who looks after the man, and in doing so confines and emasculates him. Nancy Olson as Betty Schaefer was chosen specifically as a 'new face', someone truly not a star, just an unknown to play opposite the known, but forgotten, thereby contrasting two kinds of unfamiliar cinematic presence.

The only person the camera blatantly exhibits as sexually desirable is William Holden, who towels himself down by the pool, showing off the beefcake body of a second-rank leading man. Norma is sexual, but not sexualized – though Wilder has declared that Swanson was one of only two women he was attracted to while making a film. (The other was Barbara Stanwyck during the shooting of *Double Indemnity*.)[1]

More than this, Swanson brings the history of her self to the film, the fact that she truly was just such a silent star as Norma Desmond

Erich von Stroheim watches Gloria Swanson as Norma Desmond, getting ready for her close-up, in *Sunset Boulevard* (1950).

had been. A skewed reality shares the fictional realm here; the old movie-star photographs that decorate Norma's becalmed house are simultaneously the genuine relics of Gloria Swanson's fame, her career; when Joe and Norma sit and watch the old Norma Desmond films they are in fact watching old Gloria Swanson films, thrilling to *Queen Kelly*, the movie that shipwrecked her career, and that of her director, Erich von Stroheim.

Stroheim's presence in the film as the butler who used to be Norma's director, her husband too, reframes yet again the relationship between the male director and the woman star. Max and Norma re-enact the obsessive relationship of a Josef von Sternberg with his Marlene Dietrich. Confused relations of power shift and flit through the story. As Norma's director was Max her servant or her controller? Is film the product of male anxieties and needs, or a realm where a woman's dream of herself finds its place? Reputedly, Stroheim asked

Wilder to include a scene where Max would hand-wash Norma's underwear.[2] There are unmistakable elements of masochism in this ex-husband's self-willed debasement before his former wife, the star. Max sustains Norma's dreaming, contriving endless fan letters, fostering the illusion that the crowd still love her. His muse has grown old; the photographs, the films, preserve the art they made together; a compact keeps Max attached to the person who cohabited with the image, the woman inside the star.

These speculations were apt for Wilder, a director who had come to cinema as a writer, and a man suspicious of the grand claims made for the ('hushed tones') great director. He was too much of an author to need to be an auteur. He let himself be happy with the writer's unremarked role, content with the view from the margins of it all.

The film hovers between the offhand be-bop world of the American present and a grand operatic past; it is no accident that Richard Strauss's *Salome* offers Norma's inspiration, figuring her as both a *fin de siècle* and a film noir femme fatale. The new Hollywood of quick cheap pictures, of words, confronts the silent movie world of mute gesture, of the power of the human face. Joe Gillis's voiceover represents the will of words to order the story. He's in a double sense a ghost writer, rewriting Norma's script and a dead man offering his tale; even after death, the scriptwriter keeps pitching scripts. He's a behind-the-scenes person brought into relation with the visible star of the show. His words do battle with her own images, with the power inherent in the human face. In the course of this film, Joe will collaborate on two scripts with a woman he desires, on Norma's extravagant biblical epic, and on Betty Schaefer's drama of ordinary life, the two representing at this moment distinct possibilities for the direction of cinema itself.

At the film's close, just after murdering her lover, Norma becomes a sleepwalker, a woman contained within a dream. Only the thought of the cameras upon her rouse her to a still somnambulistic action. In 1950, as the film ends when Norma descends the staircase and declares herself ready for her close-up, it was still weird, even sinister, to see someone excited by the presence of cameras. Now in the age of the selfie, more or less everyone is in Norma's position, finding themselves in a Facebook profile or an Instagram account, existing most fully in the light of an image.

When in her madness Norma breaks the fourth wall at the very end of the film and addresses the audience before the cinema screen, the people out there – in here – in the dark, she exposes the contract that cinema presupposes. The edifice on-screen, the shiftless murals of film, the very person and presence of the star would cease to exist without its witnesses. The audience, the fans, are dreaming Norma; in becoming their dream, in sharing it too, she now needs them to exist. Without them, she is nothing and no one, when the film ends its run, when she returns to herself. Without the dual existence of being both person and image, without the validation of others' glances, of their adoration, Norma becomes deathly. The death sealed into the cinema image, that strips a presence from an actual person, becomes actualized in her. For her love is murderous and suicidal; she is the woman passers-by thought was dead; she's Salome kissing John the Baptist's 'cold, dead lips'; she's the woman who kills her man to keep him. It is only after Norma's suicide attempt, with the bandages still on her wrists, that Joe and Norma consummate their relationship. Norma is dead and alive, just as Joe is; her living death expressed through a photograph, a flow of cinema images; while his is expressed in the traces of a voice, the afterlife of writing.

17

AVA GARDNER:
I AM NOT AN ACTRESS

One day Ava Gardner dropped by the studio publicity department at MGM. She wanted to take a peek at all those cheesecake photos they were always taking of her: throwing a beach ball; licking an ice-cream cone. A drawer full of images was spread out before her, and she leaned across and looked them over. After a little while she 'straightened up and kind of shrugged, and she said, "Jeez . . . From the way people went on, I thought I was better-looking than that."'[1] There's an essay to be written on the disadvantages of physical superiority, and Ava Gardner would make its perfect test case. Her beauty distracted others; people considered it an invitation, a property that never seemed her own possession. It might be lost through any accident. It made men ache and act crazily. It made people forgive her. It was something that age would take and that she could ruin, with all those late nights, with all that drink. Above all, it made her lonely. She appeared not so much herself as the sum total of other people's reactions to her.

Worse, those reactions tended to strip her of her own character and reduce her to an object, a thing of pure physicality. Al Altman, who made her screen test, had seen enough promising starlets to know that a really beautiful woman was rare indeed, in fact a 'freak'. To Howard Duff, she was the 'most beautiful thing he had ever seen'; he simply had to have her. To others, she was 'an extraordinary creature', 'the most beautiful creature I had ever seen in my life', even 'the Taj

Mahal of beauty'. Or she 'was like an animal, Ava. The sex thing.' When Howard Hughes proposed to her one more time, he romantically suggested that after three previous marriages, it really ought to be his turn. Ava replied, 'You make it sound like I'm a pony ride at the county fair.' The posters for *The Barefoot Contessa* (1954) declared its star to be 'The World's Most Beautiful Animal', and in the film itself Marius Goring helpfully declares: 'You are not a woman . . . I only see that you have the body of an animal. A dead animal.'

The most beautiful girl at Rock Ridge High, it was her looks that took her to Hollywood, and certainly Gardner was famous as a beauty before she was famous as an actress. Her best films both celebrate her appearance and yet also respond to it as a problem, almost a fate. They were always making icons of her – all those publicity stills and bathing-beauty snaps, a portrait by Man Ray for *Pandora and the Flying Dutchman* (1951), the ridiculously overblown statue for the grave-side scene in *The Barefoot Contessa* (it ended up in Frank Sinatra's California garden until one of his later wives finally had him throw the thing out).

Although others may turn her into an object, her appetites were decidedly her own. She was ready to exploit the powerful effect of her own fame and glamour. Yet somehow she could not rise above the objectification implicit in her profession. Even in Lee Server's sympathetic biography of her (2006), her body becomes at times something between an exhibit in a freak show and a commodity of pure desire. He lists her measurements (thighs: 19 inches; calves: 13 inches); he tells us of the problems caused on set by her erect nipples and the Mexican playboy seeking one place on her body that had never been kissed ('And I got to the soles of her feet and I said, "*I found it!*"'). More unusually, Server shares with us Mickey Rooney's expressive admiration for Gardner's 'cunt', which apparently had the strength and mobility of a mouth. There might be a Nabokovian completeness in such an approach, if it were not for the fact that at the same time Ava's inner life recedes from view, leaving us all too often with mere physical description or the anecdotes of her endlessly bad behaviour. In Server's favour, he also applies this treatment to some of the male protagonists in his book. Anyone interested in Frank Sinatra's endowments will find plenty to chew on there. Soon after his first entrance, we are informed that nude he resembled a tuning fork, a metaphor which left me, temporarily at least, none the wiser until things were more graphically spelled out a little later. Once a reporter asked Gardner what she saw in Sinatra, a 'hundred-and-nineteen-pound has-been'. Ava blandly replied, 'Well, I'll tell you – nineteen pounds is cock.'

Server's biography of Gardner leaves little out, and by implication brings even more in, including Gardner's rumoured bisexuality and her taste for rough sex. And yet, to paraphrase Samuel Johnson, inevitably one may gain more real knowledge of Ava Gardner from watching ten minutes of *Mogambo* (1953) than from Server's informal and studied narrative, begun with a funeral, and ended with one too.

The broad process of Ava Gardner's life is that a small-town girl becomes a Hollywood star, then a hard-drinking rabble-rouser, and finally a grand and rather sad old lady with a corgi and a maid-servant living in one of those sadly grand houses in Knightsbridge. In between, she makes some pictures. Gardner's career happened in the lulls between drinking bouts or marital fights, or simply when she needed to escape from wherever she happened to be living. Her habits were all bad ones, consisting of getting drunk, smashing crockery and picking up handsome but ultimately unappealing men. In adapting to Hollywood, she transformed herself into a sassy and worldly-wise 'broad' (her own choice of word), someone who would enquire of an English actor asking for a date, 'Do you eat pussy?' Around the same time, she declared to Vinicius de Moraes, 'Yes I am very beautiful, but morally, I stink.' She was being unnecessarily hard on herself. She pursued her pleasures and broke a few hearts in the process, but hearts are made to be broken, and it would seem that most of the men she had sex with were still happily boasting of their 'conquest' half a century later. Sexually there seems to have been little that she did not try; she hung out in brothels; she travelled; she drank; she danced with gypsies; took part in bullfights; skinny-dipped; and got herself barred from most of the best hotels in Europe. If fun is the ultimate goal in life, then she attained that goal: Ava Gardner had a lot of fun.

Gardner came from North Carolina, the last of six children in a poor farming family. Discovered as the result of a photograph seen in a New York store window, she was screen-tested and brought to Hollywood, where she spent some years contracted to MGM, waiting for a break as a leading lady. She filled in the time by getting married. She had three husbands in quick succession, two of them before she had starred in a film. All of them were famous. First was Mickey Rooney, the miniature star of the Andy Hardy pictures. Rooney embodied all the horror contained in the word 'irrepressible'. He was effervescently manic, the kind of man who would attempt to bring the house down during a quiet lunch. As the marriage disintegrated, Howard Hughes, the millionaire movie mogul and aviator, appeared on the scene. Driven by a combination of Obsessive Compulsive Disorder (OCD) and appetite, Howard Hughes saw Gardner for what she was becoming, the commodifiable woman – his unwittingly arrogant statement about his intention to marry her ('I can do no better') sounding uncannily like a strapline for an automobile ad. Gardner was not buying his attempts to buy her. She was admirably resistant to the charms of money, not out of indifference, for she certainly knew the value of cash, but more out of a refusal to be placed within the market.

Husband No. 2 was the bandleader Artie Shaw. Rooney looked up to her; Hughes stalked her; Artie Shaw tried to educate her. Shaw was an insufferable intellectual. He oppressed her with psychoanalysis and *Buddenbrooks*, and made her pack a copy of *On the Origin of Species* for their honeymoon. It was only as this marriage swiftly faded out that she made her first significant film, *The Killers* (1946). After divorcing Shaw came a period of pick-ups and cocktails, before she fell for Frank Sinatra, then about to fall into the abyss of a career low. In his own way Sinatra was just as appalling as Shaw or Hughes, faking his own suicide to get back at her, punching photographers, or hanging out dewy-eyed with the Mafia. Their arguments were the stuff of legend, but the rages at first seem in part to have been stormy

Complex, moody, restless, Ava Gardner in a publicity shot.

prologues to an equally passionate making-up. Yet soon the fights were only fights, and soon after that they couldn't live together at all.

She never remarried after the split with Sinatra. There were, however, countless lovers, from the guy who did the props to (perhaps) Fidel Castro. Though she had some disappointments with sex, in the main her erotic life seems to have been a dizzying round of pleasure.

There is no equivalent term I know of for 'womanizing', but if there were Gardner spent twenty years doing it. Her serial seductions were sometimes about sexual desire and sometimes about her fear of sleeping alone, as some men were certainly invited back merely to keep her company. Her biggest Hollywood affair post-Sinatra was with George C. Scott, the most ghastly of all her lovers, a man so repellent as to make even Sinatra seem like a paragon of sense and virtue.

Beginning this account of her with her private life may seem invidious. In fact she had no private life. Sinatra's failed marriage to Gardner inspired 'In the Wee Small Hours of the Morning', one of the great heartbreak records. Nelson Riddle commented on Sinatra's voice in this period, 'It's like a cello . . . Ava taught him the hard way.' Sinatra was transforming his 'private life' and, more importantly the publicity about that privacy, back into public art. Gardner would do the same; indeed, this process was to be the key to her career. Her affair with Sinatra, at that point still a married man, turned her briefly into a public hate figure, before her position altered through changed public perceptions following her performance as a sad, deserted woman in *Show Boat* (1951). She became instead yet another unlucky star, someone the audience could love because she was both beautiful and tortured. The scripts of her films began to make reference to a back catalogue of affairs and to her increasing fame as a drunk.

At first Hollywood hadn't known what to do with her. She waited for something to happen. She was groomed, she was photographed, she avoided being coerced onto the casting couch. They put her in a number of low-budget quickies, such as *Ghosts on the Loose* (1943), a forerunner of *Scooby Doo*, but without the wit and sophistication. And then came *The Killers* (1946), the film that made her a star. I find it a dreary and portentous film, a pseudo-tough version of *Citizen Kane*, and Gardner was not really at her best as a femme fatale. Barbara Stanwyck could play the chilling tramp, and Veronica Lake was a charming blank; Gardner just looks like a good kid from North Carolina who's got herself in trouble. She may in later life have been scary and fiery company, but she was just essentially too nice, and *The*

Killers could not help but reveal this fact. Yet, vitally, she redeems the film in one extraordinary moment. The scene begins like a thousand other scenes: the noble hero at last has the slippery femme fatale on the ropes. She's sitting in the back of an automobile with Edmond O'Brien. He is playing that standard figure of mid-1940s noir, the insurance detective. She is apparently cornered and knows it. They sit side by side in the car, her on the left, and him on the right. 'Where are we going?' she asks him. 'The Green Cat on Sultan Street,' he says. Then she is alone on the screen. She glances forward and then to the side, pissed-off and sulky. 'I thought you didn't like The Green Cat?' She's coquettish; he's tough. Yet her voice is somehow too high, a little trembly and bloodless. Her face is very pale below her dark hat and dark hair. But she is playing tough too. Only her eyes drop a little as she asks him. And then the camera focuses a moment on O'Brien, giving his hard-boiled reply, 'Only when I'm not expected,' and then glancing across at her. And here the moment comes. Again she is suddenly alone on-screen. She makes no answer, looks at him, looks forward, and then makes a barely perceptible shrug, or not even a shrug, more a faint loosening of the body, something between acquiescence and boredom with her own act, almost, one feels, with her own acting, taking the measure of the moment and stepping outside it; not a vamp, but a woman with a history, a life before the film, and then she looks out of the car window, out beyond the frame with a casual interest, as though what is going on out there catches her attention more than the rigmarole in the car. The film's director, Robert Siodmak, very likely shares in the creation of the moment's apparent naturalness. He told her what to do in minute detail, forcing her to play down her performance. Whoever was responsible, the result is a little piece of perfection, a rare instance of a muted, off-guard grace amidst the turgidity.

Gardner was never so good again, or at least not in this way. From now on, her strength would emerge in the analogous process of just being herself, whoever that was, on-screen. Her reiterated insistence that she was not an actress was not false modesty but an unusually perceptive analysis of her situation. When she came to play Pandora in the movie of the same name, she read the following description of her character: 'Complex, moody, restless with the discontent of a romantic soul which has not yet found the true object of her desires.' Ava said, 'It is almost me.' To take just one other example from many, similarly when she read the script of *The Barefoot Contessa*, she told Joseph Mankiewicz, 'I'm not an actress, but I think I understand this girl. She's a lot like me.' Well, exactly. The increasing identification of Gardner's person with her screen performances should not surprise anyone. This was how the star factory worked. They called Gardner the 'Hollywood Cinderella', but really nearly every 1950s woman Hollywood star was that, the medium itself providing the transformation that turned an ordinary Norma Jeane into a Marilyn. The films would not only be about her, but about her transformation by film.

In the case of an Audrey Hepburn, whose gamine looks were supposed to render her invisible, this process matched the sense that the actor has an unusual beauty, which the film would uncover. Hence the revelations of *Sabrina* (1954) or *Funny Face* (1957). With Ava Gardner, what was being revealed was not her singular attractiveness, which was obvious to everyone, but rather a spirit in her, something hidden behind the beauty, something natural. It would require a lot of artifice to bring out. As happened with everyone back then, the studio set out to remake her. Her voice was changed, she was instructed in how to move, all in an attempt to capture a 'quality' that they saw she had in her anyway. Film was there to throw the key light on someone and so transform them. It would draw out a hidden essence, rendering that essence as only surface, the shiny, beautiful, glow of Technicolor.

There are strong indications that Gardner experienced the move from her home town of Grabtown to Hollywood as one in which she was driven to become something new, a modern creature, distinct from the limits that life otherwise might have held for her. She had to play many roles to get by, the most notable one being the barefoot child of nature constrained by the brutality of civilization. Of course, in reality she came to exemplify a certain kind of American modernity: the Hemingway-esque, a life of fast cars, fast planes, bourbon, big-game hunting and expatriation, but one rooted in an antique American image, a new direction for the old frontier stock. She even played three Hemingway heroines, including the love interest in the dire *The Snows of Kilimanjaro* (1952), which inflated a short story into a hotchpotch pastiche of everything the Great American Writer had produced up to that point.

Some of the best directors she worked with – Alfred Lewin, George Cukor, John Huston – were specifically engaged in locating what they felt to be the private, natural quality in her so as to catch it on film. The enemy in this process appeared to be Gardner herself. She was openly shy when she was young, secretly shy when she was older, and even oddly shy before the camera. As a result, although she always looked pretty, at first she was a wooden performer. She became an actor by finding a way of presenting herself on-screen, the self she presented being in two senses a Hollywood creation: both the kind of person that the milieu there permitted, and also the package sold to the world through her relationship to the press. The quality those directors found was not the unmediated natural woman from Grabtown, but in every way the product of the industry itself.

Gardner conformed with this process, even as she seemed to rebel against it. Her rebellions were also enacted on-screen: the bad behaviour, the drinking, the player's refusal to play. Ultimately the Cinderella myth concerns the transformation of ordinariness. What was special about the Hollywood women stars of the era was that they could be at once as ordinary as you or me and also special, untouchable princesses. For the public, the women in those 1950s films existed in a discrepancy between two forms of knowledge and intimacy, both manufactured. There was the intimacy of film itself, the close scrutiny and imaginative identification with the star. And then there was the knowledge provided by the press, the gossip magazines, the newspaper photographs. Server suggests that Gardner was the model for Anita Ekberg's character in Fellini's *La Dolce Vita* (1960), a fact that in a way explains everything about who she had become in the eyes of the public and (in a word derived from Fellini's film itself) the paparazzi. Many of the fake elements that made up Gardner's public persona were there: Ekberg's enactment of a wild child given over to pleasure, adored by men but unattainable by them, strongly sexual, frustratingly innocent, pursued by cameras, and always behaving as though one were there watching her. Only the saving qualities of Gardner's capacity for affection and the genuine warmth she could not help but express were lacking.

The Barefoot Contessa (1954), Gardner's film made with Joseph Mankiewicz, brilliantly portrays the process of Gardner's immersion in Hollywood. Above all, it exposes one essential part of the Gardner myth, uniquely strong in her case, although present with every film star. You might call it the *Notting Hill* syndrome. In *The Barefoot Contessa* Mankiewicz pays tribute to the impressively egalitarian nature of Ava Gardner's sexual desire. The film's male stars cannot have sex with her; they are father figures like Bogart, weird like Warren Stevens, or impotent like Rossano Brazzi. On the other hand, Gardner's character is free to have sex with many anonymous and unseen ordinary men, gypsies, servants, men glimpsed infrequently or kept off-screen altogether. She pays for this freedom with her life. The film thereby manifests the audience's basic desire, that no matter what the private life of the star, she can still be someone whom anyone in the audience might possess. Yet she also falls victim to the film's and the audience's envious moralism, murdered by her stupidly jealous husband. Gardner's character is constrained between desire and judgement, exactly the ground she occupied in her media life.

In retrospect her career was not a bad one. She outlasted some other promising femme fatales, such as Rita Hayworth or Jane Greer, whose movie work was effectively over by the early 1950s. In the end her staying power was her strength. When nearly every one of her generation was dead, retired or in TV, she was producing what may be her best ever performance, in John Huston's adaptation of Tennessee Williams's play *The Night of the Iguana*. A couple of years later she almost played Mrs Robinson in *The Graduate*, a perfect piece of casting sabotaged by Gardner's self-doubt and reluctance to strip. She was in many bad or dull films, though she also made some good ones, notably *Pandora and the Flying Dutchman*, *Mogambo* (1953),

The Barefoot Contessa, Bhowani Junction (1956) and *The Night of the Iguana*. Yet she was never in a truly great film and all her performances somehow fail to add up to an *oeuvre*.

Years ago, when I was working in a public library, an old woman asked me to recommend something to read. I mentioned some biographies. 'Oh no!' she said, 'I don't want to read one of *those*. They always die in the end.' It is a rare biographical essay, a rare biography, that evades the melancholy of ending. Inevitably there is the frailty of old age, and then the only end of age. Gardner spent her last years walking her dog in London; she was the nicest person Michael Winner ever knew. In the 1960s sometimes people would ask her, aren't you Ava Gardner, and she would say, 'No, I just look like her.' She would watch her old films on TV. Once, after seeing *Bhowani Junction*, she rang Stewart Granger to ask him, 'Were we really that beautiful, honey?' Even though there remains an abiding impression of a rather sad life scoured out by fun, one leaves Ava Gardner with a sense that she was an extremely likeable person. She was coarse, though self-deprecatingly modest; energetic in the pursuit of pleasure, indolent otherwise; hot-tempered, easily bored and very good company. For all her doubts about her own abilities, her best films remain good company too, mostly for the imagined sense of closeness to the real woman playing in them.

18

MONTGOMERY CLIFT: HE'S NOT THERE:

I n John Ford's great Western *Stagecoach* (1939) John Wayne makes a famously striking entrance as the Ringo Kid. About fifteen minutes into the film he appears out of nowhere, legs astride, the quintessential cowboy, spinning his rifle in his right hand while his left holds up his saddle. He barks out a command, 'Hold it!', and the camera sweeps towards his face, passing out of focus, and then coming clear again, regarding him, awed, his face registering with the faintest surprise the understated apprehension that out of the blue he is facing capture by the law. Yet even that small shock bursts quickly into the brightest grin. This was far from being Wayne's debut in film, but nonetheless it was a calling card for a new intent. He announces his presence with a flourish, a youthful confidence too much in the grain to be macho, claiming his right to command, his belonging to this earth.

Pass forward nine years, a world war in between, to Montgomery Clift's first screen moment in his debut film, Howard Hawks's *Red River* (1948). Again we are fifteen minutes into the film, and we have already seen Clift's character, the orphan Matthew Garth, played by a young boy actor, and then in a few words uttered by John Wayne ten years have passed. Now John Wayne crouches on the ground, telling us how it is, and as the camera rises upwards we see grizzled Walter Brennan to the right of the screen, and Clift standing between them, a little behind, a little lower than Brennan, deferential, patient, listening, looking from Brennan to Wayne. He helps Wayne up, for the older man is stiff from squatting. Wayne talks on, and Clift chews a stalk of grass, and then the camera closes in on him. The only movement is in Clift's eyes, alert, looking up, taking in Brennan, turning to Wayne, turning thoughtful. It is the understatement that matters, his air of proud submission, his apparent intelligence. As in that moment in *Stagecoach*, it is the right to command that is in question. Clift goes on to offer a plan, but demurs when Wayne rejects it; he rolls a cigarette, but it is Wayne who is going to smoke it and Clift who will light it. This moment is a calling card of a different kind. Clift impresses, but quietly so; he is assured, but held back; at the centre of the screen, yet a figure in abeyance.

Montgomery Clift was a lush, a loser and a masochist on the public's behalf; for just over fifteen years he was also one of the finest actors in America: as Clark Gable put it, 'that faggot is one hell of an actor'. His beauty, his drinking, his homosexuality, his failure and his unaccountable talent have all reformed themselves as elements of the icon that stands in for Clift, a potent image of an abject stardom. There is a story that having seen himself in *Red River*, Clift knew that fame was coming to him and he grabbed the opportunity to get drunk anonymously one last time. In the years of his renown, it could seem as though his aim was to hold on to that foregone anonymity while in the throes of stardom. For all that he clearly loved the limelight, despite his conspicuous need to perform, Clift tried to turn celebrity into concealment. The sad joke of his career was that his fame outlived his success; after *Red River*, he couldn't even be anonymous in failure. In 1963 his miserable performance on *What's My Line* seems a prophecy of the last years that were coming, his sadly altered face and body in plain view before four blindfolded celebrities (including a young Peter Cook), all struggling to recognize him from his almost unaltered voice. And all the indignity of the situation plays out as embarrassment before the curious crowd.

The shape of Clift's career follows a tragic symmetry: eight early films from *Red River* through to Fred Zinnemann's *From Here to Eternity* (1953), and then eight later films from Edward Dmytryk's *Raintree*

Montgomery Clift diffidently there in Howard Hawks's *Red River* (1948).

County (1957) to Raoul Lévy's *The Defector* (1966), the hyphen between them provided by the spectacular car crash that wrecked his face. There are three kinds of classic American motor crash: the James Dean, Eddie Cochran legend-sealer; Bob Dylan at Woodstock making disaster an opportunity for reinvention; and the sweet Gene Vincent long martyrdom. Clift could have been another Jimmy Dean, instead apparently he was granted the Gene Vincent twilight, doomed to carry on as his own shadow, the ravenous crowd remarking on the difference. What if Clift had died in that accident? For many, he did, the later films better ignored, seen as staining the magical purity of those early performances.

In her highly interesting book *The Passion of Montgomery Clift* (2010), Amy Lawrence idiosyncratically prefers those neglected post-accident films, resistant to their mood of dejection, but alive to Clift's quieter genius.[1] It's a preference that fits her method. We all know about Clift; but Lawrence demonstrates how every element in that popular icon of the man is in fact a misconception, in particular the belittling sense that Clift is simply a male Monroe, Judy Garland as a guy. Although one of the founding members of the Actors Studio, it turns out that rightly he shouldn't even be considered a method actor, his style already fully formed by the time the method came along.

His career at first was defined by his personal beauty, the effect his face and form had on others, the bobby-soxers' dreamboat, a gay guy for the straight eye. Karl Malden declared that 'he had the face of a saint', a compliment especially poignant when we consider that it was spoken by a man with the generous face of a heavy-drinking cabbage-patch doll.

Clift made relatively few films, but nonetheless at first at least he chose well, working with most of the best Hollywood directors of the era: Howard Hawks, Fred Zinnemann, William Wyler, George Stevens, Alfred Hitchcock. In ten or so of his sixteen films, he is, by anybody's reckoning, flawless. It is not surprising that John Ford never showed an interest; the 'manly' directors that Clift did work with suspected and, in John Huston's case, tormented him. He turned down the chance to work with Billy Wilder on *Sunset Boulevard* and, it seems, was never asked again. It still rankles that he never had a chance to work with Douglas Sirk, although directors are not the issue in Lawrence's view, except when they turn into bullies. Her anti-directorial stance is at its strongest when it comes to the admittedly ghastly John Huston; if his *Freud* (1962) is as good as she believes, it is because of what Clift achieved in spite of its director.

When The Beatles spearheaded the 'British Invasion', one Tin Pan Alley songwriter reputedly lamented, 'These boys are geniuses; they're going to ruin everything.' That's one way of reading the impact that the triumvirate of Clift, Marlon Brando and James Dean had on Hollywood. Of course, there had been great actors before, but – among the men – there had been few who were renowned for intensity, for 'sincerity'. Passion and performance were for women. For men, effortlessness and dignity were the requirements through the 1930s and '40s, a laconic polish, with the tragic scenes given stoically or in quotation marks, driven by a sense that films were not quite a serious business.

Clift was the forerunner of a new generation, marked down as a youth in an industry dominated by older stars. In his early films such as *Red River*, William Wyler's *The Heiress* (1949) and George Stevens's *A Place in the Sun* (1951), Clift is someone that the mature men suspect. In the latter two films, it is a class suspicion, the closing of ranks against the interloper, but it is also a generational matter, an effect of style. Among other things Clift represented those men who had passed through the war. Although he was unfit for active service (due to the lingering effects of amoebic dysentery), there is still the presence of the war in *Red River*'s Matthew Garth. In several of Clift's subsequent films – Fred Zinnemann's *The Search* (1948), George Seaton's *The Big Lift* (1950), Alfred Hitchcock's *I Confess* (1953) – Clift is or has been a soldier, the films themselves engaging with the aftermath of the war in Europe. In *I Confess*, the war appears to suggest, while not conclusively providing, a reason why Clift's character, Michael Logan, should elect to become a Roman Catholic priest. The war had made these characters, gifting them with confidence, troubling them with memories.

So it was perhaps that the 1950s were the decade of neurosis. For all their resistance to the 'torn T-shirt brigade', even older stars such as John Wayne and Jimmy Stewart succumbed, putting the dark side of their personae on-screen. From the start Clift embodied the new unease in his combination of earnestness with charm, and in his posture and expression: Clift habitually hunched his shoulders, taking on the look of a man who expects to get hit. His apartness beguiles us; he comes across as easily hurt, a fascinating loner at a time when loneliness was cool. He brandishes his solitude like a badge. Clift was the solitary barroom pool player as existential hero. He was the romantic orphan, the placeless man. He played orphans too, a family-less character, or, as in *A Place in the Sun*, a son getting away from what little family he has. He had the orphan's sensitivity, his thin skin, there in the way he gave himself to the roles; and he could also claim the Keatsian orphan's righteous pugnacity, expressing itself in the willingness to take the punch. He gets into fights, but holds himself back, pummelled and humiliated, before he throws back the jab that justly revenges the indignity. Despite the weight of all those high-school yearbooks, this was the 1950s *beau idéal*, the lonely youth as a desirable alternative to the organization man. It was also a long-standing American paragon: from Natty Bumpo to the Ringo Kid, from Captain Ahab to Philip Marlowe. In this sense Clift's type represented nothing new, just the latest variant on a character already dear to Hollywood. Indeed, as Lawrence remarks, in the first half of his career Clift's generational struggle was as much about fitting in as rebelling; he was a defiant conformist, cosying up to the father figures he challenged, shadowing the outlaw stances that they themselves embodied. In *From Here to Eternity*, Clift's character Prewitt loves the army; he stands apart and yet embodies the ethos of the institution. He's a hell of a good soldier.

In her book on Clift, Amy Lawrence considers how we read a performance, a face, but more how we respond to it. Clift is the test case for her arguments and, given the complexities of his career and fame, he proves to be a very good one. Regarding Clift himself, this viewer is often left with mere admiration. It is like Heinrich von Kleist's tale of the self-conscious athlete in reverse, where being told he is beautiful makes the young man pitiably seek to reproduce the pose he once struck naturally. It is the watcher who falls into self-consciousness. Rather than a merging in ecstatic suffering, as Lawrence imagines the viewer of Clift's films doing, for me there is a lucid, disenchanted appreciation. If this is ecstasy, then it is one expressed in its own restraint. This is where the later films do show a new power in Clift's art; his fourteen-minute appearance in Stanley Kramer's *Judgment at Nuremberg* (1961) is stunning, the contradictions of pain and compassion almost unbearable.

Yet in his first films Clift's attraction is clear. In *Red River* he moves with such verve, the lightness in the leap with which he mounts a horse, or the ease with which he takes a step, the concentration as he lights a cigarette. In fact, he is so good in *Red River*, you wonder why he only made one Western – unless John Huston's *The Misfits* (1961) counts as another. His secret was to act like it really was happening, simulating the emotion by feeling it. He sweats at the roles, emotionally absorbed. Therefore, it is understandable that his 'real' self can be read into the performances he played, even though that self is likewise now just an image, interpretable, fantasized, but ultimately unknowable. The famous 'Taps' scene in Fred Zinnemann's *From Here to Eternity* is as manipulative and as affecting as anything in William Wyler's *The Best Years of Our Lives* (a film that Zinnemann greatly admired); it is a test case for the younger Clift's power to move us. Prompted by his response to an act of arbitrary unfairness, Clift's character, Prewitt, has given up a place in a bugle company in order to become a simple infantryman. He plays the bugle brilliantly, but has foregone the opportunity to do so. His best friend, Maggio, played by an impishly wiry Frank Sinatra, has just died, effectively having been killed as a consequence of the beatings meted out by a thuggish fellow soldier. For once Prewitt plays the bugle again for the army, though rather than an official duty he offers up instead a personal military requiem for Maggio, giving us a faintly bluesy lights out. The music fills the camp and the other soldiers pause to listen. For all the stoicism, Prewitt's feeling is on show; he's heartbroken, but nonetheless performs superbly, saturating the notes with sadness. In part we are so moved because Clift restrains himself, his face filling the screen, inscrutable for all the teardrops that run down his face.

From 1948–9, in just about a year, Clift could be seen in three films as different as the contemporary drama *The Search*, the Western *Red River* and William Wyler's costume drama *The Heiress*, an adaptation of Henry James's laconically sour novel *Washington Square* (1880). The impact of those first three films must have been immense, the nearest recent equivalent being the admiration produced by Daniel Day-Lewis's near simultaneous debut as the stuffy prig Cyril in *A Room with a View* and as a cocky rude boy in *My Beautiful Laundrette* (both 1985).

Clift's versatility is as impressive as his readiness to take risks in his choices. The male leads of *The Heiress* and *A Place in the Sun* both risk losing the audience's goodwill. In fact, Lawrence tells us that for *A Place in the Sun* Clift hoped to alienate the audience even more by having a more sympathetic actor than Shelley Winters cast in the role of the fiancée that he lets die. In later films, such as Joseph Mankiewicz's overheated version of Tennessee Williams's *Suddenly, Last Summer* (1959), playing a young psychiatric surgeon, Clift lets the women take centre stage; it is Elizabeth Taylor's film, then Katharine

Hepburn's. Here, as in *Freud*, he is a 'listener', busy only with eliciting speech from the women. Of all the early films, it is in the last, Vittorio De Sica's excellent (though butchered for u.s. release) *Indiscretion of an American Wife* (1953) that Clift takes the greatest risks. Here Clift plays an Italian trying to hold on to his affair with Jennifer Jones, an American wife and mother, while she tries to end their liaison by catching a train out of Rome. For all his beauty, Clift comes across as spoilt and unappealing, sabotaging our compassion. It is a beguilingly diffuse film, the camera drifting towards others at Rome's railway station, as though losing interest in the passionate affair it purports to be about. Other lives intrude and our gaze shifts outwards and we see what the lovers see distractedly: the crowd, the passers-by, the woman's nephew, the poor, the policemen; all of them intervening and preventing their love. Throughout the film men stare at the woman and peep at the couple, smearing their privacy. Producer David O. Selznick did his best to ruin the film, anxious as he was that Jennifer Jones, his wife, would appear morally compromised by the passion and moral complexity of Cesare Zavattini's scenario. Even so, it is one of Clift's most impressive films, even more so in the attempt to reconstruct a director's cut of it as *Terminal Station* (1983).

It is true that Clift had his limitations: a master at conveying angst, he rarely expresses joy. Yet it is his intelligence about the roles he plays that is now most striking. Lawrence provides plenty of evidence that Clift consistently sought to render the characters he played more ambiguous, more morally unsympathetic. Her attention to his annotations to his scripts reveal what an attentive and intelligent actor he was. He needed that intelligence above all when considering how to use or circumvent the facts of his private life in his public persona on-screen. Yet in the glare of later revelations about that private life, it can at times seem as though all his work can be explained by his concealed passion for men.

Clift could be understood as the American Dirk Bogarde, both being 1950s matinee idols with something to hide. There's the beguiling possibility that had he lived, Clift might have, like Bogarde, started taking roles that drew more directly on his sexual identity. In fact in the film version of Carson McCullers's *Reflections in a Golden Eye* he was due to play the part of married Captain Penderton, sadistically in love with one of his soldiers. But Clift died too soon, and Marlon Brando took the part.

However, such direct approaches to the matter may have been rendered unnecessary by a constant thread of gay subtext in his mainstream Hollywood films. In retrospect, the homosexual innuendoes in *Red River* seem obvious, and *Brokeback Mountain* not as groundbreaking as is sometimes supposed. Likewise, in *I Confess* the notion that Clift's priest and the murderer played by O. E. Hasse are doubled in guilt (the German actor was also gay) is central to an understanding of that film. Moreover, while in his public life he was busy passing as 'straight', in films too he could play someone acting to mislead others, whether in *A Place in the Sun* or *The Heiress*. In those films, he was performing a belonging to a class that would not have him; he was up against the scrutiny of the rich. Olivia de Havilland's gaucheness in *The Heiress* forces him to make the erotic running; in this instance the unconvincing quality of the straight pitch acts as the point. He acts out romance, the smiling charm of his flirtation being inseparable from the possibility that he is laughing at it all.

There is a scene in a teenage girl's bedroom in David Lynch's *Blue Velvet* (1986) where over the phone the high-school heroine (played by Laura Dern) tearfully forgives Jeffrey Beaumont, her erring boyfriend. Above her is a portrait poster of Montgomery Clift, a double for Jeffrey, dreamy with the charm of chaste desire, a sanitized wild one, a complex, divided man to nourish and coddle. Lawrence understands the ironies of this moment, Clift being for her a romantic hero who appears uncomfortable with conventional Hollywood romance. For this reason, he was arguably at his best when freed from the Romeo role. In *Suddenly, Last Summer*, love for him is out of the question, something that makes the transgression of the doctor's professional distance in his few kisses with Elizabeth Taylor doubly uncomfortable, as bad as the possible stain on his priestliness in *I Confess*. Indeed, Hitchcock's film plays with Clift's double-image as matinee idol and serious actor, presented both as the soft-focus lover within the romantic glimmer of Anne Baxter's flashback and as the alert sufferer on display in the rest of the film.

Despite, or perhaps because of his tentative approaches to heterosexual passion, he was often paired with dark, sensual women: Jennifer Jones, Liz Taylor or Joanne Dru (in *Red River*). He was paired too with the most macho of Hollywood actors, John Wayne in *Red River*, Burt Lancaster in *From Here to Eternity* and Clark Gable in *The Misfits*. Clift's self-consciousness in *Red River* prompted Wayne to become a little self-conscious, too, and to investigate his screen image; it was only after seeing *Red River* that John Ford declared to Howard Hawks, 'I had no idea that son-of-a-bitch could act.'

If it now sometimes feels impossible to watch Clift's films without throwing his gayness into the balance of understanding, there were always already other factors obscuring or illuminating his films. Most especially there was that car crash. At first Clift's beauty obscured his acting; later his supposed grotesqueness stole the attention. It can be hard to distinguish artistic curiosity from ghoulishness. In the eyes of some, his suffering body stole the attention, as though he were a man of sorrows. His face did change: a thyroid condition supposedly made his eyes bulge; his eyebrows thickened, giving him a *Thunderbirds* look. He can almost seem a different man. And then there is the wondered-about effects of the car crash itself. The temptation to moralize Clift's accident is evident: he put it down to exhaustion; others have blamed him for being drunk or stoned, or both. It is as though the smash cannot simply be a matter of chance, but must be a punishment, the payback for all that ability, all that beauty. Do we need the wreck that destroyed his life to be the car accident? Yet even setting aside the crash, there are other ways to sermonize about Clift's physical decline. In his diary entry for 24 September 1956, some few months before the accident, Christopher Isherwood already laments Clift's lost looks, putting it down to the ravages of self-indulgence. Indeed, it is hard to shrug off the notion that the face had been ravaged as much by cigarettes and alcohol as by the accident. The booze, the chain-smoking, the prescription pills, the years – it's a wonder he still looked so good.

It seems crass to admit it, but despite the accomplishment of those later films, the loss of Clift's good looks matter. It is of a piece with the palpable melancholy of his last years. His late appearance on the Hy Gardner chat show in January 1963 exemplifies the problem, the lucid self-knowledge punctuated by moments of concealment about drink, about love affairs, that leave the viewer feeling dismal, embarrassed at the lack of connection, the chain-smoking unease. Clift comes across as too bored to be bothered to conceal his own defeat. And yet at this time he was giving performances as great as any he had ever done. He was becoming a brilliant character actor, his death robbing us of the great work he would have done in the 1970s and '80s: Clift didn't live to make his own *The Godfather*.

The role of film star trapped Clift in a contradiction. He was a man burdened by beauty and bound by others' expectations, and yet committed to a very public vanishing act. After all, Clift disappeared twice: there were the last washed-up years between *Freud* (1962) and *The Defector* (1966), but before that came his three-year sabbatical from film at the height of his commercial success. He ended that sabbatical with *Raintree County* (1957): his first line, spoken of himself off-screen, and written by himself, was the revealing 'He's not there.'

Over his career Clift was given to cutting as many of his lines from the script as possible, knowing that in cinema less really is more. The premise of *I Confess*, whereby a priest's vows forbid him from divulging what he has learnt in the confessional, forces him to adopt 'I can't say' as his mantra. Here Clift offers a performance where the actor must constrain his own performance. Deprived of verbal expression, inwardness can only be displayed through the close-up, that treacherous opportunity to read the mind's construction in the face. Some criticized him for this restraint, though this vow of actorly abnegation is the entire point of the film, and even of Clift's *oeuvre* as a whole.

After all, he was an actor who had made a speciality of turning his back on the camera. If Clift sought privacy in the glare of publicity, hiding his sexuality, concealing his drinking, then he was only fooling himself. He ended up seeing the publication of Kenneth

Anger's tacky *Hollywood Babylon* (1965), a book that gloats over the diminutive size of his penis. This would be only an inkling of the revelations to come. He was to be emphatically 'outed', the signs of his inward life emblazoned for the greedy public. He began by manipulating his public image and ended up publicly manipulated. And yet, while among those options for the American victim, Clift may not have been James Dean, he may have been a prototype for Bob Dylan. For metamorphosis was Clift's secret too, ineffability and absence his keynotes, a star reinventing himself, because that was his job.

19

SETSUKO HARA:
THE STILL POINT

From the late 1930s until her death Setsuko Hara was one of Japan's most popular stars, her fame lasting long after her retirement from acting in 1962. As an outsider to Japan and to the Japanese language, I am ignorant, watching Setsuko Hara, of all she might have meant. Most of the films in which she starred are unavailable to me; subtitles convey some residue of all that her words contain; I miss her relation to the mores of her culture; most likely I misread gestures, and fail to comprehend what would have been too obvious for her primary audience to discuss. And yet, nevertheless, she moves and interests me deeply. In considering Japanese, Indian and Chinese films, undoubtedly my own ignorance of the cultures in question forms a barrier. How much of 'the person' on-screen can transcend that barrier? How far can I comprehend? In writing of them – perhaps in writing of anyone – do I appropriate them and so misunderstand them? Though I acknowledge how profoundly culture, politics and social conventions build a film, still I cannot help but believe the movie itself remains available to anyone. Some remnant, perhaps the point itself, is there.

To western audiences, Setsuko Hara is before anything else the 'Noriko' of Yasujiro Ozu's trilogy of films, each of which features a woman of that name. Together they form one of the twentieth-century's greatest works of art, and a substantial part of that greatness is down to the actress at their heart. In films that explore change and tradition, motion and rest, Setsuko Hara is always Noriko – and Noriko is always changing. In *Late Spring* (*Banshun*, 1949), she plays a daughter who resists marriage so she can remain with her widowed father; in *Early Summer* (*Bakushu*, 1951), she is again a daughter, resisting one attempt to arrange a marriage for her, before choosing her own husband, her dead brother's old friend; and in *Tokyo Story* (*Tokyo Monogatori*, 1953), she acts the widowed daughter-in-law, living alone in Tokyo, the only member of the extended family to show her husband's elderly parents any love or respect.

These films are unlike almost everything else in the history of film to that date. Each film takes the time to observe things – a door, a clock – that show themselves in balance. The camera lingers on the room after the people have left or shows the sun asleep in the empty street before a woman runs out into it. Images of stairs, of corridors, of empty rooms build for us a spatially realized world. We understand, just by watching, the way our places frame us, how they occupy us as much as we occupy them. And again, and again, images appear that suggest immobility, but include unresting motion: the sunlit staircase at a railway station where the flowers blow, factory chimneys held in place while smoke billows. Here is motionlessness in motion. *Late Spring*, in particular, unfolds like a ritual of stillness creating moments for the giving and receiving of courtesies.

To paraphrase Virginia Woolf, critics have exerted much effort in the desire to catch Ozu in the act of greatness. Fascinating work has been done, and yet the film goes missing in the analysis of its strange aesthetic. Some have looked down on the apparently simple-minded cinema audience who are busy simply being moved by what's on-screen. It has been imagined that this audience of feelers is too busy emoting to notice the strangeness, the unwontedness of much that Ozu does. Yet the aesthetics, the strangeness, is at the service of feeling itself, complex and overwhelming.

Setsuko Hara's performance enshrines the slippage between surface signs and an imagined interiority. In *Late Spring* Noriko's aunt says to the father, 'but you can't tell how she feels inside'. 'One can never tell,' he replies. Earlier, Noriko calls her uncle 'filthy' and 'foul', yet all the time maintains her polite expression. The rule remains that one must suffer yet smile. The face gives away nothing except that there is an acting self. The subtlest gesture, the smallest change in expression is everything. Such outward signs provide our only way into an inner world, while raising the spectre of the thought that this world is also perhaps only that which exists in these surface signs. Perhaps the film demonstrates and alludes to an interiority, but the surface is all.

In *Late Spring* Noriko and her father go to watch a Noh play, and we in turn watch them watching in a held attentiveness. On stage actors perform their masked, ritualized emotion, and in the audience the father's face is a reciprocal mask, dutiful, exhibiting his honest amusement. Yet the greater wonder is Noriko's expression; we regard the changing sorrows of Hara's face, watching bare feeling and her sadness and resentment and jealousy for Mrs Miwa, the widow that her father may marry. And then there follows a shot, nine seconds long, of some distant trees another tranquillity evoked.

The scene contrasts an art form dependent on artifice with one that values 'naturalness' above all else. On stage, a man plays a woman (an *onnagata*, a Kabuki female impersonator; in Japan men played women on-screen until 1918), while in the audience a woman plays herself. From the start, as in the case of the first Japanese woman film star, Aoki Tsuruko, the unaffected was what was valued in Japanese women stars.[1] Tsuruko was a Japanese woman who made her name in Hollywood, and so it was that Japanese stardom came to Japan via America, and with it arrived a perhaps American ideal of 'authenticity'.

Things change, Ozu's *Late Spring* tells us, but they also changed before. The presence of the war in the years behind this story, these people, remains transformative. The Ozu films, and indeed all the Japanese films of the period, emerge from the national experience of searing defeat. Everyone understood that Japanese society had failed and had to start again; meanwhile the film-makers were trying to establish continuities, while embracing change. These are films that centre on the family, one threatened by social change, and indeed by change itself. Above all, the family stands as an institution designed to frame and temper changefulness while committed to newness and the new generation. It holds together across generations, but in doing so has us encounter unavoidable loss and disappointment.

With its forced labour, its diseases, its destruction, the war interrupted the seemingly timeless world. And now Japan is a new place. In each film of the Noriko trilogy, trains become symbols of uprooted lives in motion. As an occupation-era movie *Late Spring* shows an Americanized Japan, with Coca-Cola signs by the sea and baseball for the kids, and a potential husband who looks like Gary Cooper.

One of the transformations wrought in post-war Japan was a top-down insistence on women's rights.[2] A conflict emerged between tradition and the new independence. As in Jane Austen's novels, though everything in Ozu's trilogy turns on 'marriageability' and family life, some scepticism arises about both. Conventional marriage can seem merely a matter of playing the game: 'All you need to do is smile at him,' we are told. The great film critic and historian Donald Richie reports a conversation with the director Shiro Toyoda:

> I asked why the men were usually such poor actors and why the women were almost invariably so good. He said it was only natural: the Japanese woman from childhood is forced to play a role – more so than in most countries. She is her father's daughter, then her husband's wife, then her son's mother. From the earliest age she learns to mask her true feelings and to counterfeit those she does not feel.[3]

One senses that the resistance to marriage voiced by Noriko reflects its difficulties, how little this institution may have to offer the 'modern woman'. Noriko's rebellions are limited to trying to stay where she is. In *Early Summer* Noriko has collected a thick album of Katharine Hepburn photos. Hearing about this, her boss wonders, 'Is she queer?' Queer or not, in this film Hara as Noriko unmistakably prefers the company of her woman friend to that of some hypothetical husband; that is, until she herself promptly chooses a husband of her own. Resistance crumbles and a new family forms. Setsuko Hara came to be nicknamed 'the eternal virgin', her own real-life resistance to marriage both scandalous and alluring, at a time when single women were looked down on and held in contempt. Both Setsuko Hara and the Noriko she plays move before us as an 'old-fashioned modern girl'; this simultaneity is the paradox she lives.

Marriage is not an individualistic act as in the West, but in the Japan of that moment it is something undertaken in relation to the family. And Setsuko Hara is not an individualistic star. The tombstone on Ozu's grave offers merely 'Mu', the Japanese character for 'Nothing'. There is something similarly elusive, similarly humble about Hara's star persona, something vanishing, something restrained and ungiven in the performance. Yet the person she plays gives everything, indeed more than almost any other actor on-screen. Her voice is perpetually breaking into laughter or tears, but almost never becomes fully either. She is self-absorbed in places and in kinship, and an individualist. For after all, she is a star, an actor. This again is her enacted paradox.

Setsuko Hara played so often the disobediently obedient daughter, the suffering wife. She symbolized stability but also that aspect of the person that is crushed by social conventions, by time itself. Her fate was both gendered, as specifically the woman's lot in Japanese society, and universal. Life, after all, crushes everyone in the end. Ozu shows us what one wants and what one cannot have, whether it is family happiness or a child coveting a 32mm model train track. The young may want everything, but for the old, and perhaps in *Tokyo Story* for Noriko, an unexpected power arises from wanting almost nothing. A strange humility justifies the characters. They enjoy quiet days, in lives marked by marriages, births, looking after the children, a grandparent visiting. Their hopes are modest, their life a sadness accepted. Setsuko Hara acts as the symbol of this residual affirmation, the living point around which things move.

So it is that politics enters into the films, enforcing the circumscription of her life. Yet it is more than a social change that is looked for. There is a longing for quietude, for changelessness. Noriko wants to be with a parent forever and, in that longing, to be happy forever in the way that she is happy now. Yet life will not allow that; in *Tokyo Story* Ozu, through Setsuko Hara, makes a film that seeks the still permanence of the photograph, but cannot find it.

In *Late Spring*, we know that what Noriko wants is wrong and resists life, and is, at worse, though sex is very distant here, a kind of incest. We understand too that her resistance to marriage is not a feminist stand: after all, she chooses one patriarchal servitude over another; she wants to serve. We cannot share her longing, and yet we do share it. We understand her; we too have wanted nothing to change.

Hara's career goes far beyond the three Noriko films, taking in impressive performances in three other Ozu films and also, among many other works, films by Akira Kurosawa and Mikio Naruse, including *Repast* (*Meshi*, 1951) and *Sudden Rain* (*Shuu*, 1956). Her versatility is astonishing. She began as a teenager when in 1935 her brother-in-law, the director Hisatora Kumagi, helped her to a contract with Nikkatsu. In 1937 she appeared in Arnold Fanck's *Die Tochter der Samurai* (1937), a collaboration between Imperial Japan and Nazi Germany. When the war started she was already a star and she went on to play in wartime propaganda films.

Post-war, Setsuko Hara became more rebellious. During the war she had been merely loyal and stoic, but afterwards she took a more 'adversarial', refractory position.[4] In Kurosawa's *No Regrets for Our Youth* (*Waga seishun ni kuinash*, 1946), the director's only film focused on a woman protagonist, she's all energy. She's sulky, skittish, discovering during the film a seriousness and commitment. *No Regrets* was precisely about regret over the Japanese militaristic past, but the title might have cut the other way too, implicitly exonerating Setsuko Hara for her questionable past. It is a powerful performance, totally unlike the Noriko she would soon play, though moral integrity is central here too. She is a well-heeled, well-educated Kyoto girl, given to playing tempestuous bursts of classical piano, who chooses to live with her dead husband's peasant parents and become a farmer. In Kurosawa's adaptation of Dostoevsky's *The Idiot* (*Hakuchi*, 1951), playing Nasu Taeko, the Nastasya Filippovna character of the 'fallen woman', passion is the key. Her ability here to reach a damned intensity, such as when she stares at Ayako, the stubborn, headstrong daughter, shows just how much the Noriko of the Ozu trilogy is a performance. Yet even here for Kurosawa, Setsuko Hara does what she nearly always does: she portrays decency. For in *The Idiot*, the meaning of the film plays on the fact that this fallen woman, this demonic figure, is in essence good.

More than most other actors, Setsuko Hara embodies the idea that film stars themselves are changing and unchanging. The stars are iconic, preserved, but also ageing and endlessly altered. In Ozu's films, in particular, Setsuko Hara makes this truth the intense concern of the film. In her last film for Ozu, *Late Autumn* (*Akibiyori*, 1960), we find the profoundest reflection on the fact of ageing. The film remakes *Late Spring*, but with Setsuko Hara taking the parent's role, a widow (Akiko) – rather than a widower – with a daughter, Ayako (played by Yoko Tsukasa), who refuses to marry. In *Late Spring* the daughter's rival for her father's attention is the widow Mrs Miwa, and here Setsuko Hara is herself a Mrs Miwa, a widow who others want to see wed.

Setsuko Hara, quiet, self-contained, devastated, in *Late Spring* (1949).

The film commences with three men assessing the beauty of women, the men in question being the old friends of Akiko's dead husband. Troubled by the widow's independent beauty and by the reminiscent allure of her daughter, the men decide to set the young girl up. Like Noriko before her, Ayako resists the attempt to marry her off. Unlike Akiko, however, Ayako no longer desires change-lessness, but really resists marriage as such, though motivated too by concern about her mother. Yet Ayako wants a love match, not the match-made marriages arranged by *miai* that had been customary only a few years before.

Everything in *Late Autumn* is vicarious; the characters make matches where they have an interest of their own, whether for the daughter as substitute for the mum, or the mum for the daughter. These schemes are rivalrous fun for the men, who plot together to cement their friendships, giving themselves a project in common and allowing themselves the illusion of power. Their desire for a plot grants the film some narrative purposefulness. It is a story with intention in it. So it is that Ozu here remakes *Late Spring* in part as a comedy; *Late Autumn* is a quietly funny film, comic for those (mostly the men) who are occupied plotting. For those who are the objects of their conspiring, especially Setsuko Hara, there is real confusion and real sadness involved.

Here Setsuko Hara has played three of the roles, both mother and daughter, and indeed also the widow who might marry the parent. When Ozu cast her for *Late Autumn* he was making use of her age, putting the actress in touch with the changefulness brought by time. All that Noriko had resisted in *Late Spring* is here embraced, the fact that in life we must pass through shifting roles, be a daughter, then a mother (as an actress too must play different parts). Setsuko Hara, whose presence had once expressed the future's potential, now possesses a past. The movie insists on her beauty having remained (it truly had), yet still places her ageing before us.

Setsuko Hara is intriguingly marginalized by the plot. Her role is not to understand what her role is. First the trio of middle-aged match-makers are the actors, and then, when they fail in their plot, attention shifts to Ayako's friend Yuriko, played by the gloriously pert Mariko Okada. The young actress is a live wire and by moral force and sheer vitality takes over the film's machinations and schemes. Independent and family-minded, as Noriko once was, she brings the sad, middle-aged men to the restaurant and bar where she is the daughter of the house, while disguising this fact from the men she is entertaining. And then, when the match is made and Ayako married, and the mother turns down her own marriage prospects and returns to widowhood, suddenly we leave the men, we leave Yuriko, and we end with Setsuko Hara again. The melancholy that had lifted from the film reasserts itself. This autumnal masterpiece begins with a memorial and ends with a wedding, one that is also a parting. As Akiko, Setsuko Hara ends the movie alone, smiling and crying, but not crying, caught between emotions in a paradox, forever.

20

TOSHIRO MIFUNE:
STUDYING LIONS

oshiro Mifune never sought to be a film star. When Toho
Studios launched a campaign for 'new faces', friends sent in
his photograph. Ever after there remained something of an
accidental quality to his on-screen presence, a sense of being more
alive than cinema itself. This is not obliquely to belittle Mifune's
acting skills, to join that chorus of voices who only perceive bluster,
misled by his physical force, that baritone bark. From the start he was
a subtle performer and his ability to convey nuances of character
and emotion only grew over the years. Rather there is a feeling of a
man throwing himself into something he had not thought of before
and doing it supremely well. Often, according to the standards of
1950s cinema, Mifune is closer to a mime than a Hollywood actor: he
moves like a dancer, a physical presence on-screen embodying force
and speed. It has been said that when readying himself to play the
peasant samurai in *Seven Samurai* (*Shichinin no samurai*, 1954), he
prepared for the role by going to the zoo to study lions.

If he was discovered once through that Toho talent contest, it was
the second time he was discovered, when he auditioned for Akira
Kurosawa, that made him the most famous Japanese star outside of
Japan. Kurosawa was stunned by the tensed unleashing of rage shown
by the young man that day, a curt capacity strikingly to enact emotion. So present, so dynamic an actor needed a film-maker with as
much restraint and power as Kurosawa unfailingly mustered from

Toshiro Mifune as the bound bandit in Akira Kurosawa's *Rashomon* (1950).

Drunken Angel (*Yoidore tenshi*, 1948) to *Red Beard* (*Akahige*, 1965). In *Drunken Angel* Kurosawa let Mifune overwhelm the movie, claiming the audience's sympathy, unsuppressable.[1]

Kurosawa is a film-maker with punch. There is a sustained fury in his films, an organized passion that fires through them. The film-maker most addicted to visually astounding effects – such as the flights of arrows thudding and splintering the wood around Mifune at the close of *Throne of Blood* (*Kumonosu-jō*, 1957), which were being shot for real at the genuinely terrified actor (both playing fear and experiencing it), and the frenetic, rain-lashed battle of *Seven Samurai*, where in the mud Mifune slashes and stumbles and strikes out at the galloping riders – found the most visually arresting of actors, a man who demands the audience's attention, a person who will not rein himself in. To Kurosawa, a man preoccupied with the experience of men, Mifune became a masculine muse, an image of human possibilities, a sustained exemplar of what it might mean to become adequate as a male.

Kurosawa's reputation is that of the least Japanese of the great Japanese directors, a dynamic creator and not a careful follower of traditions. Yet in *Throne of Blood*, at least, his adaptation of Shakespeare's *Macbeth*, he shows that the 'universal' quality of a classic may mean in practice its ability to become strange to us. For this most 'Western' of Japanese directors produces here the most un-Western film I have ever seen (only Sergei Parajanov's extraordinary *The Color of Pomegranates* (1969) is more foreign to me). Nonetheless, as a consequence of this supposed 'Western' influence, Mifune has been seen by some as an emblem of an Americanized Japanese aesthetic, an individualist in a country committed to conformity and community. It was this perceived individualism that let Mifune seem to outsiders the archetypal, almost the only Japanese star. The star too is, after all, the individual epitomized and the cult of stardom might seem no more than a personality cult. Mifune's personality, his persona in fact, offers us an image of the starkest proportions, a clearly defined, vivid and yet elusive self. Mifune's presence, artfully arrived at, drives most of the films in which he appears. And yet, when it comes to extolling individualism as an ultimate value, it is hard for me to see this as present across the sixteen marvellous films that Kurosawa and Mifune made together. Rather a quiet socialism and a compassionate humanity live at the heart of these films.

Rather than a solipsistic individualist, Mifune played best when he played against another actor. He was a living vehemence looking to find its balance in another. The master–pupil relationships so central to Kurosawa (and to his master, John Ford) were one place where Mifune's intensity could take its stand. In his earlier films Takashi Shimura acts as his guide; later he became the teacher himself, a guardian to the peremptory princess of *The Hidden Fortress* (*Kakushi toride no san akunin*, 1958), to the inept samurai of *Sanjuro* (*Tsubaki Sanjūrō*, 1962), or for the stuck-up young doctor in *Red Beard*. Class tensions entered these last relationships; Mifune is the bluff, honest older man putting privileged youth right.

In Isaiah Berlin's formulation, Shimura might appear a fox in relation to Mifune, the hedgehog, in so far as Shimura palpably could become any kind of person (so much so that sometimes it is literally hard to recognize him across films), whereas Mifune's most famous roles seem variations on the theme of the vagabond warrior. In fact, Mifune's versatility is just as great. In *I Live in Fear* (*Ikimono no kiroku*, 1955), the 35-year-old Mifune makes a creditable job of playing a seventy-year-old man, and even in such apparently similar roles as those he played in *Seven Samurai* and *Yojimbo* (1961), there is a world of difference in the ways that Mifune embodies the person he plays. With one, he bodies forth the insecure aggression of self-doubt, in the other power's un-tensed assurance. More than this, Mifune grew up on-screen; he allowed himself to embody the theme of maturity and acceptance of the world that was so central to his great director's vision. He moves from the callow, insecure hoodlum of *Drunken Angel* to the sturdy, watchful compassion of the doctor in *Red Beard*.

Kurosawa's greatest films pit violence against beauty, savagery against serenity. In *Sanjuro* the protected women sigh over the calm beauty that is genuinely present in that film, as in the camellia blossoms that float down the stream. You remember those blossoms, it is true, but more than that the last moments of the movie linger with you, where Mifune and Tatsuya Nakadai play out one of the tensest showdowns in cinema, a strained abeyance of stillness exploding into a single cut of violent motion, and a sudden spray of blood. A clear-sighted sense of human shabbiness pervades all Kurosawa's movies. Though they inspired the lovable C3PO and R2D2 of *Star Wars*, the peasant farmers of *The Hidden Fortress* are a scruffy, greedy pair, apt to grab the other's share, eager to take turns raping the runaway princess. Yet through that film we find also a humane attempt to transcend egotism and the restrictions put on understanding by social class. The spoilt princess realizes the sufferings of a peasant girl sold into prostitution, and that girl in time will be ready to stand in for the princess. A Dostoyevskian concern with the other, a wish to come into honest relation with another person, suffuses Kurosawa's films, most strongly through the person of a doctor in *Drunken Angel* and *Red Beard*, but in fact distilling itself everywhere.

Shimura is most often Kurosawa's good man, a person trying to attain a humane, spontaneous and compassionate understanding of himself and others. Yet in many films Mifune lived out that pursuit too; in his last film for Kurosawa he effectively takes on the role that Shimura had played in relation to him in *Drunken Angel*. In *Stray Dog* (*Nora inu*, 1949), with Shimura again as a compassionate mentor, Mifune plays a cop whose pistol has been stolen by a desperate criminal, doubling himself in guilt. The distance between the policeman and the criminal shrinks to nothing; both had their knapsack stolen when they left the army, both are left-handed; they are mirrors to each other. To track down his missing gun, Mifune's character plays the down-and-out his adversary has become.

Above all, despite playing a professional vagabond killer for much of his career, Mifune never seems a violent man; he's all force, and no edge. In *Seven Samurai* his killings are either done out of bravado or out of a guilt-ridden grief. He doesn't relish violence as a Lee Marvin, Clint Eastwood or even a Robert De Niro character might; it's just that he's good at it. There is a softness in Mifune and, with the exception of the rapist in *Rashomon* (1950), no matter what role he plays, no matter how gruff or repugnant they seem at first, by the end of the film we have warmed to him. His apartness, even the childlike defeated roundedness in his shoulders, touches us. It is this that guaranteed Mifune's stardom, the fact that through his own artistry and his director's skill, power could transform itself into the lovable.

21

NARGIS AND
RAJ KAPOOR:
MY HEART IS
HINDUSTANI

F ew star couples were as closely bound up in their public's imagination as were Raj Kapoor and Nargis, formative stars of the
Indian film industry in the 1940s and '50s. He was her co-star,
her director and, it would appear, her lover. The films expressed their
intimacy, something also remarked upon in interviews, while they also
publicly denied that anything 'romantic' was going on; they presented
themselves as purely 'close', just good friends.[1] In reality they were
in love, with Nargis eager to marry Kapoor, while Kapoor, who was
already married, hedged his bets and hesitated.[2] He declared that his
wife was his wife, while Nargis was his actress. There was a daring in
their being clandestinely together that was only permissible for great
stars, if it were even permissible for them; Nargis's brother, Akhtar
Hussain, reportedly beat her in an unsuccessful effort to end the two
stars' relationship.[3]

Nargis and Kapoor were likely already lovers before they first
acted together in *Aag* (1948), directed by Kapoor; in all they would
make seventeen films together. Though she had made many other
films before she worked with Kapoor, and also played alongside
Indian cinema's 'tragedy king', Dilip Kumar, it may seem that for a
while Nargis allowed her career to fall into second place in relation
to Kapoor's. In fact, she was just as much of a draw as he was and
regularly had higher billing and wages than the men with whom she
worked.[4]

Both Nargis and Kapoor began their careers as people who had been born into the world of films. Kapoor's father, Prithviraj Kapoor (1906–1972), was his mentor at first; as we will see, in *Awāra* Prithviraj played his real-life son's on-screen father. Nargis was only six years old or so when she made her debut in film. Nargis's mother, Jaddan-bāi, as a *kothewali*, belonged to the world of the professional singer and courtesan, and was herself a significant film actor; in time her mother's life would colour audiences' responses to the daughter's on-screen persona and, more especially, to her off-screen self; respectability would always elude her.[5] Nargis went to the elite St Mary's school in Bombay and had ambitions to become a doctor, before she was waylaid by cinema – and her mother's plans for her.[6] It has even been suggested that her mother sold her daughter's virginity to a Muslim prince.[7] In the 1940s, when Nargis and Kapoor achieved stardom, one strong element in their appeal was the fact of their youth, which was as central to Kapoor as producer, actor and director as it had been to his role model Charlie Chaplin or to Orson Welles. Working with Kapoor was the first time that Nargis had a director of more or less her own age. Being young, they expressed the vibrant hopes of a new nation. Meanwhile, Nargis's vital ability was to enact an extraordinary spontaneity of feeling on film and to stand at once in the audience's mind for opposed and contradictory ideas, possessing especially the ability to seem both 'modern yet pure'.[8]

Perhaps stardom means something slightly different in an Indian context than it does in Hollywood, though the continuities are as striking as the contrasts. Yet Indian films of the 1940s and '50s certainly offer another aesthetic, another way to imagine the human being, and therefore the star themselves. There has often been among critics a condescending view of the classic 'Bollywood' films ('Bollywood' itself being a potentially patronizing designation) as escapist, sentimental, silly and simple.[9] Actually, of course, they are complex and moving works, and entertainingly so. Yes, these 1940s and '50s Hindi films reach for simplicities, telling us such banalities as life is short or that youth passes. Only, of course, these 'banalities' also happen to be unalterable truths. The truisms move us because of their stark veracity, especially in situations where the film explores those artless facts in plots complicated by accident and circumstance.

Kapoor consciously saw himself as making films for the 'common people', making films to entertain the 'common man'.[10] Like Federico Fellini, he was both a fan of the clown and an avid comic-book reader, bringing something of that form's cartoon clarity to his films.[11] His collaborator, Khwaja Ahmad Abbas, the author of Kapoor's great masterpieces *Awāra* (1951) and *Shree 420* (1955), was a neo-realist writer, passionately committed to social realism; their films merrily combine cartoonish fun and realist ardour. It was Abbas who was the leftist, though Kapoor was sympathetic to socialism, and moreover in the early stages of his career never behaved as though as the star he was more important than the other workers on the film, eating his food sitting on the floor with the rest of the crew.[12] Though some demur at the idea as simplistic, Louis Dumont has suggested that in Hindu culture there were two kinds of men: those who live in the world and those who renounce it.[13] For all its naivety the distinction between 'renunciation' and 'worldliness' is in fact central to Kapoor's image of the vagabond, his borrowed and revivified version of Chaplin's Little Tramp. As with Chaplin too, that figure affirms the value of the unofficial and the free.[14] For Chaplin and for Kapoor, finding oneself below the world of economic exploitation is also somehow to stand above it. Opting for comedy enacts the turning-away from the social world of work and money, where promisingly comedic plots appear to turn tragic.

In *Awāra* ('vagabond') this hobo figure is not just a hobo, but a criminal, almost a gangster. *Awāra* is a film about a disrupted and broken family that is itself a family affair, with Prithviraj Kapoor playing the father, a prominent judge, who, because he believes his wife was raped, abandons his son, 'Raj Raghunath', played by his actual son Raj Kapoor. Shashi Kapoor, Prithviraj's youngest son, plays Raj as a child. Thrown into poverty, an enemy of the judge does his best to corrupt young Raj and lead him into a life of crime, doing so as revenge for an unjust ruling against him by the boy's intolerant father. In *Awāra* there is a turn towards a mythic ending through the redemption offered in Indian cinema's first dream sequence. In the end the errant father acknowledges his son, though only after his harshness has first led to pain and rage.

In *Awāra* Nargis plays a lawyer who represents young Raj in court, while also being in love with him, the two having formed an attachment in childhood. She stands out as a person who is both boldly independent and an adherer to traditional hierarchies. She is frankly, and transgressively, in love, and yet ready to accept her lover's brutal authority. On a day out at the seaside, Raj slaps her and she tells him, 'You want to hit me? Go ahead.' (There are indeed as many blows as embraces in Kapoor's love stories; these films are apt to punish Nargis for the very desire she arouses.)

As this might show, *Awāra*'s essence is to be contradictory things at once: a tragedy with stars and a musical with a singing, dancing chorus. Through melodrama, *Awāra* explores the relationship between nature and nurture, arguing that people are made by their environment, by social expectations and by experience. That is the film's theme, but it is not perhaps the element that has most impact on the viewer, who remembers instead the romance between Raj's and Nargis's characters, the songs (written by Shankar Jaikishan) and the scenes of emblematic tragedy.

The huge popularity of *Awāra* and, later, *Shree 420* in Russia and China propelled Kapoor and Nargis to fame throughout the 'second' and 'third' worlds, making them popular in the Middle East, Turkey, Iran, the Eastern bloc and the Soviet Union, and in South Africa and much of West Africa too. Kapoor and Nargis were in part popular in these places because what they were doing was seen to be compatible with the ideal of a socialist film. Their films' caricatures of landlords, exploiters and moneylenders could be enjoyed in Communist nations, even if the films themselves were not exactly Communist. Rather, they evinced a commitment to the people, to the land, to a mythic and transcendent understanding of familiar life.

Kapoor's feeling as a director was for lightness. He attained a very rare balance and poise between music and drama that exceeds in skill that found in the Hollywood musical in the same decades.

With the help of Abbas and the impact of collaboration, he outclasses other film-makers too in marrying a dramatized social conscience with the joy and sorrow, the exhilarations of song. His films point to real poverty via a melodramatic version of living questions and experience. There is a closeness (as in so many of the great film-makers from the 1910s to the '50s) to the exaggerated art of Dickens, and with the same risks of falling into the sentimental or the carica-ture. Like Chaplin, like Fellini, similarly Dickensian artists, he usually sidesteps those risks.

However, in *Aah* (1953), with another director, Raja Nawathe, formerly Kapoor's assistant director, in control, he overbalances and the film can be felt to fail. Inspired by Saratchandra Chattopadhyay's tragic novel *Devdas* (1917), *Aah* nonetheless kicks off with elements of screwball, somewhere between *It Happened One Night* (with his swept-back black hair and his clipped moustache, Kapoor is even a bit of a dead ringer for Clark Gable) and *The Shop Around the Corner* (1940). Kapoor plays an unconventional bourgeois, a rich man of the people dedicated to his socially conscious work on a dam deep in the country. Nargis and Kapoor fall in love by letter, as Nargis's character replies to love letters sent by Raj to her sister, as that sister cannot herself be bothered to respond to a young man so committed to living far from the city, even if her parents have negotiated an arranged marriage between them. As befits any romantic comedy of the period, the more Raj and Neelu try to get away from each, the closer they get. They fall in love with each other's words through let-ters, this being, the film seems to tell us, a way of glimpsing the inner person.

The film depends upon a benign sibling rivalry between Chandra Rai (played by Vijayalaxmi) and her younger sister Neelu Rai (played by Nargis). In parallel with the plot that positions one man in rela-tion to two women, the film shows a strong interest in symmetry in the compositions, presenting the two sisters with Raj between them; this is a movie in which things are in or out of balance. Raj and Neelu's love affair is thrown into doubt when Raj discovers that he has TB. For self-sacrificing reasons he decides to keep this from Neelu and end his relationship with her. Instead he courts Chandra, as their parents had initially arranged.

Neelu appears to us as more humble and romantic than her sister, a contrast that strengthens as the film progresses. Suffering lends depth; that is the affirmation that melodrama offers. Through unrequitedness, one becomes interesting. It is a film of close-ups, particularly of Nargis's face, showing us her abjection. The movie condemns her to silence, to not saying what is going on, while Kapoor lies and lies about himself and his feelings; instead she is made to sing, to be dutiful. The film pointlessly multiplies suffering. Raj is engaged to death, his tuberculosis explaining his apparent heartlessness. *Aah* fared badly at the box office, I would guess likely because Kapoor has to play such a deliberately unattractive figure for so much of the film; too often one forgets that he is being gallant and perceives only his staged insensitivity.

Raj's 'self-sacrifice' feels sadistic, especially as it seems he is punishing Neelu by courting her sister. He doesn't just simply bow out as anyone else might. One suspects that the film reproduces and plays with Nargis's role as mistress, even as it offers a kind of redemptive masochism for Kapoor in creating such a morally suspect and insensitive role for him to play, even if at the end of the film he is then forgiven for everything. Raj plays someone who chooses to be an actor in the situation he is in, just as Neelu writes her letters in Chandra's name. 'Why are you wearing this mask?' Neelu passionately asks him, and the audience wonders with her. He is being 'noble', but meanwhile his acting challenges the very basis of faith; soon there is no place for 'God, truth, or faith' in their lives.

In the film as originally screened, Raj dies while Neelu goes to marry, the bridal party unknowingly passing his body. Desire has led to its punishment, a repeated trope in Kapoor's films, where his yearning hero is scarred (as in *Aag*), imprisoned or left for dead.[15] Sexual longing will receive its comeuppance, hardly an inexplicable fantasy for a married man passionately entangled with his co-star, even as he was also furtively looking elsewhere for still further entanglements. This tragic ending in *Aah* is the version of the movie that audiences rejected; later Kapoor would recall overhearing the people in the auditorium on the opening night and from the 'living, palpitating' atmosphere grasping that the film had failed.[16]

Yet, at the close, in the remade comedic version, in a rebuttal of what the film had so strongly said about the loss of faith, faith is what the film finds. Against all odds, in this revised version Raj and Neelu marry, and Raj is brought back from death and deception to joy. The film's ending is extraordinary, as Raj and Neelu silently watch dancers perform an ancient tale in which Krishna defeats the demon of death. Life rises to the largeness of myth. For the run of the story, with its intimations about their private lives, the stars Kapoor and Nargis are central; but, here at the end, but not for the first time in the film, they are also displaced and put in the position of spectators. They watch with us dances and songs performed by others, just as their own singing voices are dubbed, taking their reality from performances other than their own. Similarly in *Awāra* an anonymous chorus of commentators are not the impersonal figures of the early Hollywood musicals, but people who are powerful and alive in community. The dances are rituals and the songs express greater truths. Unlike anything in the American cinema of the period, the stars regard those truths with us, and the resolution in *Aah* occurs through others, who are anonymous, yet are gods and heroes too.

Nargis and Kapoor had one undoubted masterpiece together ahead of them. *Shree 420* begins with an image of a comic and tragic mask, and as this presages, it will unite those two supposedly opposed modes. A '420' in the Indian Penal Code refers to the crime of cheating, so the title effectively means 'Mr Cheat'. The action of the film strikes a note of national sentiment, as Raj Kapoor plays an optimistic vagabond singing a song of the open road: 'My shoes they are Japanese [*Jāpānī*], my trousers are English [*Inglistānī*], the hat on my head is Russian, but my heart is Hindustani.' He is even more Chaplinesque here than he was in *Awāra*, wearing the mask of a clown and sharing (at first) in the clown's romantic chastity too. Unlike the male heroes in many Indian films of the 1960s, and despite that slap on the beach in *Awāra*, Kapoor was not often sexually virile or commanding, but was rather humorous, humble, even importunate. As I have suggested, there were echoes of Chaplin in this aspect of his persona too, but also elements of what has been named the 'Majnun-lover', 'passive, poetic, and childlike'.[17]

Raj comes to the city and takes to life on the streets. He bumps into Vidya (Nargis), an impoverished slum teacher, in a pawnshop and promptly falls in love with her. In an effort to get enough money for the two of them to marry and have children, he ends up using his prodigious skills at dealing and playing cards for shady confidence tricksters running poker games. After a shaky start he is soon rich, but in the process loses himself and wrecks his relationship with Vidya, who believes that he has taken up with the nightclub singer Maya (played by Nadira). In the end, after an attempt to con the poorest in Bombay society, Raj turns on his fellow deceivers and gets them arrested.

Through all this, as in *Aah*, Nargis must suffer and wait. This can make it seem as though the film offers no significant place for its woman star to act or change the circumstances. In this vein, the women's singing voices in the film, and of the time, are a squeaky fal-setto, a mouse-like trilling that exaggerates the difference between the sexes. Yet as is so often the case in her films, Nargis nonetheless appears strikingly self-determining, even as she remains tied to the end in marriage, her identity something that will only be fulfilled there.

In the fable of the film, it is tempting again to find an allegory of Kapoor's emotional triangle, with vampish Maya (the name meaning 'illusion') standing in for the adulterous Nargis, versus put-upon Vidya (meaning 'true knowledge' or 'clarity' – and, of course, actually played by Nargis) as his long-suffering wife. However, from the mid-1950s Kapoor also started pursuing other women, and his straying affections might in any case have led him to see Nargis as also the deceived and abandoned one. When Nargis as Vidya visits the nightclub world, she dons black to do so. Later, as she pleads for her love, a double-image of herself emerges on-screen, with Nargis there in a gleaming white sari, a dream self, expressive and loving, and her rejected self, judging and alone, in black. As Vidya, Nargis meets her opposite here, with the Jewish actor Nadira playing Maya, the film's femme fatale. Telling Raj that he is not her equal, Maya provides a glimpse of female power, an innovation that is felt within the movie to be transgressive, urban and Westernized. Often Maya dances in Western styles, sometimes evoking a Spanish Carmen, sometimes finding herself in a waltz, or singing to Latin rhythms.

He is playing a cheat, yet still Raj plays a character called 'Raj', as he often does, a rhyme that helps the audience identify the actor with the part they play. Yet Kapoor is also doubled here, more so even than Nargis is in the dream-moment described above. Within the same film, he is both the hapless vagabond and the suave con man in a tuxedo. In one scene, a suited and booted Raj talks to his past self in the mirror, dressed haphazardly there in hand-me-down clothes. 'Raj,' asks Raj, 'where have you disappeared to?' He begins to make money by fraud, that deceit perhaps being an image of the allure of cinema itself; 'you've sold yourself to a tinsel world,' Nargis warns him.

In this film Bombay, as it was then known, thrives as a snare for innocence, a web of selfish corruption. This, like the film industry of the same city, is a world where people are up for sale, where talent, whether for the deception of acting or of card-sharping, makes the person into a commodity.

As ever in the Bombay cinema of the time, the songs channel an emotional overflow and very often are the peak moments of each film. The glorious folly of dance steps into contact with genuine suffering. In *Shree 420* and *Awāra* Raj Kapoor brings dancing in touch with poverty with a spirit and a social conscience that shows up *West Side Story* (1961) for the stylized sentimentality it is. Dance here is the sign of hope amidst the hopelessness.

In the nightclub Raj stands and watches Maya's performance, just another punter unwillingly enchanted. When Raj flees that 'tinsel world' and goes back to the pavement where he once used to sleep, he meets again his fellow destitute friends. As they sing of frustrated love, 'Ramayyaa vastaavayyaa' ('Rama, will you return?'), first Nargis and then Raj become a singer in the song, no longer an observer but a participant. Here, as in *Aah*, Raj comes back from the dead as, apparently gunned down, it turns out he has already replaced the bullets in the pistol with blanks. 'In this nonsensical world,' he tells the crowd that watch his resurrection, 'one has to live by feigning death.' Kapoor represents for us a life force, the irrepressible incarnate.

Few films balance the contrast between pathos and energy so tactfully as Raj Kapoor's. *Shree 420* is circular, its end returning us to its beginning, with Raj once more setting off on the open road; only this time, as at the end of Chaplin's *Modern Times*, he does so with his love beside him, as Nargis joins – and directs – his rambles.

They leave the film together, but their relationship was coming to an end. Without informing her lover, director and co-star, Nargis was about to make a great movie that would also represent her break with Kapoor, a move towards independence in a film that celebrates the newly independent nation. With the star system in India being largely based on very few men (Kapoor, Dilip Kumar, Dev Anand), the women stars were largely seen in relation to them. This was never precisely the case with Nargis, who enjoyed great popularity in her own right, but with *Mother India* (1957), this would certainly and powerfully change.[18] Based on Pearl Buck's novel *The Mother* (1934), Mehboob Khan's *Mother India* ran in Indian cinemas for nearly forty years. Nargis had already performed in Mehboob's *Taqdeer* (*Destiny*, 1943), *'Anmol Ghadi* (Precious Watch, 1946) and *Andāz* (1949). The last of these was her third film alongside Raj Kapoor. Yet it was in *Mother India* that Nargis would attain the weight and force of a symbol of the nation.

Mehboob Khan made films in which the values of the good village confront the corrupt city, but also in which the city opens up the individual to possibilities outlawed in the constricted village. The movie traces the life of Radha, a wife and mother condemned to keep her family and then her whole village together, no matter what the personal cost. The movie encapsulates the personality of Nargis's stardom even as it portrays the abnegation of the personal in favour of the family and the community. India itself is the mother in this film, personified in Nargis's exemplary patience, and yet also the power in the face of which this patience must be exercised.

Romance in the rain between Nargis and Raj Kapoor in *Shree 420* (1955).

At the beginning of the film Nargis's character comes into being with her marriage ceremony; wordless for all the film's opening sequences, she is the reticent object of our gaze, shyly monumental, a Lakshmi bride. The bliss of marriage quickly fades, driven away by money worries, all caused by her mother-in-law mortgaging the land to pay for the senselessly lavish wedding. Again, here her husband strikes her, another instance of the oppression of the world, where her strength is to suffer.

The virtue that the world demands, and that the film affirms, is endurance. 'Because we are born, We must live in the world', one song tells us; 'If life is a poison, We must drink it.' It is difficult to imagine Tin Pan Alley coming out with a similarly stark sentiment. Beyond such stoicism, the film similarly celebrates the fecundity of the earth itself. The fields themselves are India, in one shot the wheat grown literally to the shape of the subcontinent. The film identifies Radha with the earth, and in fact soils her: the first thing we see her do is to smear a clod of earth onto her face, and when she desperately goes to the villainous moneylender and mortgage-holder Lala to give herself to him sexually in payment of the family debt, she first muddies her face. The film gives us a myth of appropriation, with the land stolen by the greedy moneylender, and with the mother's honour needing to be rescued by her son Birju (played by Sunil Dutt), who can only do so as an outlaw. Against that vision of the mortgaged land, the film itself enacts its own form of fertility; in its inordinate length the movie overflows the measure, bringing us the sense of time as Nargis's character remembers some moment now passed, rhymed now with the present scene. (The great length of the Hindi films is not surprising in a culture where plays were traditionally very long, sometimes lasting from 9.30 p.m. to dawn.)[19]

The sexual politics of the film are as muddied as Radha's skin. The husband in this film loses his arms: it is hardly his fault, but it furthers the sense that men here are emasculated, frail, to be supported by the strength of women. The film commodifies a myth of female endurance. In *Mother India* Nargis can both embody innocence and be an object for sexual desire, be young and old, passive and active.

Variety was central to how the public saw Nargis, allowing her to embody many kinds of role, playing the urban *Miss India* (1957) in the same year that she stood as the rural 'Mother India'.[20]

Nargis is the moral centre of the film, and yet for much of its last third she is marginalized as attention turns towards Sunil Dutt's Birju. It is tempting to see in this the coming shift that hit Bombay cinema in the 1960s and thereafter in which that cinema ever more emphatically centred on the male star.[21]

In ways that are apparently simple, but also profoundly resonant, the characters on-screen move us both as their limited selves and also as personifications of greed, of endurance, of revenge. Again, as at the close of *Aah*, a mythological and religious understanding of human life grounds the movie, letting Nargis's character be at once Lakshmi, goddess of beauty, *Dhartī-māta*, Mother Earth, goddess of fecundity, and Radha, the consort of Krishna and goddess of love – as well as being just herself, ordinary Radha, the village woman whose story the film unravels.[22] Similarly Nargis's ('Radha's') sons Ramu and Birju play out the contrast between Ram and Krishna, between patient goodness and impetuous mischief. The mode here is epic, the commonplace person raised to greatness by the perception of the god or goddess that shadows them; the divine appears incarnated in mundane lives.

It is not only that a religious comprehension of events underpins the film, more that its aesthetic strategies involve a sense of the human being as enmeshed in spiritual realities. The apparent instability of the film (and of certain of Raj Kapoor's films too), the mixture of comedy and tragedy, melodrama and farce, of musical and social realism, all point to an essentially large and diverse view of the kind of artistic modes that have to be called upon to depict the human being in their fullness. This expansive sense of the person does seem intrinsic to these films, though it is far from confined to Indian cinema. There are elements of it in Andrei Tarkovsky's pictures, even in John Ford; but only here do we find precisely this kind of mixing, something bound up with the formal practices of these films and not necessarily expressive of a specifically Indian mode of understanding;

other kinds of film were possible in the India of the time, as Satyajit Ray's or Mrinal Sen's works, for instance, show.

In this intensely Hindu film, Nargis acts as a Muslim playing a woman whose identity involves Hindu goddesses. In making films with Kapoor she can be seen to have joined the ranks of Hindu film-makers. By going back to Mehboob Khan as her director she was re-entering the Muslim fold, although in a film that places Hinduism at its centre. It was only truly in the afterlife of the film that Nargis's status as a Muslim began to determine how audiences perceived the movie, especially when her son, the actor Sanjay Dutt, was arrested for terrorist activities that suggested to some that he was a radical Islamic sympathizer.[23]

Sunil Dutt, her co-star and her son in the film, in reality rescued Nargis during a scene involving burning haystacks (in the film's plot she was supposed to be saving him). Kapoor and Nargis did not work together again after the making of *Mother India* and soon after, in March 1958, she married Sunil Dutt. Kapoor was devastated. Thereafter Nargis committed herself to her family, charity work and politics. She was a friend of the Nehru family and of Indira Gandhi, that other 'Mother India'. Nargis later became an MP: in a speech in parliament she denounced Satyajit Ray's *Pather Panchali* (1955) for peddling poverty and a regressive view of India.[24] Some old animosity between an internationally lauded arthouse cinema and a hugely popular but patronized commercial film industry might well have prompted her attack.

Kapoor went on to make a number of great films, notably ones that explored his own persona as on-screen clown, *Mera Naam Joker* (1970) and *Bobby* (1973). Yet nothing he did afterwards was as res-onant as the great films he made with Nargis. They lived on film together in balance, just as the best films they made represent such a balance, unifying in a gloriously shaped muddle both music and a social conscience, tragedy and comedy.

22

GIULIETTA MASINA
AND MARCELLO
MASTROIANNI:
NOTHING IS SADDER
THAN LAUGHTER

Giulietta Masina invites our love; Marcello Mastroianni embodies our desires. In the films that both of them made with Federico Fellini, they incarnate opposite roles, the suffering wife against the deceiving husband, the waif opposed to the wastrel. Together they take possession of some of the most glorious and life-affirming films ever made, as the wife and muse of the director, or otherwise complexly, differently, as his alter ego. Though she appears in a number of his movies, Masina is the heart of three Fellini films: *La Strada* (1954), *Nights of Cabiria* (*Le notti di Cabiria*, 1957) and *Juliet of the Spirits* (*Giulietta degli spiriti*, 1965); Mastroianni is the wandering centre of *La Dolce Vita* (1960), *8½* (*Otto e mezzo*, 1963) and *City of Women* (*La città delle donne*, 1980); and the two appear together at last as a reunited elderly Astaire and Rogers tribute act in *Ginger e Fred* (1986). With Masina in particular, we approach something central to our relation to some of the great stars, the fact that they evoke in us endearment, even love. Fellini's intense affection for Masina pervades these films, much as it pervades those films with Mastroianni where she is ostensibly absent and appears only as a guilt that Fellini has concerning his unfaithfulness towards her. We grow fond of Masina, the films invite us to do so, as we feel for Gelsomina and Cabiria, for Giulietta and Ginger. The love that these films evoke is a kind of knowledge, a way of being engaged with a work of art, with a person.

Several of Fellini's films express their own part naive, part worldly-wise fascination with the movie star. These are films involving stars that are themselves star-struck. In *The White Sheik* (*Lo sceicco bianco*, 1952), an innocent bride would rather adore a portly, flirty and boy-ishly self-satisfied film star than spend her honeymoon with her cautious, self-satisfied new husband. In *Cabiria*, a film star briefly plucks Cabiria from the streets into the realm of chic nightclubs and his out-of-town mansion with champagne, caviar and lobster ('I saw one of these in a movie,' Cabiria declares) served in the master bed-room. In *La Dolce Vita*, Mastroianni pursues Anita Ekberg, in part because she is so beguilingly sexy, but more largely because she *is* Anita Ekberg, a quintessential film star, her fame encouraging him to discount her vapid remarks and scatterbrained indifference. Masina and Mastroianni are stars dazzled by the stardom of others. One of Masina's proudest moments was when, after accepting the Oscar for *Cabiria*, she got Clark Gable's autograph – Gable, the star she had adored on-screen back when she was just a child.

Fellini once laid out the basic requirements for being a film direc-tor. They include curiosity, humility before life, the desire to see everything, laziness, ignorance, indiscipline and independence. While probably all these qualities pervade his films, it is their curiosity and their openness to the world that most enchants you, opening us to, as he once put it, his 'immense faith in things photographed', the sense that film might allow a moment of communion between the viewer and things, between you and a human face.

In his black-and-white films, that almost unparalleled run of masterpieces from *The White Sheik* to *8½*, Fellini stands as the Charles Dickens of cinema. Like Dickens, critics find him sentimental, exag-gerated and chaotic. Where some see sentiment, his lovers perceive a capacity to feel, not for some idealized abstraction, but for this specific character. The outsiders, the marginalized, the victims in life attract him, and he looks at them face to face, never from above, and never from a place removed from their troubling difficulty. He is close to Dickens in pursuing a politics based on gentleness, on the thought that a good society will form when this person here acts justly and tenderly to that person there. As for the exaggeration, like Dickens he actually softens and takes the edge off the unexpectedness and weirdness of others, even as he remains alive to it. When it came to people and to places, Fellini said of himself, 'my capacity for marvelling is boundless . . . I am not blasé about anything.' The chaos is admittedly there, but it is a creative one; Fellini possessed the immense gift of never settling to a fixed view about life. He condemns no one. As he suggested, his films are trials, but as seen by an accomplice, rather than by a judge.

Like Dickens too, he was nourished on a genuinely popular culture: comic strips, *Flash Gordon* and the circus. His cinema belongs to the fairground, not the museum. The comics were a seminal influence: he didn't so much write his films as draw them, making sketches, doodles and designs that would open up their spirit. At the moment where the intellectuals were moving in on that other popular art that is film, his genius was to have such an intelligent, imaginative fullness of response to that common culture, something that enabled him to recast it into some of the greatest works of cinema.

With Masina in particular in mind, it is vital to remember that Fellini worked at first on imagining his films by drawing those caricatures and cartoons. As the heavy-eyed, burdened innocent Gelsomina in *La Strada*, as Cabiria, Masina partakes of some of the static eternity of the comic-strip hero; it is no surprise that Walt Disney sought to make Gelsomina into an animated character, a human companion for the world of Mickey Mouse and Pinocchio. In those early films, Masina's characters attain something of the changelessness of the cartoon figure, sustained in innocence, caught in the firm delineated stance of an attitude, much as Little Orphan Annie wanders the world forever or Charlie Brown will be perpetually eight years old. They are exaggerations, eternal like Dickens's characters, closer to Oliver Twist and Mr Micawber than to the psychological depths of an Emma Bovary or Anna Karenina. So it was that, for different reasons, André Bazin rightly affirmed that 'the Fellinian character is timeless.'[1] In *La Strada* history collides with this timelessness when Gelsomina companion, Zampano the strongman, murders the fool. Unable to

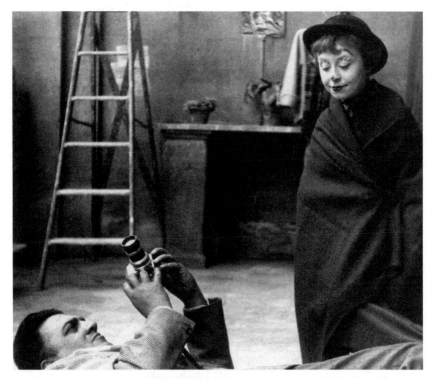

Giulietta Masina with Federico Fellini on the set of *La Strada* (1954).

reconcile herself to this cruelty, she pines away and dies, her natural changelessness irrevocably changed.

Masina reminds us too that the film star is likewise a cartoon. They too, through being memorialized on film, through being so strongly a persona, neither age nor alter. New depths may appear in them, but as stars their image is static – except that Masina and Mastroianni must, like all of us, age. In *Ginger e Fred*, Fellini confronts the transience of the person who coexists with the star persona. That film blazons an Andy Warhol world where fame is democratized and meaningless, the TV studio presenting celebrity lookalikes (doubles for Clark Gable and Kafka bustling together), saints, mafia bosses, musclemen and transvestites, all existing with the same vulgar flatness. In this cheapened world, as genuine performers, 'Ginger' and 'Fred' attain a delicate dignity, even though their own fame likewise merely echoes film stars from an American elsewhere. Stars themselves, though sadly aged,

Masina and Mastroianni here play the role of 'stars', though Masina shows herself as deeply bourgeois and ordinary, Mastroianni as pathetically unruly and boyishly bohemian. And yet when, at last, they dance on stage, the magic of performance lifts them and the genuine lightness and joy of their act transcends the lurid television studio world.

It is odd to remember just how despised Fellini was once, a man found guilty by critics on the left of sullying the doctrinal purity of Italian neo-realism with sentiment and solipsism. Such critics understood art as essentially political (or, now, as essentially 'woke'), a form that either embraced or denied true 'commitment'. For Fellini, however, film meant a free space for fantasy and memory, and a form where fantasy might transform memory into a beguiling and truthful lie. *8½* provides a devious, sidestepping response to his critics, incorporating their adverse readings into the film; 'commitment' is both the film's problem and its hero's, troubled as he is both in his career and his marriage. In a sense, it is Fellini's version of Evelyn Waugh's *The Ordeal of Gilbert Pinfold*, a record of a breakdown that leads to the hearing of many enticing or hostile voices.

Though all art finds its roots in a life, it is remarkable how very few expressly autobiographical film-makers there are: Woody Allen, Andrei Tarkovsky in *Mirror*, Bill Douglas and a handful of others, all recasting their lives as a fiction. As a man often identified with his work, Fellini is perhaps the most notable among this select group. An 'autobiographical vein' runs through many of his films, each one encapsulating a period of his life. Yet no one should think when watching his films that they are learning facts about Fellini. Like Dickens in *David Copperfield*, Fellini transfigures the past (or in the case of *8½*, the present) into artifice, a puppet theatre. He was never one to let the facts stand in the way of a good story. His films charm us with the invention of a life, the marvellous being made otherwise marvellous; not the small truths of anecdote, but the evocation of how it might have been. These films dance around the dividing line between the imagined and the real. In the charming *I Vitelloni* (1953), Ostia stands in for his home town of Rimini and in the process turns nostalgia into a stage set, an improved and refined quintessence of memory.

In his early films, the characters have either the strong simplicity of children or the complexity of the devious; they are either kids or con men. The greatest innocents of all are those played by Giulietta Masina in *La Strada* and *The Nights of Cabiria*. Both films are glorious, and *Cabiria* is certainly one of the five or so films I most love. Here Fellini's comedy, like much great comedy, works by breaking our hearts open and still finding there somewhere the muted capacity for hope. The great problem for Fellini's characters is that of loneliness. Its solution, where it can be contrived to occur, is connection between people, including the most unlikely of pairs. Masina is the soul of these stories, an actor gifted with one of the most expressive and vital faces ever witnessed on-screen. Through her, Fellini expresses his fellow-feeling for the disinherited and the unrespectable. Fellini said of his wife that she embodied his nostalgia for innocence.[2] She is a holy fool in *La Strada* and *Cabiria*, an 'Auguste' clown, a happy hooligan, gifted with rare humility; Cabiria has almost nothing, but believes she has everything; there's nothing she does not have that she wants, except that one impossible thing for her, that is, to receive and to give love. Though Cabiria defends herself against the world through anger, she is ready to experience joy at any moment, exuberance winning out over suspicion; she dances, wildly but, all too often, alone.

Mesmerized by a demonic stage hypnotist, she reveals, as a kind of theatre, her inner longing to be loved. The rough audience of men howls with laughter, ridiculing her. In that scene, even as the film reminds us that Masina is an actor, a performer on a stage, comedy turns on itself. Earlier we had laughed too, but the laughter in the film was always intertwined with affection, with a sympathy that hurts with her. Fellini said of Masina's characters that they are not women, they are asexual, figures beyond or above gender – a remarkable thought given that in *Cabiria* Masina plays a Roman prostitute, though admittedly a rather hapless one.

With *La Dolce Vita* (1960) Fellini's style shifted and we move from artful naivety to a bright, louche and fragmented world, one, as

Fellini himself put it, marked by 'the silence of God'. As a result Masina fell away from the on-screen world and Mastroianni shrugged into her place. When we next see her, in *Juliet of the Spirits*, Masina tries to take her place in this new carnivalesque and abrupt world of late Fellini, and the result is tellingly jarring. Where in *La Dolce Vita* and *8½* Mastroianni negotiates the chaos, charmingly bewildered, Giulietta (actor and part conflated by their sharing a name) is still, hesitant, amused but held back from full involvement in the chaos of images – visions that are both hers and impositions upon her, visitations that she would sooner reject. What was coming into being as 'the Felliniesque' was on the verge of defeating the human element encapsulated in Masina's presence.[3]

There is a book of essays on Fellini from the 1970s where, considering *La Dolce Vita*, the hero's angst is taken very seriously indeed and the movie compared somewhat implausibly with T. S. Eliot's *The Waste Land*. In fact, rarely has the collapse of Western civilization looked such fun: indeed 'fun' is precisely what that civilization collapses into. The film's title, 'the sweet life', is not irony, it is intoxication. More than any other film, *La Dolce Vita* preserves the enchantment of parties, even their enchanted weariness; the film bestows upon us that sense of the possibilities present in an evening out, as well as the light melancholy that falls as the possibilities dwindle. Fellini liked to drive through Rome or walk its streets, glancing at the faces, giving himself to the casual encounter; here too Rome is a place glimpsed in motion, connections forming and falling apart, as the night sobers up with dawn. As the society journalist Marcello, Mastroianni offers us the Italian Cary Grant, a man baffled by his own beauty as well as the essential elusiveness of the women he ineffectually pursues. As an actor, Mastroianni was always at his greatest when the characters he played were at their most unreliable, the incompetence undercutting his debonair handsomeness.

When I first saw *La Dolce Vita*, my first Fellini film, I thought he was a sophisticate; now, years later, I know he was a dreamer. The director's memoir of his illness is replete with reveries; Fellini much admired Carl Jung and it shows. One reason why Fellini cast his

Marcello Mastroianni baffled as Marcello Rubini in *La Dolce Vita* (1960).

wife in his films was Masina's magical 'gift of evoking a kind of waking dream quite spontaneously, as if it were taking place quite outside her own consciousness'.[4] As his career went on, his films became increasingly hallucinatory, in a way not always for the best. In his defence, other kinds of coherence are brought in, a moving away from logic and consequence. In *8½* the balance is still perfect, a film that stands in the uneasy but productive space between fantasy and the real.

It is a fabulously messy film. The eye moves restlessly over things, rarely settling. We are inside a crisis, with apparently nothing noble about it. The film's hero, the harried director Guido Anselmi (played again by Marcello Mastroianni, and clearly a stand-in for Fellini), is as silly, mean, self-regarding and empty as the film itself – and yet, for all that, this same fractured movie is superb. In the relation between the sorriness and the wonderful, *8½* casts its spell.

Ultimately *8½* is a comedy of guilt, of a life riven by untruths. In a double sense, Guido lives in breach of contract. He compromises the deal he has made with his producers, declaring he has a film in hand when truly he has nothing; and, more darkly, he undermines his vow to his wife, by his affair with another woman. A need for naughtiness, for narrative, prompts Guido's adultery; yet also we can see how it is of a piece with an overwhelming tenderness, an aptitude for curiosity about others. The film portrays brilliantly the farcical nature of shame, exposing in Guido's relationship to his mistress his shifty embarrassment, the way he both wants her there and seeks to deny all claim to her. Playing the director's mistress Carla, Sandra Milo grants us the apogee of this comedy of deceit: spotting, as she debonairly approaches, that Guido is in fact at the café table with his wife, she manages to walk in two directions at once, her legs heading leftwards as she darts to the right.

To add to the grubbiness of it all, Sandra Milo was not only Guido's lover in the film, but Fellini's lover in real life. This is only one of the ways in which *8½* draws us into a hall of mirrors, where reality and art prove indistinguishable from each other. We gaze into an endlessly receding abyss, but yet (and this is the miracle of the film) also can perceive how that abyss brims over with abundance. In the end the film seeks to imagine a loving settlement that will fulfil the promises Guido has broken: in spite of everything there is a film; his love for his wife, for everyone it seems, all the puppets he controls, is intact. The guilt doesn't matter, for there is in the end reconciliation. Some might see this resolution as venal and self-serving, using a movie to get oneself off the moral hook. And yet, as it plays on the screen, it also conjures by sleight of hand a release from shame, from doubt.

It is not the anguish, the uncertainty, but the laughter in *8½* that matters, the reflective humour of it. The film closes with a death that appears to end the possibility of Guido's film becoming real. For a moment things pause and there is an atmosphere of wistful farewell. And then Fellini pulls off his masterstroke, reclaiming life as a party, and one to be shared, the momentary establishment of an imagined imaginative space. When Guido and his wife Luisa likewise join the dance that Guido directs, not directing it any more but being a part of it, it proves to be, for me at least, one of the most moving moments in cinema. It recalls what Rilke wrote of Shakespeare's *The Tempest*, describing that moment when the artist-magus pulls a wire through his own head and hangs himself up with the other puppets, and then steps before the audience to take their applause.[5]

At the end of both *Nights of Cabiria* and *Juliet of the Spirits* Masina looks out to us in the audience and walks: in *Cabiria* absorbed and serenaded by a group of shining, guileless schoolchildren, in the latter film alone and towards the woods. Again that last glance in *Cabiria* conjures feeling with an intensity that few other movie-makers reach. Cabiria has been deceived by the man she thought loved her; she has nearly been killed and all the money she has ever earned, through long nights of selling her body, has gone. Here comedy breaks and, as Fellini put it, it tears 'open our most painful scars so that we feel them all the more strongly'.[6] Desolate, she wanders alone through the woods, until she finds herself among those teenage revellers, heading home, singing for her, wishing her goodnight. Summoned from her despair, Cabiria smiles back at them, regaining hope, her face, so defensively tough throughout the film, relaxes, and then she turns to us and offers us another such smile, a contract, a connection, in that glance. The film asks us to decide how it should end, and the responsibility for comedy, and the fate of Cabiria, of this fragile questing person, of this film star, falls into our hands.

23

JOHN WAYNE: HOW TO GROW OLD

O n screen, John Wayne aged by remaining unchanging. In an interview the director Douglas Sirk spoke of the dangers of 'petrification', of giving up on development and the possibility of becoming something new, only at once to declare: 'Wayne is a great actor because he has petrified. He has become a statue.'[1] In John Ford's *The Man Who Shot Liberty Valance* (1962), we are told that despite changes to the small western town, 'the desert's still the same'. Wayne can seem as changeless as that desert, the human embodiment of the essential landscape.

Wayne grew old without growing up, retaining a childlike quality; he had the confident boyishness of the college football star, even forty years on. In *I Am Not Your Negro* (2017), James Baldwin finds the perpetual puerility in Wayne expressive of both a moral and political failure:

> I am speaking as a member of a certain democracy and very complex country which insists on being very narrow-minded. Simplicity is taken to be a great American virtue, along with sincerity. One of the results of this is that immaturity is taken to be a virtue too, so that someone like, let's say, John Wayne, who spent most of his time on-screen admonishing Indians, was in no necessity to grow up.[2]

Yet despite this reading of his affect, Wayne precisely came for some to represent an American maturity: independent, self-reliant, stoic, competent, courteous and murderous.

In the 1960s, as Baldwin's remarks typify, a deep hostility solidified towards Wayne and all that he stood for. Questions around Wayne haven't gone away. In the election year of 2016 Steve Bannon claimed that Donald Trump was 'the John Wayne of politics', an unlikely comparison that might nonetheless trouble some of those who feel affection for Wayne. He was known to be a member of the rightist John Birch Society, a self-described believer in 'white supremacy', a defender of the genocide of the Native American peoples. As the 1960s progressed, the young men he had fostered through film, the young women who had fallen for him, were supposed to reject his proffered frontier wisdom, the stoic assurance of that presence. The propaganda film *The Green Berets* (1968), directed by and starring Wayne, with its sentimentally tough celebration of the war in Vietnam, alienated many; only two years before Dee Brown's *Bury My Heart at Wounded Knee*, there were many ready to prefer Cochise and Geronimo to Wayne's hard-edged heroes. Molly Haskell has written that although other Hollywood stars were similarly right-wing, none got 'under their enemies' skin quite the way Wayne did'.[3] And yet even then, Wayne's allure, the protection he offered, continued to offer a divided appeal. In *Slouching Towards Bethlehem* (1968), Joan Didion affirmed that 'when John Wayne rode through my childhood, and perhaps through yours, he determined forever the shape of certain of our dreams.'[4] Haskell describes 'the time he went to Harvard. The kids, who came to jeer someone they regarded as the Godzilla of American imperialism, stayed to cheer the man . . . "Yeah," he laughed . . . "We stayed up all night drinking. I guess I was the father they never had".'[5]

This big man personified the West, the frontier experience. He did not so much act as simply live on camera, the force of his performance a matter of presence. The immobility of his face – there already in Ford's *Stagecoach* (1939) – was once misunderstood by critics as woodenness. Actually, he's a natural actor, one employing the resource of his virility, his potency. If his face is impassive, then that only deepens the unreadability of the man. Wayne's terse, epigrammatic style signals his stoicism: 'that'll be the day'; '"sorry" don't get it done'. He stands for reticence, an inarticulate hero, and not a talker. He will not tell what's on his mind, what's in his heart. In Wayne, we have what looks natural, and is yet the fashioning of an image. Marion Morrison turns himself, or lets the films turn him, into a symbol, a moving expression of American masculinity and a way of ageing honourably. Wayne's characters belonged to an honour culture, one where a man asserts his own dignity; they adhere to a doctrine of independence. 'Dammit,' the director, Raoul Walsh is said to have said, 'the son of a bitch looked like a man.'[6]

Wayne succeeds purely by 'being there', the power and strength of a real presence on-screen. And yet that presence is not just the recording of something inextricably bound up with the fact of the man himself; it is also a mode of performance, a way of acting. Howard Hawks declared: 'he's a damn good actor. He does everything, and he makes you believe it. He's just a different form of an actor.'[7] As Edward Buscombe puts it, 'He brings to his roles, especially his Western roles, a massive assurance, an indomitable solidity. But it's not true that he simply performs himself, that his screen charisma is just a projection of his real-life persona.'[8]

Wayne can stand up for property, laws, the constitution, and yet his persona embraces all that is independent and free in America's ideal view of itself. He's the embodiment of a law so deeply held that it can look just like a fact of life, part of the tenor of things. Yet ferocity could be felt to lurk in him, even as it coexisted with an old-world courtesy. Wayne embodied American dignity and American violence. From *Stagecoach* on, the morally complex form of the Western always provided a clear window into the American darkness. It makes a space for the irrational and neurotic, with increasing force in the late 1940s and 1950s, a parallel to the darkening of noir.

Until these decades the Western had largely stood as a realm of almost heraldic simplicities, a moral landscape where the good and the bad square up, white hats versus black hats, and all stays firmly in its place, especially the foundational dominion that is America itself. Suddenly in the post-war world only the landscape seemed intact. Now, within this backdrop of the pristine wilderness, new disconcerting complexities became manifest. In this way, neurosis and social disorder itself could ascend to the status of legend, the petty problems of the individual soul raised up into something archetypal.

It is curious that the moral ambiguities and psychological strangeness on display in those films of the 1940s and '50s is largely the province of the middle-aged, present in men and women who had been stars before the Japanese struck Pearl Harbor. So it is that the trail from mythic sanity to mythic disintegration can be tracked most clearly in the careers of the period's two strongest Western stars: James Stewart and John Wayne. Even in his good-natured, all-American-guy phase, in the 1930s and early '40s, Stewart could always tap into an alarming irascibility. Yet watching *Mr Smith Goes to Washington* (1939) or *The Shop Around the Corner* (1940), few could have predicted the rage, the brooding compulsions exposed in *Winchester '73* (1950) or *The Naked Spur* (1953). In Anthony Mann's Westerns, Stewart finds in himself hard-edged selfishness, cruel propensities. John Wayne's descent is even more precipitous. Film-maker, critic and John Ford fan Lindsay Anderson cordially despised John Ford's greatest Western, *The Searchers* (1956). To Anderson that movie betrayed the epic simplicity, the vast decency once central to the genre. John Wayne's solid probity here disintegrates into racist hate and cruelty and an unassimilable apartness. The core of the 'great men' had turned out to be a desperate one indeed.

In *Red River* (1948) and *She Wore a Yellow Ribbon* (1949) Wayne was already playing an old man, taking out his reading glasses in the latter to read a citation. From then on, whether he wanted to or not, Wayne was playing old, perhaps the first of his generation deliberately to do so. Hollywood men more usually clung on to youth, on-screen Dorian Grays, though there were ones who could not, despite the toupees, the sympathetic lighting, hide the fact of their ageing. The ageing juvenile lead was a hangover from theatre traditions that had Henry Irving playing Romeo or Sarah Bernhardt playing young Hamlet in their mid-fifties. Beyond theatre, such casting came up

John Wayne offers an unreadable glance in John Ford's *The Searchers* (1956).

against film's 'realism', or at least its preoccupation with externals. There were other issues involved in middle-aged men continuing to choose young actresses as their romantic partners, including commercial possibilities and male fantasies of an unending attractiveness. Hence, in *The Horse Soldiers* (1959) opposite Constance Towers, or in *Hatari!* (1962), where his character marries Elsa Martinelli, a young Italian more than half his age, directors and producers had Wayne cling on to desire and youth. It was always somewhat the case that due to a perceived awkwardness with women, 'he became a character lead rather than a romantic one.'[9] And so, increasingly, for the most part he does without romance, that staple of Hollywood genre cinema. In *The Searchers* there is no romantic partner for him; he nurtures an impossible love for his brother's wife, soon lost to the ultimate unrequitedness of death; he lives alone. When romance was still on the cards, the power of the man meant that Wayne had to play opposite equally strong women – Maureen O'Hara, Angie Dickinson – people as tough, as competent, as un-self-pitying as he was. This insistent epitome of traditional masculinity needed to be in relation to an equally defined, opposite and only perhaps equal femininity. Wayne is the man of the frontier, the man's man, coming into knowledge of women.

Wayne's ageing began in earnest with *The Searchers*. Here he plays Ethan Edwards, an ex-Confederate soldier bound to track down his niece Debbie, the only survivor of a massacre that claims his brother, his sister-in-law, his nephew and another niece. Debbie has been taken by Scar, a Comanche chief, similarly consumed by a desire for vengeance. Accompanying Ethan/Wayne on the trail is Martin Pawley, a part-Cherokee adopted son in his brother's house, and someone whom Ethan had saved from another massacre when Marty was only a baby.

Making *The Searchers*, Wayne was only 47 when he played Ethan; Jeffrey Hunter as Marty was 31, and Natalie Wood as the abducted Debbie was eighteen. Only the previous year Wood had played opposite James Dean in *Rebel Without a Cause* (1955), establishing herself in the public mind as a troubled teen.

The Searchers' middle section frames Ethan's character. Here in her home, before her family, a young woman and Marty's would-be sweetheart Laurie (Vera Miles) reads a letter from Marty, written in the frontier space. The letter distances Ethan, who has become a problem to his young companion, someone unreadable, unknowable. The frontier itself shares this same elusive quality, where the doubtful signs left by Marty's 'squaw', 'Look', can be read in diverse and contradictory ways. In any case, though Ethan can translate 'Look's' words, Marty understands nothing of her delicate speech. The letter that Marty sends is likewise an act of communication that falls short, upsetting Laurie, the woman who loves him, his meaning mislaid in the poor words he possesses. In such a world, it may be no wonder that Ethan in particular should appear so baffling, so much a problem, his actions things that Marty hasn't 'figured out yet'.

The first word spoken in the film is 'Ethan?', Wayne's character's name instantly put into the interrogative mode. Wayne here is both a mystery and the quintessence of his persona's stoicism, though with a deeper gloom, a fiercer rage than is usually allotted to him. Even with this wrath, he remains a comforting figure too, a good man to have on your side, if not a good man as such. In a tight spot we can rely on this homicidal racist.

In this world pervaded by misunderstandings, Ethan is one of the very few who can interpret all. He speaks Spanish and Comanche fluently; he understands the Comanche culture through an anthropology of hatred; unlike many of the men in the movie, he reads 'real good', both the texts produced by language and civilization, and the tracks and signs left on the trail. His hate for the 'Indians' is a form of attentiveness. He knows to shoot out the eyes of a dead Comanche and that this mutilation will condemn that soul to endless wandering, a deed that both shares in the rules of an alien culture and manifests contempt for it. It is Ethan who sees things, who looks into the burning house and finds the corpses, who comes upon and buries the mutilated unseen body of his abducted young niece Lucy. In her wonderful book *West of Everything*, Jane Tompkins alerts us to the constant presence in the western of mortality, of the dead; it's death that's west of everything.[10] Howard Hawks agrees: 'The western is the simplest form of drama – a gun, death . . .'.[11] This knowledge Ethan keeps. He spares the others, and holds it within himself, bound by self-imposed rules of secrecy: 'What do you want me to do?' he shouts, 'Draw you a picture? Don't ever ask me!'

Like many of the great Westerns, a relationship between an older and a younger man is central here. Jeffrey Hunter's Marty is essentially incompetent, a blunderer, falling over himself. He is maladroit, a maker of mistakes, riding his horse to death, kissing Laurie clumsily, and even failing to protect Debbie adequately at the end. Yet Marty's failure in the frontier space is redeemed by his capacity for love, the only kind of belonging that he can find. At the end old Mose Harper (Hank Worden), the errant frontier holy fool, won't tell Ethan where Debbie is, but happily shares the secret with loving Marty. Marty is an outsider who is an insider by choosing, and Ethan an insider who becomes an outsider by experience. Where Ethan renounces his real relations, Marty choses his kin. Marty believes in a world of shared values, of love, of family. Perhaps, like Marty, Ethan stays on the quest out of love, but in his case it proves to be a dark, obsessive love, and one enmeshed in his greater hatred for 'the Indians'.

The Searchers is a film where the issue at stake is who gets to be understood as 'American'. The Mexicans, the 'Indians', the 'half-breeds', the captive whites whose 'people' are now the Comanche, the assimilating immigrants, the absent African Americans, all represent a divided and unendorsed homeland. Played as he is by John Wayne, that icon of the nation, Ethan seems securely American. His pupil is good-hearted Marty, whom he inducts into the laws of the landscape. His double, however, is Scar the Comanche warrior-chief, united by the mutual hate that is their bond, mirrored in the fact that both have lost their families to massacre.[12] And yet the violence, this race-hatred, the essential isolation of the man is felt to prevent Ethan from joining the new society. He rides the frontier, with the place inside him, in relation to the monumental forms of the American landscape, but an outsider, willed or no, to the settled world that is coming to that landscape, to that place.

Ethan's viciousness is part of a communal violence, a reciprocal deadliness. The Comanche massacre Ethan's family; but then we witness two massacres of Comanche villages by the noble 7th Cavalry. Even sympathetic young Laurie shares Ethan's racist horror of miscegenation, declaring that the Indianized Debbie is better off dead.

In this spirit, Ethan seems set to murder Debbie, but then, in one of cinema's most heartbreaking gestures, just as we think he is going to dash her to the ground and kill her, he picks her up, takes her in his arms and tells her that they are going home. The gesture as he lifts her rhymes with the moment he picked her up when she was a little girl, linking back through time. He cradles her, accepts her and together they return.

At the film's end, though, Ethan, and John Wayne himself perhaps, cannot claim a place even in this compromised society. The frontier space calls for a certain kind of killer, a loner. His actions call back into being a family that was shattered by massacre. But now the frontier is cleared, there is no home for this man in the feminine, domestic, civilized world he has helped to bring to birth. Like the Comanche whose eyes he shot out, Ethan finds himself doomed to wander between the winds. Framed in the doorway, John Wayne turns and walks back out away from the dark cave of home and into the bright dust of the desert. Lindsay Anderson scorned this moment as fake:

> the metaphor is forced. The door swings to, and rounds the story off with perfect symmetry. But of course no one in the drama closes it – why should anyone want to exclude Ethan? – it has to be the hand of an unseen assistant, standing in for the author, that motivates the symbol.[13]

Who, he asks, wants to shut the door on Ethan, who expects him to turn his back? Yet it is the wind that shuts the door and closes the film, not a human gesture but an inevitability, an exclusion just as sure as the turning of the earth.

Wayne's next Western, Howard Hawks's *Rio Bravo* (1959), was an altogether gentler affair. Though not a critical success, it was a hit with the public, who justly warmed to this comfortable, funny, tender film. In some regards it might be thought to meander for all the in-built tension of its plot of a small group of men under siege. Responding to the impact of TV drama, Hawks realized that television was not about plot, but was rather about engagement with characters, the audience just wanting to hang out with these people who are themselves hanging out with each other. In the impermanence of art, the film celebrates the casual joy of being here now, of the moment, though these series of moments are moralized, or authenticated, by an ethic of integrity, honesty, having 'guts'.

Here, with the ageing Wayne at its heart, the movie shows four generations of men interacting together, supporting each other, being friends: there is Walter Brennan (64), Wayne (who was 51), Dean Martin (42), and that restless kid, Ricky Nelson (a mere eighteen years old). They are trapped together in the jailhouse, guarding their prisoner, but this claustrophobic space is both an entrapment and a refuge for those with self-respect. Here they are, or will prove themselves to be, good enough. Wayne's role is the pivot, as he stands here as the older man rescuing and supporting his sidekick, the alcoholic Dude (Dean Martin).

In the wonderful scene where the four men play music and listen to each other (only Wayne watching, not joining in, though undoubtedly still part of their harmony), song summons up concord and unity, even as the two singers, the old crooner Martin and the young rocker Nelson compete and harmonize, while old Walter Brennan nods along, and Wayne watches. Four generations of men coalesce around the music and around Wayne as leader. The moment brings a relaxed delight to them, to us. Outside this circle of respect lurk those whom the group dismisses. Solidarity is here, and there is no world beyond, just a characterless mass of gawpers.

In *Rio Bravo*, playing opposite the wonderful Angie Dickinson as 'Feathers', a showgirl and card sharp trying to survive in the West, the contradictions of Wayne's relation to his leading lady are at their starkest and at their most charming. Inept in matters of love, here Wayne can seem fond, gentle, even cuddly, his strength turning to a masterful and still maternal solicitude, carrying Feathers protectively up the stairs. Angie Dickinson was a mere 26 years old, but to any viewer she's the one making the running here. Her throaty voice speaks of experience, recalling Lauren Bacall. Like all of Hawks's heroines, she is both an independent creature and a 'man's woman', physical, daring and confident. Their strengths are parallel, their capacity for vulnerability mutual. There is no doubt that midway through the film Chance and Feathers make love. Soon she is protecting Chance/Wayne too, someone to watch over him. It is because she chooses to stay, because she helps, that they fall for each other. For Hawks, the woman enjoys a kind of dominance, pursuing and making fools of the men. In *Only Angels Have Wings* (1939), *To Have and Have Not* (1944) and *Rio Bravo*, the leading woman delivers the same line: 'I'm hard to get. All you have to do is ask me.' She will capitulate to the man who capitulates to her; love here is mutual service.[14] It's a world without marriage, where relatedness is spontaneous and unframed, and ad hoc commitments come and go, a world where happiness carries traces either of a thin melancholy or a joyous freedom – you decide which.

Yet, lover as he is, Wayne was still busy ageing on-screen. *Rio Bravo* gives us bodies to stare at, the sweaty, trembling, dusty, greasy, stinky, decrepit body. From Stumpy's (Walter Brennan's) limp, through Dude's (Dean Martin's) suffering stench and his shakes, to Wayne's middle-aged potbelly, each appears sympathetically weak. These are not supermen, but people who really might require each other's help. After *The Man Who Shot Liberty Valance* Wayne no longer, as Howard Hawks put it, moved like a big cat, but became paunchy and stiff.[15] He's the bass note in this bitterly unembittered lament, this elegy for the West and for old Hollywood. In Henry Hathaway's *True Grit* (1969) he is a fat old man, one beyond flirtation, moving from a father figure to a grandfatherly one, though he also stands in for Kim Darby's murdered father.

Don Siegel's *The Shootist* (1976) was Wayne's last movie and something of a self-conscious coda to a life on film. The movie begins with memories of its hero, John Bernard Books, where the images of the hero's early life derive from footage of the young John Wayne, those black-and-white films standing in for a man's lost past. Death shadows the film, with Books, as Wayne was, stricken with cancer. Actors who had played alongside Wayne through his career reappear, like echoes, like nemeses: from *The Man Who Shot Liberty Valance*, James Stewart plays the doctor who diagnoses him with cancer; from the long-ago *Stagecoach*, John Carradine plays the undertaker who'll bury him. The elegiac note is clear; 'we all have our time', and Wayne's, and Books's, and the West's, and the Western's, are all together one. Death challenges the hero's fabled self-sufficiency.

And yet even here, close to the end of things, Wayne seems undiminished. His life spent on film might be thought to have splintered into a hundred or more transitory flickers. And yet, in fact, he achieves a sublunary permanence, as unchangeable in his changing as the desert beyond. This star, this man of the West, cohered across the years, a role model, a partial personification of one of the myriad things the nation stood for, a role model, a treachery, the ongoing, timebound persona for one kind of America.

24

AUDREY HEPBURN: FRANKENSTEIN'S CREATURE

s her 1964 movie *Paris When It Sizzles* explicitly informs us, Audrey Hepburn's persona was often that of Frankenstein's creature, an artless, blank, dreamy sprite of a girl conjured into something extraordinary by an older man. One of the premises of her early films, amazingly enough, was that Hepburn was a plain Jane, a kid with a funny face, awaiting the moment when the camera (controlled of course by a man) would reveal her womanly beauty. So it is with Billy Wilder's *Sabrina* (1954), with Jo Stockton in Stanley Donen's *Funny Face* (1957), with Eliza Doolittle in *My Fair Lady* (1964). Elsewhere she was sometimes accorded the right to remake herself: a virginal music student inventing a counterlife as a philandering femme fatale in Wilder's *Love in the Afternoon* (1957); barefoot waif Lula-Mae Barnes metamorphosing into a metropolitan Huckleberry-sophisticate in *Breakfast at Tiffany's* (1961); or collaborating on the script of her creation in *Paris When It Sizzles*.

When she made her great 'debut' in *Roman Holiday* (1953), her previous films hardly mattering, she embodied a new genre of beauty. In the era of the buxom, she revived the fortunes of the gamine. Still, her beauty is taken to be hidden, her nature disguised. Hepburn's transformations show her becoming fashionable – the rough clay of her face transmuted through the remoulding of externals. Her 'interesting' face is one that the screen both loves and wishes to show as peculiarly in need of transformation. As Pauline Kael said of *Roman*

Holiday, there comes a moment when William Wyler suddenly finds the radiance in her face.[1] We know she's beautiful at once, but in the culture of the period, the other characters in the films are in doubt concerning her attractiveness – it takes the eye of a photographer or an artist (Dick Avery in *Funny Face*) to perceive her attraction. Her films are not ignorant of these processes. In such sweetly throwaway songs as 'On How to Be Lovely', an ostensible exposure of the way fashion mythologizes beauty, *Funny Face* celebrates the 'beauty myth' even as it refutes it.

Audrey Hepburn was so often a person discovered through metamorphosis, becoming what she originally did not appear to be. It was her fate to be manipulated, whether by Gregory Peck's journalist on-the-make in *Roman Holiday*, or by Professor Henry Higgins, or by *Funny Face*'s Dick Avery and *Quality* magazine, or in *Sabrina* by the wealthy Larrabee family. How often in the songs in *Funny Face* her singing consists of echoing the singing of others, even as she finds in the songs some space for her own voice. She is a girl who, it would seem, can stand in need of a Svengali.

The sometimes hard-to-take age differences between herself and her leading men intensify this Svengali effect; Humphrey Bogart and Fred Astaire were even born at the end of the century before her. In *Funny Face* Astaire does his best not to look like a lecherous old man by being absolutely attentive to Hepburn as only a photographic image, while not apparently noticing her as a woman with a body, or indeed as a person at all. In *Love in the Afternoon*, as the ageing seducer, Frank Flannagan, the film cannot escape the sad wreck of the once intensely beautiful Gary Cooper's face. It does all it can to circumvent the fact – the Vaseline on the camera lens, the use of shadow – but there it is, an instance for some of a movie wrecked by its casting.

At least in *Funny Face* Hepburn is as much remade by a woman as a man for, among all her older men, there stands one significant older woman, the extraordinary Kay Thompson as Maggie Prescott, *Funny Face*'s imperious woman fashion magazine editor, the proto-version of Anna Wintour. Thompson is in control, a person who rises above her own hype. She is not interested in marriage, but is still there joining in the fun, enjoying independence. As such she embodies another kind of possibility, one outside the conventional formation of the happy couple.

This most beautiful of women can even (like Joan Fontaine in *Letter from an Unknown Woman* (1948) and Greer Garson in *Random Harvest* (1942)) hide in plain view. In both of Hepburn's films for Wilder, Hepburn's character begins by hiding (up a tree, behind her cello, washing her hair, behind a wall). In *Love in the Afternoon*, others hide too: the jealous husband, the errant wife behind the veil, her private detective father snooping. In these Billy Wilder movies, Hepburn's characters likewise reveal themselves to be people who might be forgotten, as when David Larrabee (William Holden) cannot recognize Sabrina when he meets her at the train station, or when Frank Flannagan can't quite recollect her face or recall her name (he never heard it) when they chance upon each other at the opera.

Ostensibly, at least, despite his age, in *Love in the Afternoon* it is Gary Cooper that the film wishes to gaze at, and young music student Ariane, as played by Hepburn, is happy to be the one who gazes. Her father lives as a professional voyeur, a spy on the lives of others who ultimately will be invited to spy on his own daughter. She is apparently poised to follow in his footsteps. From her room in the apartment to the balcony at the opera, she's constantly on watch over another. That the Gary Cooper who is the object of her gaze is himself so worn, so aged and still so busy watching other women himself is one of the paradoxes involved in the thin rewards that watching offers Ariane. (The film is elsewhere determined to show Cooper's continuing vigour; we are not allowed to suspect that the star is anything but virile. In connection to the picture, asked if Cooper worried about the age difference, Wilder declared, 'No. He could have fucked anybody he wanted.')[2]

The key to Hepburn's films, and one of their pleasures, is discovering how much autonomy the young actor can find within the process of transformation. In *Sabrina* she leaves behind the baron who supports her and in *Funny Face* outgrows Dick Avery even as she takes direction from him, ending by giving direction to herself.

Becoming 'beautiful', becoming an actor, becoming a woman, she is a compromised innocent caught in the machinations of the marriage plot. In fact, one of her roles, though I hope not the chief one, is to render back love and innocence to an older man, turning inveterate bachelors back into marriageable men.

In her aptness for metamorphosis Hepburn was a creature of the city, almost always at her best in urban films. In *Roman Holiday* or *Sabrina* or *Breakfast at Tiffany's*, she expresses that myth of the self-transformation that the city can enable. In *Breakfast at Tiffany's*, Southern 'white trash' Lula Mae Barnes may refigure herself as the effortlessly elegant Holly Golightly. She makes herself subject to the city's possibilities, and exploitative of them too. Like Cary Grant, another urban creature, Audrey Hepburn's voice was curiously unplaceable. It is a classless property, mostly understood as purely not American. Her voice is another thing that is there to be transformed: the Southern accent displaced in *Breakfast at Tiffany's*; the raucous cockney made over into an (over-dubbed) light opera singer in *My Fair Lady*.

Her films are a series of awakenings, repeated manifestations of the adolescent drama of entering the world. *Roman Holiday* initiates the myth by showing it in reverse: she becomes the princess who turns herself into a Cinderella, before renouncing her new-found ordinariness in favour of duty. The transformation means losing the prince (Gregory Peck as a grubby journalist, who due to the reversal is a humble commoner). Her proper fate is to become an 'actor' in the world and not simply an observer of it; as Sabrina puts it, 'I have learned how to live, how to be in the world and of the world, and not just to stand aside and watch.' As such young Hepburn's a hopeful version of filmgoers themselves, one who hopes, by proxy, to launch into the realm they have until now merely regarded. Some may feel that her transitions merely take her to a state where she leaves the public realm again, locked down in the position of regal duty or domestic marriage. My own sense of things is more optimistic; at the close of most her early films, it is hard to believe that she won't maintain forever the flourishing that the movie has witnessed.

Audrey Hepburn, overlooked in the foyer, in *Love in the Afternoon* (1957).

When Hepburn ceases to be an observer, then she must become a manipulator herself, trying in *Sabrina* to seduce David while he is engaged ('you probably want to kiss me'), turning herself into a fantasizing liar in *Love in the Afternoon,* or, in *Roman Holiday*, an economist with the truth. *Love in the Afternoon* exposes the fact that men and women lie to each other: wives deceive husbands; husbands cheat on their wives. Like all Wilder's films, it is a worldly affair. It takes pleasure in unmaking romantic clichés that it also draws upon. Hepburn must be like the others. In *Sabrina*, everyone is knowing: 'What rhymes with glass,' ponders David Larrabee, wounded in the tush by two shattered champagne glasses left in his back pockets. In *Roman Holiday* she's as understandably reluctant as the journalist Gregory Peck is to place her hand into the Mouth of Truth (the Bocca della Verità), given that it will bite off the hands of a liar. Though her lies feel brilliantly white ones, nonetheless the world unveils itself as a place where everyone deceives everyone else. To win is to stop playing the game, or to allow oneself to be outwitted. Undoubtedly there is a mythic naivety about Hepburn's persona, and she's another Candide, a 'Huckleberry friend', negotiating the compromised world.

Yet she cannot come across as too cynical. In *Sabrina* Wilder largely sidesteps the potential tensions around class and money. Humphrey Bogart enacts the benevolent, hardworking millionaire, one who, in the end, will put personal relations above finances. Sabrina herself can never be felt to be a gold-digger, someone in love with one Larrabee son after another, simply because they are rich. Nonetheless ultimately the Audrey Hepburn character is not a simple innocent abroad. Though she may be a manipulator, she is an entranced one. In *Sabrina* she is so in love with David and with her new-found sexual power as to turn the consciousness of that power into a kind of innocence – into wide-eyed, smiling, amused, bemused fun.

In *Love in the Afternoon*, a man faces her, it first seems, too insubstantial in his commitments to undergo any awakening himself. Frank Flannagan (Gary Cooper) is an individual caught up in the repetition of seduction, in a film happy to repeat itself too – playing over and over the succession of sequestered afternoons, playing over and over the same gypsy music, playing over and over Ariane's recorded list of seductions. Cooper, or Flannagan, is essentially a flirt; seriousness eludes him. In this film much hangs on the characters' relation to music: with Ariane a serious player of serious music, and Flannagan a cynical user of it, indifferent to its greater pull, employing the gypsy band as a clichéd aphrodisiac. The music student Ariane is constantly leaving her cello behind, as though its demands were something she wanted to forget. With its trip to the Paris Opéra, the film includes – and resists – the Wagnerian intoxication of *Tristan*; it is much more attuned to the Viennese schmaltz of the tune called 'Fascination', the repetitive, lulling earworm that the gypsies play to seal the deal of seduction.

It is Mozart who's in play here, not tragic Wagner. Mirroring Flannagan's flickering persona, Ariane transforms herself. She becomes for him a female 'Don Juan', someone as given to impermanence as himself. Here she is a fantasist who imagines herself and then enforces that imagination on others. She remains innocent, and yet subverts the idea of that innocence through the force of her fantasy. The ease with which she plays the part of Don Giovanni shows how much that part is already an element of her fantasy life. She finds herself in the mirror of the male Don Juan. Like her father, she has been Frank Flannagan's Leporello, the keeper of the list of his conquests, all set out in her private detective father's dossier. Returning the compliment, Flannagan becomes in time *her* Leporello, playing over and over the spoken list of her imaginary suitors. In the end, as her father balances the two files, Flannagan's and hers, it turns out that her list of imaginary figures adds up to one – her helpless love for Flannagan himself.

Hepburn's Ariane has approached life through texts, what are to her the 'romances' recorded in her father's sordid files. She will now attempt to live these romances in her real life. To her father, the stories in the files are repugnant accounts of real events (in which he takes a perverse but professional pleasure); for Ariane, they are fantastic tales of a distant world. To her, they whisper of romance.

In fantasizing herself as a Don Juan, Ariane becomes exactly the kind of woman Frank would love; in other words, she becomes a mirror of him. In her list of lovers, in her endlessly deferred revelation of the self, she's a Scheherazade entrancing the murderous Sheikh with stories; she's an inventor of a world (even if it's a world she's already found in the texts of her father's files). Like Tony Curtis in *Some Like It Hot* playing 'Shell Oil', or Monroe in *The Seven Year Itch* as 'The Girl', as 'The Thin Girl' Hepburn may embody her lover's fantasy. The film lets us imagine that she's the seductress she pretends to be. It is all but a precursor to Bernardo Bertolucci's *Last Tango in Paris*, another film where two people in Paris, one without a name, meet day after day to make love. Yet as Ariane, Hepburn remains indefatigably innocent; Flannagan laments that for all her numerous lovers, he himself hasn't even 'got to first base' with her.

Hepburn's persona was often wistfully pre-sexual. In *Funny Face* she declares, 'I don't want to be kissed by you, by anyone.' Billy Wilder said of her, 'I don't think she exudes a long sexual history. She was *Miss Audrey Hepburn.*' *Love in the Afternoon* contrives to make a young woman who meets a man every afternoon (apparently) for anonymous sex appear innocent. When Cooper works his way down a line of hotel employees, tipping each generously, and comes to Hepburn and hesitates with his money, the film flirts with the possibility that she might look no more than a prostitute. (There is a similar moment of confusion in *Roman Holiday*, where, having spent the night in his room, the cash-less princess asks Gregory Peck for a loan and the scandalized landlord darkly misinterprets the transaction.)

In *Love in the Afternoon* Hepburn takes her stand as a committed lover who must portray herself as a Don Giovanni in order to win love. Seriously involved, she must appear to turn love into a game. Though she's too young for that game, and he's too old, one pleasure of the film is the pleasure they both take in the play they make together, their sense of fun, their winking at each other. Its beauty is that, though it is Cooper who makes the move, they are both prepared to abandon the game and become serious players.

As Ariane, Hepburn's identity remains unfixed. She changes herself by putting on the clothes of more urbane women: another woman's veil, a different woman's ermine coat. Dressed as them, she can perform a version of the 'mature' femininity she hankers to embody, an absurdly enchanted courtly instance of womanly sophistication (bowing to the gypsies as she steps in, clad in her white fur coat). Her name is her own secret and all we know is that it begins with an 'A'. She's not 'Adolf'; she's 'Ann-nonymous'. If the film taps into fairy tale here, it is as a version of 'Rumpelstiltskin' and not the usual 'Cinderella'. One of the 'As' that Flannagan cannot guess is 'Audrey', the one most apparent to us, who see the real person – the star persona – concealed in the role.

There is sometimes a rage nowadays, a fury of disappointment, about the women of the past and the compromises they lived. The great women stars now may seem collusive sell-outs in a male-organized game. Their 'innocence' has become ignorance, their agency a deception. Naivety has a rough time these days, being generally thought to be only incapacity and gullibility. Few credit that innocence might also be a power. Sometimes little credit is granted to the ways in which the women stars and the parts they played parlayed their way through the social structures that framed their lives, sometimes finding the possibility of personhood in them. Something ought, I believe, to be granted to their struggles, their aliveness, their 'charm' – even though 'charm' itself can be viewed as a delimiting imposition, a public fraud.

Some readings of old films focus on the 'nothing-buttery' conclusion (to borrow Mary Midgeley's phrase) that all that was ever on display in classic Hollywood cinema was either power or its briefly licensed subversion, a simple empowerment or disempowerment. This may seem a ghastly flattening of distinctions and differences, both moral and aesthetic, the same critical card trick endlessly performed. Every story from the past becomes the same story. We fall into the most homogenized and limiting binary relation of all, that between enlightened now and the benighted otherness of the past.

Beyond the suspect fantasies of late middle-aged male sexual renewal, Hepburn played alongside such older men in part at least because her style of acting was more in keeping with the still-working male stars of the 1930s and '40s than it was with that of her contemporaries, Clift or Brando or Dean. She shared much more the lightness, the ironic artlessness of a Fred Astaire or a Cary Grant than the intensities of the Actors' Studio generation. Hepburn could be 'natural' while clearly contriving naturalness. The irony in her, which keeps the films she is in at a respectful distance, is not postmodern or cynical, not exhausted; it is light, playful, a way of being simultaneously in a film and outside it, utterly heartfelt and happy to be ridiculous. This is the irony that springs from a curious innocence. Her self is a winning joke that she herself earnestly plays.

In 1964 the film critic Simon Brett summed up Audrey Hepburn's essential conundrum: 'The chief characteristic of her skill is its apparent absence.' Hepburn lives as the shimmering embodiment of the essential unreality of classical Hollywood films. What is curious and so wonderful is how much this unreality engages and moves us. In *Funny Face* Hepburn's character Jo Stockton is a follower of 'empathicalism', a philosophy based on empathy, even as she herself stands for the feeling person with whom the viewer (of any age or gender) is invited to empathize.

Her films, and Hepburn herself, manifest their strong link to fairy tale and to comedy. Given their immersion in natural artifice, both Marilyn Monroe and Audrey Hepburn were at their best in comedies. When placed inside a tragedy, the fiction of the star disturbingly glamorizes suffering. In comedy that fiction creates an image of a brighter, more beautiful, ideal world, and the image in the cave shows as more enticingly beautiful than what lies outside. The feeling of dissatisfaction with one's own life that Hollywood can promote only finds its justification as comedy. Here the stars and the films they inhabit reveal the perfection of art, which reflects a truth about existing, without resembling life. Again and again Hepburn stands by the strength of her humour, her knowing involvement in her roles.

Her work can hardly be praised enough. In it lives one of the great interpreters of Hollywood film, and one of the brightest incarnations of the life of the star.

25

MARILYN MONROE:
THE SUFFERING STAR

Back in 1959, hearing that Billy Wilder was making a comedy that started with murders, the great producer David O. Selznick prophesied, 'They're going to walk out in *droves!*' The first test screening seemed to prove him right. Playing to a middle-aged, small-town audience, people stayed silent, some shuffled in their seats, and some indeed walked out. One person laughed, once. *Some Like It Hot* nearly died there, doomed to be buried and forgotten. At Wilder's insistence, they tried again, playing the film to a largely student crowd in a college town. They loved it. And most who see it have loved it ever since.

That first uncomprehending audience had a right to be thrown. The cross-dressing at the film's heart seemingly offered the wrong kind of daydream. Its early scenes bring in something genuinely grim; it's startling when a comedy includes the machine-gunning of a man pleading for his life. There is a rift of darkness here, from the genre-threatening killings to the passingly mentioned story of the woman who slashed her wrists when Valentino died. (There are suicide attempts in so many of Wilder's films, from *Sunset Boulevard* to *The Apartment*.) Yet it will turn out that this self-destructive woman provides the keynote to the film's love affair with fantasy, and with that fantasized person, the movie star, personified by the strongest fantasy of all, Marilyn Monroe.

Some Like It Hot begins as a strange pastiche, more *Scarface* than *Sabrina*, with George Raft ('Spats' Colombo) reprising his time as a hard-boiled 1930s gangster. By accident two burlesque musicians, Joe (Tony Curtis) and Jerry (Jack Lemmon), witness Colombo's Valentine's Day Massacre of his rival's gang. Desperate to avoid being the mobster's next victims, they run off, drag up and join an all-girl band, Sweet Sue and the Society Syncopators, headed for three weeks at Miami Beach. Joe becomes Josephine and Jerry transforms into Daphne. In disguise, Joe falls for the band's singer, Sugar Kowalczyk, aka 'Sugar Kane', played by Marilyn Monroe. Once in Florida, Sugar intends to marry rich. Aided by some slumber-party revelations, Joe decides to disguise himself as just the right kind of millionaire for her, the gentle, bespectacled son and heir of Shell Oil.

In the film it is suggested that you may prefer things classical, or like them hot; Wilder's film achieves both. A comedy of errors and cross-dressing, it is closer to Plautus than to Judd Apatow, formally perfect, yet suffused with all Hollywood's vivid vulgarity. Watching such very familiar classic films you may feel the movie has become its own tribute act, the audience hitting the punchlines one beat ahead of the performers. But the greatest films – *Some Like It Hot* among them – smash their own icon; every time I see it, there's a freshness about it that won't stale, a tautness that will not sag.

Wilder's films often leave us with the taste of a sugared cynicism, sweet and sour.[1] Yet among all his films, *Some Like It Hot* most radiates a knowing exuberance; the characters party, run, race on bicycles, slap the bass (and don't pluck it), dance, throw balls, fall over, tango till dawn and, by sheer force of energy, escape. Its great symbol is the sleepover party that takes place in the railway couchette, one that begins small and keeps growing exponentially, the narrow bed filled to overflowing with more and then still more women. Once it grabs hold of you, the laughter in the film doesn't let you go. There are a few islands of stillness in the mayhem, between Josephine and Sugar in the train's washroom, or between Shell Oil and Sugar on the yacht. These pauses of intimacy give space to a love story that proceeds almost entirely through pretence. Around them an inner vitality brightens the screen, a magnificently anarchic staving off of the threatening world.

Set in 1929, the scriptwriters Wilder and I.A.L. Diamond tease out the ironies of history. It's Gatsby's decade, an oasis of dreaming. Sugar Kane is on the hunt for millionaires, not realizing that they are an endangered species, with the Wall Street Crash only months away. A black-and-white nostalgia suffuses the film, offering a backward glance to the world of Wilder's own youth. Back there, in the days before his flight from Europe to America, there has not yet been a Great Depression, an *Anschluss*, an Auschwitz.

American dreamers beguiled the downbeat, worldly-wise, Viennese Billy Wilder. His films mark the clash that comes when a fantasist confronts a cynic, a battle in which the sceptic tends to succumb, won over or worn down by the power of dreaming. In his tales there are so many visionaries of private life, from *Sunset Boulevard*'s Norma Desmond, sealed off in a fantasy of her silent-film stardom, to *Love in the Afternoon*'s would-be female Don Juan.

Some Like It Hot has its dreamers too, not least the gangsters, self-mythologizers caught up in a vision of themselves as immaculate killers. With their sharp suits and their enacted machismo, they set up a strong version of maleness to counterpoint the film's preoccupation with an enacted femininity. With George Raft playing mob-leader 'Spats' Colombo, reprising his early 1930s roles as a tough guy, the film reveals itself as pastiche, though one in love with cinema's, and America's, past. In homage to James Cagney's breakfast-table ferocity in *The Public Enemy* (1931), Raft even threatens a henchman with a grapefruit. Parody makes it a film about films; though more vitally, it is also a film about performing the self, and therefore about the fate of the film star.

For the greatest dreamer of all is Monroe. She was more than just a dreamer for herself, she was a dream for others, an embodied reverie, apt for desire, available for imitation. In his next film, the even greater *The Apartment* (1960), Wilder joked about this fact, having one of his seedy insurance workers pick up a 'real Marilyn Monroe' in a bar. In *Some Like It Hot* Monroe's iconic position as all-American scapegoat is in play; as she sings 'I'm Through with Love', Sugar's heart breaks, but the shadowy hotel guests are dancing anyway, oblivious. Sugar's persona contains a quality of beleaguered innocence, such that no one suspects or condemns her gold-digging, the plan being too fanciful, too unworldly to look sinister.

On-screen, Monroe was unique yet generic, individual and anonymous. For seven years or so she had been merely the quintessential blonde, and even here was an invented woman, 'Sugar Kane'. In Wilder's *The Seven Year Itch* (1955) there are two dreamers, not just vole-faced Tom Ewell, but Marilyn Monroe, 'The Girl' herself (she never assumes the fixity of a name). It might appear that, as in Howard Hawks's *Monkey Business* (1952), she's no more here than the embodied answer to another person's mid-life crisis. Instead in *The Seven Year Itch*, though she would seem a shadow of other people's desires, she is brimful with yearnings of her own, for elegance, for sophistication, for New York. She is a blonde Holly Golightly in her first month in Manhattan. Monroe was yet another version of the Hollywood Cinderella, a myth of ordinariness transmuted, Norma Jeane Mortenson, the abused and abandoned child, metamorphosed into an icon of glamour.

In a sense, as Molly Haskell has suggested, Monroe is *Some Like It Hot's* third female impersonator.[2] She enacts beauty as advertised. You might not want to be her, to adopt so strong a version of what the world imagined men would like to imagine. Yet, as Jacqueline Rose has persuasively argued, her uniquely fragile impersonation of the fantasy woman itself could act as an exposure of the fantasy's limitations, its essential unreality.[3] Her palpable vulnerability, her actual intelligence, her quality of suffering undermined the enticing sheen of the image. Responsibility crept into the proffered irresponsibility of sex. And that sheen could be felt to assume its status as an artifice. For there was always something ostentatiously made-up about Monroe; in *Monkey Business* Ginger Rogers threatens her, 'I'll pull your blonde hair out by its black roots!' Wilder wondered 'whether Marilyn is a person at all or one of the greatest DuPont products ever invented'.[4] In a well-known anecdote, one of Monroe's personal assistants has recounted being on the street with the star, and how the two of them were able to walk obscurely and unnoticed. And then Monroe turned to her and said, 'Shall I be Marilyn?' In an instant, she switched on the persona, and promptly was mobbed by the crowd. Often overlooked on set, passed by on the street, Norma Jeane could assume the guise of 'Marilyn' and suddenly claim everyone's attention. Ever since her breakthrough film, Howard Hawks's *Gentlemen Prefer Blondes* (1953), where Monroe's persona emerges fully formed in an after-echo of Anita Loos's ingénue flapper, Lorelei Lee, Monroe was sealed, or sealed herself, into the glorious unreality of comedy. *Niagara* from the same year shows that Monroe could play drama. Nonetheless, though intelligent herself, she was condemned to play dumb ('just stupid, I guess'), though in doing so she proved herself as great a comedienne as anyone of her era.

By 1959 Monroe seemed lost in the uncertain ground between being an actor, a private person whose life was the subject of public knowledge and a 'sex symbol'. Tony Curtis discourteously declared that kissing Monroe had been like kissing Hitler. Perhaps there was some animus there, brought on by his co-star's unprofessional behaviour, but more than that it seems now a statement about just how far this particular woman had been transmuted into a quintessence of fame, an icon. In the end that icon would become imbued with the process of its own defeat. Ageing forms the subject of *The Misfits* (1961), as present in Montgomery Clift's face and Clark Gable's as it is in Monroe's. By now, by then, the stars are in decline.

Once again playing an unregarded girl on the make, in *Some Like It Hot* Monroe nevertheless fills the film with the alluring sheen of 'the star'. We all know that these actors are workers in 'the dream factory'. So it is that when Joe impersonates his anhedonic tycoon, he adopts Cary Grant's voice as disguise ('Nobody talks like that,' protests Jerry); it is an entirely fitting mask, the man becoming the movie star all men wanted to be, in order to woo the movie star that all men were supposed to adore. And meanwhile Jerry becomes Marilyn, turning himself from a neurotic bull-fiddle player into a gold-digging blonde temptress.

All this playing with Hollywood's pipe dreams makes perfect sense in a film whose ultimate subject is the illusoriness of love.

Wilder and Diamond explore the thought that when we fall in love with someone, we really fall for an image of our own making. Osgood, the satchel-mouthed genuine millionaire, worships Daphne, who only exists as a performance; Sugar adores 'Shell Oil', a figment of her own imagination impersonated by someone who's peeked backstage at her dreams. Finally, there's the audience too, smitten by the delectable shadows of the silver screen – just like that suicidal woman, unable to live on in a world without Rudolph Valentino. The illusions of love merge with the illusion of the film star.

Marilyn Monroe.

Cross-dressing brings in that same question about illusion, asking us if we desire the surface or the essence. The great Hollywood stars performed gender for us, inscribing it as a shimmer of gestures, in stories that held up an illusory world. On film, transvestism is the apotheosis of acting, and a symbol of performance's ability to shake up the rigidities of the social world. In earlier movies, transvestism merely reveals an assertion of essence. Discussing Greta Garbo's cross-dressing in *Queen Christina* (1933), Roland Barthes writes how through it all Garbo remains Garbo. When, in *I Was a Male War Bride* (1949), Cary Grant dons women's clothes, the joke is that he doesn't cease for a moment to be a very obviously male Cary Grant. Yet in *Some Like It Hot* cross-dressing might really invoke the possibility of becoming another. Jerry begins by having to remind himself that he's supposed to be a girl, and ends by trying to convince himself that he's a boy: 'I'm a boy, I'm a boy, I'm a boy,' he mournfully repeats. It is vital to the movie's power that Josephine and Daphne should really be like other people, that, for moments at least, their male selves (even the actors' selves) might be lost.

For the joke to work there has to be a good enough reason for them to don women's clothes. In the film it is based on, the German comedy *Fanfaren der Liebe* (1951), itself based on a French movie from 1935, it is down to simple economic necessity. Wilder and Diamond felt something more desperate was needed, and so the gangsters had to come in. If film creates narrative and identity from fragments and cuts, then the key cut in *Some Like It Hot* is the one that takes us from typical boys, Joe and Jerry, to the two of them teetering down the railway platform as high-heeled women. One of the jokes is that they are the band's most ladylike members. When he first puts on high heels Jerry staggers and stumbles, but by the film's end he is so used to them that he forgets he is even wearing a pair. With his pretty boy looks, cross-dressing suited Tony Curtis, whose first ever acting role had been playing a girl in am-dram. Through the film, Tony Curtis, the philandering wise guy, divides himself in two, becoming both an understanding woman and an ineffectual, impotent 'millionaire'. Both roles manifest previously unexplored aspects of himself, other versions of a person he might also be. In play, an actor's identity is in someone else. Joe's philandering self was anyway also a performance, as we watch him acting out his charm to get his way.

As Shell Oil, Curtis/Joe plays a frigid man, a move that forces Monroe/Sugar to be the active partner. That works as a joke about Monroe's universal desirability, something that Curtis pretends to be proof to. Yet few films are so upfront about the audience's desire to gaze at a woman's body. Curiously it feels precisely a matter of the audience's desire and not the film's (or the director's – as it might in a Hitchcock film). The film gives us what it supposes we want, lingering on Monroe's bottom and hips, or flirting with the possibility of showing us her bosom. ('I couldn't aspire to anything higher', she sings, lifting herself up towards the edge of a light that would expose her diaphanously half-covered breasts to our clear view.) Yet this gaze is not so much lascivious as essentially thwarted. In this regard, Curtis's faux-impotence exposes a crisis in the man's ability to respond to such desire, a mirrored vulnerability in relation to it.

In a strange development of the experiences of that weirdly humourless first test audience, I once met a young man who also refused to laugh at *Some Like It Hot*. By a wonderful paradox, he was a student. Curiously his immunity to the film had a political basis; he viewed it as a sham act of subversion, an apparent exposure of the artifice of gender roles that, in the end, settles down to reinforce the status quo.

Well, perhaps. Yet for its time, near the end of the film Josephine's 'lesbian' kiss of a startled Marilyn was a daring gesture. Moreover, a doctrinally motivated resistance to the film misses out on its capacity for chaos, its wit, its pleasure. Wilder and Diamond celebrate the comic ability both to get into trouble but also absurdly to get out of it, to defeat death, to defeat defeat, and then to make your escape. The film asserts its own vitality against mortality, as with its garish party blaring on behind the hushed funeral parlour. After all it begins with a massacre on Valentine's Day, and thereafter holds to that strange conjunction of murder and love. Moreover, in the end it endorses, as all Wilder's films do, a limited but humane decency. And the film's last line offers a way out of the conundrums of gender politics, and also provides an escape from the fear that desire itself is a delusion. When Osgood refuses to stop loving feisty young Daphne, despite the fact she drinks, flirts and cannot have children, even though, finally, she is a man ('Nobody's perfect'), the film beautifully shows us a real person lovable behind the facade. This millionaire doesn't love Daphne for her assumed womanliness, he loves her for something he has glimpsed in her – the Norma Jeane in the Marilyn, the unguessed at, but recognized, heart.

26

JUANITA MOORE AND
SUSAN KOHNER:
IMITATION OF LIFE

Douglas Sirk's *Imitation of Life* (1959) tells several stories at once. Its apparent main thread concerns the history of Lora Meredith, played by Lana Turner, then one of America's most beloved film stars. Widowed Lora, with her daughter Susie (Sandra Dee), finds renown as a star of the theatre. In gaining the world of theatrical fame, she loses her own soul, cutting herself off from her daughter and sabotaging her love affair with advertising executive (and would-be photographer) Steve Archer (played by John Gavin). However, this is a film with a double plot, with a pair of seeming supporting roles played by second-tier names, not stars, but character actors. In this plot an African American woman, Annie, played by Juanita Moore, also in lone charge of a daughter, Sarah Jane (played, in her adult guise, by Susan Kohner), befriends Lora and comes to live with her. Annie becomes an indispensable member of Lora's household, the hub around which the turmoil and ambition turn. However, Sarah Jane, a light-skinned child (her father, we are told, was 'practically white'), hates the fact that she is 'black' and conspires to pass as a young white woman, rejecting in the process all ties to her plainly black mother. Sirk takes this subplot and makes it the centre of our attention: the supporting actors become the main show, the people we remember, the fates with which we most sympathize. He draws our gaze from the star roles to the 'interesting parts'.[1] The film both treasures and dethrones its star, drawing our attention to the people on the margins of American success that Hollywood films so often neglected to notice, the maids, the chorus girls, those who are not 'white'.

Here ostentation and glamour, all that most characterizes the 1950s Hollywood film (Jean-Louis' costumes for Lana Turner at that point were the most expensive ever made), becomes distraction, like the diamonds that cascade downwards in the opening titles, glimmering and blocking the view. That opening glitter immediately gives way to shots of Coney Island beach in the summer of 1947, the brilliant colours preserving what is still a documentary view, with Lana Turner having lost herself and her daughter in the holiday crowds. When John Gavin's photographer takes a snap of Turner, she's just an anonymous face, though his camera's lens, like Sirk's, picks her out for our curious stare. 'My camera,' Gavin's character tells her, 'could easily have a love affair with you.' We soon learn that Lana Turner's great desire is precisely to be 'seen', to leave the mass and engross our attention.

Turner's character is an actor in a film who perpetually invites us to see the practice of everyday life as anyway a performance. Gavin and Turner go for lunch at a theatre hang-out, and Gavin wonders, 'Is everyone in here an actor?' If so, Turner is the only one in whom he believes. Turner will soon show herself again to be a convincing actor, lying her way through an audition, making herself be believable; the sleazy agent tells her, 'You were pretty good. You lied. All actresses lie. But I believed you.' (For Annie, however, 'it's a sin to be ashamed of what you are. And it's even worse to pretend, to lie.') Lora misses the audition to play Blanche DuBois in Tennessee Williams's 'new play', *A Streetcar Named Desire*, but in effect she'll play aspects of that role for the rest of the film, an ageing American dreamer clinging to the dream.

So far Turner has made the running of the film, and the whole thing appears to be playing out like an addendum to *A Star Is Born*, a Technicolor reprise of *All About Eve*. She's a woman busy trying to remake the world in the image of her dream about it. And then about halfway through things shift. Turner finds her longed-for notoriety and assumes her place in fame's unreal realm. If one stopped the treadmill of success, she would 'be sure to find out how sad [she] really is'. She competes with her daughter for John Gavin's affections, while her modern desire for independent success conflicts with her boyfriend's conventional wish to be a bourgeois husband. She is a modern woman, a free agent, and someone committed to herself; the others in her life orbit around her, supportive, reflective, at the edge of the picture. Meanwhile our attention wanders to adolescent Sarah Jane's sardonic anger and to Annie's saintly patience in response to it. These are the two conductors around which the film's energy now pulses. Kohner is all seductive energy, all restlessness, all performance. She runs, hides, she mocks and imitates, she pretends. And Juanita Moore incarnates a stoic stillness, her face and voice encapsulating an acceptance of suffering, the embrace of an enduring, rejected love.

The film counts the cost of what it means to be black in this white-dominated society. It is no surprise that Sarah Jane should resist the narrow role that the world has allotted her. Annie sighs, 'How do you explain to your child, she was born to be hurt', a lament to which the film can provide no answer. 'Was Jesus white or black?' the child Sarah Jane asks; as a real man, not a pretend one, he must be one or the other, defined by the same binary relation that defines everyone else in 1950s USA. Unlike in John Stahl's original film version (1934), it may complicate matters more than slightly that the actor playing the Sarah Jane character, this young woman who acts out of her race, is not in fact 'black'. Kohner is half-Jewish, half-Hispanic, and so she passes as one who passes. (Ironically, Fredi Washington, who took the role in the earlier movie, found her career short-circuited by the fact that she refused to 'pass', while being considered too light-skinned to play African American characters.)

Kohner and Moore are as remarkable as each other, each playing the film in a different key, in counter-tempo. Kohner forcefully refuses discrimination, while recognizing its supposed immovability. She plays the system, and in doing so tacitly accepts its premises. She blames her mother for her boyfriend's vicious racism; all would be different if only she were not 'black'. She refuses her social role by making a role of her own. In one moment, she sarcastically impersonates a southern slave, 'toting', and in doing so confronts Lora/Lana with the accusation that Annie is her slave. Sarah Jane's 'liberation' from the ties of kinship, from her connection to her mother, involves another kind of constriction, as she remakes herself as a slave of gender roles, a vaudeville performer flirting with septuagenarian punters at a seedy New York burlesque bar, or as one of the anonymous chorus girls in a Los Angeles vaudeville. She's playing sexy; she's a rebel who conforms. Her self-directed life founds itself on a lie concerning her origins. Annie asks her if she is happy, and Sarah Jane replies, 'I'm somebody else. I'm white,' and the audience may wonder to what extent she has answered her mother's question. She is as much of an actor as Lana Turner, but she, being different, will never play the star.

A moment of troubled compassion between Susan Kohner and Juanita Moore in Douglas Sirk's *Imitation of Life* (1959).

The mother acquiesces in the fantasy out of love. She's dying anyway, and her death and funeral are what close the film, in scenes that are designed to break our hearts. 'Our wedding day and the day we die are the great events of life,' murmurs Annie. It is over-the-top, it is melodrama, but it moves us. The artifice makes us weep; we know that it is all faked, merely a lie, and yet it is possible for us to believe in it.

Near the end Lora and the audience simultaneously discover that Annie has many friends. It is a surprise to us and a shock to her, and in this instant the film summons up all that until now has failed to be included in it. We glimpse a life for Annie beyond her relation to Lora and to Sarah Jane, and depths and connections hitherto undisclosed show her in a fuller reality. Above all, it reminds us how Annie, with her avoidance of the limelight, adhered to a life based on associations and kinship, on love and selflessness. For her, selfhood is not something made up, something performed, it is a world of relations into which one is born and which one forges through life. At the funeral Annie and Juanita Moore are centre stage at last, and yet wholly absent, the heart of the event and hidden away forever. All that remains of the vanished person are the people gathered who in life defined her. Too late, Sarah Jane acknowledges the pull of such connections, claiming the mother she had denied.

Douglas Sirk was that rare phenomenon, an intellectual movie-maker: an acquaintance of Bertolt Brecht, an attendee at Einstein's lectures in Berlin, a man with theories and concepts, a film-maker who approached film with the same concerns as the 1970s critics who eulogized him.[2] It is typical of him therefore that he took from Euripides the notion of a false happy ending, finishing his films in such a way that they feel unfinished, the Hollywood optimism undercut by loose ends and a sense of an arbitrary joy.[3] *Imitation of Life* summons up energies and complexities that it cannot in the end bring to rest, and in doing so it questions, as powerfully as any film ever has, the centre stage pre-eminence of the shallow star.

NEW WAVE STARS

27

JANET LEIGH
AND TIPPI HEDREN:
TORTURING THE
AUDIENCE

Alfred Hitchcock's *Psycho* (1960) and *The Birds* (1963) deal two death blows to the old cinema of coherence, their violence erasing a moral and aesthetic consensus. Above all, these films similarly enact a homicidal assault on the woman star and on the concept of stardom itself.

After *Psycho*, the Motion Picture Production Code, which had maintained the limits of the 'family film', looked in tatters. When audiences first saw the brutal shower scene, with its unprovoked murder of Janet Leigh, the film's heroine and its female star, people fainted, ran out shrieking, or walked out shocked; the realist photographer WeeGee recorded people screaming at a performance, even being given first aid. Coming to the film now, with its reputation preceding it, many find the moment anticlimactic. Has the film lost its power to shock?

In one sense, it may have. Horror films in particular are prone to upping the ante in terms of taboo-breaking; to viewers accustomed to 'torture-porn', *Psycho* may look comically tame. Moreover, Hitchcock's techniques have become clichés: what was novel can appear tired.

Yet even without its original visceral terror, the film remains hugely powerful. Particularly, as the critic Raymond Bellour has suggested, the film shatters a primary rule of storytelling: its end refuses to connect with its beginning.[1] This is one reason why Hitchcock insisted that audiences must watch the film from start to finish, so they might endure the full impact of the tear that shreds his film.

Hitchcock's take on the decline of the Hollywood star was to engineer such a star's death or, at least, her torture; to make us identify with gentle, lost Marion Crane (played by the lovable Janet Leigh), in order then to remove her from us and have her inexplicably, chaotically killed. In her place, we are given a shrewd detective (also killed) and a bland questing couple (impossible to like) looking for the missing Marion, played by the brusquely stolid John Gavin as her lover (Hitchcock nicknamed him 'The Stiff') and a lost Vera Miles as her sister. But strangest of all, the movie invites us to identify with Norman Bates (Anthony Perkins), a character as broken in two as the film in which he appears, a double man, between old and young, female and male, victim and killer. Yet everyone we sympathize with, even murderous Norman, is taken from us.

The duality in Norman finds its mirror image in a doubled America. After the Technicolor gloss of *Vertigo* (1958) and the fabulous *North by Northwest* (1959), *Psycho* has the unspectacular dullness, the low-budget anonymous look of the TV shows that Hitchcock was making at the time. This television world is commensurate with a modern, soulless America of hotels, motels and highways, a white-tiled, pre-fabricated, functional and chilling place. Yet the TV look, the black-and-white documentary feel of the film finds its dark shadow in its pull towards the Grand Guignol. The flat motel building where Marion meets her meaningless death is literally overshadowed by Norman's childhood home, all Californian Gothic, where the Victorian domestic meets Dracula's castle. In the midst of shiny modernity, the past remains to haunt and possess the present.

Psycho does all it can to conceal the split in Norman from us. On one level the film is an enormous practical joke (such as its director adored), a magician's act of misdirection; it misleads us about the value of the stolen money that apparently launches the film's plot, but that turns out to mean nothing, and dupes us about the identity of the crazed killer who haunts it. If it is a joke, then the film dwindles to the 'bit of fun' that Hitchcock sometimes declared it to be; a macabre comedy, a ruse to delude the viewers. The camera becomes a wilful deceiver.

A pensive Janet Leigh as Marion Crane in Alfred Hitchcock's *Psycho* (1960).

Yet *Psycho* impresses us as more than that. Partly that is due to the perfections of its style, its classical surface that favours – in this film given to savage explosions of hectic violence – a nervy stillness. How often the camera presents two people mirrored across the frame, static; or cut apart from each other in isolating reaction shots. Both kinds of image foster a dark immobility in the film, a perverse and isolated quiet.

Tippi Hedren contemplates as the crows gather in Alfred Hitchcock's *The Birds* (1963).

The Bates motel and house stand like places in a nightmare; the highway has moved away; the house lingers on. The spookiest moments in the film are now those indications of a morbid inertia – as Vera Miles wanders the deserted rooms, taking in the mother's heavy Victorian bedroom, the son's childhood room, with its melancholy, unhappy toys.

Psycho remains proudly, even aggressively, a shocker. Its relation to its viewers is a curious one; its scriptwriter Joseph Stefano asserted that for the entire second half of the film the intention was simply to 'torture the audience'.[2] This must refer in part to our status as dupes of the trick the film wishes to pull, but also to a desire to rub our noses in our own voyeurism. Norman likes to peek and so, the film suggests, do we. When Norman pulls back a picture of 'Susannah and the Elders' in order to stare through a peephole at Marion undressing, and so at famous Janet Leigh undressing too, this is the first moment that the film leaves her point of view; it does so, so that we can gaze at her as she strips for her shower. At least as far back as *Saboteur* (1942) Hitchcock had displayed an ambivalent attitude to the punters he entertained. That earlier film included an extraordinary moment, designed to unnerve its cinema audience, in which a villain at Radio City Music Hall randomly fires through the screen at another cinema audience. In part at least, *Psycho* seems another such assault. It subverts the comfortable expectations of the cinema-goer, yet nonetheless plagues them with a vision of their own desires, including the desire to assault the star: the old fan magazine adoration turned aggressive, the resentments of the mass – of men – laid bare. We want stars, so it gives us one; tacitly we want them hurt, and so it kills her too.

Hitchcock's next film *The Birds* perpetrates a further offence against the woman star, and therefore against stardom as such. In *Vertigo* Hitchcock had reflected on his desire to transform a woman into a fantasy of his own projection, a screen on to which his (and our) desires could be projected. Here, with Tippi Hedren as Melanie Daniels, he took things a stage further. First, he transformed a model into a movie star (Hitchcock and his wife had first spotted Hedren doing a commercial for Pet Milk), remoulding her into another version of the immaculate, cool, elegant blonde, only then systematically to rip that elegance apart. Speaking of the strangeness of being a star, Marilyn Monroe remarked that it was unnerving when people who did not know you loved you, for they could hate you just as easily with the same lack of reason. Hitchcock had long built up a reputation for sophistication and glamour; now *Psycho* and *The Birds* viciously did the dirt on the movie star's confected allure. Both films expose, uncomfortably, the hostilities that lurk in the audience's relation to the cinematic icon. Where Fellini loves his people, even the most idiotic, the most compromised, simply glad that the world should contain them, Hitchcock manifests something like real hatred in these films, victimizing the women, these stars, while on some level he at once objectifies and identifies with them.

As Melanie Daniels, Tippi Hedren offers us the modern woman as the quintessence of civilized artifice; her gestures, her make-up, her clothes, even perhaps herself, a matter of publicity. If the film assails her for those qualities, it is itself embroiled in them, being a masterpiece of artificiality, a world constructed from sodium vapour process matte shots, and highly stylized acting. (Melanie's mimed reaction shots to a coming explosion are as unnatural and extreme as Kabuki theatre.) Yet into this artful construction intrude the birds themselves, actors without wills, or consciousness, only in possession of instinct and a perverse collective impulse. These animals represent the mass, the death of the individual. The attacking birds have no care for the single life within the flock. Under their assault, lives seem meaningless, the ego shaken by that unavoidable offence of mortality.

Such resentment as is clearly directed towards its leading lady is perhaps only the most intense expression of the film's desire to show the civilized world as a precarious place. Once the birds start to attack human beings, things quickly fall apart. Melanie and the man she loves, his sister and his mother form an improvised domesticity; but the home they hide in is also a trap, a besieged and oppressive place. The key is turned on their uncertainty. Memories of Hitchcock's visit to London during the Blitz, when he cowered under attack while in Claridge's hotel, are to be found in these dark scenes, as is the fear of nuclear war (the film was shot during the Cuban Missile Crisis).

The Birds was perhaps the last film that Jean Cocteau ever saw. We know that he adored its strange atmosphere, seeing it not as a failed kind of science fiction, or even a disaster movie, but as an experience framed like a dark dream. In that case, it might harken back to some of the great American films that preceded it. But in fact its weird perplexing narrative conveyed, just as much as the crack at the centre of *Psycho*, a contempt for traditional Hollywood film structure and for how that structure had cherished and supported the star, the integral framing of continuities in an ongoing human life. In particular, *The Birds* does not so much conclude as end; its last shot, of the beleaguered human beings driving off, with the birds left in uneasy possession, leaves everything unresolved. In his early sixties Hitchcock was adopting the techniques of much younger film-makers in France and Italy. After years of making works of art, he was suddenly becoming self-consciously 'arty'. In the open-endedness of *The Birds* are shades of new and excitingly disturbing works by Alain Resnais and Michelangelo Antonioni. Yet Hitchcock marries the incomplete plot to the exposure of something missing in the star's commodifiable allure. The long love affair with a series of America's sweethearts turned sour. Hitchcock's extraordinary films mark a profound shift in modern consciousness, one perhaps always concealed within the dreams the dream factory sold. After a lifetime of more or less playing the stardom game, suddenly he forges a radical turn towards the anti-human, the anti-star, and takes the first confident steps down a path that we are still stumbling along after him.

28

AUDREY HEPBURN
AND CARY GRANT:
THE STRANGE DEATH
OF THE HOLLYWOOD
GOLDEN AGE

I n early December 1963, only a couple of weeks after the Kennedy
assassination, Stanley Donen's *Charade* opened at Radio City
Music Hall, Manhattan. According to Tom Wolfe, at 6 a.m. on
a freezing New York December morning the crowds were already
lining up down 50th Street and 6th Avenue to make sure they secured
a seat.[1] During 'the dark days' after JFK's death, *Charade* offered Cary
Grant and Audrey Hepburn (the two most attractive people ever to
appear on-screen), a Henry Mancini score, Givenchy dresses, suspense, glamour and Paris. Here Donen reproduces the Hitchcock
film, melding elegance and thrills, celebrating the star, just at that
moment when Hitchcock himself was shredding that formula. In the
midst of the dislocation and strangeness produced by JFK's death, it
must have seemed one of the few signs that life was proceeding as
normal; the world may have become strange, but Hollywood's illusions were intact. The stars were still there. Yet some months later,
Pauline Kael, the best of all American film reviewers, was writing: 'I
couldn't persuade friends to go to see *Charade*, which although no
more than a charming confectionery trifle was, I think, probably the
best American film of last year.'[2] For Kael, the film's invisibility was
a sign of the times, a retreat from all that was vibrant and vulgar and
wonderfully frivolous in American films.

Somewhere around 1963, just as sexual intercourse began (according to Philip Larkin), the classic Hollywood movie was dying. It was

a slow demise, brought on by the triumph of television, by a self-doubt
that preferred the longueurs and disruptions of *Last Year in Marienbad*
to the sheen of a movie like *Charade*, and by the death or retirement
of the classic stars (Bogart and Clark Gable, Grace Kelly and Marilyn
Monroe). The best directors were turning valedictory; there's that
touch of autumn in the air of John Ford's early 1960s films; *The Man
Who Shot Liberty Valance* or John Huston's *The Misfits* were elegies
for something departing. Even when they soldiered on into the swinging world, like Billy Wilder or Howard Hawks, some saving vitality
had departed. In such transitional films as Orson Welles's *Touch of
Evil* (1958) or Hitchcock's *Psycho* (1960) a dark candour and a fractured storytelling displaced the old consensus of self-censorship and
narrative cohesion. I am not suggesting that at this point the world
started going to the dogs; Hollywood continued to make excellent
films. Things did not necessarily get worse, but they were decidedly
different. In the transition from *The Searchers* to *The Wild Bunch*,
from *The Apartment* to *M*A*S*H*, a charm, an inconsequential grace,
an unreality was vanishing.

Right before Audrey Hepburn made *Charade*, she filmed *Paris
When It Sizzles* with William Holden, a movie that lays bare something of Hollywood's identity crisis. As we have seen in the earlier
discussion of Hepburn, it is a smart, sophisticated film that parodies
the scriptwriting business and in the process dismantles Hepburn's
screen persona of the impressionable ingénue. Hepburn looks like
she's enjoying the demolition, and there is a kind of fun about the
screen parodies, the self-reflexive exposure of the clichés of movie
romance. And yet there's something a little desperate about it too, a
post-mortem feel provoked by the dismal spectacle of Hepburn's love
interest (and real-life former lover) William Holden, all boozed-up
and bleary. It is Hollywood standing against the supposed vacancies
of the European New Wave by admitting that the game is up. The
film guesses that the audience has seen through the movie business,
and aims to get there before us in our projected boredom about the
set conventions – all that dull stuff of meeting cute, the expected
unexpected plot twists ('the switch on the switch'), and the inevitable

closing kiss. It tells us that the whole Hollywood shtick is hokum, but then sells it to us anyway. Meanwhile only Holden's self-loathing feels authentic; it is the film's stab at joyfulness that seems unreal. A preemptive weariness awaits us in the pastiche; the tongue has hollowed out the cheek.

Kennedy's murder signalled a crisis in American life; for some nothing thereafter made much sense. In the late 1950s there had already been talk of the perils of conformity, of a national failure of spontaneity, of women incarcerated behind their picket fences, of the death of the individual at the hands of the organization man. Yet in this dark American moment, this apparently moribund culture produced films like *Rio Bravo*, *Gigi*, *Some Like It Hot* and *North by Northwest*, works of a wit, a freshness and an inner joy unrivalled by any other nation on earth. And there in the moment of classic Hollywood's departure, just as the gilt of the Golden Age fades, stands *Charade*.

A limited but defensible definition of film might be that it is a medium that came into being in order to present and preserve Cary Grant and Audrey Hepburn. (And Monroe and James Stewart and Setsuko Hara and Sidney Poitier, and some few dozen others – the cast, in fact, of this book.) These are actors who were merely interesting on stage, or even out of place there; yet on-screen they were astonishing. It is sad that Hepburn and Grant took so long to make a film together and that they never made another. They were made for each other, these two creations of a studio world, these two Europeans in America, both of them busy embodying myths of what it means to be a Hollywood actor at all. They would have made a good pairing for a remake of Hitchcock's *Notorious*, with Grant rumoured to have spied for the British in Hollywood, and with Hepburn genuinely having a father with Fascist (indeed Nazi) connections. Yet at least we have *Charade*, a movie that unifies two highly compatible acting styles, both of which presuppose a strange distance from the medium that celebrates the actor themselves. On the one hand there is Grant's ironic presence, performing himself and somehow standing aloof from that performance. Then there is Hepburn's heartfelt earnestness combined with her genius as a comedienne, present in

Cary Grant and Audrey Hepburn stylishly together in *Charade* (1963).

her ability to transform in an instant her seriousness into the silly. Donen's film manifests the same double take: it is a screwball suspense movie, a comedy laced with violence, channelling the droll anxieties of Hitchcock at his lightest. The violent side of the plot plays like an updated version of Chaucer's 'The Pardoner's Tale', as one by one the greedy thieves encounter death. In its plots and counterplots, its version of an endlessly various leading man (whose identity changes four times in the film), Donen taps into the latent unease felt in relation to Grant's urbane demeanour – the potential killer of Hitchcock's *Suspicion* (1941) lurks behind his persona's unruffled calm. As such, *Charade* plays on the spy film's interest in the notion of trust as the basis of love – in a world of espionage and double agents, of deceits and dishonour among thieves. With two actors on-screen whose whole image was nourished by the contrivance of an artful naturalness, the film wants to ask how can we tell when someone is lying to us, how do we know who is merely an actor.

Charade was significant in allowing Hepburn to sidestep her usual role as Undine, while keeping her in the genre of romantic comedy where she was always at her best. She is grown-up here in ways not often allowed her in a comedy, cut loose for once from an on-screen father figure: independent, mature, in possession of herself. With the father absent, she only has a dead husband, a man, it would seem, hardly known to her. Embarrassed by the 25-year age difference between him and his co-star, Grant persuaded scriptwriter Peter Stone to have Hepburn make all the romantic running. The result is a new sense of agency in her and, for once, the absence of worry over the uncomfortable discrepancy between elfin Hepburn and her variously pensionable lovers (like Bogart, Gary Cooper or Fred Astaire).

After *Charade*, Grant had only two more films in him; he retired in 1966. Hepburn played on through the 1960s and the films she went on to make – *How to Steal a Million* (1966), *Two for the Road* and *Wait Until Dark* (both 1967) are all good stuff – yet undoubtedly some glory has departed. No one ever wanted to live inside the dismal 'realism' of *Two for the Road*. Yet maybe the world is better off without the sugared trickery of classic Hollywood? More than with any other actors, when watching Cary Grant's and Audrey Hepburn's films it proves hard to escape the ache of film, that nostalgic longing that invites us to live in that honeyed celluloid world, while knowing that we cannot. Yet for all of its 113 minutes, *Charade* presents us with a temporary entry into that brighter place, into the possibility of adventure, the vicarious possession of beauty. Acted by two Europeans in a mythic, dangerous, beguiling Paris, *Charade* remains a quintessential Hollywood film; some sixty years after Oswald's fatal gunshots, it serves to remind us of the brief, lost wonder of a specifically American beauty. The film effortlessly fuses Grant and Hepburn's private insecurity and their palpable sense of optimism; in an act of illusion it conjures up the possibility of the fullest of lives in an inimical modern world.

29

ANNA KARINA:
THE MUSE

Jean-Luc Godard had a problem with endings. So often his early films call a halt with a throwaway closure, a death, not quite real, distantly presented. His films are all middle, without coherent beginnings or ends; in between comes a system without story, a pattern of riffs and improvisations. There is no narrative pressure, and what plot there is feels imposed and silly. In that inconclusive masterpiece *Pierrot le Fou* (1965), who knows or cares to whom the missing money belongs? In Hitchcock's sense of the term, the cash is a pure 'McGuffin', a necessary element required to get people moving around the screen, and nothing more.

Yet a sense of ending nevertheless imbues his films. For Godard, love itself is a relation that is always already winding down. His lover, his wife, the muse of the best of his amazing early films, Anna Karina, embodies the problem of love, of ending, personified. The films just want to be with her, without knowing where that companionship of the screen will finish up. Whenever I watch *Bande à part* (1964) and *Pierrot le Fou* again, I really don't want these films ever to end; the deep pleasure of being in the company of Karina, and Claude Brasseur and Sami Frey and Jean-Paul Belmondo, is so beguiling that you just want the fun to keep going some small while longer. These are films in which people just kill time, delightfully. There is an energy there, a yearning restlessness of youth; in these movies people dance, or are always running, even, in *Breathless* (1960), as the life ebbs from them. When stillness comes, as in *Breathless*'s long scene in Jean Seberg's bedroom, it finds itself full with pent-up intimacy. The films play to a musical sense of rhythm, carried by a beat, a melody connecting the images. Here improvisation is liberty; plot is control. Karina acts as the living symbol of someone caught between her own spontaneity and others' constraint. She is living her life, but nonetheless stands as the victim of the directorial process, bartered by pimps, controlled, bullied and photographed.

Aged only seventeen, Karina ran away from home and hitchhiked from Denmark to France. She lived on the streets in Paris until, by a life-transforming chance, she was spotted in the café Les Deux Magots by a woman from an ad agency and launched a career as a model. Godard first caught sight of her advertising soap suds, apparently naked in a bath. When he cast her in a leading role in *Le Petit soldat* (released 1963, but made in 1960), as a 'minor' she still required her estranged mother's signature on the contract. During the making of the film, Karina and Godard began an affair; they married in 1961 and embarked on a passionate, desperate marriage that finally ended in 1965. Between 1960 and 1966, prompted by affection and despair, Godard made seven films with Karina, as well as *Le Mépris* (1963), in which Brigitte Bardot effectively impersonates her; combined they form one of the glories of twentieth-century cinema, a testament to love and art.

Each film is strongly distinct in tone and form, moving from the romantic comedy of *Une Femme est une femme* (1961) to the dystopian *Alphaville* (1965), from the skewed documentary impulse in *Vivre sa vie* (1962) to the melancholy comedy of *Bande à part*. Likewise, Karina herself proves so different in each movie as sometimes to seem another woman altogether. She is not inhabiting a continuing cinematic image in these films. Belmondo is more or less constantly Belmondo, a boy of larger growth, virile, insouciant with his boxer's poise; Karina can be anything or anyone, and yet remains herself, a person and not a persona.

Her first film with Godard, *Le Petit soldat*, is a tale of the Algerian war, an echo of Joseph Conrad's *Under Western Eyes* set in a Geneva filled with spies and double agents. It is a film of surveillance and interrogation. In a remarkable scene, the right-wing secret agent, the hero of the film, photographs a withdrawn Karina, directing her, trying to provoke her into opening up before him. Yet for all we are invited to stare at her, she remains elusive, reserved. Later in an extended sequence Algerian terrorists torture the hero. They attempt to extract information from him and he does all he can to withhold it. Compelled to share his sufferings, it is a distressing exemplum of the film's main theme: what goes on in another person's head? How can we know what another person feels or knows? This query would become Godard's brooding preoccupation with regard to Karina, the elusive beloved, the shifting heart of each movie. Hence in *Breathless* too, Seberg wants to comprehend the thoughts and feelings hidden behind Belmondo's face. Photographing Karina, intruding on her privacy, the spy gives us Godard's famous line: 'Photography shows the truth. Cinema shows the truth at a rate of 24 frames per second.' But where, these films want to know, is the truth present in another's face? In *Bande à part*, with Karina as Odile, we watch strangers in the Métro, knowing nothing about them, guessing at the unguessed facts of their lives. And, she tells us, quoting and thus inhabiting lines written by Louis Aragon, she too is one of us, this star, a woman in the subway, ordinary and hidden.

In *Une Femme est une femme*, playing a stripper, Karina could have become someone 'objectified', merely looked at; in practice, she is too much herself for that. When she strips, half the punters are too preoccupied to bother peering at her. In *Vivre sa vie* Godard plays again with our desire to watch his star, to trace the sorrows of her changing face. The film begins with Karina splitting up with her partner, the whole scene shot from behind. 'What's that look for?' she says, but with their backs to us it is a look we cannot ourselves see. Her husband, a schoolteacher, quotes a child's essay to her: 'A bird is an animal with an interior and an exterior; remove the exterior you see the interior; remove the interior, you see the soul.' From then on Godard constructs a portrait of Karina, putting a life, his love for her, on-screen, trying to find that soul by way of the exterior. It is inexpressibly beautiful. The character she plays, Nana, is perhaps no more than an anagram of Anna K. herself. When she visits a cinema to see Dreyer's *La Passion de Jeanne d'Arc* and watches the enrapt attention bestowed on Maria Falconetti's judged, suffering face, she is a witness to a parallel case. Karina's tears in this film would move a stone. Here we are brought face to face with essential loneliness on-screen.

Nana/Anna lives her life, but that life is one pursued as an image, a beguiling beauty that others will pay to possess. The film toys with a long-standing slur that connects the actor to the prostitute. Playing a frustrated actress, Karina here allows us to entertain the thought that Arthur Rimbaud's famous, ungrammatical paradox 'I is an other.' which she quotes in the film, may be, for the actor, a practical truth. She is caught among a set of contradictions: that she is an extraordinary person, uniquely valuable, and still she may just be a pretty face, no more than the sum of the reactions she provokes; that the vivid palpable presence on-screen, those tears, so real, may merely be the artifice of acting; and that art, this process of making a memorial of her, is both life and death. Her lover wants to go to the Louvre; paintings bore Nana, but he attempts to persuade her, saying 'art and beauty are life.' Yet the Poe tale he reads out is the story of a man whose painting of his beloved robs her of life, art supplanting the real, human woman it attempts to memorialize. At the film's end, in another of Godard's apparently offhand conclusions, Nana is trapped between men, shot by both sides. It is both melodrama and a political point, the woman's symbolic fate.

In one of the greatest moments in this great film, as Nana, Karina dances. It is a solitary surrender to movement in a film that laments and records her isolation. There is a wonderful, uninhibited silliness to it; we enjoy, from outside, that freshness in her, an irresponsibility that the film shares, the camera prowling the room with her, following the impulse of the loping bass guitar. And then, for a moment, we are inside her point of view, playing the room with her, until the pimps catch sight of her and once again we are onlookers too.

In a fabulous transformation, Karina followed the alienated poise of Nana in *Vivre sa vie* with gauche, gamine, maladroit Odile in *Bande à part*. She frowns, ineptly flirts, large-eyed and troubled. There is a

Anna Karina living her life in Jean-Luc Godard's *Vivre sa vie* (1962).

dance sequence here too, the Madison performed in the café by Odile and her two boyfriends. This time Karina dances with others, but still remains alone; the three of them mirror each other and stay separate, Godard's voiceover reminding us of their concealed, private thoughts. Remembered as a movie about companionship, in fact it exposes the separation and disjunction, the coercion and rivalry that shadow the trio's inconsequential idyll of togetherness. For most of the movie they remain on formal 'vous' terms. It is a cold February film, the trees bare, the waters dead with the late winter. As everywhere in these early films, Godard invests the movie with an irony that nonetheless evokes the poetry that it resists. In consequence, for all the fact that it is drenched with melancholy, it nonetheless exudes a fragile joy; you finish it, feeling that bit more reconciled to life.

Bande à part also exposes one essential fact of cinema; in the absence of plot, the time must pass somehow, and so the trio help it pass, dancing in the café, having a minute's silence, breaking the speed record for getting through the Louvre, playing cops and robbers. *Pierrot le Fou* is even more invested in this thought: it is a film that constantly struggles with (and overcomes) the fact that films and life are boring. It flirts with the duty to entertain, its characters and the audience both wanting distraction, all the more necessary in view of the absence of connected plot. Imbued with outlaw-chic, Belmondo and Karina move between a Jules Verne idyll and a hard-boiled thriller, taking up or dropping the frame provided by genre. In the process it gives us, as few other films can, the aching invitation of charm. It is a very funny and very desperate film; it closes with murder and suicide, because it has to close somehow.

At the end of Godard's time with Karina comes *Made in u.s.a.* (1966), firmly at the start of a new phase in his career. Experimental, Maoist, committed, these later 1960s films are no doubt intellectually stimulating, but, to this viewer at least, they are a misery to watch. The lightness has thickened; Karina and Godard were already divorced and it shows. In a sense *Alphaville* provides a more fitting coda to the films they made together. It is a strange precursor of *Blade Runner*, a noir-esque science-fiction film, similarly preoccupied with a flight from feeling. Here, more than anywhere else perhaps, Godard frames Karina as an actress with the power to move us. Inhabiting a society where feeling is alien and coldness is all people learn, she nonetheless moves towards gentleness. The film shows her discovery on-screen of the human qualities of compassion, of love; in the coldness of film, she makes a space for human warmth. It is a small miracle, and a miracle repeated in nearly all her films with Godard, a frail embrace of tenderness that we never want to end.

30

CELIA JOHNSON AND JULIE CHRISTIE: THE ADULTEROUS STAR

Both *Brief Encounter* (1945) and *Doctor Zhivago* (1965) came into the world looking set to fail. The British critics loved *Brief Encounter*, while audiences more or less let it pass by; the critics savaged *Zhivago*, though the public adored it. The reputations of both films remain mixed. It is striking how most of the legends about *Brief Encounter* involve people finding it ludicrous. While Lean was filming *Great Expectations* in Rochester, *Brief Encounter* was screened to a predominantly working-class audience; one woman at the front started giggling at the love scenes and pretty soon most of the audience were laughing with her. At a preview, the critic James Agate loudly provided a running commentary on the film's faults. It is rumoured that in France the movie appeared blankly mystifying; if the two protagonists longed for each other so much, why didn't they just go to bed? Its afterlife involves a sense of its Home Counties excess being somehow mortifying, the feeling that feeling itself has dwindled to a clichéd stoicism. *Zhivago* too has seemed an embarrassment, the whole movie an extravagant instance of 'white elephant' art, the large, empty schmaltz that hip 1960s critics once so despised.

Yet *Brief Encounter* and *Doctor Zhivago* are surely two of the greatest love stories committed to film. Now, more than fifty years later, it is much clearer that the scale of *Zhivago* forms the measure of its appeal, and its gorgeousness can be agreed to be intrinsic to one of cinema's virtues. With Chaplin, Hitchcock, Carol Reed and Michael

Powell, David Lean is one of the greatest film directors Britain has produced. Like all among this company, he is a romantic, and romanticism was his subject-matter: the flourishing and the breaking of inordinate desires, the dangerous pull of beauty, of adventure, the untrammelled life. It is the romantic version of the individual, of the star, that he affirms. Both films inevitably present the impossibility of an illicit love finding a place in the world. In *Brief Encounter* social convention and decency prevent it; romance flourishes only to be worn out by the talk of casual acquaintances. In *Doctor Zhivago* it is history and the political realm that show themselves to be love's enemy.

Brief Encounter's structure lays down its resignation from the start; the story begins with the end of the affair. Laura (Celia Johnson) finds herself torn between her children and her impassive, crossword-solving husband Fred, as opposed to the overwhelming mutual longing she shares with a handsome married doctor, Alec Harvey (Trevor Howard). The film plays out as a story told to Fred silently in Laura's head, a tale offered and withheld, never to be heard by the man to whom she does and does not tell it. Alec and Laura first meet by accident at a station

In *Brief Encounter* (1945) Celia Johnson allows herself, briefly, to dream.

café. Here their affair finds a comic parallel in the relationship between the café's owner (Joyce Carey) and the stationmaster (Stanley Hollo-way). They pass quickly through the vibrant collusion of laughter, the conspiracy of shared concern; they sit together in a cinema, mutually dismissive of the grand passions on sale there; they run together to catch a train; step by step, they fall in love.

Playing in Noël Coward and David Lean's *In Which We Serve* (1942), Johnson slots into the wartime ethos of the community; the ship is the centre, the protagonist even, with the men and the women who wait for them finding their reality in relation to it. The war required such sacrifice of self, hence all those films of the time that enact the process by which we may satisfyingly lose ourselves in the group: *The Way Ahead* (1944) or *Millions Like Us* (1943). In a war, as Bogart once told us, the love problems of the individual don't amount to a hill of beans. There are no stars in Coward and Lean's first collaboration or its nostalgic successor, *This Happy Breed* (1944); these are ensemble pieces, interlacing multiple plots. And then the pleasures and pressures of the individual life return in *Brief Encounter*, with a vengeance.

Johnson is no longer many people's idea of a film star. She's thin, intense, long-limbed, feline-faced, a Barbara Pym heroine ready, in *This Happy Breed* at least, to solve all problems with 'a nice cup of tea'. Yet hers is a face made for the cinema screen – the strong eyebrows, the large eyes – a face on which nothing is lost. She's so talented, so enormously far from the clipped, cold suburbanite of caricature. Her voice softly breathes diffident desire; here emotion lives in the experience of its suppression. There is her constant brisk, clean-cut refusal of self-pity or sentiment, an attitude of mind that carries with it the risk that one also sweeps from one's life all passion. She stands for a heightened, unalienating drabness, someone wary of getting above themselves, the embodied archetype of 'The Wife'. The aim is to be 'sane and uncomplicated', not dull, just 'awfully nice'.

Celia Johnson was an everywoman for the British middle classes. This identification with her emerges in part from the way that *Brief Encounter* not only makes her an actor in her own drama, but just as often presents her as a spectator, in the audience watching a film just as we are, catching a lunchtime concert, looking on, as we too look on, at the café owner and stationmaster's romance. As she watches them with us, in such moments she becomes our representative, her perceptions not distinct from that of the audience who feel with her. In stark contrast, twenty years later, Julie Christie raises up the aspirations of the time, glamour, the alluring remoteness of beauty. The 1940s' depressive fatalism looks easily trounced by the 1960s' optimism, a last sigh of possibility before the three-day week and Margaret Thatcher.

Brief Encounter is parochial, small, unemphatically tragic, whereas *Zhivago* covers the expanse of Russia, is epic, poised between the personal and the great event. Yet it would be wrong to make too much of the obvious differences between the films. For all the contrasts, there are deeper connections. There was already a touch of the Russian about *Brief Encounter*; Laura almost shares Anna Karenina's fate, struck down on the tracks of a railway station. The earlier film plays like a Chekhov tale set to Rachmaninov, that music summoning up the vehement feelings concealed in the ordinary day, the ordinary place. (There's perhaps a self-reflexive joke in *Zhivago* in the moment where, at a private concert, a distracted Ralph Richardson counters his wife's suggestion that the music they are listening to is 'genius' with the riposte, 'I thought it was Rachmaninov.')

Yet divergences remain, not least in the striking dissimilarity of affect between Johnson and Christie, Laura and Lara. At that early stage in her career Christie was not a 'thinker' on film, but a profound 'feeler', not conveying an intellectual life but a rich affectual one, a life of feelings, moods, impressions. We take in the fact that Johnson, contrariwise, intensely reasons and reflects, for all that she aims to portray herself as femininely dim. Discussing medical matters with Alec, Laura professes herself to be lost, but her dullness plays as her playing up to the conventions of the time, enacting for them both the kind of nonsense a woman was supposed to say to a clever man. The moment is, I believe, a false note, a betrayal of who she actually is. For all the time, her affair hurts her into a knowledge that she actively possesses, even though she is only just able to bear it.

A pensive Julie Christie as Lara, keeping warm in *Doctor Zhivago* (1965).

In both films, the male leads are doctors, but only Zhivago seems a healer. In *Brief Encounter* the leading man's status as a physician places him as respectable, a figure of authority; he has something of the smugness of the locally important man. Otherwise his medical knowledge is a symbolic property by which he confidently enables Laura to see, removing the grit from her eye. Where Laura is briefly a kind of patient, Lara and Zhivago are healers together, a step towards the emancipation that the era promised.

Previously, in John Schlesinger's films *Billy Liar* (1963) and *Darling* (1965), Christie personified youthful impulse and freshness, though in the latter film that freshness sours. Back in 1965, fresh from these successes, it was remarked of Christie that she was becoming a film star, while belonging to a milieu (the 'swinging London' set) where to be a film star was considered 'a bit square'. That un-hipness derived from the sense that the film star passed a life without freedom, in so far as they could no longer live in privacy. They were as constrained in their own way as Celia Johnson once had been, as trapped in the public role as any Soviet citizen. The films that present them may explore and celebrate the private life, but the stars themselves had none. The authentic life was led away from publicity. It is not accidental that

Zhivago's great theme is that of the value of the private life, of family, of love, even of the affair; in the midst of history, someone must go on quietly, tumultuously, with living.

In this way Christie manifests a paradox of the period, a movie star who somehow looks down on the very notion. This is only one of the ways in which *Doctor Zhivago* looked both ways at once, into a future yet caught up in a dying tradition. Now it seems drenched in 1960s modishness, but in fact the film stands uneasily above the revolutionary experimentation of the era, wedged between the MGM epic and the oncoming strangeness of *Repulsion* (1965) and *Bonnie and Clyde* (1967). It unites the new faces of the British new wave – Rita Tushingham, Tom Courtenay and Julie Christie – with such embodiments of the old guard as Ralph Richardson and Alec Guinness (sometimes improbably made up as an insurrectionary youth). Geraldine Chaplin signals some of the film's Janus-faced properties, being both a 'new face' and a reminder of cinema's long history, inevitably being perceived as her famous father's daughter. Boris Pasternak's novel itself possesses this investment in the old-fashioned, a fiction in the spirit of Stendhal and Tolstoy published in the heyday of the *nouveau roman*. It provides the pleasures of an adherence to a nineteenth-century belief in the life revealed in time, set against the disjunctions and incomprehensibility of the modern world. The plot interweaves destinies as improbably as any Dickensian fiction; there may be modernist glances at interruption, the false start, accident and missed moments, but the world nonetheless promises coherence.

Lean's *Brief Encounter*, *The Bridge on the River Kwai* (1957) and *Lawrence of Arabia* (1962) are all questioning films; they face up to dilemmas that cannot be resolved. *Zhivago* questions nothing. Instead it accepts everything. This acceptance can make the movie look facile and yet is also the root of its ultimate affirmation. The film signals Zhivago's life as a poet by making him a passive, receptive, attentive character, as Laura had sometimes been in *Brief Encounter*. He stands and watches, and by watching absorbs the world. He is a witness to life, perceiving the loveliness even in the sweat-soaked would-be suicide; for him, there is no such thing as the sordid. Confined in a railway truck, alongside a handcuffed Klaus Kinski consigned to a forced-labour camp, among dying fellow-passengers, passing burnt-out villages, Zhivago gazes through the frosted window at the snowbound expanse of Russia and simply finds it beautiful. Perhaps romanticism is given too easy a ride in *Zhivago*. Here the lovers are destroyed from outside, while Peter O'Toole's T. E. Lawrence hollows himself out from within. In Lean's previous films characters break themselves, but in *Zhivago* they are simply crushed, like Lara probably consigned to a camp and forgotten. Here romanticism finds its justification in its enmity to the remorseless cruelty of history as embodied in the cold ideals of Lenin and Stalin.

One of the things that Zhivago's gaze falls on is the similarly lovely Lara, someone real, striving, a person in a star. *Doctor Zhivago* raises no questions about the adulterous love at its heart; Zhivago's affair brings guilt but never recrimination. No one minds the deceptions; all blame is absolved. The revolution may unmake everything, and yet within Zhivago's circle it remains a courteous world. Everyone is gentle here, all are good. If the film is to work upon us, we must feel that Zhivago and Lara are destined for each other and that somehow his relationship with Tonya (Geraldine Chaplin) is a mistake. Tonya is attractive, admirable – in a film where all the major characters but Komarovsky (played by Rod Steiger) are at one time or another described as admirable. Yet she feels like a sister, too bound up with Zhivago's childhood, brittle and childlike herself, and to be protected; she gives the impression of someone playing at being grown-up. Lara, however, is womanly, a capable nurse, and so different from Zhivago in terms of class, as well as so unlike in appearance, her blondeness set against Omar Sharif's dark looks.

It should not be so perhaps, but the leading actors' beauty renders their adultery forgivable, just as the film's beauty acts as its guarantee – a loveliness that is not kitsch, nor sentimental, but romantic, an opening up before life that enfolds even ugliness in glamour. Omar Sharif's and Julie Christie's extraordinary handsomeness somehow justifies everything. Morally this is ridiculous; but in aesthetic terms it graces us with the profound meaning of film itself, and its enraptured relation to the real. *Zhivago* has been found wanting because it is so gorgeous. Yet the surface spectacle of it is identical to its deepest meaning. Colour here is significance. It is a film of greys and reds, the sky's faded blue and the whiteness of snow. Even flesh looks somehow grey or white, as pale as Christie's colourless lips. Against this drained pallor the movie sets the allure of colour. Colour is both the surface and the heart of the film – in a historical moment where Whites battled with Reds. There is a scene where Bolshevik troops unwittingly massacre a company of boy soldiers in a sun-enfolded wheat-field. It is a harrowing image of pointless death, and yet the film swathes it too in colour's enchantment, its tones a visual rhyme for Christie's wheat-coloured hair. Elsewhere there are the sunflowers that weep in the abandoned hospital, the brilliance of the sunflowers in spring. Cinema can also present this fabulous beguilement, enchanted and ensnared by a vision of the world.

The film invites us to partake in its own embrace of life, that unbearable romantic impulse; it is there in the way we are shown the forests, the snowbound houses, the streets at night, the gilt, plush ballrooms and evanescent parties. Where *Lawrence of Arabia* had summoned up moments of meeting, figures arriving and riding towards us from beyond, *Zhivago* gives us people receding, the eye straining to catch the last glimpse of a loved one moving away from us, dwindling through distance into air. Here people are lost; running in a crowd, the hand that holds us lets go. We run after lovers that we cannot catch up with, we try to call to those too far away to hear. Perhaps both of Lean's romantic masterpieces indulge too much the melancholy they invite. Yet a place undoubtedly remains for such an impractical sadness and for these yearning celebrations of human failure.

31

SIDNEY POITIER:
THE DEFIANT ONE

O ne of the least remarked-on powers of cinema is that it simply presents the consolation of a human presence. Yet in political terms, that consolation may prove to be everything but simple. Sidney Poitier's skill was that more than almost any actor of his time he embodied an essential reassurance; Poitier's problem was that in the era of Bobby Seale and Eldridge Cleaver, reassurance looked like collusion. He was the Martin Luther King of cinema, a character entirely dignified. As King's influence dropped away, so Poitier's star passed its zenith. To worried whites, there was little that was comfortable about a man like Malcolm X, whose very persona was a sharp rebuff. Three years after *To Sir, with Love* (1967), Tom Wolfe was writing about 'Mau-Mauing the Flak Catchers' and the game was playing up defiance. It was the paradox of his career that Poitier's genius should be expressed in a culture that found consensus suspect. The audience that he won over was no homogeneous entity, but a crowd imbued with contention.

At a time when the anti-hero was asserting his power on-screen, Poitier was so often someone truly heroic. Given to the good, he was rarely, if at all, allowed a capacity for corruption. In 1967 the critic Hollis Alpert celebrated Poitier's place on-screen, one he saw as being as archetypal as Gary Cooper's or John Wayne's.[1] At the inception of the 'permissive society', Poitier stood as the restrained, courteous and uncorrupted star. There was something outmoded about Poitier, a formal quality in an age of informality. He played men to be respected.

It now seems that what we see in Poitier's extraordinary run of films from *The Defiant Ones* (1958) to *Guess Who's Coming to Dinner* (1967) is the record of a divided America's growing desire to unite around their affection for this shyest of stars. Race complicates this bashful love; Poitier's apartness is what is being screened. For all the fact that he is so often granted the family context unavailable to his contemporary white stars, he manifests as they do an existential solitude. In *Touch of Evil* (1958), where does Orson Welles come from? In *Notorious* (1946), what was Cary Grant's childhood? We neither know nor care. Yet with the people that Poitier plays, we find so often some identifying trace of an earlier home life. Unlike theirs, his is an Americanness with roots. In *Lilies of the Field* (1963) he is another of the period's wanderers, but one with a specific Baptist culture behind him and a Bible in his jacket pocket. Though all rebellions are political, unlike for Paul Newman or Warren Beatty, the simple fact of Poitier's self-assertion took on a political aspect. His reiterated attempt to avail himself of the dignity of being an adult man is a social project, an assertion of the deepest possible civil right.

American cinema had long offered a simple split in the way it represented African American characters. They were either (though rarely) villainous and terrifying, or (more often) contented and comic. Comforting stereotypes prevailed, of comic laziness, of selfless devotion, and mixed-race characters of tragic placelessness, and films, like the stirring *To Kill A Mockingbird* (1962), made to prick (or soothe) the white audience's liberal conscience. In a 1967 interview, Poitier declared that when he first began appearing in films,

> the kind of Negro played on the screen was always negative, buffoons, clowns, shuffling butlers, really misfits. This was the background when I came along 20 years ago and I chose not to be a party to the stereotyping. I felt an awful lot of work needed to be done. I deliberately chose other parts . . . I want people to feel when they leave the theater that life and human

beings are worthwhile. That is my only philosophy about the pictures I do . . . I have four children including two teen-age girls . . . They go to movies all the time but they rarely see themselves reflected there.[2]

Poitier was the first black star strongly to engage the American national consciousness. Yet there were striking forerunners, like James Edwards in *Home of the Brave* (1949) and other war films of the 1950s, or Harry Belafonte, in films like *Carmen Jones* (1954) or *Island in the Sun* (1957). Still the prevailing image of a Hollywood film star in mid-century was that of someone white. It would be difficult to overstate the strength and structural depth of the prejudices that an actor such as Poitier had to overcome. In the South, films such as *Imitation of Life* (1959) (see Chapter 26) were simply banned. With this in mind it is all the more extraordinary that in 1968 Poitier was named in the *Motion Picture Herald* poll as the number one money-making film star in the world.

The demographics of cinema were changing too and were, in part, responsible for this and for Poitier's powerful presence in the 1960s. As the centres of cities experienced 'white flight', the big old picture houses that remained there were sometimes attracting 100 per cent attendance by African Americans. There were moves to integrate cinemas. Both meant an increase in the African American audience in ways that impacted upon film production.

Although he had made films before, Poitier's time as a leading star strongly began with Stanley Kramer's *The Defiant Ones*, a film that has Poitier on the run from the chain gang while handcuffed to a racist fellow-con, played by Tony Curtis. On-screen Poitier was often paired up, even bound together, with racist characters. In *Pressure Point* (1962), he is a prison psychiatrist obliged to treat a pathological American Nazi (played by Bobby Darin). *The Defiant Ones* displays a strange captivation with the physical proximity between the two men, a closeness always threatening to turn to violence, and yet strongly desired. In the end, even when they are freed from the chain that binds them, and with Curtis (and certainly not

Poitier) having the possibility of running off instead with a frustrated young mother, they still prefer to be together. It is a staging of a baffled and beguiling, and to James Baldwin a crazily impractical, closeness between black and white that will run through many of Poitier's greatest films.

In *A Raisin in the Sun* (1961) Poitier is firmly, and desperately, at home with a nearly all-black cast, a thwarted son and husband blocked in his attempt to step out of the 'ghetto' and find independent wealth. In this screen version of Lorraine Hansberry's great 1959 play, Poitier can define himself in relation to other African American characters, a route to maturity he was rarely offered in his other films. The film uses many of the original Broadway cast and unfortunately it shows; there is a lot of larger-than-life theatre acting here, but even with that proviso, it is a warm and powerful film.

What I would take to be Poitier's greatest role, and the one for which he won the Golden Globe and the Oscar, is as Homer Smith in Ralph Nelson's *Lilies of the Field*. It is hard to think of a less fashionable film; in a secular Britain, no film that ends with a resounding 'Amen' is likely to be especially popular again. Poitier is a drifter who finds himself co-opted by a group of German-speaking nuns eager to have him build for them a chapel in the middle of the Arizona desert. There could be something Kafka-esque in Poitier's repeatedly foiled attempts to escape the nuns' peremptory clutches. However, the movie finds its interest elsewhere. *Lilies of the Field* creates a utopian space, remote as it can be from racist whites (the only person in the film to express racist attitudes is a middle-aged white boss). It makes up an American parable, establishing a realm for hard-working migrants, German and Austrian nuns, Hispanic workers, an Irish American priest. (It is extraordinary that seven years later, in 1970, its director would make the terrifyingly bleak Western *Soldier Blue*.) The nuns' German origins lets the shadow of Hitler fall across the film, only to dismiss it. It is hard to think of another mainstream American film that shifts so often into foreign (un-subtitled) speech, that unites Germans and Americans, Baptists and Catholics. Only the recalcitrant white stands outside the circle. The 'Amen' that closes the film is key to its meanings; this is a film made to foster agreement. That 'Amen' is absolutely apt in a story about coming together, about reaching accord. Contracts and then promises knit lonely selves together in a communal project. In its final moments a hymn-singing Poitier looks out from the screen directly towards us, drawing us in to the unity of the movie. The film becomes a space for comradeship, exuberance, even the sharing of prayer. There are racial stereotypes at work here, certainly, but also something bigger, the overspill of pleasure.

The Bedford Incident (1965) is one of the most colour blind of all Poitier's films of the decade, in so far as it pays almost no attention to his blackness. He is not 'an African American', but just a journalist. Here Poitier allows himself to slip into the supporting role; he is an interviewer, an observer, a confidant, but it is really Richard Widmark's film as the neurotic, bullish navy captain who, through pig-headedness, starts a nuclear war.

In Guy Green's *A Patch of Blue* (1965) Poitier plays an office clerk who decides to help out a young blind woman, a kind of Southern Kaspar Hauser, an adolescent who has been kept confined to her room by her manipulative mother (an Oscar-winning performance by Shelley Winters). Set in a racist Southern city, it is a type of fable about relations between the races: Selina (Elizabeth Hartmann) is not only blind, but 'colour blind'. She only takes in the fact of Poitier's kindness, humour and concern, and although she discovers he's black (after her mother tells her), she does not stop loving him. Selina's mother is a prostitute, and Selina ends up being pushed into prostitution herself. It is a grimly sexualized world, and in the midst of its voyeuristic complicities only Poitier seems to stand above the ruthlessness of desire.

Poitier above all offers audiences the reassurance of goodness, of decency. It is a truism, and also a truth, that in the films of the 1950s and '60s Poitier really was not allowed to display much, if any, evidence of sexuality. At the time some critics worried that Poitier's apparent lack of an erotic interest in blind Selina was a cop-out, a refusal to own up to adult desires and, moreover, a conscious neutering of the feared (and desired) virile black man. Certainly there was

317

an investment at the time in imagining Poitier as chaste. (There may be parallels here to the unease over reports and rumours about Martin Luther King's philandering.) The reassurance that Poitier offers is itself 'sexy', I feel, though in part because it transcends the possibility of actual intercourse.

That sexiness would be most at issue, perhaps, in his playing a charismatic schoolteacher in James Clavell's *To Sir, with Love* (1967), where the context insists on Poitier's wistful avoidance of Judy Geeson's schoolgirl crush. Here his self-imposed restraint makes sense; undoubtedly if he flirted back or responded in kind, we would think less of him. The film makes explicit the ways in which Poitier's films preoccupy themselves with the exploration of his on-screen appeal. Playing one of his young East End pupils, Lulu speculates, 'You're like us, but you ain't'; she's not referring to the obvious difference of his blackness. Poitier was always 'like us', while being in indefinable ways better and therefore different: more courteous, more courageous. Poitier here places himself on one side of the generation gap,

Sidney Poitier as the schoolteacher in *To Sir, with Love* (1967).

standing in for an authority that youth might still respect. (One of the unspoken ironies of *To Sir, with Love* is that a dozen years earlier Poitier had himself played a classroom hooligan in *Blackboard Jungle* (1955), where Poitier's character is both a ringleader and someone allowed the possibility of redemption.)

In his two other great films of 1967 he is much more firmly on the boundary between the two generations, an earnest policeman and an example of young African American self-assertion, a mature doctor and a rebellious son. It is clear from all three films of that year how Poitier became necessary as a way to figure a route out of the conflict and dissent of late 1960s American life. He was on both sides at once, not as a quisling or an 'Uncle Tom', but as a genuinely responsible, realized man.

In 2016, Poitier won a BFI poll for the best-ever performance by a black actor for his role as Virgil Tibbs in Norman Jewison's *In the Heat of the Night* (1967). It is one of Poitier's best films certainly, though in terms of his acting it is remarkable chiefly for how fiercely he puts himself under restraint. He broods and stands back, or rather merely stands up for himself. It is a stylish, sweaty, sultry southern night of a movie, scored by Quincy Jones with a potent blues lament. With what's on show being Poitier's self-command, it is more than ever a film about our distance and closeness to the hero. Three times the movie enacts a ritualized moment in which our hero tenderly touches the white characters, crossing an indefinable borderline. We see it in the compassionate attentiveness with which he examines the murder victim's body; it is there in the careful grasp with which he caresses the first major suspect; it is present most tentatively in the held-back but still-given touch with which he endeavours to comfort the grieving widow. It is a film about needing help, and the detective plot is a mere McGuffin around the sympathetic reaching out enacted between bullish, put-upon Rod Steiger and Poitier. The parody of these intimacies comes with the returned slap that Poitier gives to the racist plantation owner. That hard blow shows he is no cheek-turning Christian, but a person asserting himself in the world. It is a response in kind. Watching Poitier's films, I lose count of the moments where white characters call him 'boy'. In this context, the simple statement 'They call me Mr Tibbs' is itself a declaration of independence, the right to be a realized social being.

If we want to place these touches in context, it is good to remember the scandal caused in March 1968 when singer Petula Clark and Harry Belafonte touched arms on television, or the furore around the first TV 'inter-racial' kiss that November, between Uhuru and Captain Kirk on *Star Trek*. In the U.S. it was only in 1967 that anti-miscegenation laws were recognized as unconstitutional. There was a fear of affection at work here, an enormous terror around the concept of race, where the feelings inspired by Poitier must remain attenuated, distanced ones. It is especially good to bear all this in mind when watching Stanley Kramer's *Guess Who's Coming to Dinner*. It's a glossy, artificial, easy-listening world, a cotton-wool unreality of a movie. Katharine Hepburn and Spencer Tracy's bubbly innocent daughter is set to marry Poitier, a widowed, older, African American doctor, and they, and his parents too, are unhappy about it. Such a plot device was, for the time, revolutionary. There had been the example of John Cassavetes's *Shadows* (1959), though there the relationship is inadvertent, the man is white, and the actress (the wonderful Lelia Goldoni) was in any case Italian American. (In *Broken Lance* (1954), Spencer Tracy had an 'inter-racial' marriage of his own with a Native American princess.) As far as they understand it, Hepburn and Tracy do not oppose the marriage because they are racist, the film tells us, but only because they worry about the problems and prejudices such a couple will face. In the end, love conquers all, of course. The movie's real subject is again the generational divide, with Poitier a 37-year-old who is still primarily a son. In *Raisin in the Sun*, Poitier's character becomes a man, by becoming like his father, adopting the probity of the older generation. Here he stands up for the younger generation, declaring to his dad, 'You think of yourself as a coloured man, I think of myself as a man.' It was, in its way, Poitier's key statement of belief, an assertion of his right to be a person on film.

After the great year of 1967, Poitier kept making films, but nothing ever again matched the impact and power of those he had made in the previous eleven years. He trod old ground, reprising the role of Virgil Tibbs, twice, and even doing a TV movie of *To Sir, with Love II* (1996), relocated to Chicago; he played Nelson Mandela alongside Michael Caine as F. W. de Klerk (1997), and was as good as ever. Yet, sadly, American cinema could no longer find a significant place for him. Still the impact of those films of the 1950s and '60s, and the ways they changed American life, remains; Poitier will always be a living example of a star, a man carrying film acting and movie stardom, even the idea of personhood itself, forward through a period of profound change.

32

DUSTIN HOFFMAN: LITTLE BIG MAN

An intriguing history of film might be written based around the films that were never made and the star performances that never happened. In some parallel universe Cary Grant is the star of Hitchcock's *Rope*, Montgomery Clift performs the washed-up screenwriter in *Sunset Boulevard*, Grace Kelly embodies the object of desire in *Vertigo*, Jane Fonda is *Chinatown*'s Evelyn Mulwray and James Cagney takes centre stage in *Casablanca*. And in that other world Robert Redford acts the handsome star of Mike Nichols's classic of the generation gap, *The Graduate* (1967).

Redford would have been closer to the Benjamin Braddock envisioned in Charles Webb's novel, for Webb's hero is cool in several senses of that word: handsome, disabused, hip. If Redford had been Ben, the 21-year-old lover of Mrs Robinson (Anne Bancroft), his father's partner's wife, and then the romantic pursuer of Elaine, her college-student daughter, the erotic complications of the situation would have themselves looked cool, a modish set of complications for what was fast becoming a swinging America. With Dustin Hoffman in the role, the love affairs become hapless, even improbable entanglements, something that first, with the mother, swamps a passive and wholly receptive character, and then, with the daughter, advances a kind of illusion that he wills himself to run after.

Above all, Redford was an established star, already known for *Inside Daisy Clover* (1965) and *This Property Is Condemned* (1966), as well as numerous TV roles. Established actors bring continuities from their other roles to a part and echoes ring in their screen performances. After the success of *The Miracle Worker* (1962), Anne Bancroft was also a known quantity, familiar already. (As we have seen in Chapter Seventeen, Ava Gardner might have played Mrs Robinson.) One way in which cinema signals youth is by casting actors who have no such resonances. The new face stands for youth. In the 1950s and '60s, in particular, the debut star could embody a freshness longed for in the culture as a whole. We see it in earlier films in images of the desirable young girl, such as with Ingrid Bergman at the start of her Hollywood career in *Intermezzo* (1939) or with Lauren Bacall in *To Have and Have Not* (1944). Later it is there with a novel kind of male star, first with Clift in his apparent debut in *Red River* (1948) and then fully formed with James Dean's role in *Rebel Without a Cause* (1955). At the end of the 1960s, although it was not in fact her first screen role, when Olivia Hussey played the ardent young lover in Franco Zeffirelli's *Romeo and Juliet* (1968), she stood for an incarnated youthfulness, for all that was bright and unsullied and new.

The 1930s and '40s had seen the star as a figure of elegant maturity, someone expressing the competence of an already realized self. The pop stars of these decades were worldly-wise crooners, experienced men of a certain age, representing solidity and suave knowingness. From the late 1940s onwards it was the drive and unthoughtful charm of youth that would be most admired. By the end of the 1950s and certainly the early 1960s the great male stars of the Golden Age were getting too old plausibly to play romantic leads. It was the time of the baby boomers, those who had seen through the plastic culture around them. Wisdom was now something that one lost with age.

In 1967 Dustin Hoffman was a complete unknown, a new face. It was all the easier to accept him as identified with his role. Novelty connected the film star to the immersion in the present moment that characterized the budding culture of pop. Hoffman's later varied and distinguished career removes us from the sense of just how unfamiliar and atypical he then was. At one point in the film, hunting desperately for the soon-to-be-married Elaine (Katherine Ross), Ben finds himself in the changing room of a jocks' college fraternity house. There he stands, a diminutive, tentative, dark-haired Jew eagerly trying to outwit a pack of identikit blonde blue-eyed hunks, cookie-cutter versions of another generation of implacably confident professional men, the arrogant who inherit the earth. If it had been Redford in the role, one blond would have faced the others. Redford was the star as figure of aspiration, graced with a handsomeness that few in his audience would share. Instead Hoffman offers us the star as everyman, his Jewishness signalling an unillusioned expectation of defeat at the hands of life, but also the determined decision to try for victory anyway. He is not smarter than us, he is not more handsome; he is wonderfully ordinary. His ineptitude acquits him of looking predatory, his pursuit of Mrs Robinson punctuated by his nervous small gulps and whimpers. He plays cool, without being it.

In the context of a 1960s culture salted by the contribution of Jewish Americans – Bob Dylan and Paul Simon, Lenny Bruce and Woody Allen, Joseph Heller and Philip Roth – Hoffman's unconventional star presence seemed of a piece with a larger movement, an internal critique of American conformity by men whose outlook was creatively jaded, the gift of the world-weary outsider. Mike Nichols asserted that the movie portrayed the 'Los Angelization' of the world, the replacement of people by things and the 'plastification' of the person.[1] When Ben laughs at Elaine's conception taking place in a Ford ('in a car, you did it?'), he expresses a comprehensible contempt for the mass-produced world offered to the young, a place where (in the complacent eyes of the middle-aged) the future means 'plastics'.

As that list of Jewish American culture stars shows, although there were such great exceptions as Cynthia Ozick, the new spirit was plainly dominated by men. In Hollywood terms, moreover, the late 1960s and the '70s were dominated by the male star, where rebelliousness, the style inherent in revolt, the cool guy's refusal of conventions and bourgeois happiness was embodied in a set of impressive white guys: Paul Newman, Robert Redford, Warren Beatty, Steve McQueen, Al Pacino, Jack Nicholson, Robert De Niro and Gene Hackman. There were, of course, striking women actors in these years, notably Jane

Fonda, Faye Dunaway, Barbra Streisand, Sissy Spacek, Ellen Burstyn and Shelley Duvall; but regrettably their roles were more limited, their impact on the culture as a whole more muted. Hoffman was somewhat different from the main run of men in not being noticeably tough, but like them he made his name by looking unlike stars were meant to look, by embodying a negative to the closed-down lows of American middle-class aspirations.

The Graduate was emphatically not about healing any generation gap, but rather sought to tear it wider. This was a film meant to be understood above all by the young: one audience survey revealed that 72 per cent of the viewers were under 24, 24 per cent were aged 24 to thirty, and only 4 per cent were over thirty years old.[2] The film was fighting back against an adult America that was sending young men to die. Even the apparently conformist gesture of Benjamin and Elaine's eagerness to marry likely finds its source in this young man's attempts to avoid the draft; he has been ineligible as a student, and as a husband he will be safe again.

At the end of the film's first act, two Simon and Garfunkel songs play: 'Sound of Silence' and then 'April Come She Will'. The sequence lasts a few minutes, in which a whole summer passes, the young man's identity caught in the passing of time. Here the film puts on-screen an inner perception of time's duration. We are inside the confusion and doubling of Benjamin Braddock's summer, one spent between a hotel room with his older married lover and a family house, monitored by dad and mum. He lives between the Taft Hotel, where he borrows his adult persona as 'Mr Gladstone', and his parents' home, where he remains, despite having reached the age of majority, defined as a son. The Oedipal energies of the film – films then never strayed far from the fashionable psychology textbooks – are exposed in the confusion made by the sequence's transitions. Months vanish in rhyme with the changes recorded in Paul Simon's modernization of the ancient folk-poem 'April Come She Will', updating the unchanging story of the cuckoo, an apt choice for a young man who is busy cuckolding his father's partner. Above all, time moves elliptically here, resolving into moments that are not yet epiphanies, but rather fragments of an oscillating emptiness. What we see are snapshots from a confusion, post-coital waiting, pool-drifting, instances of disconnection.

Ben begins the film as a track star in abeyance, his energy latent, his passivity intense. As he passes through Los Angeles airport, he stands on the moving walkways, carried along like his own suitcase on the carousel. Glimpsed often behind glass, or submerged by water, or behind dark shades, his character confronts us with a lacklustre reserve. During the date with Elaine, as Stanley Cavell has pointed out, Hoffman starts to run, and runs thereafter through the second half of the film, after buses, across the lawns of Berkeley, down the dusty roads of Santa Barbara.[3] His contact with Elaine brings him to vivid life; suddenly for the first time in the film he actually wants something. Hoffman would run often thereafter, most notably in *Marathon Man* (1976), where his ability to be fleet of foot is what keeps him alive. On the other hand, Elaine's fiancé, Carl Smith, a prematurely aged, tweed-jacketed young fellow, is dismissed as no more than 'a good walker'.

For, above all, Ben runs from involvement with the compromised, morally empty and Martini-drinking middle-aged and towards con-nection with the natural, decent and gum-chewing young. In the era of Vietnam, to choose the young over the old acquired a righteous air. Despite being one of the greatest comedies of the 1960s, *The Graduate* is a film suffused with melancholy; it constantly regrets the youth, the summer, that it preserves in film. 'You'll never be young again,' laments Mr Robinson; 'I know,' murmurs Ben, in deadpan response. Watching *The Graduate* now, we are returned to a moment when Hoffman himself was young and was no one but this one character he played. American culture had long worried over the problem facing the American adolescent, whether Huck Finn or Daisy Miller, Holden Caulfield or *The Member of the Wedding*'s Frankie, that no society could offer sufficient freedom or beauty to match the potential per-sonified in such selves. At the end of the film, as newly married Elaine and her 'other man', Ben, ride off at the back of a bus filled with the curious old and middle-aged, few have mistaken the air of unease about what lies before them. Ben has grabbed what he wanted; and what should he want now?

For the next decade and more, ahead of Hoffman, anyway an ageing youth of nearly thirty years old, was a lifetime of American possibilities, a series of roles that would express the complexity of a nation in crisis: *Midnight Cowboy* (1969), *Little Big Man* (1970), *Kramer vs. Kramer* (1979), even *Tootsie* (1982). He would specialize for a while in playing out the failures of the nation, while creating characters who could hold their own in the chaos. It was all incipient there in that first role, the decade's finest, funniest, most unsettling portrait of American youth and the new men that were to be the next generation of American stars. From film to film, Hoffman would act out the energy of transformation, becoming one thing after another, discrepant, incommensurable, with each role both a new beginning and another accomplished addition to his portfolio of selves.

At the centre of it all is a star signalled as an unwilling solitary. In Hoffman's late 1960s and '70s films, connections are made between people, but raggedly, fleetingly. In film after film Hoffman lingers at the centre of a web of loneliness. These films reflect back to us an estranged world. Hoffman moves here as a lone wolf, ending *Marathon Man* in solitary connection to the dead: his father, his brother, his girlfriend, all gone to him. He begins and ends the film circling the wide, empty lake at the centre of Central Park, sealed within the loneliness of the long-distance runner.

Against that disconnection, Hoffman plays out simultaneously a series of counterculture buddy films, celebrations of friendship's unlikelihood. *Midnight Cowboy* is a near contemporary of that other Manhattan pairing *The Odd Couple* (1968), and few couples were ever so ill-matched as Jon Voight's Texan dreamer, Joe Buck, and Hoffman's romantic cynic, Ratzo Rizzo. Here Hoffman can only run in his fantasies, in 'real life' he's a cripple, stumping down the unforgiving sidewalks of New York. Buck and Rizzo are counterculture figures by virtue of their failure, even though they stand outside the world of the Andy Warhol-esque faux-Factory crowd, a pack clinically keen to co-opt the two friends' authentically seedy lives.

In Arthur Penn's *Little Big Man* (1970) Hoffman's protean qualities flicker before us most fully, most comically. The film establishes a

Dustin Hoffman in *Little Big Man* (1970).

counterculture appropriation of the frontier space, taking the West back from John Wayne. Hoffman lives here as the anti-Wayne, a small, inept, bewildered, Jewish nebbish. In his Westerns John Wayne was always one thing; here Hoffman is everything. Wayne was changeless; Hoffman gives himself over to the flux.

In *Little Big Man* all the preoccupations of the hippy movement can be found intact: the environmentalism and the dream of going back to the land; the male-centred happily sensual sexuality, with the willing Native American women like *Playboy* bunnies (and Aimee

Eccles, who played Sunshine, was indeed later a one-off *Playboy* model); the off-key, grating jokes about rape; the revulsion felt at a white culture that believes only in death and killing.

Here, even more than with Wayne's films, it is death that is central, witnessed in the mutilated bodies, the genocidal violence; corpses are everywhere in the film, from its first shots to all but its last. Yet it is a film about resurrections, as Hoffman manifests the life-spirit as such (he fails even to kill himself). He comes back from a myriad possible deaths to survive, even as he wonders whether this world is worth living in. 'It's a good day to die,' declares Hoffman's foster father, Old Lodge Skins (played by Chief Dan George). However, death will not come. The film's tale is told, after all, by the last living survivor, a man who, in his 121st year still cannot bring himself to die. For Hoffman's character, old, young, white, Cheyenne, settler and the displaced, only memory persists, and within those memories that constitute the body of the film itself, only more movement, more changes, more carnage. Hoffman's mutable self parades before us, showing us a frontier person, both a white man and an 'Indian', or as the Cheyenne themselves put it, in a telling phrase for this book, a 'Human Being'. Hoffman and his character meld with this border environment, negotiating the spaces between. They are both an actor, inhabiting one by one the cartoon or the archetypal roles of the Wild West: Indian brave; hymn-singing boy; gunfighter; the dude who keeps the store; cavalry scout; frontier hermit; town drunk; the aged teller of tall tales, including the tall tale of his own life. Hoffman assumes all the various roles allotted to masculinity in the frontier space, and through all of them, the same face – the star's face – appears, unchanged and changing. He takes the part of a whole-hearted actor, adopting poses and social positions as though they are theatrical roles, never one thing nor the other, but still resiliently Dustin Hoffman, with all the cultural freight he had accrued from *The Graduate* and his other films borne with him. There he is, found again, the round-shouldered, hangdog, energetic, plucky, comically willing anti-heroic hero of it all. The supposed 'hero', the Errol Flynn part goes to General Custer, played by an actor (Richard Mulligan) few remember except fans of the soap opera parody *Soap*; Custer's the man who ought to be the 'star', who thinks he is the 'star', but is actually a bit-player, a scoundrel, a charlatan and a fool.

Until the radical instabilities thrown up by his cross-dressing role in Sydney Pollack's *Tootsie*, Hoffman would not quite be so nakedly split into performing selves on-screen. Instead he takes on the role of plucky victim, the little guy standing up against the conventions, the machinations of the state. In *Marathon Man* he's post-graduate, post-young, a superannuated student still caught up, Hamlet-like, in confronting the death of his politically radical father. Everything about Hoffman's character is as yet unsettled; he's off the cuff, intensely low-key, a nonconformist for a decade that treasured the single stand against 'The Man'. He's related to his 'straight' brother, played by Roy Scheider, though Scheider is far from being the businessman he plays. He's a CIA man, an agent for the government, both competent and morally compromised, as his work has led him to an accommodation with a renegade Nazi doctor. Inevitably, given the myths of the times, Hoffman becomes an unwilling rebel, the little guy ostensibly weak and busy only with his self-preservation (in that renowned decade of 'Me'), who nevertheless finds himself standing up for decency, for political virtue, combatting the rogue elements of the 'Deep State', even as he also visits retribution on the paradigmatically wicked figure of the Nazi. (Hoffman's and Scheider's Jewishness is an unspoken presence in the film.)

In Alan J. Pakula's *All the President's Men* (1976) he stars again as a buddy, a dishevelled Carl Bernstein to Robert Redford's Ivy League Bob Woodward. In bringing down corruptly square Richard Nixon, Hoffman enacts here the liberal dream of the age, a man undaunted and unconventional. He is a Jewish white knight, a fearless pursuer of the truth, as much excited by the dynamics of the narrative he uncovers, and therefore constructs, as he is by idealistic outrage at the corruption and compromise of the straight world. He is the journalist as counterculture hero, long-haired, a newspaper man since the age of sixteen, undeterred and intelligently hip. In *Kramer vs. Kramer*, there were signs of the counterculture world that had first nourished

Hoffman's star persona giving up on itself, turning to self-critique, a fine instance of a coming 1980s backlash against the progressive advances of the previous fifteen years, particularly as that pertained to the improved social position of women.

Yet for fifteen years or so Hoffman was more than a brilliant actor, more than a man who commanded the attention of the audience on-screen. He was the exemplary new face, a symbol of cultural change and of new possibilities in the idea of the American self, the American hero, the American star.

33

WOODY ALLEN:
THE DIRECTOR AS STAR

T homas Hobbes declared that all laughter depends on sudden
contempt, that flash of superiority when the other chap slips
on the banana skin and we don't. When we smile, we show
our teeth. For this reason, he warned against the self-deprecatory gag,
for after all who wishes to pull down contempt on himself? No one
seems to have told Woody Allen.

With Alfred Hitchcock, Allen must be the most recognizable
director in the history of cinema. In Hitchcock's case, it was his TV
series that sealed his presence in the public mind; for Allen, his fame
emerged from the way he combined the role of director and star, his
films exploring a peculiarly distant form of intimacy, another way
of putting a life on-screen. Like all the greatest stars, Allen was both
himself and a fantasized persona, sometimes literally so: in 1984 an
anthology was published devoted to people's dreams about him. To
like his films long meant to like him, their personal vision one that
somehow can best be accepted personally. Perhaps the peculiar intimacy of his relationship to the audience stemmed from the fact that
he had been a stand-up comedian. The early films maintained that
sense of performing to their audience: *Annie Hall* (1977) is as much
about the faux-intimacy of addressing the viewer as is *Alfie* (1966).

There is nothing more intimate or more immediate than a joke.
Allen knows this all too well, and in *Annie Hall* he dramatized that
fact, showing the way that jokes establish sympathy with another

person; they call for a response – you either get them or you miss them. It is there realized in the heartbreaking moment when Alvy Singer (played by Allen) tries to repeat with another woman the laughter he had shared with Annie Hall (Diane Keaton) over their attempts to catch and cook a still-living lobster. His new girlfriend gazes at him in unsmiling bemusement; she just can't see the gag. We in the audience are similarly free to laugh along or not; if we don't, then what is at stake is perhaps not just our sympathy with the movie or its director.

Over the last 25 years or so the unresolved accusations regarding what may or may not have been an act of child abuse have complicated and darkened the relation of many in the audience towards the man. For some sympathy has thickened to contempt. The films themselves have come to seem polluted purely through their relation to him. In a complex and persuasive essay entitled 'What Do We Do with the Art of Monstrous Men', Claire Dederer takes Allen to be the 'ur-monster', truly as bad as it gets.[1] His centrality to the creation of his films, as writer, director and, often, actor, now make his films seem all the more culpable. Some actors who have appeared in his films are deemed to be complicit with him as abuser, despite the fact that the accusations of abuse have never been proven, and that much doubt remains concerning what happened between Allen and his ex-partner's daughter. Such disdain and anger that now exist towards Allen are particularly disruptive in watching his films, in so far as they depend on the elusive sympathies of the shared joke. A gloom hangs over Allen now, destroying the connection his films had hinged upon.

For all these reasons it is hard not to approach Allen's films biographically – both his and the spectator's. Of course, the man on-screen was always a persona, and yet the works have seemed like fragments of a great confession. Regarding *Annie Hall*, both Allen and Keaton had been lovers (her real name is Diane Hall); *Radio Days* (1987) is memoir on the slant (though one where Allen himself for once does not appear). It is symptomatic that so often when he imagines a character writing, what they produce is part autobiographical-fiction, part wish-fulfilment. For me, as an adolescent in the 1980s, Allen's films opened a door to sophistication – not that alluring knowingness of defeat that permeated a movie like *The Third Man* (1949), but a world of dinner parties, love affairs and cultural consumption. The first time I heard of the possibility that someone could enter psychoanalysis was through Woody Allen. A film like *Love and Death* (1975) appealed to the teenage me who had just discovered Russian novels, loved them and yet could find it funny that I loved them, a turn of events that little in my environment allowed for. With a film like *Hannah and Her Sisters* (1986) it proves hard for me to be objective; it seems so personal to me, it is sometimes a surprise that other people know it, like discovering another life for a friend.

Allen has lamented that his work has had no cinematic influence, that he has no followers. If that is true, he may console himself with the certainty that for a couple of generations his art, and with it his presence, his perception of the world, extended into people's lives. Few of us (it is to be hoped) have had a Scorsese moment or met a Coppola character. Yet who has never felt that they were, even for a moment, inside a Woody Allen film? And who has never met (or been) a Woody Allen type, neurotic and self-effacing? By engaging with everyday life, he has permeated it.

In the 1970s Allen looked irreverent, hip, a part of the new Hollywood generation. In an age of auteurs, he was the auteur personified, the writer, director and star of his films, active in the editing, choosing the soundtrack, initiating the projects. His modishness stemmed from his films' willingness to talk about sex; no one noticed as yet that, until *Match Point* (2006) at least, they modestly held back from depicting the act itself. He was modern enough to seem part of a contemporary social problem, the exemplar of the modern narcissist, the distracted consumer of 'relationships'. In his 1970s jeremiad *The Culture of Narcissism*, Christopher Lasch worried about Woody Allen's use of the self-wounding joke.[2] Allen, he asserted, was using humour to defend against the serious. Yet Allen's wit was always more than that, a pre-emptive strike against one's own pretensions, but also a bright disruption offering the possibility of insight.

Yet even while he was in vogue he was already out of time, an old-fashioned guy aghast at contemporary vulgarity. He was already in his early 40s when *Annie Hall* came out; his music was Sidney Bechet and Duke Ellington, not Hendrix or The Eagles. In an era of unconventionally good-looking leading men, Allen presented the most unlikely romantic movie hero of all; the balding, bespectacled nebbish up against smouldering Al Pacino. The mood of the times was for anti-heroes, for unhopeful rebellion. But by virtue of his ordinariness Allen was the greatest rebel of all, offering a way to be male without being a conventional Hollywood he-man like Robert De Niro or Jack Nicholson. You can see it in the way the two types drive: in one case Gene Hackman weaving and speeding down a one-way street in *The French Connection* (1971), and in the other Allen sputtering out of Manhattan in *Broadway Danny Rose* (1984), a man ill at ease with the mechanical environment. Both types derived from old films – for one the Western hero or film noir tough guy, and in Allen's case, Bob Hope. Allen was sexual, but no 'stud', sensitive, courteous, above all, both funny and ultimately earnest. Strangely enough, considering his contemporary reputation, one of his great gifts to cinema has been to portray through his own acting and through the casting of men like Owen Wilson in *Midnight in Paris* (2011) a decent way to be a man.

Yet, even before the accusations of abuse, many people hated Allen, and therefore Allen's films. Like Bob Dylan, he has always lost his form and yet the current work strikes everyone as a comeback. More accurately, he has always made some weaker films, had some bad runs (most notably since 2011), but he clearly has it in him to produce at every turn in his career vibrant, spirited movies: a late film like *Midnight in Paris* is possibly a slight work, but is also (in my eyes, at least) a joy.

Some avoid his films, feeling they know in advance what they are going to be offered. They can indeed feel, when viewed at a distance, as though they are just more of the same forever: the older man and the younger woman, the shrinks, the neurotic loser, the architects and writers and theatre people. It can seem as though everything takes

Woody Allen.

place in an insulated Upper East Side world, exploring the travails of an arty, intellectual, comfortably white Bohemian middle class that hardly exists anymore except in fossilized state. Even out of New York in a film such as *You Will Meet a Tall Dark Stranger* (2010), there was a sense of business as usual. And yet, close up, what strikes us now is both the remarkable consistency of Allen's vision and the surprising

336

variety of his films – and of the ways he has acted in them: from a modern fable like *Zelig* (1983) to the science-fiction farce of *Sleeper* (1973), from the fantasy of *The Purple Rose of Cairo* (1985) to the problem play that is *Crimes and Misdemeanors* (1989). Above all, his subject-matter has matured as he has. The early works depict the archetypal young adult about the city, but later he turned to the problems of middle age and, more recently, old age.

If it had not been for the horrible stain on his public image, Allen might now have still seemed a comfortable figure, the official bard of bourgeois Manhattan. In fact he has long been one of cinema's disrupters and a great experimentalist in narrative, a man devoted to finding out as many different ways as possible to tell a story. The fruits of his years in psychoanalysis are apparent here. *Annie Hall* tries every means possible to fragment the individual and its story: split-screen scenes, empty frames, black frames, subtitling (to show what people are really thinking), a disembodied soul drifting off during sex, a cartoon version of Woody, confrontations with the younger self, the man up on TV versus the same man on the street. It's tightly structured, but the film's surface is nonetheless non-linear, digressive and self-questioning. If the early films seemed self-obsessed, Allen responded by moving on to the group portrait, creating narratives that were diffused and decentred, with double or even triple plots. The central star and the couple ceded place to the ensemble. Such films produced a complex image of their social milieu. Allen is a man immersed in Americana who has also been sceptical about America. His inclination towards European cinema might account for his perceived lack of success with the American audience. Without his penchant for W. C. Fields and Mort Sahl, he might have fully been what he almost is, the American Éric Rohmer.

In fact Allen had the enormous gift of creatively loving both Vittorio De Sica and the Marx Brothers, Ingmar Bergman and *Born Yesterday* (1950). This complex taste is really the source of all that is best and all that is most contradictory in his films. He plumps for European slowness, yet his own films evidence a preference for American rapidity: a cut-to-the-chase rhythm that feels urban, that suggests New

York. Sometimes one suspects that, like Graham Greene, he divides his films into 'novels' and 'entertainments'. As with Greene, it's apparent that many of his most profound works belong in the latter category.

At his darkest, he proffers comedy without affirmation, an unrelentingly desolate view of life. In *Crimes and Misdemeanors*, Lester, the fatuous director of sit-coms (played by Alan Alda), repeats his possibly absurd mantra, 'In comedy, things bend, they don't break.' Yet in several of Allen's best 'comedies', breaking is precisely what things do. Like Thomas Hardy, he clearly feels that in a world without God life is meaningless; like Hardy too, there is a reliance on coincidence and the unlikely accident to twist the plot. Art has loaded the dice. Increasingly his characters are caught up in the machinations of design. They may invite such contrivance, for after all they so often seek to disrupt their own lives, to break up marital bliss for a risk. In Allen's comedies the ordered life is always provisional. Collapse comes with an affair, a mix-up. If order is restored, then that too is a makeshift solution. In works such as *Crimes and Misdemeanors* and *Husbands and Wives* (1992) there is existential grit in the oyster, an undercurrent of real despair. Such films tell us that life is pretty awful and we can only hope to get through it the best way we can. Morals are valued, but their efficacy doubted.

And yet Allen's jokes don't always believe in this troubled vision. For all that he is so morose, he cannot be reliably bleak. He tried to be a philosopher, but cheerfulness kept breaking in; he tried to be a clown, but philosophy kept him doubting. *Melinda and Melinda* (2004) demonstrated his problem: the same story is told twice, once tragically, and once comically; while I can delightedly remember almost every aspect of Will Ferrell's comic descent into suffering, the tragic part of the film is lost to me. Apparently lacking a faith in the essentially comic nature of life, Allen has nonetheless done most of his most valuable work in comedy. At his best, he tenders a contrary vision of art as healing illusion, a step into a fantastic world that holds out an antidote to despair. He has deserved something of his reputation for angst, but there are as many films that celebrate the silly. He is a great praiser of things, a lover of cities and cinema. His films are often best understood as tributes to film. That sweet stroke of genius *Manhattan Murder Mystery* (1993) is *Blue Velvet* (1986) remade by Bob Hope, the dull couple launching themselves into hapless adventure.

His great subject is the illusion offered by art. Watching films, and making films, has offered him – and us – a place of escape. In *Hannah and Her Sisters*, Woody Allen's character Mickey Sachs has his faith in life restored by a Marx Brothers movie; to paraphrase Kenneth Williams, if life is a joke, then we might as well make it a good one. Yet a more recent film, *You Will Meet A Tall Dark Stranger,* exposes the fatuity of our sustaining illusions – the beauty of the woman in the window opposite, the flattering promises of New Age 'spirituality', the thought that death and old age might be evaded with a treadmill and Viagra. The delusions unravel, or not, but are seen through and sent up. In his warmest films, *The Purple Rose of Cairo* or *Midnight in Paris*, there is a gentler unmasking. He acknowledges the glamour of the silver screen and the magnetism of the past. When the films return to the real, they do so honourably, knowing and accepting that, while sometimes disappointing, the best kind of life is the life that actually is.

Allen never produced a single universally accepted *chef d'oeuvre*, no *Godfather*, no *Raging Bull*. Instead over the years, he has made a multitude of small things, comic novellas rather than great novels, pleasurable and rewarding works of art that without trying to be great have accumulated greatness, remaining tentative and lovable. In sketching these films, he was also sketching over and over versions of himself, his own identity fragmented into tentative fictions, held together by the most downbeat of movie stars.

34

ROBERT DE NIRO: FOR REAL

Through the 1970s into the early twenty-first century Robert De Niro stood in the public mind as the epitome of the actor, a man who defined the possibilities of performance on-screen. Particularly in the run of films he made with Martin Scorsese, some nine feature films, from *Mean Streets* (1973), through *Taxi Driver* (1976), *The King of Comedy* (1982), and *Goodfellas* (1990), to *The Irishman* (2019), De Niro became a muse of the new Hollywood, the personification of its tough, authentic male actors.

In particular he became, I want to argue, a focus, a muse, for Martin Scorsese and a means whereby the director through a series of classic films examined his and our relationship to fame. Scorsese has declared that he has always been excited by celebrity, especially that of the actor on the screen.[1] In *Taxi Driver, New York, New York* (1977), *Raging Bull* (1980) and *The King of Comedy* we follow a sequence of films in which fame and notoriety are dissected and celebrated, picked apart and endlessly found, in the person of their star, De Niro. In those films De Niro stands both for the distortions wreaked on us by fame, and for the recalcitrance, the vitality and violence of the person as such, unstable, unassimilable, for all that it can be put on to a screen. Fame's illusions meet here, again and again, with an actor who signalled authenticity.

Already in his first movie for Scorsese, *Mean Streets*, De Niro adopts the bravura swagger of the neighbourhood guy who in his own mind is a star, Jumping Jack Flash, the cock of the walk. That free self-celebration, the belief that transforms each dive bar into your own private stage, turns nastier in De Niro's next Scorsese film, *Taxi Driver*.

The film's writer, Paul Schrader, had originally intended the film to be austere in the existential Robert Bresson style, with the purity of non-actors central to the work of art; the moment De Niro came on board that austerity, that purity, was touched with movie-star glamour and so departed. In fact, however, the presence of a big new celebrity in the film, the playing of alienating Travis by this young, bankable star, introduced complexities and nuances that could never have been there otherwise.

In *Taxi Driver* for the first time there emerges a question that became a continuing preoccupation with De Niro's characters and his on-screen presence: how can we sympathize with such a man? His films begin to operate in a space where revulsion and attraction co-exist. As Travis Bickle, the returned Vietnam veteran, an insomniac Yellow-Cab Jeremiah, De Niro becomes both the audience's representative, the manifestation of their own puritanical disgust, their own voyeuristic lust, and that which stands always on the far side of empathy: someone who disturbs our moral sense and troubles our compassion. Travis is the 'righteous man' and a hypocritical viewer of porn, drawn – as we are – to that which repels him. Travis acts out Scorsese's New York nausea, and Paul Schrader's, and the star's, De Niro's own. Scorsese asserts that, reading Schrader's script, he realized that this 'was exactly the way that I felt', and that the violence that followed was an almost legitimate exorcism of that loathing of the corruptions of city life, all the pimps, the whores, the junkies, the johns, and that he had 'the impression that De Niro felt that too'.[2] Scorsese confessed that he, like Travis, knew the 'killing feeling'.[3]

The audience must abide with Travis's aversion for a long time, waiting on the violence within him, starting to long for it to be expressed. When it comes, as Travis assaults the tenement building where Jodie Foster's underage prostitute works, De Niro expected a kind of shrinking back from Travis, a withdrawal from him, and from the identifications that the film had woven. Instead audiences whooped and cheered, as Travis becomes the Mohawk revenger, a suicidal killer, expunging the dirty others so as in the end, if he but could, to expunge himself. Instead of that explosive self-erasure, Travis finds himself elevated to the role of 'hero', a minor celebrity graced with the absolution of fame. The newspapers, and the public they cater for, anoint him as a 'good man', his image preserved. It's a bitter, cynical ending, prompted in part by the presence on the cover of *Newsweek* magazine of Lynette 'Squeaky' Fromme, Manson Family member and would-be assassin of Gerald Ford. What mattered now was not goodness or decency, but fame itself, the balm that justified any action.

De Niro's next film with Scorsese, *New York, New York*, toned down the darkness a few notches, though the star remains fascinatingly hard to like, even as – or if – we feel with him. Most often regarded as an interesting failure, the film nonetheless plays its part in engraving De Niro's presence as a 'Hollywood star', even as his roughness, his aggression, his vitality, his very presence, militate against the packaging understood in that concept. The film staples together a delight in the artifice of old Hollywood, the blatantly fabricated sets, the off-key slickness in the attempt to render the 'real', with something jagged-edged, something recalcitrant and uncompromising in the film's main characters, the saxophonist and the jazz singer, played by De Niro and Liza Minnelli (the daughter of a star and a star-director). The fake conventions of classic Hollywood cinema are shown to contain something that is also 'for real'. The movie's use of improvisation cut into the synthetic stylishness of the sets, costumes and make-up, the felt-for dialogue striking against the put-on and feigned. The relationship between Minnelli's character and De Niro's turns on their mutual pursuit of art, success and, in time, fame. They are a double act whose yearnings pull them apart, and De Niro comes across, as he so often does in these films, as perverse, closed-in on himself and his own ambitions. Minnelli's cute quirkiness cannot help but make De Niro's macho pride look brutish and uncouth. His refusal to see his own newborn baby plays, as it must, as weirdly unsympathetic and yet comprehensible, even of the self-absorption that it reveals.

Robert De Niro in *Raging Bull* (1980).

It was in *Raging Bull*, the greatest of all of their collaborations, that fixed forever the kind of film star that De Niro would be, a star who was an actor first, indeed an anti-star, prepared to take risks for the sake of doing things 'for real'. It's the fullest and most extreme realization of the meanings he brought to the concept of 'stardom'.

In *Raging Bull* De Niro embodies Jake LaMotta, first as one of the great boxers of the mid-century, and then, in his decline, as a reciter, but always a man performing and displaying his body on stage. As a performer LaMotta stands as a mirror, an other, to the audience, and also to the actor who performs him. *Raging Bull* was a riposte to *Rocky*, an antidote to triumphalism and an ominous, searching film of American failure and self-destruction. It was De Niro who drove the project.[4] It's a ferocious and compassionate movie, the record of an American hero's ascent into the brutal compromise of a brief notoriety. It tells a life in flashes, much as LaMotta imagined his own history:

> Now sometimes at night when I think back, I feel like I'm looking at an old black-and-white movie of myself . . . Not a good movie, either, jerky, with gaps in it, a string of poorly lit sequences, some of them with no beginning and some with no end.[5]

Halfway through the film, in a solitary intrusion of colour in this otherwise black-and-white picture, Scorsese cuts to a montage of home movies contrasted with re-enactments of LaMotta's classic fights. The sequence makes a financial point, showing how LaMotta's growing wealth has its roots in violence; family life and fighting interconnect. But it also poignantly juxtaposes the public and private man. The home movies stand for the genuine, the backstage truth, but are really only another kind of fantasy, LaMotta's presentation of himself, the invention of family happiness, with compulsory smiles and the strains of a vanished festivity.

The crux of the film lies in LaMotta's appallingness, his violence to women and to his brother, his insecure ferocity, his stumbling intellect, his aggressive and self-consuming jealousy. The jealousy he feels regarding his wife, the suspicions he inflicts on his brother, demarcate a desperation about himself, an inner, unappeasable insufficiency. Even the film's makers could not evade the question of whether or not LaMotta was worthy of the attention of a film. Most movingly of all, LaMotta undoubtedly shared that contempt: on a piece of folk-art given to Scorsese, a framed portrait of LaMotta, the artist had inscribed the legend, 'Jake fought like he didn't deserve to live'.[6] LaMotta's shtick, his one great talent, and the urge that perhaps facilitated his fighting, was the ability to take punishment on the ropes. In the boxing ring, he expiated a guilt and self-loathing that filled him. The key writer on the film, Paul Schrader, felt that his task was to grant LaMotta 'a depth, a stature he does not possess'.[7] At a meeting with the production heads, one of them blandly told Scorsese and De Niro that LaMotta was a 'cockroach'.[8] De Niro was furious, and heatedly responded, 'He's not a cockroach! He's not!' And yet the comment belongs with a series of metaphors and comments in the movie itself that puts LaMotta down as an animal, truly a raging bull.

The new generation of 1970s male American film stars were typically ready to play the part of the anti-heroic hero. Alongside Jack Nicholson's tour de force as the insane Jack Torrance in Stanley Kubrick's *The Shining* of the same year, turning the countercultural hero into a demonic louse, De Niro's LaMotta pushes this trend to its furthest point. As embodied by De Niro, LaMotta is there to test the limits of what counts as human, to probe for us the boundaries of our empathy. In this man who communicates with his fists before words, a person who best comes into contact through aggression, we are invited to find a reflection of the human, to find the person in the beast. To be human also means this. Near the end, in frustrated fury LaMotta pummels and beats his head against the wall of a prison cell; as he does so, he bellows and howls to himself, 'I am not an animal! I am not an animal!' In this ragged scene of rage and utter defeat, the film presents someone who seems to stand beyond the limit of sympathy, a man bound to a passion too extreme for us to share. And yet, we truly might share in it, we might reach out and understand this wretch.

Certainly De Niro was ready to share LaMotta's position in the most physical way possible. First, he trained as a boxer with LaMotta, becoming good enough in the old fighter's estimation to have the potential for a sportsman's career. De Niro needed to understand what it was like to possess such a body, to have those muscles, that strength, to be the owner of that ready power. LaMotta's lacerating jealousy resides in the inescapable fact that sexual possession is not the same as the possession of the other's apartness, their free and unexpressed mind. For LaMotta, other people slip beyond his control, their other-ness a challenge to him. If De Niro could not see into LaMotta's mind, his imagination, he could nevertheless inhabit, at one remove, what it meant to live in such a body. As LaMotta's physique fattened and lost definition, as his agile tautness turned heavy, De Niro set out to share LaMotta's decline too. The actor travelled around Italy, growing plump on pasta, so that on-screen he could, for real, feel what LaMotta felt, look as LaMotta looked, and be in the flesh that other man.

René Girard has affirmed that the pleasure of impersonation is that it permits our attempt to be, to become, the model you impersonate.[9] The pleasure for the actor is that of becoming others, impersonating them (while remaining oneself). De Niro's identification with LaMotta appears to belong to this mechanism of desire, the co-inherence of acting. And in tandem with De Niro's embodiment of this other man, the audience's projections echo this yearning, while standing outside and judging the man, the men, in the movie. The cinema audience imagines with the actor, and the film becomes an artifice created between ourselves and the people on-screen. Yet because the actor in this case is a film star, because it is De Niro, we enjoy the imperson-ator as a model; the star remains a star, and De Niro, for all the work he does, for all that he inhabits this other man's life, remains always De Niro. So it is that we take pleasure in the excellence, the astonish-ment of De Niro's acting. It pleases us to see him become LaMotta, and in relation to that becoming, modelling ourselves, while standing outside in judgement and compassion.

Throughout *Raging Bull*, this deeply expressionist movie, Scorsese would have us share LaMotta's view of things. When the film stutters and slows down, when sound drops away, we perceive the world as LaMotta does. We are taken inside that unique perspective on things that is LaMotta's, with all its bafflement, its self-loathing, its thwart-ing. Later in his career, in Penny Marshall's *Awakenings* (1990), De Niro would play again with the process of empathy, enacting a cata-tonic person enclosed by torpor, making himself into a statue coming to life, to personhood. Here compassion humanizes, and the revived man is at heart a good one, in love with the world. This man locked in by encephalitis lethargica comes to communicate with others; the dark energies of Scorsese's vision find themselves healed.

Raging Bull's great theme is incarnation. It is there in all the religious iconography scattered through the scenes, telling us of the spirit that flesh would rise to, the flesh that the Word became. It is there too in the thought that the person is merely animal, one ascetically denying the flesh, beating it and having it beaten in the ring. And it is there, above all, in the physical presence of the actor, doubling another man, standing in for a real person, beyond the movie screen. LaMotta joked, 'I asked if I could play myself in the picture, but they said I wasn't the type.' De Niro becomes that type, his face transposed onto LaMotta's face. Faces here are unreadable, telling us little of the mind's construction they conceal. It is against the face, that index of the soul, that the violence is perpetrated, that the blows are struck. The movie yearns for – and takes its revenge upon – those fragile features.

In the last scene of the film, the ageing, overweight LaMotta warms up in his dressing room. He looks into the mirror and flatly gives us the speech that Brando makes to Rod Steiger in the back of a car in *On the Waterfront* (1954): 'I could have been a contender; I could have been somebody', he says; 'it was you, Charlie; it was you.' Scorsese remarked that in this moment De Niro plays Jake LaMotta playing Marlon Brando playing Terry Malone.[10] And Malone is the mirror image of the man in the seedy dressing room, the 'you' he confronts. In playing Brando here, De Niro is staking a claim to be an actor as the inheritor of the great method man's supremacy, placing himself in a genealogy. He is also, in character, accusing his brother, or himself, or merely placing himself in another man's position. No one, not even the actor or the director, could decide which. Yet in this recession of mirrored images, this mirroring without narcissism, comes the place where the wonder of De Niro's acting makes its stand. Passion and skill make significance; this is the self-abnegation and the realization of the star.

After the peak of *Raging Bull*, *The King of Comedy* risks looking like an addendum, an afterthought. In fact, it is a film of enormous wit and intensity, a last great opportunity for Scorsese and De Niro to explore the tensions in De Niro's star persona. As Rupert Pupkin (the name is often misspelt, often mispronounced, he tells us), De Niro is a would-be comedian, a salesman busy attempting to sell that unshiftable property, himself. Pupkin would do anything to secure his place in the TV world of celebrity, the self-sufficing realm where attention is guaranteed for those who have already caught the world's attention. The talent that warrants that attention seems an afterthought to him. He relentlessly pursues Jerry Langford, comic and TV late-night host (played by Jerry Lewis), badgering him for a slot on his show, and when normal channels fail, bagging that slot by kidnapping Langford and threatening his life. *The King of Comedy* draws on the comedy of embarrassment, of social collapse. Pupkin's ego-driven ignoring of all social rules or niceties drives the film, his ignoring too of the fact that the star he badgers is actually only another human being, and as such entitled to the dignity of distance, to courtesy. The film tells us that fame, that stardom, is precisely the acid that corrodes normal human social interactions. Faced with a star in real life, social intercourse becomes strange and desperate. In the movie's reiterated confrontations between the star and the world, the neediness in our relation to others out there is put on display, cruelly unveiled. One moment someone's flattering the star and calling for an autograph, the next, after the smallest and most natural rebuff, they are wishing the star should die of cancer. It is all but unbearable to watch.

The King of Comedy poses a question that echoes through this whole book. What do we see in a star? And, more than that, what is it that we want from them? One answer the film supplies is that we see ourselves in the star, and what we want to do is to replace them with ourselves. Love and hate flows along the connections made in the identifications framed in a film. Fame – their fame, our own longings for it – becomes a vicarious way to assert our own importance, a way not to change or develop as individuals, but to become, like the star, an imagined thing, a changeless image.

After this glorious exposure of the sickness of fame, the entrapment that the star must experience, De Niro would go on to make many other great films, with Scorsese and without him. Yet it is in the run of films explored here that his relation to his own persona, to his own stardom, is most blankly exposed. There are incomparable films from an era ready to take films very seriously indeed, that could see in the pop culture world something gorgeous, something complicated, something real.

POSTHUMAN STARS

35

HARRISON FORD:
BLADE RUNNER AND
THE REPLICATION
OF THE THE PERSON

I t is entirely apt that a film dedicated to replication should itself exist in multiple versions: there is not one *Blade Runner*, but seven. The film star too can be seen as someone who exists in multiple versions, renewed and remodelled in each film and each character, always the same, and always newly fashioned. Aptly too, repetition is written into the film's plot, which sees Deckard (played by Harrison Ford) as an official assassin or bounty hunter (or 'Blade Runner') consigned to hunt down, one after the other, four 'Nexus-6' 'replicants' (genetically designed artificial human beings, intended as slaves for Earth's 'off-world' colonies). One by one, our equivocal hero seeks out the four runaways: worldly-wise Zhora (Joanna Cassidy); stolid Leon (Brion James); the 'pleasure-model' Pris (Daryl Hannah); and the group's apparent leader, the ultimate Nietzschean blond beast, Roy Batty (the wonderful Rutger Hauer). Along the way Deckard meets and falls in love with another replicant, Rachael (Sean Young), as beautiful and cold as a porcelain doll.

In *Blade Runner*, as in all science fiction, the 'future' is a style. Here that style is part film noir and part Gary Numan. We are back in the world of Welles and Peter Lorre. The 1940s influence is everywhere: in Rachael's Joan Crawford shoulder pads, the striped shadows cast by Venetian blinds, the palpable atmosphere of unillusioned defeat. It is not just noir. Ridley Scott also taps into 1970s cop shows and films, which themselves tapped into nostalgic style with their disconsonate jazz and their sad apartments. Deckard even visits a strip joint as all thorough TV detectives must. The film remains one of the most visually stunning in cinema history. It plots a world of perpetual night, a landscape of shadows, rain and reflected neon (shone on windows or the eye) in a world not built to a human scale; there the skyscrapers dwarf us like the pyramids. High above the Philip Marlowe world, hover-cars swoop and dirigible billboards float by. More dated now than its hard-boiled lustre is the movie's equal and opposite involvement in modish early 1980s dreams; in the age of John Foxx the soundtrack by Vangelis was up to the minute, while the replicants dress like extras in a Billy Idol video, a USA post-punk, synth-pop costume party. There are traces too of Kraftwerk's propensity in those years to alienate the audience from that near-equivalent of the film icon, the pop star, making themselves as corporate and neatly featureless as possible, replacing their presence on stage with showroom

Harrison Ford beside Sean Young as the replicant Rachael in *Blade Runner* (1982).

354

dummies and unmoving robot figures. Within this, particularly in that moment where, as Pris, Daryl Hannah feigns being a lifeless marionette, resides a long fascination with the uncanny puppet, back from Hoffmann's *Der Sandmann* (1816) up to Hans Bellmer's dead, lustful figurines. (It seems apt that one of Hannah's other key roles was a very human, other-than-human mermaid in Ron Howard's *Splash*, 1984.) However, in this medley of influences it is noir romanticism that wins out, gifting the film with its forlorn Californian loneliness.

It's a starkly empty film, preoccupied as it is with the thought that people themselves might be hollow. This predicates too a hollowness in the film star, someone who fills in the roles they play. The plot depends on the notion that the replicants must be allowed to live no longer than four years, because as time passes they begin to develop raw emotions. Why emotion should be a capital offence is never sufficiently explained; but it is of a piece with the film's investigation of a flight from feeling – what psychologist Ian D. Suttie once named the 'taboo on tenderness'.[1] Intimacy here is frightful (everyone appears to live alone), especially that closeness that suggests the replicants might be indistinguishable from us.

This anxiety may originally have had tacit political resonances. In the novel that the film is based on, Philip K. Dick's thoughtful *Do Androids Dream of Electric Sheep?* (1968), the dilemma of the foot soldier plays out, commanded to kill an adversary considered less human than ourselves, yet troubled by the possibility that the enemy are in fact no different. Shades of Vietnam darken the story, as well as memories of America's slave-owning past. We are told that the replicants can do everything a human being can do, except to feel empathy. Yet how much empathy do we feel for faraway victims or inconvenient others?

Harrison Ford's Deckard may or may not be as gripped by uncertainty about his job as was Dick's original 'blade runner'. In any case, his own brusque 'lack of affect' provides one of the long-standing puzzles of the film: is he also a replicant? Certainly Ford's perpetual grumpiness (it sometimes seems his default acting position), his curdled cynicism, put up barriers to feeling that suggest emotion is as

disturbing for him as it is for the hunted Leon or Roy. In the late 1970s
and early '80s Ford offered one key version of masculinity, a mercenary
ready to melt into commitment in the *Star Wars* trilogy, an action hero
in the *Indiana Jones* films who is poised between the adventurous
yearning for the things of the world and an overwhelming sense that
he has already wearily seen everything in it. In *Blade Runner*, irascible
Ford has less opportunity to melt; he looks battle-hardened, worn out
by killings he has carried out before the film even begins. If he turns
towards feeling in the end, it is a process only permitted through suffering and pain. Though some still doubt, it seems clear that Deckard
is indeed a replicant, his imaginings and memories downloaded from
some database, his life as transitory as that of his victims. However, in
watching *Blade Runner* Deckard does not *feel* like a replicant; he is
dour, unengaged certainly, but lacks his victims' detached innocence,
their staccato puzzlement at their own untrained feelings. The antithesis of scowling Harrison Ford, Rutger Hauer's Roy Batty is a sinister
smiler, or someone whose face falls at the brush of an unassimilable
emotion.

After all, the replicants that are Deckard's quarry are in a sense
children, none of them older than four; it should hardly be surprising
that they act like kids too. ('Gosh,' murmurs Roy, as he gazes at a menag-
erie of living puppets and dolls, 'you've really got nice toys here.') It is
through their resemblance to children that we perhaps learn to warm
to them, for all their chilling potentiality for violence. They are children
too in relation to the man who (quite literally) made them – Tyrell, the
Frankenstein-father to Roy Batty's outcast creature. In this regard the
film's Oedipal impulses are inescapable: when pressed about his mother,
Leon replies 'let me tell you about my mother' and blasts the inquir-
ing blade runner in the groin; when Roy demands of Tyrell, 'I want
more life, fucker,' it's the first and only swear word in the film, all the
stronger for it, and more aptly placed than most in being addressed
to a 'father' who has unfeelingly engineered him, and not out of love
fathered him at all.

Tyrell is the Murdochian head of the 'Tyrell Corporation'. One
of the good guesses *Blade Runner* made about the future is that it

would be corporations, not governments, who would really run things. Indebtedness to commercial power depersonalizes the people in this film: more even than dispensable workers, the replicants are not makers of the product, they are the product; otherwise Deckard is a man scoured out by being a functionary on behalf of what he himself names 'the business'. Against this dehumanization, first the replicants and then Deckard strive to create ways that will restore the personal to their lives. Leon attempts to do so by clinging to photographs; one of the key things that Ridley Scott brings to Philip K. Dick's story is an attention to film itself, and to how it makes meaning for us. Leon's sentimental snapshots are lit like the paintings of Edward Hopper, though in them the human figures are almost absent, obscured by gloom, hidden in mirrors. Film would hold on to such fugitive moments, screening remembrance for us. Otherwise memories are lost, as Roy tell us, 'like tears in rain'; but are his memories real or artificially implanted ones? Are the photographs that decorate Deckard's piano authentic or fake?

Yet *Blade Runner* does not gloss over the fact that film can also participate in the dehumanizing procedure, turning others into objects for our voyeurism. Our own resistance to this process can be measured in our responses to the replicants' deaths. Wearing a stripper's bikini and a see-through plastic mac, Zhora's murder is a soft-porn, slow-motion spectacle, played out to sad music; but is sadness for her what we feel? When Pris dies, she does so like a beetle thrashing and screeching on her back; the strangeness of it repulses sympathy. Yet minutes later we shall see Roy mourning her, her death for him not a matter of disgust but of lament. In a sense, the entire film re-enacts the Voight Kampff test that is repeated through it – an attempt to register the presence, or absence, of human empathy in us, the film's remote audience.

The replicant embodies the Nazi category of *das unwerte Leben*, the life that is unworthy to live. They are all that our society would render abject, the migrant, the slave, the dispossessed. Standing outside the social contract that draws us together, outside too the 'thou and I' relationship that frames the human, they are merely threatening and therefore ripe for destruction. We may kill them with impunity; it is not a crime to murder them, but 'justice'.

A strange confusion haunts this movie. In a way it is not surprising that often we respond to the replicants as human beings, for it is always apparent that the actors playing them are human. They are caught in that same conundrum that faces the stage actor who, in Shakespeare's *The Tempest*, embodies Ariel, some boy or girl, man or woman, put in the place of an unsexed, unhuman spirit. And the replicants too, for all they are only this actor, this actress, are also machine-people, traces left by a technology, the spectre of a person in film.

Deckard's own path away from cruelty and disconnection occurs, equivocally enough, in his rejecting the values of the 'business' and allowing himself to fall in love with Rachael. There are three love scenes between them in Deckard's apartment, each played out with gathering closeness: the first is hardly a love scene at all, as the two stalk in different rooms, doors closed between them; the second, just after Rachael has saved Deckard's life, shows him disturbingly violent towards her, bullying her into saying that she loves him, forcing the words into her mouth. The last scene achieves at last both tenderness and reciprocity; as in a fairy tale, he awakens her from what really might be death with a kiss. 'Do you love me?' he asks. 'I love you,' she replies. 'Do you trust me?' 'I trust you.' After these words, still a kind of mirroring perhaps, Deckard denies his role as blade runner; the two of them end the film on the run, as Pris and Roy have been, their unrelenting mortality running with them.

Feeling connection to the beautiful Rachael is one thing; coming into connection with brutal, terrifying Roy Batty is quite another. Since Edgar Allan Poe's Dupin, arguably the first detective, sleuths have solved crimes by putting themselves in the position of the criminal, by becoming what Poe called a 'double Dupin'. For much of the film Deckard refuses to identify himself with his prey; after all that might make him no better than an organic machine. Yet throughout the replicants are busy trying to make him feel as they feel, to share the unnerving experience of 'living in fear'. In one of the film's most brilliant sequences, Roy and Deckard pursue each other through a murky apartment, playing out a vicious child's game of hide and seek. As they do so the similarities between them grow stronger – both are hunter and hunted, both are in pain, both struggle with a hurt, claw-like hand. If at this point, the film suggests a connection here that Deckard himself might still deny, at the very end doubt falls away. Roy's life closes with an act of pity, one that raises him morally over the commercial institutions that would kill him. If Deckard cannot see himself in the other, Roy can. The white dove that flies up from Roy at the moment of his death perhaps stretches belief with its symbolism; but for me at least the movie has earned that moment, suggesting that in the replicant, as in the replicated technology of film itself, there remains a place for something human.

36

MAGGIE CHEUNG:
CENTRE STAGE

aggie Cheung represents the survival of the personality
on film, a latter-day *mensch*. By challenging herself as an
actor, she became an icon of human possibility, not a
body-hacked superwoman, but a character opening up aspects of
herself on film, and readier than most in the period to question the
processes of stardom, and of film acting, that made her fame.

In a new century where China is the key global power, the Chinese
star becomes the new figurehead of international stardom.[1] What is
striking about Cheung is how international her life and her career has
been, how open to hybrid identities, to global citizenship. Born to
Shanghainese parents in Hong Kong, from the age of eight to eighteen
she lived in Bromley. She's fluent in Cantonese, Mandarin, English
and French, and adept at Shanghainese too. In 1983 she returned to
Hong Kong, where she began as a beauty queen, being first runner-up
in the Miss Hong Kong beauty pageant and winning the accolade of
Miss Photogenic. She soon landed roles in Hong Kong films. Although
she had already been recognized as an up-and-coming actress, she truly
found fame with her role as Jackie Chan's petulant, inept but cute girlfriend in *Police Story* (1985). For nine years or so Cheung worked at
an almost manic pace, appearing in dramas like Clara Law's *Farewell
China* (1990), superhero films such as *The Heroic Trio* (1992) and its
sequel, *Executioners* (1993), and light comedies like *Boys Are Easy*
(1993). Bored with the idea of coasting, she reached out for more

challenging roles, moving into arthouse film while maintaining a place in the mainstream.

Wong Kar-wai's *As Tears Go By* (1988), Ann Hui's *Song of the Exile* and Wong Kar-wai's *Days of Being Wild* (both 1990) marked this new direction, with Maggie Cheung playing a series of characters who are sidelined, displaced. In Hui's broadly autobiographical *Song of the Exile,* Cheung's character moves between London and Hong Kong and the Japan that was her mother's birthplace. In *Days of Being Wild*, she is unrequited, abandoned, given over to a dreary seriousness, a native of Macau adrift in a drifting Hong Kong.

Stanley Kwan's *Center Stage* (1991) takes Cheung's burgeoning status as film star and uses it to explore the life of one of China's foremost stars of the silent era, Ruan Lingyu (1910–1935), a woman whose young life was ended abruptly by her suicide, aged 24. With Cheung playing both herself and Ruan, the film is as self-conscious a meditation on the meanings of film and the film star as any explored in this book. *Center Stage* begins with stills – blurred, remote – of Ruan, and then shows the director himself talking of Ruan's roles as being all too often 'merely decorative', the films she played in not allowing her talent to thrive. 'Just like me,' laughs Maggie Cheung, there as herself, reflecting on the woman she is to play. Elsewhere in the film Carina Lau gazes at a video interview with Li Li-Li, the actor she plays in the movie. These Brechtian interventions disrupt the narrative of the film, with actors and directors reflecting on Ruan's life and on the films she played in, breaking up the staged re-enactments of that life and of those films. We share in the artifice of film, regarding a death in the falling rain, and then raising our eyes to see the watering cans that poured that rain, or looking back down to the breathing person who was just now that lifeless body. Scenes restaged by Kwan with Cheung as Ruan are placed beside clips from the original films themselves. Kwan tells us that Ruan 'became what she played'. Cheung acts scenes over that Ruan acted, doing so silently, reproducing too moments from vanished films, where there is no original to pit against its re-enactment. We see Cheung remake films we have and films we have lost. There is both a tang of nostalgia and a desire for resurrection in this. In performing again these once-performed moments, Cheung plays with another style of playing, on the far side of naturalism, her face painted white, the way she holds her body stylized and self-conscious. Cheung imitates Ruan, as we know that Ruan imitated Marlene Dietrich; cinema selves find themselves through others. We move between scenes of Cheung embodying Ruan as she was in life, and then playing Ruan as she remains as an image on film, disembodied, a photographed person. In one moment Cheung talks to Kwan in a mirror, discussing Ruan, contemplating herself.

The film begins in 1929, in an all-male bathhouse, where the men discuss the essence of Ruan Lingyu's acting, of her presence on film. Ruan both exists to herself and lives her life in a movie. In the latter case, we are asked to doubt how much of who she appears to be is determined by the visions of men. The film reiterates scene after scene where a man directs Ruan's performance. Often Ruan knows more than the man who directs her, yet she mediates herself by knowing what they want of her, by a giving that comes from her talent to respond. Acting is what she does, the person on-screen a version of who she is, but still it is also something directed, looked at, called upon by men. These men – both her directors and her lovers – seek to read things in Ruan's face, as in Cheung's.

Ruan began her career being noble and tragic, and midway turned to playing robust and austere roles, a suitable actor for the new politically engaged revolutionary film. To achieve this metamorphosis, all that is required is for Cheung as Ruan to wipe off her lipstick, deglamorizing herself in a single gesture. She had played victims, and now in an instant becomes 'a positive woman'.

Behind all the bustle of movie-making and parties, Cheung, as Ruan, projects an unhealable sadness. As Ruan, Cheung cries on-screen, and each time Ruan's acting, and therefore Cheung's, blurs the border between theatre and truth. Is the distress we see feigned distress or the real thing? Forced or forced upon us, a tear is still shed. The film does not know, as none of us know, what separates the artifice from what the actor finds within themselves. Ruan, in particular, has been understood as playing on film the emotions and scenes of her private life.[2] In the movie, the scene ends, but we watch it play on, as Cheung as Ruan still weeps, performing genuine distress or merely lost in performance. After watching one such scene, one of her directors tells her to save some tears for him; and she does so, crying uncontrollably in another later scene, as he lets the cameras roll on. Her co-star Li-li Li remarks that, after playing a suicide on film, Ruan 'couldn't stop crying for most of the day'.[3]

As the actors in the film themselves suggest, Ruan's suicide secured her legend, an early death freezing in time her image of youth and beauty – and bringing to it the taste of tragedy. Gossip about Ruan's love affairs, her life torn between the amorous covetousness of two men – Zhang Damin and Tang Jishan – become the story, and such gossip flits fast beyond the control of the person they concern. The public person possesses this strange vulnerability of being subject to the potency of the story. The press crucified Ruan; she acted modern women on-screen, and then was hounded to death for her modernity in real life. Like Dietrich, Ruan played the element of sensuality in the abject. And yet this sensuality is both consumed and suspected. Here, as elsewhere (in *In the Mood for Love* (2000) and *Clean* (2004), for example), Cheung plays a rather unmaternal mother, her daughter pushed to one side of her life. Several times Ruan played noble prostitutes, as in Sun Yu's *Spring Dreams of an Old Capital* (1930) and Wu Yonggang's *The Goddess* (1934). As in India, the actresses of the 1930s and '40s were often seen in terms of the traditions surrounding courtesans. Ruan's bad position was in part perhaps caused by the fact that, though she played virtuous women on-screen, her private life was regarded as highly compromised; audiences and newspaper editors would not countenance this split in her.[4]

In the end, the viewers brought down Ruan. The judging masses and the newspapers who sustained her career provoked her suicide. They turned this person into an icon of themselves, of their own suffering and possibilities, into someone scapegoated and adored. *Center Stage* plays out the private life and the public image, both turned into commodities for the crowd. It is still strangely difficult to believe that the stars exist in private, that they own their lives. For what they offer in the cinema feels so real, for all that it is only a fabrication of reality. Kwan screens scenes of off-screen intimacy, publishing the privacy that Ruan once protected. With the star, the public own the person enacted on film. Ruan pursues death so as to fly the pitiless force of gossip. Ruan had to die because, as Kwan tells us, 'she was a star, not an ordinary woman,' a public person pressed down by public opinion. Ruan's funeral was attended by more than 100,000 mourners; three women committed suicide during the rite, their deaths echoes of the infectious influence of the star.

Though it is done in response to the gossip of the press, Ruan's private suicide can be read as the one thing she directs herself. This dismal scene she must act alone, taking the sleeping pills while her lover dozes, unknowing. Afterwards, beside her, the men respond to her dead body, reading it as they had once read the person they witnessed in the public space before the screen. Here at its end, the film mourns Ruan and resurrects her in death; we see Cheung holding her breath to be the suicide, and then breathe again, alive in the moving picture, before we see Ruan, truly dead, trapped in the perpetual stillness of a photograph.

In Cheung's next major film, *Ashes of Time* (1994), Wong Kar-wai explores the thought that to be human is to live with memory, that we need its cohering force if we are to understand our lives as an ongoing story. Yet the film cuts up any such attempt at coherence; for much of the time, the average viewer simply struggles with the difficulty of knowing what's going on. The structure slips on ellipses, and the persons of the film are fragmented, inconsistent with themselves; one reviewer at the time dismissed it as 'an exquisite photo album masquerading as a motion picture'.[5] Brigitte Lin plays both sister and brother, Mu-rong Yin and Mu-rong Yang, and I for one was never clear if these really are two distinct persons, or the confusing product of a cross-dressing ruse. In the midst of these bafflements, Maggie Cheung's character provides a moment of stillness, representing something permanent in the flux. It was to be this heady stability in Cheung, her holding steady amidst life's chaos, that would characterize her next great roles: the tangible sadness in her, the apartness mirroring as calm the hectic world. She would not be proof to its instabilities, but would offer them back as reflection.

In Olivier Assayas' *Irma Vep* (1996) Maggie Cheung plays Maggie Cheung. It is a film about the condition of being a film star, lost in the chaos of film-making. She's flown from Hong Kong to Paris to play the role of 'Irma Vep' in a remake of Louis Feuillade's masterwork, the urban crime serial *Les Vampires* (1915–16). Irma was originally played by the streetwise dark-eyed French vamp Musidora, a Parisian Theda Bara. As the wayward director, Jean-Pierre Léaud, tells 'Maggie', 'I don't want you to act . . . I just want you to be in the film . . .' She, Maggie Cheung, outstrips the character she is set to play in importance, and once again she is to pay homage to and somehow inhabit the persona of a dead star from the silent age.

Casting Cheung as Irma Vep draws on the internationalization of cinema, in a production that is both very French and yet plays for much of the time in the new lingua franca of English. Unable to speak French, the film within the film condemns Cheung to silence. The replacement director, brought in when Léaud's character has a breakdown, rails against the casting of a 'Chinoise': casting Cheung is an invasion from abroad, an assault on Frenchness. To him Irma Vep is the 'Parisienne' personified, she is Arletty, not some actress from Hong Kong.

Irma Vep multiplies moments of awkwardness and of rapacity for another. The desire to make trouble prompts many of the characters, from the older woman who sabotages the costume designer's desire for Cheung, to the young actress Zoé, or the male co-star rehearsing with her. The director, Jean-Pierre Léaud, declares that he cast Cheung in order to see her in the bondage costume. 'That's desire,' says Cheung, only a little thrown, 'and I think it's OK, because that's what we make movies with.' 'It's just a part,' she says, 'it's like a game.' 'It's not a game!' rages the director, 'It's very important!' Fantasized on-screen, keeping her head through the filming, Maggie keeps herself to herself. 'She's like a plastic toy,' muses the costume designer who fancies her, a simulacrum of a person to play with. She's a 'cartoon character', a fantasy version of a human being. We see Cheung with her body-double,

Maggie Cheung in Olivier Assayas' *Irma Vep* (1996).

performing the stunts the star cannot. Later, in a scene between fantasy and reality, she plays out becoming the part, acting the role of a jewel thief in 'real life', stealing into a room where a naked woman rows with her lover on the phone, and snatching the stranger's necklace while she's distracted. No one can tell if this theft is a fantasy that Cheung has, or that the 'Cheung' in the movie has, or if it is a 'real' event. The reality of what we see shifts – and it is precisely this transformation in the seen that this film tells us that cinema permits – and permits precisely through the generative possibilities of particular faces, the screened presence of the star.

As in *Center Stage*, Cheung must re-enact a silent film performance, one we watch with Maggie and the director. This Maggie, like the actual Maggie, has become famous in action films, ones that she herself rather looks down on. *Irma Vep* shows other possibilities for cinema, as silent mime, as committed social commentary, as action movie, a form that operates between technique and inspiration. The film evokes stress and exhaustion, while itself brimming with life. At its close we see the short sequence that Léaud edited immediately prior to his breakdown. Nothing we have seen up to this point prepares us for the scenes that follow, where Stan Brakhage-like scratches on the negative turn Cheung and the photographed scenes into half-animated figures, the energy in the characters darting from the eyes, or shimmering electrically about the outlines of the body. Watching the film in the cinema on its first release, these closing moments utterly stunned me. Is the film, as some have argued, at the end 'defaced'? I see it rather as a tribute to the face's power, a spirited simulation of the energies intrinsic to the person, drawn out, etched in, flickering with the frames of a film.

Cheung married Assayas after making the film, but they divorced in 2001. Meanwhile in *The Soong Sisters* (1997) she rather improbably played Madam Sun Yat-sen. The film is everything that *Center Stage* was not, a rather grand and pretty unreflective bio-pic. After the manic early years of her career, she was making fewer films. Yet her greatest triumph was about to come.

With Wong Kar-wai's magnificent *In the Mood for Love*, Maggie Cheung revives memories of the great Taiwanese and Hong Kong women stars of the 1950s and '60s.[6] Married and grown-up, Cheung plays Su Liz-hen, who she had already played in *Days of Being Wild*, and would be again in *2046* (2004), the character and the actor existing beyond the individual film, growing old in discrete stories. Su Liz-hen has turned into Mrs Chan, whose husband is having an affair with their next-door neighbour, Mrs Chow. Drawn together by their partners' infidelity, Mrs Chan and Mr Chow (played by Tony Leung) become close and before our eyes fall in love. Bound by ideas of integrity, they repress desire, though it remains unclear who would be hurt by their coming together.

The mood that *In the Mood for Love* establishes is slow, broody; moments repeat as the melancholy waltz from another film similarly repeats, as the two stars pass each other on the stairs, as they shelter from the rain. Wong Kar-wai filmed light-hearted scenes of dancing or cooking together: all were cut. The would-be lovers live next door to each other, lodgers in adjacent apartments, sealed off and separate, but also interconnected, just as their marriages interconnect and criss-cross. Lonely with others, they inscribe a ring around their own companionship, forbidden and policed as it may be. They meet in urban Hong Kong, an unbeautiful, un-green world, only urban and dirty and constrained, though this film discovers what beauty it has. Indeed, above all, beauty is what we take from the film, whether it's Tony Leung's, Maggie Cheung's or the faded city's.

Ackbar Abbas has suggested that 'stories about Hong Kong always turned into stories about somewhere else'.[7] (I shall return to this concern with displacement in the elucidation of place when considering the position of another 'Chinese' film star, Shu Qi.) And therefore perhaps the political world, the post-colonial realm, shadows their shared dream. Shanghai proves to be present in Hong Kong, as the landlady Mrs Suen, Mrs Chan (Maggie Cheung) and Wong Kar-wai himself all come from there. The city is a hybrid locale, whose culture comes from everywhere; Nat King Cole plays, in Spanish, in early 1960s Hong Kong.

The two deceived spouses re-enact their partners' affair, doubling it. They rehearse imagined scenes that the others might have played, and in the process play them too for each other, using the theatre of what they imagine to express and displace their shared desire. We do not need to see their spouses, because our heroes will anyway re-enact and reimagine what they have said or done. The adulterous relation-ship and the passionately repressed friendship are performed by the same couple. As in all adulteries, the illicit lovers will reproduce the absent spouse. Here, in these scenes of fantasy and rehearsal, the trace of those moments from *Center Stage* reappears, where some man directs the woman star. But now Cheung makes up her performance together, mutually. Mrs Chan and Mr Chow also write together, pro-ducing martial-arts serials for the papers, making a joint enterprise of doing so; they are making up others' stories, in order to invent their own. Sometimes the viewer experiences a double-take, where we are uncertain if we witness candid, honest speech or merely a perfor-mance. Tony Leung plays her husband, the deceiver; she plays the mistress, his wife; as our heroes fall in love might not their spouses similarly have fallen, the deception forgivable, as theirs is, by the measure of their reciprocal passion?

Watching it, your heart breaks with them. The audience too falls illicitly in love; we have their affair, imaginatively, in their place. This is a film about an 'affair' that wants to resist the structures and clichés of the affair film; instead it becomes a movie about the keeping and sharing of secrets. *In the Mood for Love* dwells in the unsaid; it proceeds by indirection, making a narrative from glances. Your secret is yours, and your story cannot be confessed. When Mr Chow confides his secret to the hole in the wall at Angkor Wat, we may guess what he says, but never know for sure if we are right.

In the Mood for Love remains, for now, the highpoint of Cheung's career, and indeed one of the very greatest films of the last twenty years. Cheung has declared that in her films with Wong Kar-wai and Olivier Assayas she has fitted into how the two directors perceive beauty, bringing out Wong's desire for the sensual as easily as she finds Assayas' 'internal and modern' version of beauty. In so doing, Cheung accepts the moulding of her self in drama according to the vision of the man who directs her. As we have seen, this was once Ruan Lingyu's plight too.

In the glorious *Hero* (2002) with Zhang Yimou as director, she and Tony Leung together find complexity and an operatic melancholy in the martial arts action film. That film sustained the high that *In the Mood for Love* had reached. However, Cheung had one more chance to outstrip herself, and to pursue a new kind of role on-screen. In Olivier Assayas' *Clean* she plays a widowed junkie, whose early career as a former MTV-style VJ and her position as a famous rock star's wife has left her on the edge of the 'cool world'. After her part in her husband's overdose leads to a spell in a Canadian prison, Cheung's character moves down in the world, flying back to Paris and finding work in Chinese restaurants or a department store. She still hopes to become a rock star herself, and the movie ends with Cheung performing a track for a prospective CD in tuneless tones reminiscent of Marianne Faithfull's album *Broken English*. More vitally, the heart of the film consists of her nervous attempts to reconnect with her estranged child, to be something other than lonely.

Clean is a rootless, dispersed film, playing out in Canada (on tour), Vancouver (where Cheung's character's son lives with his grandparents), Paris, London and San Francisco. Families here are scattered and Cheung stands as the embodiment of that scattering.

Cheung is hugely accomplished in this film, but she is dedicating herself to what feels like a hollow entity, as bleak as the heroin-chic culture it commemorates. Again, as in other of Cheung's films, *Clean* attaches to the life of stardom, asking what it is we project on to the famous. It features real music stars, with Tricky playing 'Tricky', and Canadian singer Emily Haines similarly playing herself. Cheung's character is complex, human, always comprehensible. Yet the film's fabric is one in which relations are always strained, where others disappoint, where the death of an ex-lover hardly elicits any emotional response, where people do not connect, but 'hang out', don't deepen, but seek to belong to a realm of fame where no belonging lasts.

Reprising and riffing on *Days of Being Wild* and *In the Mood for Love*, Wong Kar-wai's *2046* examines the continuities and discontinuities in the fact of film, breaking up and stitching together Carina Lau's and Tony Leung's characters from the earlier films, themselves and not themselves, ageing, regretful. It is a film where Tony Leung, reacting against the serious passions of *In the Mood for Love*, turns into a smug seducer, the film structured by his serial involvements with a series of leading ladies: Carina Lau, Gong Li, Faye Wong, Zhang Ziyi. In *2046* Cheung's role as Mrs Chan has her stand as the ideal woman, someone loved and let go of. Failing at his chance for permanence, Tony Leung's character opts for the temporary. It is a film about memory and therefore it is not surprising that Cheung's few appearances in this film are reminders of the earlier film, flashbacks so that, unlike Tony Leung, she cannot appear as she now is, aged four more years. Cheung has appeared in very few films since *2046* and *Clean*. To her credit, she turned down a role in *X2* (2003), resisting the pull to sustain a career through the compromises of the Americanized action film. Her two scenes in Quentin Tarantino's *Inglourious Basterds* (2009) were cut from the completed movie. She has spoken in interviews of the problems created by ageing for women actors, not yet ready to play the grand-mother roles, but too old to play the heroine's best friend.

Cheung's absence from current cinema is surely a loss; yet she already has lived in the future of film. Cross-cultural, international, she stands beyond the limitations of any one national cinema, com-mitted to a Hong Kong that is both a locality and a bridge between places. Above all, she has brought to the screen an image of home-lessness, even as she brings to the roles she plays a fiercely protected embeddedness in the privacy of a life, screened, recorded, felt through and felt with, but always remote from us, moving on to places beyond any one story's end, still breathing and resurrected as the character she plays departs.

37

NAOMI WATTS:
MULHOLLAND DRIVE

I n 2001 David Lynch's career was at a crossroads. At this stage in
his trajectory, after the golden period that extended from *Blue
Velvet* (1986) to the first season of *Twin Peaks* and *Wild at Heart*
(both 1990), Lynch was in the doldrums following the sceptical critical reactions to the films *Twin Peaks: Fire Walk With Me* (1992) and
Lost Highway (1997). With its slow, folksy charm, *The Straight Story*
(1999) was to some, including myself, a welcome departure from what
had come to seem Lynch 'doing Lynch', playing over the same hand
of absurdist cards. However, not for the first time in his film-making
career, Lynch seemed all but down and out. As part of this low,
Mulholland Drive (2001) might have been forever incomplete. The
American network ABC commissioned a pilot for a series from Lynch.
When they sat down to watch what he had come up with, shocked
and offended, they pulled the plug on the deal. With the intervention
of Alain Sarde and Canal Plus, the finished film developed out of this
rejected pilot, some 45 minutes of additional material being added
to the 95 minutes that had already been completed.

Out of this amalgam of a film came what may be one of the
greatest movie acting performances of the twenty-first century. Here
Naomi Watts did what her character wanted to do: she became both
a great actress and a movie star. In the process, she and Lynch dreamt
up one of the most ferocious and intense and beautiful meditations
on film-making and on the nature of the human being ever made.

To précis this film is an impossible task, so busy it is with false starts, twists, unfinished business, to say nothing of the mysterious, interpretation-defying complexity of its main plot. On Mulholland Drive, a young woman (former Miss USA 1985, Laura Elena Harring) is about to be murdered, when a car crash rescues her from certain death. The sole survivor, concussed, confused, she wanders down into the Los Angeles streets below and hides in a newly vacated apartment. Here, the apartment's next occupant arrives, Betty Elms (played by Naomi Watts), a chipper young woman from Ontario, come to Hollywood to try to find fame as an actress. The apartment has been lent to her by her aunt, herself a Hollywood actor. Finding the young woman already in possession of the place, Betty assumes that the mysterious stranger is a friend of her aunt's. Instead it quickly emerges that the woman, who names herself 'Rita' (after a poster of Rita Hayworth in *Gilda* that she finds in the bathroom), has lost her memory (shades of Ronald Colman in *Random Harvest*). Attracted and intrigued, a thirty-something would-be Nancy Drew, Betty decides to help Rita solve the mystery of her identity. Meanwhile a young director, Adam Kesher (Justin Theroux), is being pressured by the Mafia (and by forces behind the Mafia) to cast a young woman, Camilla Rhodes, as the star of his next film. Betty and Rita enter an ever-deepening mystery, discovering the decomposing body of Diane Selwyn, who may perhaps have been Rita's friend or housemate. The two young women become lovers and go to a mysterious nightclub, where a strange box, to which Rita already has the key, appears in Betty's handbag. On their return Betty vanishes and Rita is left alone with the box; she opens it and the camera rushes inside. From now on, the film doubles into a darkened version of its first half. Rita becomes Camilla Rhodes, a movie star, in a floundering relationship with Diane (now played by Watts), but ready to give it up for marriage to her director, Kesher, while also clearly involved in an affair with the young woman who played Camilla Rhodes (Melissa George) in the film's first half. Things darken and disintegrate; Diane hires a hitman to murder Camilla, but instead, threatened and harried, she shoots herself.

In *Mulholland Drive* once again we fall into Lynch's world, and yet here the 1950s nostalgia, the corridor-prowling camera, the mysterious brunette, the criminal conspiracies, and all the rest of the paraphernalia of Lynch's imagination return freshened and renewed. The film's 'postmodernity' strikes us in its abrupt, illegible collisions of tone, its hectic veering between cruelty and kitsch, suffering and absurdity. For all its gloom, for all its unnerving anxieties, it is also at times a very funny movie. A scene with an incompetent hitman is ruthless, but also bleakly comedic. The movie immerses itself in Lynch's *oeuvre*, but without tiredness, plotting interconnections. As with the greatest artists, Lynch's primary source is himself, his own work and his own world. To take only a few examples of this: Betty comes from Deep River, Ontario, while Dorothy Vallens (Isabella Rossellini), the femme fatale mother of *Blue Velvet*, lived in Deep River Apartments; the film's preoccupation with car crashes takes us back to *Wild at Heart*; the camera's going down into the box reprises its descent into the eye-slit in the Elephant Man's head-covering or into the ear in *Blue Velvet*, the film taking us via those openings into an hallucinated realm.

Betty's ambition is to be 'discovered and become a movie star', though she would rather be a 'great actress than a movie star', though 'sometimes people end up being both'. Harring's Rita finds herself identified too with a star, imprinted with Rita Hayworth's dangerous femme fatale, Gilda. The history of noir pulses through Harring's immeasurably beautiful, distressed presence. Indeed, the whole film opens itself up to film history, with Harring a convincing double to Ava Gardner in *The Killers*, with The Cowboy who haunts the film just an uncanny movie country-and-western cowboy, a vestige of film tradition. It is a film that, like its leads, does not have one identity either. Genres cross and leave traces. The film spreads before us, a site for dreaming, not one thing but many.

It would be wrong to say the film hinges on any one scene, or even set of scenes; it is too jarring and disparate for that. Yet it proves ready to present us with moments in which action stills and we pause to regard someone's performance. We join up with the audience on-screen and together contemplate the show. Such instances open

Mulholland Drive up to the charge of being 'self-reflexive', a movie about movies, and certainly that would be a credible reading of the film. However, the impact of those scenes does not stop there. They show the film as more than just another investigation of the actor and of the star.

It would be easy to multiply occasions in Lynch's films where people stand aside and watch some act: in *The Elephant Man* (1980) there are those freak show spectacles; the frenzied metal gig in *Wild At Heart*; *Blue Velvet*'s vicious Frank Booth torn and tearful as he listens to Dorothy Vallens sing, or mimes along with white-faced Ben (Dean Stockwell) lip-synching to Roy Orbison's 'In Dreams'. In *Mulholland Drive* there are four or five such moments: the pair of auditions in the film studio where women sing (or act out singing) early 1960s pop songs, Connie Stevens's 'Sixteen Reasons' and Linda Scott's 'I've Told Ev'ry Little Star'; Betty and Rita roughly rehearsing Betty's audition piece alone together in the kitchen at Betty's aunt's place, and then before the director and casting agents Betty's mesmerizing performance at the audition itself; and, above all, Rebekah Del Rio's soaring 'Llorando', a cover of Orbison's 'Crying', staged in the mysterious nightclub or theatre Silencio.

In each of these scenes, the cinema audience finds itself merged with the audience within the scene, so that when Betty auditions, she auditions also for us. Moreover, when Rebekah Del Rio sings, we watch her with Rita and Betty, while watching too how they are moved to tears by the power that lacerates her singing. Our feeling doubles due to the fact that they seem to feel it too; if while watching pornography we are aroused in another's arousal, and in horror we are afraid in another's fear, here we are moved, in part, because others are moved. Our reaction to the film becomes a shared state, something linking us to others in the cinema audience, and across the divide with those on the screen. It is not so much a self-reflexive moment as a moment in which we merge with the reflections of ourselves offered to us by the film.

In these moments the narrative melts into the contemplation of an act. We, who are involved in a work of art, partake with others within the film of their own involvement with another work of art. When someone 'performs' (as, of course, the actors are in fact performing throughout the film), then we take that performance as offering us both themselves but also someone different from who they ordinarily are. A moment finds itself framed, and around that framing accrue conventions and rules, of attentiveness, of distance, of judgement. When we sing, dance for others, play or act, we mark out a moment distinct from our everyday self, that self being now found in what it chooses to do. Despite what the sociologist Erving Goffman argued, we cannot always be performing. Moreover, undoubtedly although when we perform we engage in a ritual, an event that is distinct from quotidian reality, nonetheless that performing self is also a heightening of who we are, perhaps a best version of the self. As Philip Larkin said of his poems, 'they are better than I am, but I am more than they are'.

During an interview Lynch has suggested that amnesia and acting are interconnected, the latter like the first a kind of self-forgetting. What is so magnificent about Del Rio here, and about Watts's and Harring's response as they watch her, is how much they allow themselves to lose themselves in the moment of artistic creation. It is an assertion of self that comes with the forgoing of the ego. At the peak of Del Rio's glorious rendition, the singer closes her mouth, stops, and then faints; and despite her collapse her song continues without her. Those who do not know that it is in any case truly Del Rio who sings, and even those who do know this, experience in this moment a sense of betrayal. The compère has told us in advance that it's an illusion, that all is recorded, lip-synched, and yet, entranced by the power of what we have seen, we forget – or choose to forget – that fact. Here we have perhaps no more than another moment in a Hollywood movie where the human voice is shown to be alienated from the human image, like at the end of *Singin' in the Rain*, when Lina Lamont is exposed as merely mouthing the words that Kathy Selden truly provides. Yet this moment is different; it is Del Rio, after all, who sings, lip-synching to her own performance, borrowing her own voice. It is the intervention in the sense of presence that hurts, that

Jaded and falling apart, Naomi Watts plays the troubled Diane in David Lynch's
Mulholland Drive (2001).

feeling the movie gives us here that the encapsulated humanity of
that song, of that voice, is real, but also deferred, derailed. The self is
there, and elsewhere; before us on the screen, but actually that image
has detached itself from the person that it holds and records.

'Solutions' to the film's mystery that have Diane in its second part
dreaming Betty in its first are intriguing, but ultimately unconvincing
as a final explanation of the film. When I first saw it, at its UK premiere

at the London Film Festival, where Watts and Harring shyly came out on stage when the movie ended, I know that I saw the second part as Betty's nightmare, a solution no better, but maybe equally plausible. As in Elizabeth Bowen's time-loop short story 'The Happy Autumn Fields', two characters in two distinct tales may just be dreaming, or remembering, or foretelling, each other. Who dreams whom? Or, as Lewis Carroll put it, the dream is which?

The film creates conundrums about identity that cannot finally be solved. In *Vertigo* such doublings as we have here bring us back to the actor. The disruptions in other films give us an unstable self, but one still found perhaps in performance, in the arch made by the story. Here, under the influence of Transcendental Meditation (and Lynch is a great exponent of its techniques), while still reflecting on the nature of the actor, and therefore of the human being, the dissolution of identity that *Mulholland Drive* forges comes out of a profound disbelief in the existence of the self, per se. All are one; the self is illusion. Identities are porous and permeable, elusive and strange. Watts dissolves into the other women in the film, the star sinking into the bit-part players: the woman who plays the waitress at the diner, the actress who plays the street hooker. Choosing amnesia, losing the self, Watts vanishes into other roles; she's an actor becoming anything, in a film where the devilish figure who controls all the wickedness sends out people like puppets to do his will. (At the start of the film Rita may herself be seen to look like a marionette when she stumbles and staggers from the scene of the car crash.)

When Watts as Betty prepares the audition with Rita, she is rough, hackneyed, emotive but clumsy, hardly taking her own acting seriously. In the actual audition, we see the scene played again (one of the innumerable mirrorings and repetitions woven into this film), and this time her acting is stunningly good, potently real. We see in practice how a scene can be different, even as it is the same. The rehearsal begins as an abuse of power, the older male actor who plays her lover forcing himself on the auditioning wannabe. But Betty plays along with it and tops his bullying by the power of her own performance, turning his control into a mutual seduction and then, at its end, rejecting and diminishing him. When she tells the older man, 'you're playing a dangerous game here', we wonder if the line is delivered to the character or the actor.

From this scene on, if not before, having seen what Watts can achieve, we are always aware of Naomi Watts's acting. The doubling that she must embody places the virtuosity of her performance at the heart of the film. Throughout this film she acts so brilliantly, with such verve, such conviction, such lostness in each moment: and yet, due to the film's construction, to its ironies and its sardonic removal from the placid, plastic normalities of American life, we always think of her as, in fact, acting.

In the history of cinema it is one of the recurring problems of films that they should sometimes include moments where we step back from the pretence we have been lost in and we regard the actor acting. These moments are usually associated with clumsiness, with doing a bad job. The break in the illusion comes from the jolt provided by ineptitude. But with Watts in *Mulholland Drive* this consciousness of her as an actor transforms into an excellence. Due to Watts's talent, she joins wholeheartedly with the movie's unmasking of cinema, an unmasking that exposes another mask beneath, and another one under that, mask after mask, layer after layer. It is not a tired 'meta-cinematic' playfulness, it is a glittering darkness of artifices.

To Lynch, the movie is a love story, and there is much to be said for that as a way to understand the film. The first sex scene between Betty and Rita is erotic, tender, loving; even more their closeness when they go to the nightclub theatre together is gently touching. But even here, though Betty twice tells Rita that she's in love with her, Rita does not offer a word in response. Mostly love here is a dim business, a matter of obsession and betrayal. Later, in the film's second half, there'll be another sex scene between Diane (Watts) and Camilla, and here it's not affectionate but raunchy, driven, on the edge of being brutal. The conspiratorial paranoia that informs the movie's preoccupation with the Mafia and networks of evil finds its personal counterpart in reiterated scenes of sexual jealousy and revelations of infidelity. People are threatening, or disappointing, or both. Sex dwindles to masturbation, as Diane sobs and rubs herself, wanking out of anger, despair and loneliness.

We are told that Watts's tears in the masturbation scene were real tears, provoked by her sense of humiliation in having to thrust her hand down her pants in front of a movie crew. The reality of those tears is a strange double to the 'in quotes' acting of the film's first part. Here we find another recurring trope in film, a moment where someone on-screen is perhaps not acting at all, but is merely there, recorded and doubled while in the process of being themselves. Watts risks herself here for the sake of the film, and in total it is her courage that one takes from the film, someone giving all of themselves for the sake of a person they are not.

38

SCARLETT JOHANSSON: A NEW KIND OF EMPTINESS

I n her short career Scarlett Johansson has played so many roles and embraced so much human variety that it can prove hard to characterize her. She has operated beyond the limits of one persona, and she has not, as Marilyn Monroe or Audrey Hepburn once did, come to mean one complex thing, to make up one strongly delineated way of being in the world. From her many parts, however, one may tease out a particular thread that sheds more light than any comparable star's career could on the contemporary meaning of the film star, and by extension of the contemporary idea of the person.

Johansson began her adult career as the 'other woman'. In Sofia Coppola's *Lost in Translation*, in *Girl with a Pearl Earring* (both 2003), in Woody Allen's *Match Point* (2006), or *The Other Boleyn Girl* (2008), she comes to life in relation to an unlicensed male desire. As late as *Her* (2013) she was still operating in the thin territory allotted to her own wishes as opposed to someone only called into being by a man's interest or will. In *Under the Skin* (2013) and Luc Besson's *Lucy* (2014), she has lived on to become the sometimes violent rebuttal of those masculine fantasies. In Johansson's films, particularly those she has made with Woody Allen, men confront her with what they call her 'sensuality' and are pleased to discern if she understands her effect on men. Yet in all those wonderful early films Johansson's characters mark out their distance from that effect, and prove apt to refute or outsoar those illusions.

For no one is going to blame Charlotte, Johansson's character in Coppola's charming *Lost in Translation*, even if she teeters on the edge of an adulterous affair with Bill Murray's film star character. She is here as a complex, completely likeable person, and a directionless young woman in a self-consciously directionless movie. Indeed, she's a revision of Dustin Hoffman's graduate, caught in the hesitancy of arriving adulthood and consoling herself with an older love. (The covers band – 'Sausalito' – at the Tokyo hotel where they meet even offers up a cheesy repeat of 'Scarborough Fair'.) Her own rival for her husband's attention is just the kind of self-obsessed, blondely narcissistic film star that Charlotte is not. Charlotte, like Johansson herself back then, seems just a person in a film, and not yet a star. In her sweetly unconsummated relationship with another film star, played by Bill Murray, the key to Charlotte's success with him is that she pays no heed to the fact of his fame. Is it that she has failed to recognize him? It seems rather that she approaches him quite naturally as one person to another, unfazed by his stardom. They pair their mutual loneliness, their insomniac sojourn in the temporary world of a Tokyo hotel. In his own way Murray is as directionless as she is, though we also see him as the constantly 'directed' film star, bullied into enacting himself, which often also means becoming others, channelling Sinatra or Roger Moore for a TV commercial. The movie's sweet karaoke scene, with Murray revealing himself as a closet crooner, a would-be Bryan Ferry, is another instance of this film's preoccupation with how we might lose ourselves, never live life on our own lines, but exist only as echoes of others, using those others to reveal otherwise unexpressed aspects of ourselves.

In the midst of all this alienation, when it comes to Charlotte/ Scarlett, above all, we simply appreciate her, just as Murray does, and just as her errant photographer husband fails to do. In this, Johansson carried over some of the laconic goodwill accrued in the sweet indie movie *Ghost World* (2001), based on the graphic novel by Daniel Clowes. For this viewer at least, that vicarious feeling of amity for Johansson persists up to the present, even as her later films have deliberately set out to throw it into question.

In an interview connected to *Girl with a Pearl Earring*, Johansson remarks on how differently one may approach the woman in the Johannes Vermeer painting that inspired the film, that sometimes she can seem brutal, ugly, and at others mesmerizing, so that one must stare and stare, hopeful of finding the reason for her attraction. Johansson's young women were similarly apt to exist between those two poles of interpretation. In *Match Point* Johansson's character's ex-fiancé remarks that he has seen her on the street and that she looked quite 'hard'. As the movie progresses, and her affair with the young married Jonathan Rhys Meyers ends up with her falling pregnant, she dwindles from sex symbol to demanding harridan. In her films with Woody Allen we may detect a tendency alternately to adore and resist Johansson's beauty, both to dote upon her and to make cheap gibes about the potential for hardness in her face, even, in a harsh joke in the otherwise charming *Scoop* (2006), for her to look 'piggy'. It is as though these films want both to venerate and to resist her extraordinary attractiveness.

This instability in the persona of the star was hardly new, and in it Johansson's characters showed their propensity to fall into long-standing ways of understanding a woman protagonist. *Girl with a Pearl Earring* shows Johansson's character turning, as Johansson herself might be thought to be doing, into a work of art. In the painting that Vermeer makes of his young servant, motion stills, and breathing life acquires the stasis of apparent permanence. Yet the artwork that Vermeer, and the film, fabricates is one that is impossible to read. The painting shines forth a caught moment, where the relation to the artist and to the viewer becomes mysterious, the persisting sign of a narrative that the film has contrived. When Vermeer's wife sees the painting, she cries out, 'It's obscene!', and perhaps a mere sexual exposure might be read in it, were it not also for the fact that we also feel that we glimpse in that surface glance a soul, caught in a relation to a person.

In *Hitchcock* (2012), a film based around the making of *Psycho*, Johansson took the part of Janet Leigh, reproducing therefore cinema's most vicious assault on the concept of the film star. It was around this time, beginning with *Iron Man 2* (2010), with her move from the world

Scarlett Johansson in *Lost in Translation* (2003).

of largely independent films to the action movie, that a significant change occurred in her on-screen persona. This change is resonant both for our understanding of her as an actor, but also, on a larger scale, as a symptomatic shift in our relation to the film star and to the idea of the human.

In the Marvel films, as the Black Widow, Natasha Romanova, Johansson plays an enhanced human being in the superhero mould, passing easily beyond the limitations of ordinary life. More recently, in *Ghost in the Shell* (2017) she has likewise taken the role of Major Mira Killian, a cybernetic person enclosed within a full-body prosthetic shell.

Questions about the divide between body and soul increasingly permeate Johansson's films, as though her own perceived physical perfection, at once so humane and vulnerable, has been reimagined as something remote from us, something post-human, perfect, only realizable in the mechanisms of film. In Spike Jonze's *Her*, where Johansson appears only in the form of a living voice, the aural manifestation of an artificially intelligent Operating System, all depends on the question as to whether she is a person, or not. I first watched the film in ignorance of the fact that Johansson was playing 'Samantha', the os. Undoubtedly, knowing that this warm, emotive voice is hers can direct our sense of the film, and, in a way that on that first screening I could not do, we summon up the absent presence of the star, so familiar to us from all those films, all those websites and 'news' stories, filling out the character's virtual elusiveness with memories of the woman whose voice she has.

In the disconcerting but highly interesting film *Under the Skin*, Johansson plays an alien driving the roads of contemporary Scotland, picking up men for some not-quite-understood purpose of her own. These men are enticed by this alien Lorelei into a strange undetermined place, where as they strip before a receding nude Johansson something dreadful submerges them; it all functions like aversion therapy for the lecherous. It is a depressing, dissonant movie, its tone of disruption framed by the camera's unemotive gaze, and by Mica Levi's discordant music on the soundtrack. Here we learn just how cold, without affect, the camera's eye can be; to paraphrase W. H. Auden, the eyes of the crow and of the camera look out on the same objective earth.[1] Blankly anxious, only in control when she's 'on', that is flirting so as to catch her prey, Johansson's alien stares at an alienated world; faces look strange when you're a stranger. (It's an open question why an alien would be so indifferent, why they might not be imagined to be what could be called 'humane'.) We are at the opposite end of the scale from De Sica's *Bicycle Thieves* here, trapped in a vision of the world as empty, sordid, where human deaths occur without an inkling of tragedy.

As in *Her*, where Johansson was present but invisible, part of *Under the Skin*'s power derives from the fact that the star drove and walked around Scotland, anonymously, with interactions with 'ordinary people' filmed surreptitiously using hidden cameras. Among other things, this process exposes the ways in which a young woman negotiates a world of pick-ups and catcalls. The black wig that Johansson wears acts like a disguise and genuinely seems to have allowed one of the world's biggest film stars to roam the shopping malls of Scotland unrecognized. Yet this apparent loss of her star identity is always undercut by the fact that this woman remains to us Scarlett Johansson, and that as much as anything else we perceive the blunt incongruity of her presence there, a Hollywood star on these dreary, provincial, winter streets.

The film's director, Jonathan Glazer, has remarked that the moment where he knew Scarlett Johansson was the right actor to play the alien's part came when he watched the star's face fall at the end of the video for her song, 'Falling Down', where after being made-up and celebrated in a world of privileged fame, her face slips back to neutral as she returns to privacy. There's a relation back to that other pop star film star, David Bowie, in *The Man Who Fell to Earth* (1976), with the pop-cultural human, that fabricated fiction of otherworldly excellence, summoned up by Johansson too. In the end, Johansson's alien, so expressively inexpressive, does reach towards compassion and concern, mimicking the human in a world where to be human is both courageously to endeavour to save a drowning stranger and, equally, to rape a solitary woman.

With the ambition, if not the vision, of Kubrick's *2001: A Space Odyssey* (1968), Luc Besson's *Lucy* is a film that operates on an evolutionary timescale. The subject of the film, embodied by Johansson, is the human species itself. Lucy is the name ascribed to the first human being, and now here becomes the name too of the individual who will make the next evolutionary leap, an earthbound Star Child and an incarnation of the movie star as blonde, American *Übermensch*. Indeed, at the end of the film, in a parody of God's reaching to the reclining Adam on the ceiling of the Sistine Chapel, the godlike modern-day Lucy darts off on a classic paradoxical causal loop, travelling back in time to meet our common ancestor, squatting, simian Lucy, and, finger to outstretched finger, communicates to her the shift in intelligence that kick-starts human evolution. The crouching ape-woman Lucy might as well be reaching out to one of Kubrick's Monoliths.

Someone who had begun the twenty-first century playing such flawed, intelligent and humane characters as Charlotte in *Lost in*

Translation, Sondra in *Scoop*, or Griet in *Girl with a Pearl Earring*, in its second decade was playing people who were more than human, acting out a species of perfection signalled anyway in the public mind by Johansson's existence as movie star, as Internet meme. In *Lucy* she tells us, 'I don't feel pain, fear, desire. It's like all the things that make us human are fading away.' Losing humanity, she also loses vulnerability and becomes, as is typical of Besson's fantasies, a resilient, pitiless, gun-toting action hero. The endlessly desirable invulnerability of the computer-game and comic-book hero or heroine offers to its audience here, and elsewhere in the Marvel films, and all the other summer blockbuster franchises, an image of superhuman imperviousness. Nothing hurts such demi-gods, nothing scares them; they soar away from human frailties, including those frailties most entwined with our compassion.

Like the alien in *Under the Skin*, Johansson's Lucy presents to the viewer's gaze a flatness of affect often mistaken for 'cool'. What we end with, in Besson's evolutionary fantasy, is a human being who can perform magic – a magic made possible by the illusions offered within cinema. Such sorcery upends the old understanding of the human condition, one comprehended through limitations, contingencies and through relatedness. Magic grants the magician, the superhero, the post-human and the star control over every aspect of their lives. They manipulate time, control objects and others, who are merely one more species of object. They are not bound by the rules of physical space or the frailty of the body. Above all, they transcend, as photographs might transcend, mortality itself. At the end of both *Her* and *Lucy* Johansson's characters elude death and achieve entry to some other space, uploaded onto a computer, as Ray Kurzweil has dreamt, heavenly, ineffable, omnipresent though vanished. As Lucy, Johansson is one of a kind, a lonely, perfect magical self, one only viable on-screen: that is, in other words, a movie star.

39

SHU QI:
A PLACELESS HEAVEN

Born in Taiwan, at the age of seventeen Shu Qi travelled to Hong Kong to pursue a career in films. She found herself working in soft-core porn, making films and appearing in the Chinese edition of *Playboy*. Spurred on by an award-winning success with a self-reflexive role in Yee Tung-Shing's *Viva Erotica* (1996), a comedy on the Chinese 'adult film' industry, she soon made the difficult leap out of porn and into mainstream films. She suddenly became all but ubiquitous, appearing in six films in 1997 and ten more in the following year. Indeed, she has made so many films, so quickly, that it proves hard to keep up with her or to pin down her persona. Any account of her is bound to be partial and to miss much of what she has done in cinema. However, in international terms, her place as one of the key and most characteristic film stars of the new century rests on her ongoing involvement with the extraordinarily talented Taiwanese director Hou Hsiao-hsien.

Shu Qi's status as a Taiwanese actor reflects something of her homeland's indeterminate status, as well as something of the global transactions of this (supposedly) 'late-capitalist era'. Money moves across territories and the individual must move with it. These 'citizens of nowhere' (and the writer of this book is just another of these) are everywhere; especially for the film star, the nowhere they are citizens of is the place where the films happen, the screen worlds. Shu Qi's career has moved between Hong Kong, Taiwan and China, the whole of what Gary G. Xu has named the 'Sinascape', but also brought her to France, with *The Transporter* (2002), and the USA, with *New York, I Love You* (2008).[1] She is a crossover star, mediating territories and languages, betwixt and between.

In a world powered by money and the ability to embody a rapidly changing, 'liquid' self (to use Zygmunt Bauman's phrase), Shu Qi encapsulates the possibilities and the distractions of contemporary life. She is both rooted in a time and place, and able to slip out of her time, to shift that place. Sometimes she stands for an improbable virtue; at other times, she is blank with the bewildered vacancy of the present. She acts, she advertises, she graces the covers of magazines. Her face sells a fragrance, she speaks for a fashion house. Her appeal spreads horizontally, at once consumable and unreachable.

What I write of Shu Qi is true for a multitude of other stars of the contemporary world. It is the intersection between the selling of uniqueness and the distance from it that constitutes modern celebrity. Shu Qi's untroubling beauty, the advertised flawlessness of her image, could be reproduced by dozens of other stars, from Deepika Padukone to Brad Pitt, or from Keira Knightley to Shah Rukh Khan. The actor flits between the movie industry and the fashion industry, traversing media opportunities. The films hardly matter, as what we are sold is a fetishized beauty, only a packaged identity. It is all so flawless, so Photoshopped. There is something threatening about these unthreatening versions of the person. They are messengers from some other immaculate realm.

And yet, in Shu Qi's case certainly, the films do matter. And moreover, they matter in a large and living sense, because of her presence in them. And the screen worlds that I mentioned above turn out in Hou Hsiao-hsien's vision indeed to have the specificities of a particular place, and therefore of both complex and un-erasable histories.

Hou Hsiao-hsien is a great Taiwanese director, who is without much of a Taiwanese audience. He remarked of his film *Flowers of Shanghai* (1998) that his audience for the film was 'twenty thousand in Taipei, two hundred thousand in Paris'.[2] For all their lack of popularity at home, his films are rooted in a revisionary sense of place and an understanding of local history.

In *Millennium Mambo* (2001) and *Three Times* (2005) Tapei bustles before us, grey, smog-bound, rapid. In the earlier film, time and space interweave in segments, giving us a kaleidoscopic city.[3] The film offers us 'real' instants, and especially what might seem to be the 'real' Shu Qi, the star playing out low-key moments of ordinary life, just cooking, getting ready for bed or compulsively smoking. We glimpse people through 'real' cameras, framed in images on monitors, or cast in unnatural light, or hidden behind foreground objects. Shu Qi is our focus and the person we cannot read, for all the fact that her voiceover, from the 'future' of 2011, directs the flow of the film. The bar and nightclub scenes are those moments when she's 'up', but even here we see her take these pleasures sadly. She and her friends do a good impression of 'having fun', but mirth is absent here. People's primary relations are to machines, to video games, to the computerized beat of 'techno', and to the unreciprocated love of drugs. Sex proves perfunctory and passionless, and puerilely bullying too. Shu Qi's 'Vicky' is a person adrift in an impersonal world.

The boring cool of the film could be put down to its effortful wish to be beguiled by these flattened-out figures from what has been called the 'E-generation'. Certainly, Shu Qi could play far otherwise, playing smart and cute, for instance, opposite Tony Leung in *Yau ching yam shui baau* (*Love Me, Love My Money*), released the same year. In terms of the argument of this book, something more serious is perhaps marked in *Millennium Mambo*. The advent of the star began back with Mary Pickford and Valentino, Buster Keaton and Pola Negri, with the entry of 'personality' into film, the image of a self, vivid, characterful, delineated. With this film and with the culture it apparently celebrates, cinema has reached a moment where personality departs, leaving with lingering glances; only image, only 'cool' remains. Twice Shu Qi's character, Vicky, visits the film festival in the snowbound city of Yubari. There this modern film star trudges by images of earlier stars, Charlie Chaplin and 'Torajiro', old movie posters commemorating the picture personalities of the past. For us there is only Shu Qi, seeming herself, seeming natural as, happy for once, she plays in the freezing snow.

Hou Hsiao-hsien's farewell to Taiwan, the portmanteau film *Three Times*, explores three relationships between the same two actors, Shu Qi and Chen Chang, at three very different moments of Taiwanese history. We receive here something done three times, but also truly three 'times', three historical contexts in which people are caught. The film focuses, as the literal translation of its Chinese title makes clear, on what might be the 'best times' of a life, 'not the prettiest or most fun times, but rather, those moments that only exist in our memories, those moments that can be conjured up but never relived or replicated'.[4] At their best Hou Hsiao-hsien's films drift and pause, overleap the weeks or linger in some fugitive moment, pulling the viewer into a dreamy, 'filmy' state, lost to the sense of time.[5] The critic Tonglin Lu argues convincingly that these intimate memories belong with and are interpenetrated by the collective memories of a nation, blurring together the private and public.[6]

One of the incarnations of Shu Qi in Hou Hsiao-hsien's *Three Times* (2005).

Above all, what we see in Shu Qi in the first two sections of *Three Times* is a human being who might be said to shine. After the cool of *Millennium Mambo*, we feel here the presence of a living person. The 1911 section of the film plays out like a silent movie, and this stylized return to the origins of film show again the enshrining of character. This film within a film is a patient ceremony, one that bears witness to the eroticism of the unspoken. In these first sections, from 1966 and 1911, Shu Qi seems fabulously alive. Yet the women she plays are both employed to entertain – truly, to 'shine' – to please, in particular, the male customers they serve, whether as a hostess in a pool bar or as a courtesan.

The last section gives us Shu Qi as our contemporary, in a world where there is, we are told, 'No past. No future. Just a greedy present.' Here, as earlier in the film, things turn on acts of communication. But where previously letters had been cherished and used to track down a loved one, now in the world of text and email there is only elusiveness and miscommunication. The empty present gives us a beautiful absence. Shu Qi is lovely, and the film knows that, and has her photographed as she sings (in English) on stage, turned into an image by the adoring male photographers. In 1966 she laughs and is free; in 1911 she must be patient in her forsaking and, unmarked, weep; now she is free, but indefinably anxious. There are tears for the modern woman too, though, welling up from the face that masks its own sadness.

Like Scarlett Johansson and Maggie Cheung, in order to follow a career in contemporary cinema Shu Qi has necessarily had to become an action hero. Her most recent film at the time of writing with Hou Hsiao-hsien is *The Assassin* (2015), one that reconstructs what such a film does to the stars that make them. The action-adventure hero takes us back to the first people on film, who were not precisely actors, but were 'models' and mannequins, posing and not playing. The cinema of sensation, the summer multiplex action film may require 'stars' as a measure of its bankability, but not persons, for it is not interested in the human scale. It wants cyphers, daemons in our place. The action star is an avatar, closer to the video-game substitute than to a living personality. They play out the thrilling sport of violence, standing in for us, drained of difference so that they might more feelingly become our looking-glass self.

Corey Yuen's *So Close* (2002) provides a good template for this new virtual home for the star. Computers, the Internet, the speeding car and the gun, all are central here and all have equally opened up for the frail person a sense of power more than human. *So Close* entices us with the fantasy that we can enjoy such power – and look 'hot' at the same time. In the stylish mayhem of this movie, Shu Qi is the nearest thing on offer to a human being. Her boyfriend tells her that he can feel her sadness 'even through the computer' through which they communicate. Similarly, the audience senses something of the person through the computer-manipulated flow of the film. Selves are mediated through the camera, consciously so, in a film where in a battle the fighting women are doubled with images of themselves that aren't there, merely CGI traces on film, where Shu Qi's character's sister is constantly filming, and where, after her on-screen death, Shu Qi remains alive on the close-circuit TV, her sister laying her to rest by burying the camera that recorded her.

So Close is the action film as one expects it to be, though it is nevertheless a thrilling and intriguing piece of work. More than that, *The Assassin* offers us pleasures and beauty often found in films such as *Crouching Tiger, Hidden Dragon* (2000) and *House of Flying Daggers* (2004). Yet it does so in ways that are stranger and stronger than perhaps we have seen before. As in Zhang Yimou's *Hero*, the human factor withdraws and yet the film is profoundly humane. Here Hou Hsiao-hsien gives us a hymn to Shu Qi's presence in a film predicated on her near-absence. As the assassin of the title, she lives in this film all but invisibly; there are a mere handful of moments where she faces us and speaks. She hovers on the edge of sight, stealthy, secretive, observant, but all but beyond observation herself; when she fights, her skills operate at a speed where the body dazzles and what happens grows indistinct. So often the film deals with her seen at a distance, walking, or as a figure in the natural scene, like a person distantly contained within a landscape by the ancient Chinese painters Jing Hao or Ma Yuan. Landscape, the natural world itself, is the hero of this film, while Shu Qi's character flits through its beauty, present in it for a while, clad all in unnatural black, distinct from it and extraneous. Her face is hardly seen, but is serious, thoughtful, afar. The person is there, but vanishing, and the star retreats to the edge of things.

40

ANDY SERKIS:
LEAR'S SHADOW

Film stars live through recognition, yet Andy Serkis can pass through a film unseen. At the cinema, I watched both Steven Spielberg's *The Adventures of Tintin* (2011) and Peter Jackson's *King Kong* (2005) unaware that Serkis was performing a major, and even indeed the central, role. Andy Serkis is a new kind of movie star, ubiquitous and invisible. Though he has many notable 'live' on-screen roles to his credit, as, for example, Ian Brady in *Longford* (2006) and as Ian Dury in *Sex & Drugs & Rock & Roll* (2010), he is best known for roles where, in a sense, he doesn't appear on-screen at all, talentedly present and strangely absent. As a 'performance capture' actor and as a voice in computer-animated films, he has played Gollum (also known as Smeagol) in Peter Jackson's *Lord of the Rings* films and the first part of *The Hobbit* (2012), as Kong, for Spielberg as Captain Haddock, as Supreme Leader Snoke in the rebooted *Star Wars* films (2015, 2017), and as Caesar in the latest *Planet of the Apes* trilogy. The immense variety of Serkis's performances is extraordinary; not only has he evaded typecasting, with the help of the digital vision, as no actor could have hoped to have done before him, he has transcended the limits of his physical body. In doing so, he subverts another key element in our idea of the film star: that is, that they should stand for a particular mode of individuality, an instance of personhood contained in one mortal frame. Instead he offers a chameleon identity, almost a romantic ideal of the actor (not the star), someone absorbed in and yet still expressing himself through a myriad kinds of otherness.

I first saw Serkis in 1993, playing The Fool as a drag queen in Max Stafford-Clark's Royal Court production of *King Lear*. Over the years I'd forgotten who played Lear (it was the excellent Tom Wilkinson), but Serkis's Fool has long stayed with me, ferocious and vulnerable as he was, going on, as I remember it, to hang himself at the play's end. Serkis was amazing that night, standing, in his folly and aggression and compassion, for all kinds of humanness. The stage seemed his place; I never thought I'd next see him living through a puppet as a digital double of a time-decayed hobbit.

Inevitably in watching Serkis's intensely felt performances, all mediated by technological intervention, questions of the continued presence, or absence, of the human arise. If Scarlett Johansson and Shu Qi represent the piecemeal arrival of the post-human on film, then Serkis might appear to advance that invasion several leagues. Yet in many ways Serkis stands for the resilience of the presence of the human spirit on-screen, a living exemplar of our ineradicable interest in persons. For all the intervention of computers, as Gollum, as Kong, as Caesar, even especially as Supreme Leader Snoke, that desiccated, malevolent Bing Crosby simulacrum, he's still human and his humanity, his personhood, informs all that he does.

It is striking how often, in talking of his work, Serkis refers to the honesty of a performance, the finding in acting of a character's emotional truth. As I have argued at various moments through this book, when we watch an actor, the very skill of their performance raises the question of how we distinguish a pretended emotion from a real one. If our robots and computers imitate feeling, then is that feeling 'real' or not? The question of technology merges with the question of the existence of other minds – and when the digital other lives in a fiction film then that throws the question of the actor into the mix. The destabilizing possibilities of pretence draw these three problems together, drawn into one by the technological apparatus of film.

In all his motion-capture films, though his doing so is mediated by computer, Serkis finds the person in the 'other'. Yet watching him

Andy Serkis as Smeagol in Peter Jackson's *The Lord of the Rings* trilogy.

and watching the other that is him, we cannot help but wonder how much of Serkis is there. In one sense the entire performance is, as it says, and as Kong and Caesar are, 'captured', taken from Serkis's self; in another, it's hard not to feel it's all a conjuration, a version of the marionette theatre. Serkis's motion-capture as Kong was supplemented, seamlessly enough it seems to me, by keyframe animation; who can tell which bits refer to Serkis, and which are filled-in? Serkis himself has suggested that he is the voice, the emotions, the movements of such characters, but that he cannot be their body.[1] In *The Lord of the Rings* the Smeagol we see on-screen replicates Serkis's performance, but is therefore something distanced from it, an artifice within an artwork. In commentaries on his films, Peter Jackson has spoken of the actors morphing into a 'computer puppet'. Making *King Kong*, all the actors had 'digital doubles', including Naomi Watts, of course, metamorphosing into modelled lifelike versions of themselves that could do on-screen what no human being could do, or could survive, in life. When watching the film we shift from watching traces of the actor themselves to scenes or moments where they are replaced by their own marionette.

There is notably an attempt among computer scientists and AI experts to show their digital machines and algorithm-spawners as 'creative', capable of writing novels, composing symphonies, painting pictures. Taryn Southern, a YouTube personality, has collaborated with computers who make music for her; it's curious that the resulting melodies sound more human than she does. There is an element of thrilled ambition in all this, but also of usurpation, and of a radical debunking of art as such – reduced to memes, discourse, generic properties, reproducible tropes and techniques. The critical notions that gave us 'the death of the author' now happily seek out the death of the human presence in art.

Elsewhere, there have been other radical attempts to displace the human actor from film. *Sayonara* (2015), a film by Koji Fukada, has cast an android as the lead actor in a movie. Like many such 'robots', the android is gendered as a woman actor – of course, for the production of femininity is so often the point in such endeavours. Geminoid F has her own (its own?) IMDb webpage; here it declares, 'Geminoid F is an actress'. In the film, based on a 2010 short play by Oriza Hirata, Geminoid F plays 'Leona', though in what sense she/it plays anyone is open to question. The creation of the roboticist Hiroshi Ishiguro, Geminoid F is already a performance, a replication of a human being, framed in imitation. Ishiguro's earlier robot was Geminoid HI-1, designed, either with candid narcissism or Warholian mischief, to be a robot double of himself; the name 'Geminoid' likely draws on 'Gemini', the twins. If Geminoid HI-1 is an uncreating mirror to the creative self, then Geminoid F, his/its twenty-something sister (based on the maker's daughter) embodies a prevailing myth of modest, sexy beauty, plastic, facile and amenable. Ishiguro has stated that his aim is to understand what a human is.[2] He has done so by fabricating 'autonomous' puppets.

All this, to me, reaches a depth of emptiness that is at some distance from Jackson's and Spielberg's films and even more from Serkis's inspiring motion-capture acting. The thought that it is all done by machine, and hence is purely unreal, is a beguiling but misguided one. The computer work that makes those digital doubles, those virtual people is truly a craft, the painstaking work of skilled and diligent artificers. Moreover, as Serkis consistently shows, the possibility enshrined in motion-capture is dazzling. It offers us, for instance, a symbolic version of art's attempt, and acting's endeavour, to see the world from another's perspective. This includes the possibility of a genuine transgenderism, where we might, on-screen, if not in truth, live through another body, albeit a virtual one. In this regard, in the recent *Planet of the Apes* films, it is particularly pertinent that Karin Konoval plays the male orang-utan Maurice, and does so in such a way that no one considers for a moment the gender of the human actor embodied in this sage and reflective character,

Serkis broke out as an obscured movie star playing Gollum in Peter Jackson's *Lord of the Rings* films; indeed, he was, by quite some distance, the best thing in them. As a lifelong Tolkien fan, I was sceptical of any movie adaptation and, as it turned out, rightly so. For the most part, Jackson weirdly fritters away the suspense and menace, the homeliness and the nobility of Tolkien's narrative, replacing these with an inflated and rushed unmeaning violence. Tolkien's novel creates places that are touchstones of beauty and goodness – Rivendell, Lorien, Tom Bombadil's house, Fangorn forest, the Shire itself – using these sacred sites as examples of all that stands against the cruelty and destruction practised by Saruman and Sauron. The movie reduces those shining places to kitsch; Jackson's Rivendell in particular could come out of a painting by Roger Dean. The films give us a celebration of the natural in a technological package, and its oases are those brief instances where the personal finds its breathing space, where conversations happen, where kindness is given and taken.

The Lord of the Rings and *The Hobbit* films provide a cinematic sublime, while conveying little of the humane. Tolkien's passion was for the resilience and courage of the humble, who are exalted. Jackson's focus is instead on the vast. It is not Middle Earth that is the centre of the film, it is not the individual, it is New Zealand, a real place. The landscapes of his films are undoubtedly beautiful, but the way they are shot minimizes the person. Ostensibly about 'fellowship', the nine, and friendship, the dominant unit on-screen is instead that of the horde. In Tolkien's books of *The Hobbit* and *The Lord of the Rings*, as befits someone who had been a frontline soldier, battles are seen from the point of view of the more or less bewildered participant; in Jackson's films, they are spectacles of mass violence, seen from above, the personal element lost. Jackson willingly sacrifices realism of presentation and, with it, emotional depth and reality, for effect – for excess. The power of the image takes precedence over the human meaning of the film, and we must assume that for Jackson this power was the point.

Against that tumult, in moments of quiet, there is Serkis as Smeagol, interacting with Frodo and Sam, and in the process, without even trying to do so, blowing the actors who play them off the screen. In playing Smeagol, Serkis expresses all the complexity of Tolkien's portrait, showing the character to be in turns hideous and cute, malign and generous. Bald as a baby, he's extraordinarily aged, bulging-eyed, wide-mouthed, snaggle-toothed. Smeagol is in two minds: he is both the vestige of himself, abject and eager to please, and the creature he had to become to survive his addiction, 'Gollum', vicious, wily, and insidious. On-screen Serkis is likewise split in two, there and not there. In the end-titles to *The Return of the King*, where each actor's name appears beside a drawing of their character, Serkis is there drawn twice, once as 'Gollum', and once as himself.

Gollum is a degenerate being, an evolutionary atavism, someone who prefers the raw to the cooked. Evolution is central to *King Kong* and the *Planet of the Apes* films too, with Kong and Caesar being both the less than human and the superhuman, a person brought to life by technology. In *King Kong*, as 'Lumpy', the ship's cook (his other role in the film), Serkis declares that on the island there lurks 'a creature neither beast nor man'. In this film humans and animals swap places; humans become prey; Adrien Brody plays a writer who sleeps and works in an animal's cage. The movie even reproduces, and deepens, the colonialist racism, tinged by warped evolutionary theories, of the 1933 original, with its South Sea islanders being crazed and malign to the point of incomprehensibility. As always in *Kong* films, Kong himself seems relatively more human in comparison with these debased evolutionary throwbacks.

Like most of Jackson's films, *King Kong* is scaled to the director's taste for gigantism; even the centipedes are supersized. With its penchant for a brutal kitsch, here the beauty that killed the beast is cinema itself. Everything natural in the film is unnatural, bigger than life, bloated. The sunsets, symbolic of yearning beauty, look Photo-shopped, 'painted', a stage-set sundown. This embellishment of nature focuses on two opposed locales: the weird supernatural presence of Skull Island; and that other island, the denatured, art deco epitome of modernity that is Manhattan.

Frequently Jackson's *King Kong* takes on the nightmarish quality of the original too, and also draws on the way that it may sometimes rise to the dreamlike; there's a 'good' primitivism at work here too alongside the ignoble savage shtick. Kong himself embodies the force of nature, all that the artificial space of the theatre cannot contain, even as film creates and frames it. Cinema history permeates the film, playing up Jack Black's role as a monomaniacal movie director, some-one who places the image above a human life. In this way *King Kong* follows the trajectory of Hitchcock's *The Birds* (1963), moving from screwball comedy to apocalypse; Naomi Watts takes the beleaguered Tippi Hedren role.

Like *The Birds*, too, the film encapsulates the plight of modern women, particularly the woman film star, condemned by male demands to be cute and 'entertaining'. As Ann Darrow, Watts knocks out a breathless, life-saving vaudeville performance of pratfalls, jug-gling and comedy dancing. Left to be sacrificed to this mighty ogre of a gorilla, Watts finds herself facing the defaced, re-faced face of Andy Serkis as Kong, as well as an ape who takes on the displaced qualities of the human. Though Serkis 'humanizes' Kong, it is really Watts who is the emblem of the human here. She is made special first by being the only woman on board, and then by being the object of the great ape's adoration, the only human being who can connect to the beast. Later she endures the worst fate of the musical heroine, returning to the anonymous ranks of the chorus line, taken away from the centre of things and condemned to ordinariness.

Meanwhile across town, Jack Black as the theatrical impresario has a scene enacted on stage that reproduces the racist, s&m-tinged parody that the film itself already was. This second time around a chained blonde (the wrong blonde, it turns out) hangs before a chained Kong. Enraged that it's some substitute extra, and not Naomi Watts, the beloved, the actual movie star, Kong bursts his chains and devastates the theatre, and then the streets of Manhattan beyond. He snatches up blondes one by one, checking to see if they happen to be *the* blonde, and when they are not, he tosses them aside, back to the street from whence they came. In these distorted and furious (and curious) ways, the film plays out some fantasy of loving for the man, of being loved for the woman – of being special, of being the star.

In the *Planet of the Apes* trilogy, through the mask, Serkis conveys something human, and something simian too. Regarding *Rise of the Planet of the Apes*, Serkis has described Caesar as 'a human trapped in an ape's body'; for the second film, he found himself drawing out the ape within the character. Throughout he is not aping being a chimpanzee, he is playing the person. For all the fabulous rigmarole of the technology, he is just acting as actors have always acted.

Yet in these new techniques something has undoubtedly been lost. The Czech surrealist film-maker Jan Švankmajer has spoken of the centrality of touch to the experience of film.[3] He understands, of course, that film is an audio-visual medium, but he is surely right to stress the tactile quality of films, and how central to our understanding and perception of the person is the fact of touch, the sharing of a grasp, the holding of another. So it is that touches, gestures, blows and caresses pulse through the films memorialized in this book. Through technology, we feel that a sense has been lost from our repertoire of five. We see Frodo and Sam wrestle with Gollum, and once they truly were wrestling with Serkis himself; but we sense the absence of heft in those touches, the fact that that face, that body, is weightlessly there. It is precisely in those moments when Kong touches Naomi Watts that the film has recourse to her digital double, or to props. He cannot hold on to *her*. As touch departs, some element of the human takes flight with it.

With Andy Serkis and with motion-capture acting as such, at times we may feel we are witnessing the return of 'broad' acting, the near-mime of silent cinema revived. However, as with the best of silent cinema itself, in fact Serkis's performances are nuanced and restrained in their potent expressiveness. It is the precision and subtlety of what he does that most amazes. With motion-capture, with digital doubles, we may feel that the human presence is emptying from the screen. Yet whatever he does from now on, wherever film goes from here, Serkis reminds us that the central concerns of cinema remain intact. Through the technology of film, human beings express their interest in each other, in the innumerable manifestations of human possibility, all brought to life by the actor and, above all, the star. As they have for more than a hundred years of narrative cinema, over a hundred years of stardom, the actor still embodies one kind of uniqueness, being ineradicably their own person and yet letting us share, through the magic of films, a life in connection to other perspectives, to the endless vulnerability and fascination of the celluloid shadow of the human face.

Trying to be a *mensch* – Shirley MacLaine approaches Jack Lemmon at the insurance office in Billy Wilder's *The Apartment* (1960).

AFTERWORD

I n a scene in Billy Wilder's happily downbeat Christmas movie *The Apartment* (1960), Dr Dreyfus, Jack Lemmon's Jewish neighbour, advises the apparently philandering and hedonistic star to 'be a *mensch*'. When Lemmon looks puzzled, the doctor promptly translates for him, 'a *mensch* – a human being!' That command is itself both baffling and all too understandable; for it is precisely our humanity that human beings stand most in peril of losing. With its deep roots in Charles Dickens's *A Christmas Carol*, the Christmas film often falls back on the thought that one might precisely lose the element in ourselves that we consider 'humane'. We gain the whole world or, at least, the key to the executive washroom, but in the process we may lose our souls. Dickens's fable, and its stage productions and cinematic manifestations, counter the long slowing down of the heart with a fable of renewal, redemption and (even for the old) the hope of a second chance. In Frank Capra's *It's a Wonderful Life* (1946), Jimmy Stewart as George Bailey desperately resists the humdrum, yet finds himself trapped in small-town life by loyalty to wife, family, friends and his community. Hemmed in by debts, he decides to throw his life away, only to find himself restored to who he was, reconciled to the wonderful concealed in his ordinary life. Both Lemmon and Stewart played variations on the 'little guy' motif, someone small standing up for a humanity that the great structures of the social realm overlook. These are stars who express and transcend the virtues of ordinariness; what they play on-screen is the *Menschlich* in all of us.

In these films Stewart and Lemmon are the star as 'everyman'. As this word indicates, likely some gendered expectations around the concept of the self play into their roles. When it comes to the way Hollywood cinema in particular portrays the woman star, another side to things darkly emerges. Curtis Hanson's *L.A. Confidential* (1997) pits illusion against reality, with Los Angeles as a city of tarnished dreams centred on the fictions spun out by Hollywood. A pimp runs a call girl agency where the girls are 'cut' (given plastic surgery) in order to resemble more closely those movie stars who are the exemplars of erotic desire. This film shows us that these buyable women stand in for the women on-screen. In this belated film noir the prostitutes are all versions of film noir movie stars – Rita Hayworth, Lana Turner, Ava Gardner – and sex with them promises an experience of a walk on the wild side, a flirtation with the femme fatale. On the other side of the tracks, the police detectives are celebrities too, playing things for politics and for the cameras, advising on unconvincing TV police shows whose characters fake the real workings of the law. As the critic Andrew Sarris has remarked, everyone in *L.A. Confidential* is just a reflection of everyone else. This both means that characters are morally entwined with one another, but also that the people they are depends on parts that they and others are playing, and that others have elsewhere played, on the lies they're living. As the 'cut' prostitute, Kim Basinger's position exemplifies this confusion of selves most strikingly; she's plain Lynn Bracken from Arizona, and she's a living facsimile of the film star Veronica Lake. Here the actual real-life mobster Johnny Stompanato, played by Paolo Seganti, hangs out with an actual real-life film star, Lana Turner (played by Brenda Bakke), who was indeed his lover in reality. The question arises: how do you tell a 'hooker' cut to look like Lana Turner from Lana Turner? (Or from an actress hired for a 1990s movie specifically because she resembles Lana Turner?)

If Hollywood is the factory that offers dreams that money can buy, then the film star brothel is a dream house, where a copy of that dream may be fondled and possessed. The films invade consciousness and unconsciousness, taking possession of our dreams, as those dreams possess the real women onto which they are projected. More recently, the tensions of desire witnessed in *L.A. Confidential* have been democratized by the invention of 'Deepfakes'. Here, using digital technology, the faces of (most often) women stars merge in video with those of porn doubles, Emma Watson's or Natalie Portman's features melded onto those of some anonymous Pornhub person. There are older, less sophisticated versions of this process, where the famous are Photoshopped onto nudes, or the rather different interest in genuine nude photographs of Marilyn Monroe or Joan Crawford, or, yet more intrusively, in stolen private images of stars like Jennifer Lawrence or Kirsten Dunst. In those AI-created images, desire and desecration, the dual impulse that manifests the public's relation to the star, appear together. It is noteworthy that Audrey Hepburn has been most often the older star to be reshaped in this way. Her aloof and intelligent charm has opened her to the fantasy that she can be sold and sullied. The Deepfake makes the star ordinary, 'dirties' them, stripping them down to just a body like any other, even though the body in question is not their own (any body will do), confined to basic and sellable physical longings, making them simply people to be 'had'. Love after all seeks connection to a particular person; lust anonymizes the object of desire. As a front-page story in the *New York Times* suggests, the technology could just as easily work the other way, potentially merging us with the stars, inserting our faces into classic films or onto images of celebrities. The article shows the journalist Kevin Roose metamorphose into Ryan Gosling, Chris Pratt and Jake Gyllenhaal, the unremarkable man becoming, via technology, a film star.[1] The films invade our imagination, and as a society we in reciprocation feel free to invade the privacy of those stars who manifest the movie dreams.

In the past, the virtual manipulation of the woman star was done more brutally, with cuts and additions closer to mutilations. Evelyn Waugh's uncompromising satire *The Loved One* (1948) describes a young woman star manipulated by the Hollywood studio to which she is contracted, made up by the whims of men, transformed through plastic surgery, hair dye, dentures and the imagination of the publicity department from Spanish beauty 'Juanita del Pablo' to Irish rebel Kathleen FitzBourke. 'Juanita' (née Baby Aaronson) queries her remaking and the question arises for her harried agent: 'did his client exist? Could you legally bind her to annihilate herself? Could you come to any agreement with her before she had acquired the ordinary marks of identity?'[2] This malleability of the star that Waugh portrays as perverse and darkly shallow would be seen by others in the culture as liberating, an intensified version of the free choices opened by modernity to all when it came to choosing a self. In the modern world you could dream yourself and become that dream. By this route, the film star became the ideal human being, transformed, as in the personae of David Bowie, into the pop person, someone malleable as an image, with an identity put off or pulled on with each new suit of clothes.

If the world of film hallowed persons, it did so by thinking of them as being very like works of art. At other times it would dehumanize another to treat them as though they are precisely an artwork, merely an object. Yet the film star, the actor, truly is in any case a person who is a work of art, caught up in a frame and a narrative that celebrates – and fabricates – their personhood. From the start film was an iconographic medium, one permeated by the profound simplicities of popular art, closer to the caricatures, the thrills and the happy endings of Dickens than to the conscious subtleties of a Flaubert; its natural tendency was to varnish people into icons.

However, against the static quality of the icon, when it comes to persons, film establishes continuities from selves broken up into discrete images most often not even recorded in order, from moments, gestures, scenes, even individual frames. If, as John Ellis has suggested, within the film the star's performance is a matter of fragments, of pieces, then that process also pertains to the star's identity across films, both persisting and yet also disjunct and broken.[3] Each film is yet another performance, a variation of an identity to be played with or explored again, but one never fixed or univalent.

Yet both with Lemmon and Stewart, as with Basinger and Veronica Lake, what we look for in films is company, a solace that assuages our loneliness. As we become persons through our attachment to others, some at least of those others are figures of art, the actor in this particular film, but also, the figure of the film star, people encountered variously over and over, familiar and recognized. The erotics of film, that which finds its dark expression in the Deepfake, also more brightly links to the affections touched by film, the connections, the concern we feel for another person. It is this personal element in films, most vividly expressed by our fascination with the star, that drives this book.

Among other things, every work of art is busy defining the nature of the person, exploring one version of the possibilities open to us. This relation to personhood, to concepts of what a human life consists of, is central to film. Yet over the last century, and with gathering force in the last few decades, we have been living through a deepening crisis in our sense of 'the person', and in consequence in our view of human beings as such. In a commodified world, 'now-ism' prevails and the art of the past loses its connection to us. For all its numerous benefits, our online realm has meanwhile created conditions hostile to the formation of the integral person: a world where people look and rarely see, where the human being dwindles to data and a templated self, an image demanding attention and never itself attending to others. The 'person' reduces to the bare species identity of being merely 'human', a loss of status achieved either by aggrandizing the animal and the machine, or by diminishing the human being. Stephen Hawking's dictum that 'the human race is just a chemical scum on a moderate-sized planet' is in fact what many people now believe or, worse, suspect to be the case. In *Straw Dogs* (2002), John Gray informs us that humanity (or, as he renames us, '*homo rapines*') 'is only one of many species, and not obviously worth preserving'.[4] As our belief in the value or truth of inwardness departs, we are left with ourselves as no more than images or meat machines. A new misanthropy stalks abroad. There is a growing lack of concern in the fate of human beings, and even a wearily delighted acceptance in our potential extinction. The weight of history, the sharp rise in population, our cruel treatment of animals, our indifference to the plight of refugees or those who die far from us, and our destruction of the living world inform this new contempt. Matters are not helped by the dehumanizing effects of porn or the nihilistic violence of cinema and computer games, and the selling of 'gross-out' videos.

In the shallowing of the human being to a surface, cinema may be taken as having exemplified and furthered that process. The medium itself with its commitment to exteriority, with its sense of the human being as no more than a transformable set of surfaces, was instrumental in presenting us with this flattened-out form of the person. Yet, through its commitment to narrative and to a transcendent idea of the person found in those images, it simultaneously offered a site of resistance to those negating forces. Film played against the concept of the living person, but also for it, with its affirmation intertwined with the negation, and the negation permeating the affirmation.

The 'person' is a concept that is open to being 'historicized'. It comes into force slowly, touching on but somehow distinct from the facts of biology, and even from our socialized and culturally framed selves. The person involves those elements, but is somehow beyond them, a way of alluding to the threatened, fragile uniqueness of one singular perspective on the world that is ours. I take it that every human being is at once an object to be looked at, a single instance of the species *Homo sapiens*, and a person, capable of making and keeping promises, with a history and memories in relation to others, a member of a specific culture, and someone living through the fable of their life.

Cinema may draw upon this blank cheque of a concept, presenting innumerable kinds of person. Yet ultimately, for reasons intrinsic to the medium itself, it is most drawn to those versions of the person that may best be presented aesthetically: to the stylish and stylized, to the vivid and striking, to the 'interesting'. Such vivid, forceful and idiosyncratic types as are summoned by the various film stars presented a possibility for the audience (you too may be like this, the films tell us) and a distant impossibility (they live in a realm where you cannot set foot). Cinema forms part of a twentieth-century suspicion of the average and the conformist. It is made for the consumer and the suburbanite that it also looks askance at. Films, especially Hollywood films, choose images of extravagance, of the extraordinary, and posit that those qualities are perhaps available to all. The essential morality of Hollywood film is primarily aesthetic, not praising 'goodness', but its interesting appearance (at which point goodness quietly vanishes).

Nowadays, billions market themselves as inimitable via templates that stress their unexceptional alikeness. Technologies make a space for us to frame our longings, our likings, our status. Once only cinema provided such a mechanical space for the preservation of the person. Long before it became true of us too, film stars were people made in relation to a machine.

Back in 2002, during a Brighton Festival on-stage discussion on the 'nature of the human', I debated with an author who had recently published a book on our 'cyborg' future. His work celebrated the augmented selves we would create, the new post-human beings to be made by our melding with technology. I listened to him with gathering bewilderment until, all but forgetting we were meant to be rationally arguing, I blurted out, 'but you're talking as if human beings were no more than relatively incompetent machines!' For reply, he just grinned and nodded. Finally, I had got it.

Even before the Deepfake technology, contemporary cinema was rolling out the death of the perception that what we saw on film was in any sense a real person. In *Rogue One: A Star Wars Story* (2016), Peter Cushing reprised his role as 'Grand Moff Tarkin', despite the inconvenience of having died some 22 years earlier. The CGI effects were uncannily unconvincing, with Cushing's face imposed upon Guy Henry's motion-capture performance, though the lack of human presence in the person was perhaps apt for a uniformed officer of the Death Star. In one sense, all actors on-screen are dead, and there's nothing exceptional about such digital tricks; and yet the mind resists that notion, finding life in the flickers of light on-screen. When we humanize our dolls, our toys, they don't become human: instead the sweetness, the humanity, the love comes from us. In films such as *Blade Runner*, and with motion-capture performances such as those created by Andy Serkis, in cinema as such we turn the star into a breathing person, the human being forged by our relation to what happens on-screen, created by what George Eliot termed, 'long interchanging influences'.[5]

We now live haunted by the thought that a machine may replace us. What we do they can do, perhaps better than we do it. Yet there are many things that are only done at all when a person performs them. If I read a bedtime story to my child or a robot does, the result is, in one sense, the same: a story has been read. Yet most people understand that for the adult and child involved it is not the same at all; the closeness, the intimacy, the concern, the liveliness of a living voice, the sense of being held together in the story, in the event, the sense of time being taken and shared, is only possible or meaningful between people.

The person on-screen may be made by technology, but our sense of them outstrips the mechanics of the thing. Nonetheless, the ghastly career of Evelyn Waugh's Juanita del Pablo shows that the film star might be taken as the demise of the concept of the person, fallen into the manipulations of artifice and the demands of the business. Perhaps on film the self is alienated from its own image, the movie experienced not in the presence of the person, but from the disjunction between person and film, between actor and role.

With the weight of the stardom industry upon them, the film star is maybe no more than the person as raw material, transformed and put inside a product, and then sold. The film historians Robert C. Allen and Douglas Gomery describe the star as the 'combination of screen role and actor, of filmic persona and off-screen personality'.[6] In *Visible Fictions*, John Ellis argues that the star is a mere marketing device, an element within the process of commodification, one selling point being the publication of aspects of their private life.[7] The star is the face, the person, the soul, become a product.

There is truth in this, but is it altogether true? In a sense, even though I've read about them in articles and books, I am often not particularly interested in the personal life of any star. Reports of a star's private life may colour how we take their films, but there is also something of a genuine separation. I greatly enjoy almost every performance that Cate Blanchett has made, but somehow I have never read an interview with her, or seen very many, beyond a few moments from DVD extras. I have glimpsed her at Sadler's Wells when she was in the audience and seen her on-stage in David Hare's *Plenty*, but I don't think it helps me to know her better. I don't even know if Blanchett is married or single, straight or gay, a parent or not, left-wing or right-wing, ill or well; I know her purely from the films. That's what I take in, that is what I enjoy, taking pleasure in her acting, the way she acts, I warm to and assess or judge her through the trace of her in the role, and the person who is the role herself (or himself, when she plays a man). (For the record, she is married to the playwright and director Andrew Upton and for five years they were joint artistic directors of the Sydney Theatre Company.)

Beyond what is being commodified is that which engages our interest. The stars have certainly ascended to fame through the aid of publicity machinery. Yet, concerning the long-dead movie stars of the 1920s, '30, '40s and '50s, we can still like them without the support of the paraphernalia of publicity. I enjoyed Cary Grant before I knew that was his name, much as I loved Audrey Hepburn in *Funny Face* and *Charade* without knowing who, beyond the parts she was playing, Audrey Hepburn was. Our affection arises from the films themselves; as Kavanagh puts it in his poem 'On Reading a Book of Common Wild Flowers', I was in love with them before we were introduced. I approached those films innocently, ignorantly, but still adored the people in them. This is true especially of 'foreign films': I received Setsuko Hara and Toshiro Mifune, Jean Marais and Anna Karina entirely without the intermediaries of publicity or marketing. I simply fell in love with the performances themselves, and with the person performing them.

Above all, I didn't merely decode Cary Grant – I was charmed by him, sympathetic to him, warmed to him because of the way he was in the film he was in. Later I recognized him again, certainly, and the more films I saw by him, the more I began to expect certain kinds of pleasure from him. Yet that pleasure was more akin to coming across a friend at a party of strangers than anything like the deciphering of a code.

And yet Richard Dyer and the other critics who have followed him in analysing the stardom industry are undoubtedly also right. I was only watching Cary Grant at all because of his secure place in the movie industry, his undisputed place in an informal 'canon' of stars. To understand any star and stardom itself as a phenomenon, one needs the context of the publicity machine, the star's *oeuvre*, their place in the work of any one director, the ways in which they contrast to other stars working in the industry, and their immersion within a culture, caught up in understandings of gender, race, class and of the 'person' as such. The star, like all of us, exists in a tension, being both an individual, understood in connection to him or herself, a person existing in relation to others, and a construct, impressed with forces and concepts from without.

However, while cinema indeed concerns the male gaze (and other kinds of gaze), expresses discourses of power, sells commodification and imparts indoctrination, it also voices an interest in the vulnerable person and hallows the human face. In film, as in life, we are drawn by the light in someone's eye, and the appeal of smiles, tears, blushes are all involuntary, and in each we feel in touch with the other person. That is not purely sentiment. This book investigates the question of what it means when the actor fakes these signs, and to what extent they are faked and not a giving of something within the self as a natural artifice. Still a radical doubt may set in – that the actor is not real, not themselves; although the actor's acting pleases us in theatre and film, this slippage is akin to the disorientation felt through the Turing test or in our interaction with a bot or android, the fear that all our sense of another's personhood may be subjectively faked.

The performance of a film puts a frame around human deeds and behaviour, offering us an image of who we can be, of who we are. In film the thing that is shown is embodied; though the body itself is thinned to its image, the people are truly there, and yet forever somewhere else. In watching a film we witness a series of relationships, between the persons on the screen and in the story, and, through the camera, between them and us. In the past art reached for permanence and entered tradition, and the individual who made it was ephemeral, preserved in an object that was removed from themselves. In film the art that lasts is an image, a permanent performance of the fleeting self that is contained in it. The star is the artwork, the person a fiction. Films are works of art, but so are the stars themselves. Politically cognizant, morally aware, we enjoy them and take delight in them.

Counter to the tawdriness and vulgarity, the essential insincerity of the movie-star construct, at times the film star may stand for the exemplary person, the epitome of personhood. The film historian Richard Griffith's idea that a star is a dream of a culture convinces me. The film star embodies the wishes and fantasies of a particular society, although this dream can become available to those in another culture, fed by congruent, but likely variable energies. Leo Braudy declares that the star forms 'part of the audience's story about itself'.[8] As Molly Haskell remarked on Mary Pickford, all stars are 'types', people bound to a cultural moment, but also, I would argue, drawing life from that moment too.[9] On film and through the 'film star', the person becomes a 'screen' for the projection of a communal desire and fantasy, and hostility, while also seeming themselves. Especially in the Hollywood fiction film, the 'reality' on-screen exists in a bubble of unreality, sustained by the fantasy that we know the actor in a dream of intimacy. 'The model' stands as the nearest equivalent to the film star and also as a limiting case, because what is added to the movie star is the fact of acting, the performing of a role. Though it is true of some models that they are actors too, and Kim Kardashian and similar figures may be taken as performers of everyday life, along-side vloggers and tweeters and Instagram 'influencers', what the film does that they rarely do is to embed the person in a fiction, to make of them a figure woven into a complex work of art.

The film star faces the public. They stand as a version of a self before a mass, existing in the tension of individualism, both a self alone and yet only living as a star in relation to the audience. As we saw Shah Rukh Khan's character declare in *Fan* (2016), 'I am nothing without my fans.' What they play out is a version of that audience's desires, as 'an *incoherent image*. It shows the star both as an ordinary person and an extraordinary person.'[10] The person that they enact and are gives a myth of the private life to those who watch them, a vision of ordinariness. How often the star packages a back story of being discovered, rescued from anonymity, spotted on the street, or at a beauty pageant, some potential glimpsed in a glamour-girl photo. More than anyone, the film star lives on both sides of the public and private realms, inhabiting a role that is not them, and yet putting their uniqueness up for sale.

The star belongs to an elite; they are the golden ones. As such their distance from us renders them open to resentment. Yet they are also just like us, our representative, the mirror of our yearnings. In the last decades, both left and right have come to agree in hating 'elites', the left who see them as 'privileged' and the right who see them as self-appointed and stuck-up. The amateur rules; experts are suspect. A belief in the making of 'good work' is itself seen as elitist, an offence against equality. Talent possesses an authority that is despised. The star is merely lucky, or there on the basis of their unearned advantage. On YouTube everyone can become their own movie star, a sellable image, but with a face turned towards ours, talking to camera, importunate and desperate.

After 'the death of God', the great problem of modernity is that of obscurity, the suspicion that our lives will not matter. What if it is our destiny to be unknown, unregarded? Much of the paraphernalia of contemporary life exists to protect us from this suspicion, ranging from the cult of celebrity to the dopamine rewards of social media, the fostering of a healing narcissism. The actor, the film star, combines the validation provided for the great artist with the flattering attentions afforded for the famous. Meanwhile the films they play in dramatize and argue for (or did) the centrality of the person, for the thought that when it came to the individual human being attention must be paid. On film, lives are made visible.

Still, the person lifted onto the screen is one mediated through art and artificiality. Film opens itself to the real, including the real person, and yet (as André Bazin affirmed), film is a language, an artifice made of conventions.[11] In relation to the real, we may wonder if that language, those conventions, is a self-sufficing, sealed-off but ragged system, or something that bears witness to the truth of a person. For the philosopher Stanley Cavell, what is on-screen, including the star themselves, is both there and absent; there is a sign of a person there, and not the person themselves, though that absent person may still be summoned up even by not being there.

Ideas of inwardness are particularly relevant to cinema, just as they are particularly put to question by its methods. In a medium devoted to exteriority and the external self, a self also presented in relation to the context of environment and the contingency of others, signs of the inner life are more eagerly sought, more uncannily fugitive than in any literary text.

In place of inwardness, cinema gives us the close-up, coming very close to the subject as though in that way we might elude unknowability. Yet sometimes the same close-up more emphatically displays the ignorance we possess regarding the inner life of the person we regard.

Most critics who have written on stardom have seen the stars themselves as an empty proposition, one filled out by a culture industry and an industrial culture in the interests of mass control. In *A Lover's Discourse*, Roland Barthes informs us that: 'Mass culture is a machine for showing desire. Here is what must interest you, it says, as if it guessed that men are incapable of finding what to desire by themselves.'[12] For the highly influential and gifted critic Richard Dyer, the star enacts a normalizing image of the person as understood by the dominant (bourgeois, capitalist) ideology. There is not a person at the centre of our interest in the film star, there is 'a complex set of cultural processes'; the star is a function of those processes, not a person in themselves.[13] This moving site of discourses can sometimes nonetheless be the 'author' of a film, at least in the sense that they signal and direct the kind of film it might be.

In these readings, inspired by Michel Foucault and others, the 'self', any self, is purely a cultural product, with a body that is itself also a cultural product, inscribed with concepts. Moving away from the apprehension of a person, even a personality, to the notion that personality is itself a construct has much in its favour. Yet, it removes us from some aspects of the star more interesting to me, namely their presence in the films themselves and how those films might reflect on the nature of the performer, on the reality, and unreality, of the player. In films the insubstantial self turns into an equally insubstantial shadow on film. And yet up there we find also the trace of something never to be found elsewhere, of something intrinsically theirs, interacting with the meanings and suggestions created within the work of art that is the film itself.

Oscar Wilde wrote: 'To look at a thing is very different from seeing a thing. One does not see anything until one sees its beauty. Then, and then only, does it come into existence.'[14] That distinction between looking at and seeing seems to me to be central to film, as to art in general. It is both an appeal to the aesthetic and by implication to the ethical, for when we see we rise into awareness of the endless value of the artwork or of the other person. Animals and robots, we may assume, look at things, but do not, in Wilde's sense, see them. It is our gift to trade in, or to treasure. If to see is to see the beauty in something, in someone, then this is what cinema can do to human beings, and what in the main Internet porn or YouTube does not do. There, online, we look at; in the great films, and with the stars explored in this book, we *see* them, not only as figures of glamour, but as persons. The great Polish film-maker Krzysztof Kieślowski lamented the fact that nearly always film was a literal medium; when you watched it a tree was just a film of a tree, a candle just a film of a candle.[15] And yet sometimes something transformative would occur, and within the frame of the film, ordinariness would be transformed, and you would not be looking at the thing, but seeing it. While remaining themselves, the tree would be more than a tree, the person would become a star, and at the very highest the star would show what had always been hiding there in sight; that is, a person.

REFERENCES

PREFACE

1 Erwin Panofsky, 'Style and Medium in the Motion Picture', in *Three Essays on Style*, ed. Irving Lavin (Cambridge, MA, 1995), p. 116.
2 Ibid., p. 98.
3 Paula Cohen, *Silent Film and the Triumph of the American Myth* (Oxford, 2001), p. 134.

PART ONE: **THE SILENT STAR**

I MARY PICKFORD: THE BIOGRAPH GIRL

1 Maxim Gorky, newspaper review of the Lumière programme at the Nizhni-Novgorod fair, 4 July 1896, quoted in *In the Kingdom of Shadows: A Companion to Early Cinema*, ed. Colin Harding and Simon Popple (London, 1996), p. 5.
2 Rudyard Kipling, 'Mrs Bathurst', in *Rudyard Kipling: A Critical Edition of the Major Works*, ed. Danny Karlin (Oxford, 1999), pp. 284, 286–7.
3 Erwin Panofsky, 'Style and Medium in the Motion Picture', in *Three Essays on Style*, ed. Irving Lavin (Cambridge, MA, 1995), p. 93.
4 Ibid., p. 95.
5 George Edgar, ed., *Careers for Men, Women, and Children*, 4 vols (1911–12), quoted in *In the Kingdom of Shadows*, ed. Harding and Popple, p. 177.
6 'Mr Wells and the Cinematograph', in *The Times*, 10 January 1914, quoted in *In the Kingdom of Shadows*, ed. Harding and Popple, p. 103.
7 Richard Abel, *The Ciné Goes to Town: French Cinema, 1896–1914* (Berkeley, Los Angeles, CA, and London, 1994), p. 237.
8 John Palmer, 'Mr Bunny', *Saturday Review*, 11 April 1914, quoted in *In the Kingdom of Shadows*, ed. Harding and Popple, pp. 166–8.
9 Janet Staiger, 'Seeing Stars', in *Stardom: Industry of Desire*, ed. Christine Gledhill (London and New York, 1991), p. 6.
10 *Motion Picture Story Magazine*, I/1 (February 1911), pp. 13, 30, 65.
11 See Anthony Slide, *Inside the Hollywood Fan Magazine: A History of Star Makers, Fabricators, and Gossip Mongers* (Jackson, MS, 2010), pp. 11–15.
12 Richard deCordova, 'The Emergence of the Star System in America', in *Stardom: Industry of Desire*, ed. Gledhill, p. 17.
13 Paula Cohen, *Silent Film and the Triumph of the American Myth* (Oxford, 2001), p. 136.
14 Quoted in Staiger, 'Seeing Stars', p. 10.
15 DeCordova, 'The Emergence of the Star System in America', pp. 17, 19.

16 Mary Pickford, *Sunshine and Shadow* (London, 1956), p. 114.
17 See 'Stage Celebrities in Cinema Relate their Experiences before the Camera', *Strand Magazine*, L (December 1915), pp. 646–53, quoted in *In the Kingdom of Shadows*, ed. Harding and Popple, pp. 183–4.
18 Panofsky, 'Style and Medium in the Motion Picture', p. 115.
19 Pickford, *Sunshine and Shadow*, pp. 122–3.
20 Cecil B. DeMille, 'Foreword', in Pickford, *Sunshine and Shadow*, p. 10.
21 DeCordova, 'The Emergence of the Star System in America', p. 20.
22 Pickford, *Sunshine and Shadow*, p. 47.
23 Ernest A. Dench, 'Leaving the Pictures for the Halls', in *London Life*, 2707 (12 April 1913), p. 28.
24 Cohen, *Silent Film and the Triumph of the American Myth*, p. 132.
25 Pickford, *Sunshine and Shadow*, pp. 169–70.
26 Ibid., pp. 190–92.
27 Panofsky, 'Style and Medium in the Motion Picture', p. 95.
28 Pickford, *Sunshine and Shadow*, pp. 128–9; Molly Haskell, *From Reverence to Rape: The Treatment of Women in the Movies* (Chicago, IL, and London, 1987), p. 59.
29 Haskell, *From Reverence to Rape*, p. 61.
30 Pickford, *Sunshine and Shadow*, p. 241.
31 Haskell, *From Reverence to Rape*, pp. 58–9.

2 POLA NEGRI: INVENTING THE STAR

1 Marjorie Clapp quoted in Mariusz Kotowski, *Pola Negri: Hollywood's First Femme Fatale* (Lexington, KY, 2014), p. 3.
2 This chapter draws on Kotowski's *Pola Negri* and, especially, Pola Negri, *Memoirs of a Star* (New York, 1970).
3 Siegfried Kracauer, *From Caligari to Hitler: A Psychological History of the German Film* [1947], ed. Leonardo Quaresima, rev. edn (Princeton, NJ, 2004), pp. 52–3.
4 Quoted ibid., p. 55.
5 Scott Eyman, *Ernst Lubitsch: Laughter in Paradise* (Baltimore, MD, 2000), p. 62.

3 CHARLIE CHAPLIN: THE TRAMP

1 Quoted in Joan Mellen, *Modern Times* (London, 2006), p. 14.
2 Robert Warshow, 'A Feeling of Sad Dignity', *Partisan Review*, XXI/6 (1954), in *American Movie Critics: An Anthology from the Silents until Now*, ed. Philip Lopate (New York, 2006), p. 180.
3 Charles Maland, *City Lights* (London, 2007), pp. 45–6.
4 From an article in *Theatre Arts Monthly* (November 1930), p. 908, quoted in Donald Crafton, *The Talkies: American Cinema's Transition to Sound, 1926–1931* (Berkeley and Los Angeles, CA, 1997), p. 374.
5 Quoted in Simon Louvish, *Chaplin: The Tramp's Odyssey* (London, 2009), p. 237.

6 Charles Chaplin in an interview with Richard Meryman, 'Chaplin', in *Life* (10 March 1967), p. 89.

PART TWO: THE GOLDEN AGE
4 'ASTA' AND 'CHEETA': THE ANIMAL STAR

1 James Lever, *Me Cheeta: The Autobiography* (London, 2008). Part of the following chapter derives from my review of this book in the *London Review of Books*, XXXI/2 (29 January 2009), pp. 28–9.
2 Lever, *Me Cheeta*, p. 189.

5 PETER LORRE: CHARACTER ACTOR

1 From an interview with Michael Powell by Ian Christie (1985), in *Michael Powell: Interviews*, ed. David Lazar (Jackson, MS, 2003), p. 132.
2 Scott Proudfit appears to have coined the 'Laurel and Hardy of crime' comment in *Backstage* (3 June 2003).

6 FRED ASTAIRE, GINGER ROGERS, GENE KELLY: A STAR DANCED

1 Lincoln Kirstein, 'Dancing in Films', *New Theatre* (September 1936), pp. 11–13, quoted in *American Movie Critics: An Anthology from the Silents until Now*, ed. Philip Lopate (New York, 2006), p. 101.
2 In relation to this, see the discussion of the contrast between Astaire and Kelly in Leo Braudy, 'Musicals and the Energy from Within', in *The World in a Frame: What We See in Films, 25th Anniversary Edition* (Chicago, IL, 2002), pp. 139–63.
3 See John Franchesina, *Hermes Pan: The Man Who Danced with Fred Astaire* (Oxford, 2012), p. 56.
4 Quoted in Braudy, 'Musicals and the Energy from Within', p. 154.
5 Kirstein, 'Dancing in Films', in *American Movie Critics*, ed. Lopate, p. 101.
6 Franchesina, *Hermes Pan*, p. 57.

7 KATHARINE HEPBURN AND CARY GRANT: THE PUBLIC IMAGE

1 Quoted in Robert Evans, *The Kid Stays in the Picture*, rev. edn (London, 2004), p. 152.
2 Cukor quoted in Peter Bogdanovich, *Who the Devil Made It* (New York, 1997), p. 446.
3 Peter Swaab, *Bringing Up Baby* (London, 2010), pp. 36–7.
4 Stanley Cavell, *Pursuits of Happiness: The Hollywood Comedy of Remarriage* (Cambridge, MA, 1981), pp. 123–5.
5 Joseph McBride, *Hawks on Hawks* [1982] (London, 1996), p. 79.
6 Pauline Kael, 'The Man from Dream City', *New Yorker* (14 July 1975); quoted in Graham McCann, *Cary Grant: A Class Apart* (London, 1997), p. 113.

7 Ibid., pp. 197, 210.
8 Molly Haskell, *From Reverence to Rape: The Treatment of Women in the Movies* (Chicago, IL, and London, 1987), pp. 223ff; Maria DiBattista, *Fast-talking Dames* (New Haven, CT, and London, 2001), pp. 176ff.

8 VIVIEN LEIGH: RUINOUS SELVES

1 See Molly Haskell, *From Reverence to Rape: The Treatment of Women in the Movies* (Chicago, IL, and London, 1987).
2 Molly Haskell, *Frankly, My Dear: Gone with the Wind Revisited* (New Haven, CT, and London, 2009).

9 VERONICA LAKE: HALF-OBSCURED FACES

1 Andrew Sarris, *'You Ain't Heard Nothin' Yet': The American Talking Film, History and Memory, 1927–1949* (Oxford, 1998), p. 317.
2 James Harvey, *Romantic Comedy in Hollywood, from Lubitsch to Sturges* (New York, 1987), p. 587.
3 Sarris, *'You Ain't Heard Nothin' Yet'*, p. 316.
4 Bazin quoted ibid., p. 317; Maria DiBattista, *Fast-talking Dames* (New Haven, CT, and London, 2001), p. 126.

10 CAROLE LOMBARD: THE SCREWBALL HEROINE

1 As Peter Barnes suggests in his short book *To Be or Not to Be* (London, 2002).
2 Quoted by Hannah Arendt, in 'Interview with Roger Errera', in *Thinking Without a Banister: Essays in Understanding, 1953–1975*, ed. Jerome Kohn (New York, 2018), p. 504.
3 William Blake, *Milton*, Book the Second, Plate 35, line 42, in *Complete Writings*, ed. Geoffrey Keynes (Oxford, 1966), p. 526.
4 Barnes, *To Be or Not to Be*, p. 72.

11 GREER GARSON AND JOAN FONTAINE: THE FORGOTTEN STAR

1 I was first introduced to *Letter from an Unknown Woman* while taking Stanley Cavell's class on 'The Aesthetics of Opera and Film' at Harvard University in 1996. The discussion in that class undoubtedly suffuses what follows in this chapter, and I am much indebted here again to Cavell's reading of the film, published later that year in *Contesting Tears: The Hollywood Melodrama of the Unknown Woman* (Chicago, IL, and London, 1996).
2 See Michael Troyan, *A Rose for Mrs Miniver: The Life of Greer Garson* (Lexington, KY, 1999), pp. 138–9.
3 W. H. Auden, 'Song of the Master and Boatswain', from 'The Sea and the Mirror', in *For the Time Being* (Princeton, NJ, 1944).

4 Hannah Arendt, *The Human Condition* [1958], 2nd edn (Chicago, IL, 1988), pp. 18–20.

12 ORSON WELLES: THE FILM STAR AS FRAGMENT AND FAILURE

1 David Thomson, *Rosebud: The Story of Orson Welles* (London, 1996), p. 159.
2 Orson Welles and Peter Bogdanovich, *This Is Orson Welles*, rev. edn (New York, 1998), p. 70.
3 Ibid., p. 84.
4 Ibid., p. 262.

13 INGRID BERGMAN: INTERMEZZO

1 Charles Lamb, 'Stage Illusion' [1825], in *The Last Essays of Elia*, in *The Works in Prose and Verse of Charles and Mary Lamb*, ed. Thomas Hutchinson (Oxford, 1908), vol. I, p. 674.
2 Patrick Kavanagh, 'Bluebells for Love', in *Collected Poems* (London, 1964), p. 69.
3 Robin Wood, *Hitchcock's Films Revisited*, rev. edn (New York, 2002), p. 303.
4 Ibid., pp. 312–13.
5 See Umberto Eco, 'Casablanca: Cult Movies and Intertextual Collage', in *Travels in Hyperreality* [1986], trans. William Weaver (London, 2014), pp. 197–212.
6 Maurice Schérer, '*Notorious*', *Revue du Cinéma/Image et Son*, n.s. 3, 15 (1948), pp. 70–72.
7 For this reference I am indebted to Stig Björkman's brilliant documentary portrait of Bergman, *Ingrid Bergman: In Her Own Words* (2015).

PART THREE: **NATIONAL CINEMAS – STARS FOR THE NATION**
14 LAMBERTO MAGGIORANI AND MARIA PIA CASILIO: ABSENT FILM STARS IN VITTORIO DE SICA'S FILMS

1 Robert S. G. Gordon, *Bicycle Thieves* (Basingstoke, 2008), pp. 27, 113.
2 Ibid., p. 26.

15 MOIRA SHEARER: THE MARIONETTE

1 Michael Powell, *A Life in Movies* [1986] (London, 2000), p. 653.
2 Jack Cardiff, *Magic Hour* (London, 1996), p. 96.
3 Powell, *A Life in Movies*, p. 628.

16 GLORIA SWANSON: HAVING A FACE

1 Cameron Crowe, *Conversations with Wilder* (London, 1999), p. 146.
2 Ibid., p. 47.

17 AVA GARDNER: I AM NOT AN ACTRESS

1 Berdie Adams, quoted in Lee Server, *Ava Gardner* (London, 2006), p. 57. Most of the quotes and remarks that follow in this essay are from Lee Server's excellent biography.

18 MONTGOMERY CLIFT: HE'S NOT THERE

1 See Amy Lawrence, *The Passion of Montgomery Clift* (Berkeley and Los Angeles, CA, 2010).

19 SETSUKO HARA: THE STILL POINT

1 Daisuke Miyao, 'Nationalizing Madame Butterfly: The Formation of Female Stars in Japanese Cinema', in *The Oxford Handbook of Japanese Cinema*, ed. Daisuke Mayao (Oxford, 2014), pp. 152–71.
2 Ayako Saito, 'Occupation and Memory: The Representation of Woman's Body in Postwar Japanese Cinema', in *The Oxford Handbook of Japanese Cinema*, ed. Daisuke Mayao (Oxford, 2014), p. 329.
3 Donald Richie, *Women in Japanese Cinema* (New York, 1976), p. 3.
4 Ayako Saito, 'Occupation and Memory', p. 330.

20 TOSHIRO MIFUNE: STUDYING LIONS

1 As Kurosawa described in an interview, in Joan Mellen, *Voices from the Japanese Cinema* (New York, 1975), p. 48.

21 NARGIS AND RAJ KAPOOR: MY HEART IS HINDUSTANI

1 Bunny Reuben, *Raj Kapoor: The Fabulous Showman* (New Delhi, 1995), p. 88.
2 Ibid., p. 118.
3 S. Theodore Baskaram, 'Nargis', in *Bollywood's Top 20: Superstars of Indian Cinema*, ed. Bhaichand Patel (London, 2016), unpaginated.
4 Parama Roy, 'Figuring Mother India: the Case of Nargis', in *The Bollywood Reader*, ed. Rajinder Dudrah and Jigna Desai (Maidenhead, 2008), p. 111.
5 Gayatri Chatterjee, *Mother India* (London, 2002), p. 26; Vija Mishra, *Bollywood Cinema: Temples of Desire* (London and New York, 2002), p. xvi.
6 Roy, 'Figuring Mother India: the Case of Nargis', p. 111; Parama Roy, *Indian Traffic: Identities in Question in Colonial and Postcolonial India* (Berkeley and Los Angeles, CA, 1998), p. 156.
7 Roy, *Indian Traffic*, p. 157.
8 Anil Saari, *Indian Cinema: The Faces Behind the Masks* (Oxford, 2011), p. 66.
9 Ajay Gehlawat, for example, criticizes this approach in *Reframing Bollywood: Theories of Popular Hindi Cinema* (New Delhi and London, 2010).
10 From an interview with Kapoor in Saari, *Indian Cinema: The Faces Behind the Masks*, p. 2.

11 From an interview with Khwaja Ahmad Abbas, ibid., p. 18.

12 Ibid., p. 13.

13 Louis Dumont, 'World Renunciation in Indian Religions', in *Contributions to Indian Sociology*, 4 (1960), p. 33. For a demurral, see Mishra, *Bollywood Cinema*, p. 83.

14 Vijay Mishra, 'Towards a Theoretical Critique of Bombay Cinema', in *The Bollywood Reader*, ed. Rajinder Dudrah and Jigna Desai (Maidenhead, 2008), p. 37.

15 Mishra, *Bollywood Cinema*, p. 100.

16 Reuben, *Raj Kapoor: The Fabulous Showman*, pp. 107–8.

17 Sumita Chakravarty, 'The National-heroic Image: Masculinity and Masquerade', in *The Bollywood Reader*, ed. Rajinder Dudrah and Jigna Desai (Maidenhead, 2008), p. 88.

18 Mishra, *Bollywood Cinema*, p. xv.

19 Anil Zankar, 'Scriptwriting: In and Out of the Box', in *Routledge Handbook of Indian Cinemas*, ed. K. Moti Gokulsing and Wimal Dissanayake (London and New York, 2013), p. 273.

20 Chatterjee, *Mother India*, p. 28.

21 Chakravarty, 'The National-heroic Image', pp. 89–90.

22 Chatterjee, *Mother India*, p. 29.

23 Mishra, *Bollywood Cinema*, p. 64; Roy, *Indian Traffic*, p. 169.

24 Baskaram, 'Nargis', in *Bollywood's Top 20: Superstars of Indian Cinema*.

22 GIULIETTA MASINA AND MARCELLO MASTROIANNI: NOTHING IS SADDER THAN LAUGHTER

1 André Bazin, '*Cabiria*: The Voyage to the End of Neorealism', in *What Is Cinema?*, trans. Hugh Gray (Berkeley, CA, 2005), vol. II, p. 85.

2 Federico Fellini, *Fellini on Fellini*, trans. Isabel Quigley (New York, 1976), p. 54.

3 Hollis Alpert, *Fellini: A Life* (London, 1986), pp. 169–70.

4 Fellini, *Fellini on Fellini*, p. 205.

5 Rainer Maria Rilke, 'Der Geist Ariel', in *Ahead of All Parting: The Selected Poetry and Prose of Rainer Maria Rilke*, trans. Stephen Mitchell (New York, 1995), pp. 108–11.

6 Fellini, *Fellini on Fellini*, p. 54.

23 JOHN WAYNE: HOW TO GROW OLD

1 Jon Halliday, *Sirk on Sirk* (London, 1971), p. 71.

2 Quoted in *I Am Not Your Negro* (dir. Raoul Peck, 2016).

3 Molly Haskell, *Holding My Own in No Man's Land* (New York and Oxford, 1997), p. 150.

4 Joan Didion, *Slouching Towards Bethlehem* [1968] (London, 1993), p. 30.

5 Haskell, *Holding My Own in No Man's Land*, p. 157.

6 Quoted in Didion, *Slouching Towards Bethlehem*, p. 31.

7 Quoted in McBride, *Hawks on Hawks* [1982] (London, 1996), p. 142.

8 Edward Buscombe, *The Searchers* (London, 2000), p. 25.
9 Haskell, *Holding My Own in No Man's Land*, p. 152.
10 Jane Tompkins, *West of Everything: The Inner Life of Westerns* (Oxford, 1992).
11 Quoted in McBride, *Hawks on Hawks*, p. 138.
12 See the excellent account of the film in Buscombe, *The Searchers*, pp. 21–3.
13 Lindsay Anderson, *About John Ford* (London, 1981), p. 154.
14 Robin Wood, *Rio Bravo* (London, 2003), p. 44.
15 Quoted in McBride, *Hawks on Hawks*, p. 145.

24 AUDREY HEPBURN: FRANKENSTEIN'S CREATURE

1 Pauline Kael, *Deeper into Movies* (London, 2000), p. 381. Over the years and in several essays, Kael consistently used the word 'radiant' in connection with Hepburn in Wyler's *Roman Holiday*.
2 Cameron Crowe, *Conversations with Wilder* (London, 1999), p. 147.

25 MARILYN MONROE: THE SUFFERING STAR

1 'But every bitter pill had enough sugar somewhere for the public to be able to swallow it': David Thomson, *A Biographical Dictionary of Film* (London, 1994), p. 813.
2 Molly Haskell, *From Reverence to Rape: The Treatment of Women in the Movies* (Chicago, IL, and London, 1987), pp. 256–7.
3 Jacqueline Rose, 'A Rumbling of Things Unknown', *London Review of Books*, XXXIV/8 (26 April 2012), pp. 29–34.
4 Quoted in Alex Madsen, *Billy Wilder* (London, 1969), pp. 116–17.

26 JUANITA MOORE AND SUSAN KOHNER: *IMITATION OF LIFE*

1 Jon Halliday, *Sirk on Sirk* (London, 1971), p. 130.
2 On Sirk and Einstein and Brecht, see Gary Morris, '"An Unhappy Happy End": Douglas Sirk', in *Action! Interviews Directors from Classical Hollywood to Contemporary Iran* (London, 2009), pp. 21–3.
3 Halliday, *Sirk on Sirk*, p. 132.

PART FOUR: NEW WAVE STARS

27 JANET LEIGH AND TIPPI HEDREN: TORTURING THE AUDIENCE

1 Raymond Bellour, 'Psychosis, Neurosis, Perversion', in *A Hitchcock Reader*, ed. Marshall Deutelbaum and Leland Poague, trans. Nancy Huston, 2nd edn (Oxford, 2009), pp. 341–2.
2 Stephen Rebello, *Alfred Hitchcock and the Making of Psycho* (London, 1990), p. 42.

28 AUDREY HEPBURN AND CARY GRANT: THE STRANGE DEATH OF THE HOLLYWOOD GOLDEN AGE

1 Tom Wolfe, 'Loverboy of the Bourgeoisie', in *The Kandy-kolored Tangerine-flake Streamline Baby* (London, 1968), p. 131.
2 Pauline Kael, 'Zeitgeist and Poltergeist: or, Are Movies Going to Pieces?', in *I Lost it at the Movies: Film Writings, 1954 to 1965* (London, 1965), p. 26.

31 SIDNEY POITIER: THE DEFIANT ONE

1 Quoted in Paul Monaco, *The Sixties, 1960–1969*, vol. VIII of *History of the American Cinema*, ed. Charles Harpole (Berkeley and Los Angeles, CA, 2001), p. 150.
2 Edward Lipton, 'Negro Stereotype – In a Lost World: Poitier', *Film Daily* (29 September 1967), p. 3.

32 DUSTIN HOFFMAN: LITTLE BIG MAN

1 Quoted in Paul Monaco, *The Sixties, 1960–1969*, vol. VIII of *History of the American Cinema*, ed. Charles Harpole (Berkeley and Los Angeles, CA, 2001), p. 184.
2 Quoted ibid.
3 Stanley Cavell, *The World Viewed: Reflections on the Ontology of Film*, rev. edn (Cambridge, MA, 1979), p. 78.

33 WOODY ALLEN: THE DIRECTOR AS STAR

1 Claire Dederer, 'What Do We Do with the Art of Monstrous Men', *Paris Review* (20 November 2017).
2 Christopher Lasch, *The Culture of Narcissism: American Life in an Age of Diminishing Expectations* [1979] (New York and London, 1991), pp. 18–21.

34 ROBERT DE NIRO: FOR REAL

1 Gavin Smith, 'The Art of Vision: Marin Scorsese's *Kundun*', in *Martin Scorsese: Interviews*, ed. Peter Brunette (Jackson, MS, 1999), p. 254.
2 Martin Scorsese in *Scorsese on Scorsese*, ed. Ian Christie and David Thompson (London, 2003), pp. 60–62.
3 Martin Scorsese quoted in Guy Flatley, 'Martin Scorsese's Gamble', in *Martin Scorsese: Interviews*, ed. Brunette, p. 56.
4 Kevin Jackson, ed., *Schrader on Schrader* (London, 2004), p. 133; Peter Biskind, *Easy Riders, Raging Bulls* (London, 1998), p. 254.
5 Jake LaMotta, *Raging Bull: My Story* (Englewood Cliffs, NJ, 1970), p. 2.
6 Quoted in *Scorsese on Scorsese*, ed. Christie and Thompson, p. 83.
7 Biskind, *Easy Riders, Raging Bulls*, p. 386.
8 Ibid., p. 390.

9 René Girard, *A Theatre of Envy* (Oxford, 1991), p. 59.
10 Quoted in *Scorsese on Scorsese*, ed. Christie and Thompson, p. 77.

PART FIVE: **POSTHUMAN STARS**

35 HARRISON FORD: *BLADE RUNNER* AND THE REPLICATION OF THE PERSON

1 See Ian Suttie, *The Origins of Love and Hate* (London, 1935), pp. 8off.

36 MAGGIE CHEUNG: CENTRE STAGE

1 Yingjin Zhang and Mary Farquhar, 'Chinese Film Stars', in *Chinese Film Stars*, ed. Mary Farquhar and Yingjin Zhang (London and New York, 2010), p. 2.
2 Mette Hjort, discussing Bérénice Reynaud's thoughts on Ruan's acting, in 'Ruan Lingyu: Reflections on an Individual Performance', in *Chinese Film Stars*, ed. Farquhar and Zhang, p. 40.
3 Quoted in Richard Meyer, *Ruan Ling-Yu: The Goddess of Shanghai* (Hong Kong, 2005), p. 50.
4 See Mette Hjort's discussion of Michael Chang's research in this regard, in *Chinese Film Stars*, ed. Farquhar and Zhang, p. 36.
5 Paul Fonoroff, from *South China Morning Post*, 23 September 1994, quoted in Wimal Dissanayake, *Wong Kar-Wai's Ashes of Time* (Hong Kong, 2003), p. 130.
6 Rey Chow, 'Fetish Power Unbound: A Small History of "Woman" in Chinese Cinema', in *The Oxford Handbook of Chinese Cinemas*, ed. Carlos Rojas and Ellen Cheng-Yin Chow (Oxford, 2013), p. 494.
7 Quoted in Vivian P. Y. Lee, 'The Hong Kong New Wave', in *The Chinese Cinema Book*, ed. Son Hwee Lim and Julian Ward (London, 2011), p. 131.

38 SCARLETT JOHANSSON: A NEW KIND OF EMPTINESS

1 W. H. Auden, 'Memorial for the City', in *Collected Shorter Poems, 1927–1957* (London, 1966), p. 289.

39 SHU QI: A PLACELESS HEAVEN

1 See Gary G. Xu, *Sinascape: Contemporary Chinese Cinema* (Plymouth, 2007).
2 Quoted in Tonglin Lu, 'Taiwan New Cinema and its Legacy', in *The Chinese Cinema Book*, ed. Son Hwee Lim and Julian Ward (London, 2011), p. 122.
3 As set out in Hou Hsiao-hsien's guidelines for the film, transcribed in Xu, *Sinascape*, p. 116.
4 Hou Hsiao-hsien quoted in Lu, 'Taiwan New Cinema and its Legacy', p. 128.

5 See Hou Hsiao-hsien's comments on his films quoted in Jean Ma, *Melancholy Drift: Marking Time in Chinese Cinema* (Hong Kong, 2010), p. 19.
6 Lu, 'Taiwan New Cinema and its Legacy', p. 128.

40 ANDY SERKIS: LEAR'S SHADOW

1 Andy Serkis, *The Lord of the Rings Gollum: How We Made Movie Magic* (London, 2003), p. 19.
2 See 'Human Meets Humanoid', a 'Science Channel' programme, www.youtube.com, 17 June 2014, accessed 25 January 2018.
3 During a talk at the International Film Festival Rotterdam, 28 January 2018.

AFTERWORD

1 Kevin Roose, 'Inevitably, Now an App Can Create Fake Videos', *New York Times* (7 March 2018), pp. 1, 8.
2 Evelyn Waugh, *The Loved One* [1948] (London, 2000), p. 24.
3 John Ellis, *Visible Fictions* (New York, 1982).
4 John Gray, *Straw Dogs* (London, 2002), p. 151.
5 George Eliot, *Middlemarch* [1870–71] (Oxford, 2008), p. 383.
6 Robert C. Allen and Douglas Gomery, *Film History: Theory and Practice* [1985] (Columbus, OH, 1993), p. 172.
7 Ellis, *Visible Fictions*.
8 Leo Braudy, *The Frenzy of Renown: Fame and its History* (New York and Oxford, 1982), p. 593.
9 Molly Haskell, *From Reverence to Rape: The Treatment of Women in the Movies* (Chicago, IL, and London, 1987), p. 49.
10 John Ellis, 'Stars as a Cinematic Phenomenon', in *Visible Fictions*.
11 André Bazin, 'D'autre part le cinéma est un langage', in *Qu'est-ce que le cinéma* (Paris, 1958), p. 19.
12 Quoted in James Donald, 'The Hollywood Star Machine', in *The Cinema Book*, ed. Pam Cook (London, 2007), p. 110.
13 Ibid., p. 111.
14 Oscar Wilde, 'The Decay of Lying' (1891), in *De Profundis and Other Writings* (London, 1986), p. 79.
15 Krzysztof Kieślowski, in *Kieślowski on Kieślowski*, ed. Danusia Stok (London, 1993), pp. 194–5; he actually uses the example of someone lighting a cigarette.

ACKNOWLEDGEMENTS

I especially thank Ben Hayes and Michael Leaman at Reaktion Books for their encouragement, advice and support. I am much beholden to the expert help of Amy Salter, Alexandru Ciobanu, Susannah Jayes and all at Reaktion's office. I am grateful to my generous editors, Deborah Friedell and Mary Kay Wilmers, and the editorial staff at the *London Review of Books*, and Paul Laity and Nicholas Wroe at *The Guardian*, who commissioned versions of some of the essays that make up this book (some seventeen of its forty chapters, though, in most cases, these are much rewritten). Thanks are also due to the teachers and colleagues who inspired my attempts to think through the meanings of films: Philip Horne; David Trotter; the sadly missed Stanley Cavell; and Michael Wood. My indebtedness to Professor Cavell is deeper than I know; as he did with others he both justified my own interests and left me sharing his own. I thank my colleagues and friends Peter Liebregts, Jan Frans Van Dijkhuizen and Evert Jan Van Leeuwen for their support and interest, and all my students, including especially Laura Quarto, Eddie de Oliveira, Fleur Melker, Christian van Dam, Svetlana Skripkina and Mark Broughton for keeping the immense value of cinema in mind. I am happily indebted to my friends Richard Allen, Jason Whiston, Lorna Gibb, Stephen James, Lee Sands, Catherine McLoughlin, Olivia Horley, Cristian Popa, Christopher Hamilton, Gregory Dart, Vibeche Standal, Richard Hamblyn, Jo Lynch, Nienke Venderbosch and Anousch Khorikian, with whom I saw and talked over many of the films discussed in this book. I am hugely thankful to my mother and father, Liz and Clive Newton, for their unfailing love, support and concern, and to my daughters Alice and Hannah, for all that they bring to me just by being there. My father died in the month I completed this book, and thoughts of him are everywhere in it. My gratitude goes too to my sister and brother-in-law, Jane and Phil Cole. And I could never be done thanking Lena Müller for all the good things she has given me, and for the help without which I would never have finished this book; it was written through the years we have known each other, and with her patient encouragement, and it is only fitting that I gratefully dedicate it to her.

PHOTO ACKNOWLEDGEMENTS

Library of Congress, Washington, DC: p. 16.

INDEX

Page numbers in *italics* refer to illustrations

2046 367, 370
8½ 240, 241, 244–5, 247–9

Aag 226, 231
Aah 230–32, 233, 234, 238
Abbas, Ackbar 368
Abbas, Khwaja Ahmad 228, 230
Adventures of Tintin, The 395
African Queen, The 84
Alekan, Henri 106
Agee, James 51
Alfie 332
All About Eve 281
Allen, Robert C., and Douglas
    Gomery 412
Allen, Woody 43, 65–6, 244, 324,
    332–39, *336*, 381, 383
All the President's Men 330
Alpert, Hollis 313
Alphaville 300, 304
Anastasia 156, 161–2
Anchors Aweigh 78
Anderson, Lindsay 253, 258
Anna Karenina 106
Annie Hall 332–3, 335, 337
Antonioni, Michelangelo 292
Apartment, The 271, 273, 295, *404*, 405
Arendt, Hannah 123
Ashes of Time 364
Assassin, The 392–4
Assayas, Olivier 365–7, 369
Asta 60–66, *64*
Astaire, Fred 73–82, *79*, 240, 269, 298,
    423
    as Dick Avery in *Funny Face* 262–3

As Tears Go By 361
Astor, Mary 21
Auden, W. H. 123, 132, 385
Autumn Sonata 162
Awakenings 346–7
Awāra 227, 228–9, 232, 234
Awful Truth, The 62–3, 65, 89

Bacall, Lauren 85, 93, 259, 323
Baldwin, James 250–51, 316
Bancroft, Anne 322–3
Bande à Part 299–304
Band Wagon, The 74, 79–80
Banks, Leslie 72
Bara, Theda 29, 365
Bardot, Brigitte 300
Barefoot Contessa, The 190, 196, 198,
    199
Barker, Lex 60
Barnes, Peter 119, 424
Barrymore, John 115–17
Barthes, Roland 277, 417
Basinger, Kim 406, 408
Battisti, Carlo 169
Bazin, André 114, 139–40, 242, 416
Beatty, Warren 85, 314, 324
Bedford Incident, The 317
Beerbohm Tree, Sir Herbert 19
Belafonte, Harry 315, 320
Bellour, Raymond 287
Belmondo, Jean-Paul 299, 300, 301,
    304
Bells of St Mary's, The 151, 152–3, 156,
    158, 162
Benny, Jack 118–19

Bergkatze, Die 47–8
Bergman, Ingmar 162, 337
Bergman, Ingrid 33, 86, 150–63, *159*, 323
Berkeley, Busby 75
Bernhardt, Sarah 31, 39, 253
Besson, Luc 381, 386–7
Bhowani Junction 199
Bicycle Thieves, The 167–73
Big Swallow, The 25
Birds, The 287, *290*, 291–2, 401
Blade Runner 304, 353–9, *354*, 411
Blake, William 118
Blanchett, Cate 412–13
Blue Dahlia, The 109–10
Blue Velvet 208, 339, 372, 374, 375
Bogarde, Dirk 207
Bogart, Humphrey 84, 85, 86, 93, 155, 198, 262, 266, 295, 298, 307
Bogdanovich, Peter 85, 142, 147
Bow, Clara 21
Bowen, Elizabeth 378
Bowie, David 11, 135, 386, 408
Brackett, Charles 185
Brando, Marlon 107, 203, 208, 269, 347
Braudy, Leo 415
Breakfast at Tiffany's 261, 264
Breathless 299–300
Brecht, Bertolt 69, 117, 284
Brechtian, the 71, 361
Brennan, Walter 200–201, 258–60
Bresson, Robert 341
Brief Encounter 305–10, *306*
Bringing Up Baby 62, 65, 84, 88–9
Broadway Danny Rose 335
Broken Lance 320
Bunny, John (Jack) 20
Buscombe, Edward 252

Caesar and Cleopatra *104*, 106
Cagney, James 273, 322
Capra, Frank 405
Cardiff, Jack 81, 177, 178
Carmen 30, 33
Carradine, John 260

Casablanca 72, 155–6, 322
Casilio, Maria Pia 167, 169–72, *171*, 174
Cassidy, Joanna 353
Cavell, Stanley 326, 417, 424
Center Stage 361–4
Chandler, Raymond 109
Chaplin, Charlie 27, 30, 33, 38, 43–52, *49*, 75, 88, 120, 185, 227–8, 230, 232–3, 235, 305, 390
Chaplin, Geraldine 310, 311
Charisse, Cyd 74, 77, 80
Cheeta 55–66, *59*
Chen Chang 391
Cherrill, Virginia 45
Cheung, Maggie 360–71, *366*, 392
Chimes at Midnight 138, 144, 146–8
Christie, Julie 85, 308–12, *309*
Citizen Kane 12, 138–44, 146, 194,
City Lights 44–51, *49*, 120
Clean 363, 369–70
Clift, Montgomery 41, 107, 168, 183, 200–211, *202*, 269, 275, 322, 323
Cocteau, Jean 106, 292
Cohn, Nik 135
Colman, Ronald 88, 121, *123*, 127, 129, 132–3, 373
Color of Pomegranates, The 223
Conrad, Joseph 142, 300
Cooper, Gary 215, 262–3, 266–8, 298, 313
Coppola, Sofia 34, 381–2,
Cotten, Joseph 138, 145, 158
Courtenay, Tom 310
Coward, Noël 307
Crimes and Misdemeanors 337, 338
Crosby, Bing 110, 156, 396
Cukor, George 84–6, 156, 197
Curtis, Tony 267, 272, 275, 277–8, 315
Cushing, Peter 411

Darin, Bobby 315
Days of Being Wild 361, 367, 370
Dean, James 202, 203, 211, 255, 269, 323
deCordova, Richard 21–3

Dederer, Claire 333
'Deepfake, The' 407, 409, 411
Defiant Ones, The 314, 315–16
de Havilland, Olivia 94, 96, 101, 103, 129, 208
Del Rio, Rebecca 375–6
DeMille, Cecil B. 23
De Niro, Robert 33, 225, 324, 335, 340–49, *343*
Dern, Laura 208
De Sica, Vittorio 167–73, 174, 207, 337, 385
Diaghilev, Sergei Pavlovich 175
Diamond, I.A.L. 162, 273, 276, 277, 278
DiBattista, Maria 92, 114
Dick, Philip K. 355, 357
Dickens, Charles 37, 47, 230, 241–2, 244, 310, 405, 408
Dickinson, Angie 254, 259
Didion, Joan 251
Dietrich, Marlene 33, 40, 57, 138, 145–6, 186, 362–3
Disney, Walt 40, 80, 113, 242
Doctor Zhivago 305–6, 308–12, *309*
Dolce Vita, La 197, 240, 241, 245–7, *247*
Donen, Stanley 29–30, 74, 83, 151, 162, 261, 294–7
Douglas, Bill 244
Dreyer, Carl Theodor 302
Dr Jekyll and Mr Hyde 154–5, 156
Drunken Angel 222, 224–5
Duse, Eleonora 31, 39
Dutt, Sunil 237–9
Duvivier, Julien 106
Dyer, Richard 414, 417
Dylan, Bob 202, 211, 324, 335,

Early Summer 213, 215–16
Eccles, Aimee 328–9
Eco, Umberto 155
Edison Trust / Company, The 18, 22
Edwards, James 315
Ekberg, Anita 197–8, 241
Elephant Man, The 374, 375

Ellis, John 408, 412
Ewell, Tom 274
Eyman, Scott 35, 422

Fairbanks, Douglas 27, 39
Falconetti, Maria 302
Fan 9–11, 415
Fanfaren der Liebe 277
Femme est une femme, Une 300, 301
Ferrell, Will 66, 338
Fields, W. C. 43, 64, 337
Fire Over England 93–4
Fitzgerald, F. Scott 30, 149, 184
Fleming, Victor 99, 150
Fonda, Henry 169
Fonda, Jane 322, 324–5
Fontaine, Joan 77, 86, 120–21, 122–5, *124*, 128–31, 133–4, 136, 263
Ford, Harrison 353, *354*, 355–6
Ford, John 169, 200, 203, 209, 223, 238, 250, 251, 253, 295
Foster, Jodie 341
Foucault, Michel 417
Freud, Sigmund 129
    Freudian, the 130–31, 179
Freud 203, 207, 210
Friends 25
From Here to Eternity 201, 205–6, 209
Fukada, Koji 398
Funny Face 196, 261–3, 267, 269, 413

Gable, Clark 8, 94, 96, 99–100, 102, 201, 209, 230, 241, 243, 275, 295
Garbo, Greta 38, 39, 40, 152, 277
Gardner, Ava 183, 189–99, *193*, 323, 374, 406
Garland, Judy 73, 77, 202
Garson, Greer 120–23, *123*, 125, 127–34, 136, 263
Gaslight 156–7, 158
Gavin, John 280–82, 288
Geminoid F 398
Gentlemen Prefer Blondes 275
George, Chief Dan 329
George, Melissa 373

Ghost in the Shell 384
Ghost World 382
Gielgud, John 71, 72, 146
Gigi 296
Gilda 373–4
Ginger e Fred 240, 243–4
Girl with a Pearl Earring 381, 383, 387
Glass Key, The 109
Glazer, Jonathan 386
Godard, Jean-Luc 299–304
Gone with the Wind 8, 58, 94–103
Goodbye Mr Chips 127
Goring, Marius 178, 190
Gorky, Maxim 17, 421
Graduate, The 198, 322, 325–6, 329
Grant, Cary 10, 130, 136, 157, 162,
    169, 246, 264, 269, 275, 277,
    314, 322, 413–4
    and Audrey Hepburn in
    Charade 294–8, *297*
    and Katharine Hepburn
    84–92, *90*
Grauman, David 27
Grauman's Chinese Theatre 29
Gray, John 409
Great Expectations 305
Greenstreet, Sydney 69, 72, 155
Griffith, D. W. 20, 23–5, 27
Griffith, Richard 415
Guess Who's Coming to Dinner 314,
    320
Guinness, Alec 310

Hackman, Gene 183, 324, 335
Hagen, Jean 77
Hannah, Daryl 353, 355
Hannah and Her Sisters 334, 339
Hanson, Curtis 406
'Happy Autumn Fields, The' 378
Hara, Setsuko 211–20, *218*, 296, 413
Harring, Laura Elena 373, 374, 376,
    378
Harrison, Rex 94, 107
Haskell, Molly 27, 28, 92, 101–2, 251,
    274, 415
Hathaway, Henry 260

Hauer, Rutger 353, 356
Hawking, Stephen 409
Hawks, Howard 62, 84, 86, 89, 115,
    200, 202, 203, 209, 252, 256,
    258–60, 274, 275
Hayworth, Rita 144, *147*, 198, 373,
    374, 406
Hebel, Johann Peter 11
Hedren, Tippi *290*, 291–2, 401
Heiress, The 204, 206, 208
Hemingway, Ernest 144, 149, 196–7,
Hepburn, Audrey 11, 77, 86, 196,
    261–70, *265*, 294–8, *297*, 381,
    407, 413, 428
Hepburn, Katharine 55, 77, 84–92, *90*,
    95, 136, 185, 206–7, 215, 320
Her 381, 384–4, 387
Hero 369
Hidden Fortress, The 223–4
Hilton, James 120, 127, 129
Hitchcock, Alfred 33, 65, 89, 103, 109,
    119, 278, 294, 295, 296, 297,
    299, 305, 322, 332, 383, 401
    and Ingrid Bergman 153, 156–9
    and Janet Leigh and Tippi Hedren
    287–93
    and Joan Fontaine 128–30
    and Montgomery Clift 203, 204,
    208
    and Peter Lorre 69–71
Hitchcock 383
Hitler, Adolf 30, 32, 40, 117–18, 119,
    275, 316
Hobbit, The 395, 399
Hoffman, Dustin 322–31, *328*, 382
Hoffmann, Ernst Theodor Amadeus
    37, 179, 355
Holden, William 184–5, 263, 295–6
Holiday 84, 91
Hope, Bob 110, 335, 339
Hopkins, Miriam 38
Hotel Imperial 39, 40
Hou Hsiao-hsien 388, 389, 391–3
Housman, A. E. 124–5
Howard, Leslie 96, 100, 102, 103, 154
Howard, Trevor 306
Hughes, Howard 190, 192

Hui, Ann 361
Hunter, Jeffrey 255–6
Hussey, Olivia 323
Huston, John 84, 197, 198, 203, 205,
    295

I Confess 204, 208–9, 210
I Live in Fear 224
I Married a Witch 110
Idiot, The 217–18
Imitation of Life 280–84, *283*
Indiscreet 151, 153, 156, 162
Indiscretion of an American Wife 207
Inn of the Sixth Happiness, The 162
L'Ingenu 57
Intermezzo 153–4, 156, 323
In the Heat of the Night 319–20
In the Mood for Love 363, 367–70
In Which We Serve 307
Irma Vep 365–7, *366*
Iron Man 2 383
Ishiguro, Hiroshi 398
It's a Wonderful Life 405
I Was a Male War Bride 277

Jackson, Peter 395, 397, 398–400
Jannings, Emil 34
Jewison, Norman 319
Joan of Arc 158, 162
Johansson, Scarlett 381–7, *384*, 392,
    396
Johnson, Celia 306–9, *306*
Jones, Jennifer 168, 207, 209
Jones, Quincey 319
Jonze, Spike 384
Jourdan, Louis 121
Journey to Italy 151, 160–61
Judgement at Nuremberg 205
Juliet of the Spirits 240, 246, 249

Kael, Pauline 89, 91, 261–2, 294, 428
Kapoor, Prithviraj 227, 228
Kapoor, Raj 226–35, *236*, 238–9
Kapoor, Shashi 228

Karina, Anna 299–304, *303*, 413
Kavanagh, Patrick 151, 413
Kazan, Elia 106
Kelly, Gene 29–30, 73–4, 77–8, 81,
    82, 83
Kelly, Grace 65, 86, 295, 322
Khan, Mehboob 235, 239
Khan, Shah Rukh 9–10, 415
Kieślowski, Krzysztof 418
Killers, The 192, 194–5, 374
King of Comedy, The 340, 347–9
King Kong 395, 397, 400–402
Kipling, Rudyard 17–8, 23
Kirstein, Lincoln 76, 80
Kohner, Susan 280, 282–4, *283*
Korda, Alexander 175
Kotowski, Mariusz 31, 422
Kracauer, Siegfried 34
Kramer, Stanley 205, 315, 320
Kramer vs Kramer 327, 330–31
Kubrick, Stanley 345, 386
Kumar, Dilip 226, 235
Kurosawa, Akira 217–18, 221–5
Kwan, Stanley 361–2, 364

L.A. Confidential 406–7
Ladd, Alan 109–10
Lady from Shanghai, The 144–5, *147*
Lake, Veronica *108*, 109–14, 194, 406,
    408
La La Land 73, 81
Lamb, Charles 151
LaMotta, Jake 343–7
Lang, Fritz 67–9, 72, 74
Larkin, Philip 294, 376
Lasch, Christopher 334
Last Year in Marienbad 295
Late Autumn 218–20
Late Spring 213–5, 217, 218–19, *218*
Lau, Carina 361, 370
Laughton, Charles 94, 175
Laurel, Stan, and Oliver Hardy 43, 72
Lawrence, Amy 202, 203, 205, 206,
    207, 208, 426
Lawrence, D. H. 46
Lawrence, Florence 20, 23

Lawrence, T. E. 311
Lawrence of Arabia 310, 312
Léaud, Jean-Pierre 365, 367
Lean, David 305–12
Leigh, Janet 146, 287–8, *289*, 290, 383
Leigh, Vivien 93–108, *104*, 120, 129
Lejeune, Caroline 34
LeRoy, Mervyn 103, 120
Leung, Tony 367–70, 390
Levi, Mica 385
Lewis, Jerry 348
Lemmon, Jack 272, *404*, 405–6
Letter from an Unknown Woman
    120–31, *124*, 263
Lever, James 55–6, 59, 61, 62, 423
Lilies of the Field 314, 316–7
Li Gong 370
Li Li-Li 361, 363
Lin, Brigitte 364
Linder, Max 19–20, 23
Little Big Man 327–30, *328*
Little Lord Fauntleroy 24, 26
Little Princess, The 26, 28
Lolita 61
Lombard, Carole 38, 115–19, *116*
Loos, Anita 62, 275
Lord of the Rings trilogy 395, 397, *397*,
    399–400
Lorre, Peter 67–72, *70*, 155, 353
Lost in Translation 381–2, *384*
Love and Death 334
Loved One, The 407–8
Love in the Afternoon 261–3, 265–8,
    265, 273
Love Me, Love My Money 390
Loy, Myrna 62–4, *64*
Lubitsch, Ernst 33–9, 117–18
Lucy 381, 386–7
Lynch, David 146, 208, 372, 374–9

M 67–9, 72
McCarey, Leo 62, 89, 152–3, 156
McCrea, Joel 110, 113–14
McDaniel, Hattie 58, 99
Madame DuBarry 34–5
Made in USA 304

Maggiorani, Lamberto 167–9, *168*
Magnani, Anna 160
Maltese Falcon, The 71–2
Manhattan Murder Mystery 339
Mankiewicz, Joseph 196, 198, 206
Mann, Anthony 253
Man Who Knew Too Much, The 70–72
*Man Who Shot Liberty Valance
    The* 250, 260, 295
Marathon Man 326, 327, 330
Marshall, Penny 346
Martin, Dean 258–60
Masina, Giulietta 240–49, *243*
Massine, Léonide *176*, 178
Mastroianni, Marcello 168, 240–49,
    247
Match Point 334, 381, 383
Me Cheeta: The Autobiography 55–61,
    423
Mean Streets 340–41
Melinda and Melinda 338
Melly, George 135
Menjou, Adolphe 30
Mépris, Le 300
Metropolis 74–5
Midnight Cowboy 327
Midnight in Paris 335, 339
Mifune, Toshiro 221–5, *222*, 413
Miles, Vera 65, 255, 288, 290
Millennium Mambo 390–91, *392*
Miller, Arthur 171
Milo, Sandra 248
Minnelli, Liza 342
Minnelli, Vincente 74
Miracle in Milan 172–3
Misfits, The 205, 209, 275, 295
Mitchell, Margaret 95, 98, 99, 101
Mitchum, Robert 109
Modern Times 43–4, 75, 235
Mogambo 191, 198
Monkey Business 274
Monroe, Marilyn 66, 86, 196, 202,
    267, 270, 291, 295, 296, 381, 407
    and *Some Like It Hot* 271–6, *276*,
    277–9
Moore, Juanita 280, 282, *283*, 284
Moore, Kieron 106

Moore, Roger 382
Mother India 235, 237–9
Mozart, Wolfgang Amadeus 266–7
Mr and Mrs Smith 119
'Mrs Bathurst' 17–18, 22
Mrs Miniver 127
Mulholland Drive 372–80, *377*
Mulligan, Richard 329
Mulvey, Laura 128–9
Murray, Bill 382
My Fair Lady 261, 264

Nadira 233–4
Nargis 226–7, 228, 230–39, *236*
Naruse, Mikio 217
Negri, Pola 29–42, *36*, 183, 185, 390, 422
Neilan, Marshall 28
Nelson, Ralph 316
Nelson, Ricky 258–9
Newman, Paul 314, 324
New York, New York 340, 342
Nichols, Mike 322, 324
Nicholson, Jack 324, 335, 345
Nielsen, Asta 66, 183
Nights of Cabiria 240–42, 245, 249
Nijinsky, Vaslav 75, 175
No Regrets for Our Youth 217
North by Northwest 288, 296
Nothing Sacred 117
Notorious 153, 156–7, *159*, 296, 314

O'Brien, Edmond 195
O'Hara, Maureen 254
Okada, Mariko 220
Olivier, Laurence 93, 103, 106, 107, 129–30, 145
Olson, Nancy 184–5
On the Town 82, 83
On the Waterfront 347
Ophüls, Max 120–22, 126–7, 130–31
Orwell, George 111, 122
O'Sullivan, Maureen 56, *59*, 63
Ozu, Yasujiro 212–19
Pan, Hermes 81

Pandora and the Flying Dutchman 190, 195–6, 198
Panofsky, Erwin 12, 18, 26
Paris When It Sizzles 261, 295–6
Pascal, Gabriel 106
Passion de Jeanne d'Arc, La 302
Patch of Blue, A 317
Peck, Gregory 262, 264, 265, 268
Peeping Tom 67, 180–81
Perkins, Anthony 288
Peters, Susan 121
Petit Soldat, Le 300–301
Philadelphia Story, The 84, *90*, 91–2
Pickford, Mary *16*, 17, 20, 22–8, 39, 185, 390, 415
Pierrot le Fou 299, 304
Pitts, ZaSu 26
Planet of the Apes trilogy 60, 395, 398, 400, 402
Place in the Sun, A 204, 206, 208
Poe, Edgar Allan 302, 358
Poitier, Sidney 13, 296, 313–21, *318*
Police Story 360
Pollack, Sydney 330
Poor Little Rich Girl 26
Powell, Michael 67, 174–8, 305–6
Powell, William 62–5, *64*
Pressburger, Emeric 174–82
Pressure Point 315
Psycho 146, 287–92, *289*, 295, 383
Purple Rose of Cairo, The 337, 339

Qi Shu 368, 388–94, *391*, 396
Queen Christina 277

Raft, George 271, 273
Raging Bull 339, 340, 343–7, *343*
Rains, Claude 155, 157
Raisin in the Sun, A 316, 320
Random Harvest 120–5, 127–9, 131–4, 263, 373
Raintree County 202–3, 210
Rashomon 222, 225
Rebecca 103, 128–30
Rebel Without a Cause 255, 323

Red Beard 222, 223–4
Redford, Robert 322, 324, 330
Red River 200–201, *202*, 204, 205, 206, 208–9, 253, 323
Red Shoes, The 81, 174–82, *176*
Reed, Carol 103, 145, 305
Reinhardt, Max 33, 37
Renoir, Jean 151
Reynolds, Debbie 76
Richardson, Ralph 106, 308, 310
Richie, Donald 215
Rilke, Rainer Maria 249
Rio Bravo 66, 81, 258–60, 296
Rogers, Ginger 73, 75–7, *79*, 81, 86, 240, 274
Rogue One: A Star Wars Story 411
Rohmer, Éric 157, 337
Roman Holiday 261–2, 264–5, 268, 428
Romeo and Juliet 323
Rooney, Mickey 55, 190, 192
Rose, Jacqueline 274
Rossellini, Isabella 374
Rossellini, Roberto 103, 150, 151, 153–4, 158, 160–62, 169
Ruan Lingyu 361–4, 369

Saboteur 290–91
Sabrina 196, 261–6, 271,
St Martin's Lane 94
Sandrich, Mark 75
Sarris, Andrew 112, 113, 406
Sayonara 398
Scheider, Roy 330
Schrader, Paul 341, 345
Scoop 383, 387
Scorsese, Martin 33, 334, 340–49
Scott, Ridley 353, 357
Searchers, The 253–8, *254*, 295
Seberg, Jean 300, 301
Secret Agent 70–71
Selznick, David 95, 99, 154–5, 169, 207, 271
Serkis, Andy 395–403, 411
Server, Lee 190–91, 197
Seven Samurai 221–2, 224–5
Seven Year Itch, The 267, 274

Shakespeare, William 8, 46, 61, 63, 73, 74, 87, 89, 131, 144, 146–8, 223, 249, 358
Shall We Dance 75–7, 80
Sharif, Omar 311
Shaw, Artie 192
Shaw, George Bernard 31, 106
Shearer, Moira 81, 174, *176*, 177–82
Shimura, Takashi 223–5
Shining, The 345
Shoeshine 170–71, *172*
Shootist, The 260
Shop Around the Corner, The 230, 253
Show Boat 194
Shree 420 228, 229, 232, 234–5, *236*
Shu Qi *see* Qi Shu
Siegel, Don 260
Simon, Paul 324, 325
Sinatra, Frank 190–94, 206, 382,
Singin' in the Rain 29, 74, 76, 80, 83, 376
Siodmak, Robert 195
Sirk, Douglas 203, 250, 280–84
So Close 393
Some Like It Hot 66, 88, 267, 271–9, 296
Song of the Exile 361
Soong Sisters, The 367
Southern, Taryn 398
Spacey, Kevin 10
Spellbound 156
Spielberg, Steven 395, 398
Stagecoach 200–201, 251, 252, 260
Stanwyck, Barbara 185, 194
Star is Born, A 281
Star Wars 224, 356, 395
Stefano, Joseph 290
Steiger, Rod 311, 319, 347
Stella Maris 26
Sternberg, Josef von 33, 71, 186
Stevens, George 203, 204
Stewart, James 204, 253, 260, 296, 405–6, 408
Strada, La 240, 242, *243*, 245
Stray Dog 225
Streetcar Named Desire, A 106–7, 281
Sturges, Preston 110–14

Stroheim, Erich von 184, *186*
Stromboli 158, 160
Suddenly, Last Summer 206–7, 208
Sullivan's Travels 108, 110–14
Sumurun 36–7, *37*
Sunset Boulevard 41, 183–8, *186*, 203,
    271, 273, 322
Suspicion 128, 130, 297
Švankmajer, Jan 402
Swaab, Peter 88
Swanson, Gloria 41, 57, 183–8, *186*
Swift, Jonathan 57, 137
Swing Time 79, 80
Sylvia Scarlett 84, 87–9, 185

Tales of Hoffmann, The 179
Tarantino, Quentin 370
Tarkovsky, Andrei 238, 244
Tarzan the Ape Man 58, *59*
Tarzan and his Mate 56, 62–3
Taxi Driver 340–42
Taylor, Elizabeth 206, 208
Taylor, Robert 103, 105
Tess of the Storm Country 27
Theroux, Justin 373
Thin Man, The 62–4
Third Man, The 103, 144–5, 334
This Gun For Hire 109
This Happy Breed 307
Thompson, Kay 262–3
Thomson, David 140, 141,
Three Times 390, 391–2, *391*
Throne of Blood 222–3
To Be or Not to Be 38, 115, *116*, 117–19
To Kill A Mockingbird 314
Tokyo Story 213, 216–7
Tolkien, J.R.R. 399–400
Tolstoy, Leo 99, 106, 310
Tompkins, Jane 256
Tootsie 327, 330
Top Hat 76, 78
To Sir, with Love 313, 318–19, *318*, 321
Touch of Evil 138, 144, 145–6, 295, 314
Toyoda, Shiro 215
Tracy, Spencer 84–6, 320
Trouble in Paradise 38

True Grit 260
Tsukasa, Yoko 218
Turner, Lana 95, 280–81, 283, 406
Twentieth Century 115–16, 118–19
Two Gentlemen of Verona, The 61, 63

Umberto D. 169–72, *171*, 174
Under Capricorn 157–8
Under the Skin 381, 385–6, 387

Valentino, Rudolph 30, 32, 39, 271,
    276, 390
Veidt, Conrad 155
Vertigo 157, 288, 291, 322, 378
Vivre sa vie 300, 301–2, *303*
Voltaire 57

Walbrook, Anton 177, 180
Walsh, Raoul 252
Warshow, Robert 44
Washington, Fredi 282
Waterloo Bridge 103, 105
Watts, Naomi 372–80, *377*, 397, 401–2
Waugh, Evelyn 244, 407–8, 412
Wayne, John 66, 136, 200–201, 204,
    209, 250–60, *254*, 313, 328–9
Webb, Charles 322
Weber, Max 86
Weissmuller, Johnny 55–6, 59–61, *59*
Welles, Orson 12, 137–49, *147*, 227,
    295, 314, 353
Wellman, William 117
West, Mae 86, 87, 184
West, Rebecca 120, 131
White, Pearl 20
White Sheik, The 241
Wild at Heart 372, 374, 375
Wilde, Oscar 418
Wilder, Billy 41, 203, 295, 405
    and Audrey Hepburn 261, 263,
    265–7
    and *Some Like It Hot* 271–8
    and Gloria Swanson in *Sunset
    Boulevard* 183, 185, 187

Williams, Tennessee 106, 198, 206, 281
Wilson, Owen 66, 335
Winters, Shelley 206, 317
Wodehouse, P. G. 62
Wolfe, Tom 294, 313
Wong, Faye 370
Wong Kar-wai 361, 364, 367–9, 370
Wood, Natalie 255
Wood, Robin 153
Worden, Hank 256
Wyler, William 103, 127, 203, 204, 206, 262, 428

You Will Meet a Tall Dark Stranger 336, 339
Young, Sean 353, *354*
Yuen, Corey 393

Zavattini, Cesare 172–3, 207
Zhang Yimou 393
Zhang Ziyi 370
Zinnemann, Fred 201, 203, 204, 206
Zweig, Stefan 120, 126